full circle

a search for
the world that
comes next

scott ludlam

C000142287

Published by Black Inc.,
an imprint of Schwartz Books Pty Ltd
Level 1, 221 Drummond Street
Carlton VIC 3053, Australia
enquiries@blackincbooks.com
www.blackincbooks.com

Copyright © Scott Ludlam 2021
Scott Ludlam asserts his right to be known as the author of this work.

ALL RIGHTS RESERVED.
No part of this publication may be reproduced, stored in a retrieval system,
or transmitted in any form by any means electronic, mechanical, photocopying,
recording or otherwise without the prior consent of the publishers.

9781760640835 (paperback)
9781743821688 (ebook)

A catalogue record for this
book is available from the
National Library of Australia

Cover image: Scott Ludlam
Text design: Tristan Main
Typesetting: Typography Studio
Illustrations: Alan Laver

Printed in Australia by McPherson's Printing Group.

full circle

for stephanie,
and for eve

The most common way people give up their power
is by thinking they don't have any.

ALICE WALKER

fireground

'A wind change occurred late in the afternoon, with the easterly coming in. This has caused a few spot fires in open country . . . 2 graders are currently en route to assist.'

In the terse language of the Rural Fire Service, that's bad news. On the map the fire reads as a little grey polygon, tractable and neat, drawn from direct observation and satellite hotspot mapping. On the ground it's the opposite: roaring, lethal and formidably out of control. A blaze sparked by a lightning strike days ago is being fanned into a monster. Now eight hundred and fifty hectares of unceded Yuin lands are on fire in difficult and inaccessible escarpment country. While the RFS are bulldozing containment lines across its path and calling in water bombers, this easterly is sending burning embers out in advance of the front, igniting spot fires. They post photos to social media, footage of the thing they are trying to contain – mesmerising walls of ash pouring slow-motion into the sky. From this distance, the bombers look like tiny fireflies against the face of it.

We've been watching that polygon for days, hitting refresh while charred leaves drift to the ground in silence. Every twenty-four hours it's a different shape, extending, elongating; other polygons appearing alongside it, still dwarfed by the giants burning to the north.

Hit refresh. 'It's been a pretty difficult day for fire crews on the fireline today. RFS, Forestry Corporation crews, 3 dozers, 2 graders, 2 bulk water carriers and 1 helicopter all worked to try and establish more containment on the north, south and west divisions of the fire. They were plagued by spotfires starting new fires outside control lines, while also trying to hold existing control lines.'

Under a nightfall that's come too early, we pack some essentials just in case and confer with our neighbours. The air has a different timbre to it,

1

acrid and sharp against the dead ambience of ashfall from the Shoalhaven fires we've been breathing for weeks.

While we sleep, a gusty norwester hits and it makes a run. Today was meant to be a birthday party. Waking, disoriented, to Flick banging on the door. We have to go. Fumbling, hit refresh; the polygon has grown two hideously outstretched rectangles, temporary placeholders for a thing moving too fast to map. 'EMERGENCY WARNING – The fire has moved quickly. If you're in Cobargo or Coolagolite, it is too late to leave. Shelter in place.' Fuck, it's close. It has already crossed the highway just to the south of us. Up and moving now, to throw our stuff into the car, assuring Sirius that although this isn't the walk he was promised, it will happen soon – now get in the car. An hour before dawn, the wrong horizon is aglow, deepest red. *Get in the car.*

The twilight highway is empty of traffic but for two tankers speeding towards us, directly into the path of the thing we're fleeing. The sun won't rise this morning; we'll see it days later as a flat orange disc behind the smoke. The quiet holiday town of Narooma is abuzz, headlights of caravan traffic queuing for fuel; rumours that Cobargo is burning. Coffee from a nervy little cafe just before the power dies across the whole town. Silence falls. It's begun. Lesson one: when it hits, a power grid made of exposed wires and wooden poles will immediately fail, taking out traffic lights, water pumps, petrol stations, refrigeration, whole categories of amenity we won't realise are gone until we try to call on them.

Our phones are serving up a glitchy pastiche of destruction: beach evacuations, tortured wildlife, a freeze frame of Cobargo's main street alight. It's killing people now, in vapour fires and kilometre-high firestorms. I can't bear it; hit refresh one last time before the phone network goes down. Our polygon is taking its place among the other giants; they are merging and combining into a 2000-kilometre-long fireground stretching from East Gippsland all the way to the Queensland border. We withdraw to the little park on the estuary which normally has sweeping views back towards the mountain. Today it's a sombre carnival of bewildered dogs and campervans, kids on swings and this impossible, shifting half-light. Lesson two: life continues, flows around, makes a way.

Under a blackout that will last for days, we dial up the national broadcaster on AM radios, share information with people we have only just met, make a plan that's good for the next few hours. Sirius makes a dozen new friends, gets his walk like it's no big deal, the weirdo.

'Recent projections of fire weather suggest that fire seasons will start earlier, end slightly later, and generally be more intense. This effect increases over time, but should be directly observable by 2020,' wrote Professor Ross Garnaut back in 2008.

Sitting on a park bench at the end of the world, the air a dead colour, visibility down to about a hundred metres on the last day of 2019, can confirm: the effect is directly observable. Even without a phone signal, I know the timeline is awash with a thousand examples like this right now; reminders of the warning signs and reports and red flags stretching back decades. This one feels personal, I guess; Garnaut's draft report was tabled four days after I'd climbed up, wide-eyed, onto the privileged soapbox of a Senate term. Finding myself somehow in this benighted park twelve years deeper into what people have begun calling the Anthropocene; record drought, record temperatures, record fires, all of them predicted to several decimal places.

A bloc of transnational resource sector investors control the ministerial wing of parliament and hold absolute majorities in both chambers. One of our major political parties is wholly owned, the other is divided, traumatised and compliant. A tenacious green insurgency is holding the line in there, but in a building where numbers matter we don't have enough of them yet.

Garnaut's work is a demonstration of the credibility and accuracy of our scientific institutions, side by side with the near-total capture of our political ones. He's asked by a journalist for his reaction to seeing his report, twelve years on, circulating in news feeds and social media posts amid the falling ash. 'It's one of sadness, that I was ineffective,' he says. 'Having been given the opportunity to talk to Australians on this issue, that I was ineffective in persuading Australians that it was in our national interest to play a positive role in a global effort to mitigate the effects of climate change.'

Mate. Same. He's had the grace not to drop a passive aggressive 'I told you so', but where does this leave us? On the strength of his report and the

3

work of thousands of others, backed by resurgent social movements and some adept parliamentary work, we won clean energy reforms and saw the ship begin to turn. Those laws lasted for exactly 730 days before coal and gas investors had them repealed, by 39 votes to 33.

The polygon now encloses nearly a quarter of a million hectares. Quite the birthday party, Flick. Here, with the phones blank, the roads closed and nothing to do but wait under a plume that has snuffed out the sun itself, it's time to work out what it means when your theories of change are burned to the ground.

PART 1

the motive power of fire

> The grounds for hope are in the shadows,
> in the people who are inventing the world
> while no one looks, who themselves don't
> know yet whether they will have any effect . . .
>
> REBECCA SOLNIT

the road to wattle

Early summer, 1998: a dozen people are working by torchlight and gas lanterns, miniature figures under giant trees. Bent in exertion, they're tearing into the bush track with spades and star pickets, taking turns to shovel the damp earth aside, bearing closer to the concrete culvert a few feet below. A short way back down the track, the warmth of a small fire lights the faces of another half-dozen people, and a pot of coffee is coming to the boil. A tarp has been slung across the roadway, sheltering a scatter of cushions and mattresses, a couple of sleeping kids. It's sketchy but homely.

Quiet conversation, laughter, and the subsonic rush of the forest behind the hectic racket of a twelve-foot trench being cut across the access road.

This forest. The traditional ground of the Pibelmun Noongar; walled cathedrals of silver trunks, a vaulted canopy framing a drift of stars. Some of these great old ones seeded three hundred years before the founding of my city. Tiers of understorey home to an intricate community of birds, insects, frogs and marsupials that live nowhere but here. You can't see them, with all the noise we're making. But you can feel the watchfulness: that sense of multitudes of eyes-on.

There's a minor celebration when we hit the buried culvert, and now the conversation turns to the best recipe for quick-set cement. I'm too new to this work to really understand what they have in mind: several lengths of chain are passed under the culvert, and a mess of wet concrete is being batched up on a big sheet of plastic. A couple of friends are admiring a two-foot section of steel pipe with an odd reverence; encrusted with welded spikes of rebar and scrap metal, it clearly has an important part to play in whatever is being done here.

I'm covered in mud, stepping back to the little campfire for another mug of coffee, as happy as I can recall being in a while.

Suddenly, a car is moving silently down the hill towards us. Headlights dipped; I can't tell who's steering, but there is quiet gravity in the sight of this battered station wagon rolling towards us, tyres crunching on the gravel. The earthmoving team pauses, leaning on their shovels. Now comes the hard part.

At the bottom of the trench, the concrete is already beginning to set, entombing the chains they've looped around the culvert and encasing all but the very end of that medieval-looking length of pipe. We line up and heave at the car, slewing it sideways across the track. Without really knowing how, we have shoved it into the trench and now here it lies, sunk up to its axles in the roadway. We begin to backfill, crude ramparts of an improvised roadblock.

It's ready sometime after midnight. A young woman crawls across the front seats onto a cramped bed of pillows and cushions, and I finally realise what it is we've done. A hole cut through the floor of the car lines up precisely with the lock-on pipe buried in the setting concrete. Into this, she extends her arm and clips a carabiner chained to her wrist onto a slender bar welded within the pipe. Ragged hair, focused eyes, a smile; thumbs up with her free hand.

Come the morning, if it's your job to police the passage of logging and earthmoving equipment through here, you have three options now. One: let them roll over the top and kill the woman in the car. Two: persuade her through legal threats or exhaustion to unclip and come off voluntarily. Three: dig out around the car and jackhammer through the concrete until you can put an angle grinder to the pipe, bearing in mind that it now encloses a fragile human arm.

In this particular place and time, option one is unthinkable. Options two and three will take many hours. Until the police and contractors show up and decide how they want to play it, the road into this small corner of the wild southwest is closed.

People are returning to the fire, dispersing, fatigue washing in. I'm too wired on caffeine to turn in quite yet, so let's sit a while as the firelight sets shadows dancing.

8

These memories are more than twenty years old now, but I'll never forget the sight of the sacrificial station wagon appearing out of the darkness; a battered piece of surplus technology repurposed and turned against a much larger and more complex machine.

To be clear, what we're doing here is unlawful. Chopping up access roads and implanting cars in them is against the law. Occupying such a vehicle and refusing an order to leave; that's unlawful too.

In contrast, it is entirely lawful to bring scrub-rolling dozers into this forest to pulverise the understorey and kill everything that doesn't flee; the state has granted an explicit licence for the contractors to do just that. It is also lawful to turn machines with tank-tracks and tungsten saws against these silvered giants, sending them thundering to the ground and turning this valley into a moonscape over the course of a fortnight.

So here's the problem: this localised extinction disaster is institutionalised. It has the full weight of global supply chains auspiced by modern industrial states behind it. Putting yourself in front of a bulldozer only slows it temporarily; the larger system learns, it adapts, and on some mornings it sends police in to lawfully beat the shit out of the people camped here.

I don't know what brought you here – I'm not even sure if we've met. But me, I'm one of the fortunate few – I'm here by choice. I hitched down here because it felt right, because I know and trust these people, and because the campaign has hit a tipping point and it's wild to be part of it. My family supports me being here. I work as a freelancer, so this has cost me literally nothing. I'm a temporary visitor from the comfortable bulge in the middle of the privilege bell curve, the university-educated part, where you are taught about bell curves but not about privilege. I haven't been forced into this campaign because my life depends on it, or through ancestral obligations to Country. Until quite recently, 'the environment' was just something I read about in books.

That changed the first time I stood at the edge of a working clearfell. Watching a living place being violently dismantled breaks something inside. Felling is dangerous work, and the teams are methodical, professional and terribly effective. Trees that had anchored these hillsides for more than five hundred years were being loaded onto trucks, soon to be shredded into low-value woodchips for the international pulp market. We'd get some of it back in a few months' time, as plastic-wrapped toilet rolls and blocks of perfectly white copy paper. What was left on the ground in that ruined place was then pushed into piles and torched – and all of this, not to labour the point, was lawful.

That's why we're here, around this little crackling fire: to prevent that from happening right where we're sitting. Some of the most brilliant people I will ever meet have managed, over the course of more than thirty years, to turn the tide on this terrible destruction. Camped in the mud, organising demonstrations in the city, training two generations of newcomers, carefully working the politics. They don't know it yet, but they're about to succeed, swinging an election on the strength of this mobilisation and the presence of the place itself. Direct action gets the goods, so they say. They will silence the chainsaws, not just here but across a huge extent of this ancient ground. The law will change,[1] and this powerful win will pass into activist folklore, even as new national parks are being drawn up, along with retraining packages for affected logging communities.

The larger system learns, and it adapts. In its current configuration it demands a certain tonnage of woodchips, no matter what. International buyers will now hit Sarawak a few million tonnes harder, and Vietnam, and places where putting your arm into a lock-on pipe absolutely could get you killed. None of this is the fault, or the intention, of the people who put themselves on the line here. But we can't pretend that this isn't happening everywhere, or that we aren't now descending the rapids into a full-blown planetary extinction crisis. Turn the prism, and it looks like a climate crisis. And a crisis of democracy, of militarism, of poverty.

Years ago, I came across this old story about a village by a river. A group of villagers are washing clothes on the riverbank, and one of them looks up to see a young child floating past, clearly in distress. She wades in and rescues her, a little shaken. A shout – one of her friends has spotted another kid in the water, and then another. They drop their washing and set about rescuing these stricken children as they float past.

---

1   Although, at the time of writing it remains illegal to implant station wagons in logging roads.

More kids are drifting helplessly down the river, and then more. Finally, in a fury, the original rescuer abandons the riverbank and strides away. 'Wait!' her comrades shout. 'We need you here. Where are you going?' Over her shoulder, she calls back, 'I'm going to find the monster who's throwing them in.'

Here, under these immense trees, we are organising a rescue. People in villages far from here – from Mathare to Mongolia to Minas Gerais – are organising other rescues. Soon we'll set sail and meet with some of them, to learn a little of the rivers they stand in and the monsters they contend with. This traverse will take us from the floor of the Senate to a Hadean beach, from the winter of the Great Depression to a rebellion against extinction. While we travel, social movements working across every time zone will invoke one of those rare moments in history when they begin to converge and discover each other.

There are a great many children in the water, so it's time to be up and moving. The first hints of dawn are touching the sky. With the access road bottled up, the forest protectors will be able to move many more people onto the main road into the logging area, where the confrontation will be easier for television news crews to reach. Later, I'll catch the smell of woodsmoke on my clothes, and it will bring back how this improvised extinction roadblock looked under the torchlight. It looked rough, and clever, and beautiful, like the rising global movement it is a part of.

Because we were here, there will be no logging in Wattle Forest today.

the oldest book in the world

On the eastern shores of the Mediterranean, in present-day Lebanon, stands the ancient city of Byblos. It is one of the oldest continually inhabited cities in the world, and somehow you can feel it. Walk these streets with someone who knows how to read the place, and the jumbled layers tell a story. The mountains behind are hazy, decked with unregulated apartment stacks built in a hurry for those fleeing the war in 2006, and the civil war before that. Closer to the coast, a mess of freeways and concrete tilt-up intersect with graceful architectures of the mid-twentieth-century French mandate.

We step back further, down cobbled streets past the Ottoman-era Sultan Abdul Majid mosque with its sky-blue dome, evening call to prayer echoing across the rooftops. Deeper, now: blocky ruins of a twelfth-century Crusaders' castle the highest landmark in the old city, still bearing the scars of capture by Salah ad-Din. Archways of a Roman amphitheatre built a thousand years earlier. We call the city by its old name now, Jbeil, as we walk back through the years of occupation by Alexander the Great, hundreds of years as a Persian client state before that, Assyrians before them, Egyptians before them.

Shorelines reconfigure as the centuries unfurl; the original seaport silted up and only recently rediscovered. In your mind's eye, watch as Phoenician merchant ships slip out of port laden with cedar bound for Memphis and Alexandria. They'll return carrying precious papyrus, upon which scholars will write in the earliest recognisable forms of the Latin alphabet.

Deeper. Curved foundations of palaces long gone. Layers of trauma and war; walls built and ruined and built again. Bronze Age pottery fragments. The plastered floors of vanished houses laid down by a fishing community in the early Neolithic. The narrow avenues of the old souk still bustle with commerce and culture, lending continuity to the generations of families who built every age of this place. From some time after the closing of the Ice Age, these streets have shifted and reconfigured, languages and whole bodies of law have come and gone, and the city has endured.

There is a much older story here, if you know where to find it.

Down one narrow laneway, we step into a vaulted shopfront that looks, from the outside, like some kind of gallery. We are welcomed by a genial curator and his knowledgeable young son, both of them eager to share. On the walls hang intricate friezes in fine-grained limestone – fossil silhouettes of fish and crustaceans and rays preserved in the most extraordinary detail. These distant creatures lived in the long-vanished Tethys Sea a hundred million years ago – a span of years ten thousand times the age of this city.

At the back of the gallery, a heavy rack holds a block of these stone tablets, sliced vertically in a way that allows you to leaf through them, carefully, like the pages of the oldest book in the world. A form of geological memory can be recalled here, achingly fragile lives smothered by marine sediments under a younger sun, pressed into the fossil record as the seasons turned, and turned. If you know how to read them – as the curators of this small gallery clearly do – you can infer things about the world these creatures inhabited: how hot it was, what they ate, a little of how they lived.

Among those who have spent their lives trying to read meaning into these ghostly pages, the book is divided into chapters marked by relatively sudden changes in the geological narrative. The chapter they call the Permian ends with a mass extinction a quarter of a billion years ago. The more recent disappearance of the dinosaurs marks the sudden end of the Cretaceous chapter. All the way down into more recent times, when new technologies and more intact sediments mean the book can be read at higher and higher resolution.

Follow the storyline now through two and a half million years of Pleistocene Ice Ages broken by warm interglacial periods. The ice in retreat as shorelines advance, arriving, finally, in the long, eleven-thousand-year Holocene summer, in which the city of Byblos, and the entirety of our written history, is made and remade.

Into these most recent strata of the geological record, something new. In changing sedimentation patterns around river mouths, geologists read the quiet aftermath of ancient deforestation in Europe. In air bubbles trapped in an Antarctic snowstorm five thousand years ago, faint traces of increased methane levels from rice cultivation in China.

In the late 1800s, the signal becomes unambiguous. A thin film of localised ashfall in the British Midlands proliferates rapidly as industrial coal-burning hopscotches across the northern hemisphere. Radioactive isotopes of caesium and plutonium, falling out downwind of nuclear-weapon detonations in the 1950s and '60s. In the background, slowly, trace amounts of carbon dioxide in the atmosphere and oceans continue to rise, exhaust gases building up faster than the planet can draw them down.

At a conference of the International Geosphere-Biosphere Programme in 2000 – an event that sounds like an absolute riot – one Nobel laureate's throwaway line brings things to a momentary standstill: 'We no longer live in the Holocene, but in the Anthropocene.'

The Anthropocene. Ever since that conference, the word has steadily diffused out of academic journals into popular culture. It has a certain ominous mystique to it; in my mind's eye the great-grandchildren of the fossil curators of Byblos are reading the closing of the Holocene and the incendiary dawn of a new geological age, leafing through the ash-smudged fossil record and wondering at the sudden silencing of the world.

Palaeontologists and earth systems scientists are still skirmishing over what this Anthropocene concept even means, and when this new age began. With the coal burning? The methane in the air bubbles? One view is that we passed through an invisible inflection point in the 1950s, as our industrial and agricultural bootprint transcended local environmental impacts and began tilting the earth system as a whole. The 'great acceleration', some of the IGBP scientists call this lift-off moment. 'Only beyond the mid-20th century is there clear evidence for fundamental shifts in the state and functioning of the Earth System that are beyond the range of variability of the Holocene and driven by human activities,' wrote Professor Will Steffen and his colleagues in 2015.

But which humans? Which activities? Immediately, this geological conversation is veering into oncoming political traffic.

For earth scientists, the Anthropocene is a sedimentary event layer signifying a new chapter being bulldozed into the oldest book in the world. For fossil curators, this layer will record the passing of the scimitar oryx, the Floreana giant tortoise and the Saint Helena olive, in a gathering cascade of extinction. It will hold the memory of a changing atmosphere and the acidification of the oceans, for as long as the planet exists.

Most of us aren't earth scientists or fossil curators. Most of us are just trying to get by, yet somehow we've jumped from localised ash fallout to a full-blown planetary extinction emergency in just the faintest blink of geological time. How we got here is hard to comprehend, particularly for those of us conditioned to accept rocket-fuelled great accelerations as somehow normal.

To organise any kind of coherent response to what's been unleashed here, the oldest book seems momentarily too slow a metaphor. Imagine instead a scorched black eucalyptus leaf fluttering out of an ashen sky, coming to rest on an empty chessboard extending from horizon to horizon. Out here, we'll try to face up to the scale of the thing.

Dear future generations: Please accept our apologies.
We were rolling drunk on petroleum.

KURT VONNEGUT

coins of the anthropocene

Have you heard the one about the original creator of the game of chess, this wily mathematician who submits his invention to the ruler of the country? Asked by the delighted queen what he wants by way of reward, the mathematician requests to be paid in gold. He proposes the queen place a single coin on the first square of the chessboard, two on the second square, four on the next, eight on the one after that, doubling the number of coins on each successive square up to the sixty-fourth.

The queen, perplexed that the mathematician would ask such a meagre reward for his creativity, nonetheless orders her chancellor to total up the coins. In disbelief, the chancellor calculates that this simple sequence of sixty-three doublings has the queen owing the mathematician 18,446,744,073,709,551,615 coins. The coin stack on the sixty-fourth square will reach a little over nine trillion kilometres from earth, nearly a quarter of the way to Alpha Centauri.[2]

Variations on this story are sometimes told in maths classes to give students an idea of how rapidly a system undergoing exponential growth will punch a hole through the ceiling. To understand what it means for us right here and now, imagine the chessboard expanding invisibly to cover our battered old planet, and instead of coins let's travel back in time a short distance and play the game with metallic ores. Iron ore, bauxite, copper, nickel, every tonne of it.

Start in the year 1901. The anti-colonial Boxer Rebellion in China reaches its bloody conclusion, the parliament of Australia sits for the first time, and welfare campaigner Emily Hobhouse reports on appalling

---

2   That's assuming the coins are 1 millimetre thick and there are
     9,223,372,036,854,775,808 coins on the sixty-fourth square.

conditions in British concentration camps in South Africa. Drop about 150 million tonnes on the first square of the chessboard – that's the total estimated figure of metal ores mined, shipped and smelted by the world economy in that year. Call it the queen's first coin.

Jump forward a quarter of a century to 1925: the first public demonstration of television transmission is given in London, and Adolf Hitler publishes the first volume of *Mein Kampf*. Total metal ores mined and traded: 326 million tonnes. Two coins, give or take.

Twenty-seven years and a shattering world war later, we drop four coins on the next square. It's 1952: the US government successfully tests the world's first hydrogen bomb, and the Mau Mau launch a guerrilla uprising in Kenya. We're up to 620 million tonnes.

The next doubling to 1.2 billion tonnes drops in 1967: it's the Summer of Love in Haight-Ashbury, Suharto takes office as the second president of Indonesia, and the Israeli military occupies the Gaza Strip, the West Bank and the Golan Heights in the Six-Day War.

Sixteen coins in 1995: the year in which the World Trade Organization is established, and Typhoon Angela slams into the Philippines and Vietnam.

Thirty-two coins in 2009, the booming globalised economy now trading more than 4.8 billion tonnes of metal ores in the year the United Nations COP 15 climate negotiations end in failure in Copenhagen.

Smooth out the zigzags of global commodity markets, peer past the dust and dinosaur forms of colossal pieces of mining equipment and bulk freighters the size of city blocks. This is what a mild-sounding 3 per cent annually compounding growth rate will do. An increase of 3 per cent a year will double the number of coins on each successive square about once every quarter-century. Non-metallic mining – that's all the limestone, sand, gravel and whatever – has grown slightly faster since 1901, doubling every twenty years. Coal, oil and gas are a little slower, doubling about every thirty years. You get the idea.

The simplest explanation for this explosive growth is that it coincides with the rapid and unprecedented expansion in human population – from a little over 1.5 billion people in 1900 to more than 7.8 billion at the time of writing. But simple explanations are sometimes wrong. World population growth hit an inflection point in the late 1960s and began to decline as women's literacy and access to primary healthcare improved across the Global South, and reductions in child mortality led to smaller family sizes. Nobody suggests our population is set to double again; barring catastrophe, it appears to be headed for a plateau later this century. But there is no indication that the material consumption of the world economy is slowing, by any measure. If anything, the growth curves for key commodities have become even steeper over recent decades.

A better fit for the accelerating growth in material consumption can be found in something non-material: money. If you add up the total monetary value of all the goods and services produced in a country in a year, you arrive at a magic number called the Gross Domestic Product, or GDP. The world's combined GDP has been growing at about 3 per cent a year, doubling more than five times since 1901 and almost perfectly tracking the surging growth of the industrial tonnage out on the chessboard.

Is this correlation, or causation, or just coincidence? Answering that is harder than it sounds, but for the moment the key thing to notice is that one of money's main functions is just to multiply itself. And because it only exists as symbolic transactions between people and institutions, it is free to multiply into infinity like the mathematician's imaginary coins.

The physical flows and fabrics of a living planet are not so free. Between 1901 and 2015, the human infrastructures of mining, farming, factories and quarries processed a staggering 3.4 trillion tonnes of raw materials in total. By the unyielding mathematics of compounding growth, in fourteen decades' time we're expected to churn and burn through that amount every single year.

GDP figures accurately track the one-way consumption torrent of the modern economy: from mine to landfill, with a brief pause in the hands of people this kind of economy calls consumers. When particular flows or commodities or workforces buckle or collapse, the doubling shifts somewhere else. To the financial system, the physical flows are almost beside the point; they are simply intermediaries, carrier waves for the duplication of money.

In the glossy annual reports, all the focus is on the input side: tonnages ripped and shipped, board-feet slabbed and chipped, gigalitres pumped and burned, annually compounding metrics of a planet in liquidation.

The architects of this locust economy never sought to design waste retrieval and recycling systems for this growth machine, so it piles up on the edge of town. We've brought materials into circulation that have no known disposal path – an ocean of plastics, incomprehensible new chemicals and murderously long-lived radioactive isotopes. The one that is raining scorched leaves onto the chessboard, the one we can't even see, is the invisible pollution from coal, oil and gas combustion: a careless elbow in the face of the planet's highly strung thermal regulation systems.

These are the coins of the Anthropocene, and this is what they buy us. Our present political and economic leaders are unswervingly determined to deliver the next stack twice as high on the next square, no matter what. Anybody who suggests that this is an impossibly dangerous way to organise our economy is treated like a freak.

That's a problem. In the 1990s, US public-policy thinker Joseph P. Overton introduced an idea that would end up carrying his name. He proposed that public debate is characterised by ideas that are considered reasonable and worthy of discussion. These ideas lie safely within the Overton window. Outside this window lie all the ideas considered extreme, ridiculous or outright unthinkable.

The assumption that coin-doubling growth is good and necessary and normal is so mundane, so beyond question, that most days it's all you can see through the Overton window. There do seem to be some freaks outside, banging on the glass about extinction or something, but because the window has become so firmly fixed in place it's hard to understand what they are on about.

Joseph Overton suggested that over time, cultural and political tides can move the window, with activists and innovators bringing ideas previously considered extreme into the range of matters that sensible centrists feel comfortable talking about. But today things seem askew: everyone knows something is horribly wrong, but the window refuses to shift.

We were checkmated the moment we bought into the mathematician's coin-doubling scam. Across much of the industrialised world, the consequences of endlessly doubling down now infuse popular culture like background radiation. Dystopian premonitions hover at the intersections of documentary and science fiction, an annoying cohort of doomers and whole sub-genres of apocalypse porn flirting with the aesthetics of global collapse. A few billionaires are even proposing to go and set up colonies on Mars, but as much as we might wish they'd just fuck off and live under a plastic dome millions of kilometres away, it wouldn't stop people from being crushed under the next drop of their coins. The window seems to be jammed, stuck somehow, and so rather than continue trying to shift it politely, maybe it's time we put a brick through it.

the systems game

Sometime between this coin-doubling and the next, the chess game ends because the board is on fire.

While we're thinking about that, here's a different game, one that's played with only one rule. It works pretty well with about two dozen people; you just need a little bit of space. Here's how it goes. Everyone stands in a circle, facing inwards, about an arm's length apart from one another. Each participant has to choose two other people at random – silently, without letting on who they've chosen. Ready? Okay – here's the rule. When the game starts, you have to move so as to stay an equal distance from the two people you've chosen. You don't have to stand directly between them, just try to keep the same distance away from both of them at all times.

That's it. That's the rule.

Go.

I first came across this game years ago, just before the night we closed the road into Wattle. It was introduced as part of a workshop series on nonviolence and civil disobedience, co-hosted by American author and anti-nuclear campaigner Joanna Macy. In addition to practical techniques for locking down equipment, dealing with police and understanding your legal rights, Joanna Macy stirs in a measure of deep ecology, Buddhist philosophy and something I'd only tangentially read about before, something she calls systems theory. Instead of dropping a bunch of academic papers about chaotic attractors and scale-free networks on us, she starts with this game.

The moment she calls 'go', the circle dissolves. The two people you're following, now they're moving too, trying to keep an equal distance from the two people they've chosen. In your peripheral vision you're trying to keep track of where your people are, avoiding collisions with others, aware that everyone is now weaving and careening around each other in a complex, unpredictable and strangely hilarious dance. Give it a few minutes, and unplanned crowd dynamics will arise; the tempo will slow, or everyone will begin to bunch up, until someone makes a move that drags two other people out of the flow and suddenly you're all in wild motion again.

Just one rule, everyone in the game applying it as best they can in real time.

No supercomputer will ever be able to predict where we'll all be standing when Joanna calls 'stop'. Nobody is in charge of where we end up. We're all exercising a certain amount of agency, but none of us is completely free of the influence of those we're bound to. Everything that happens in the game depends on everything else that is happening, and trying to orchestrate or direct a particular end state would seem to be formally impossible. My enduring memory of all the times I've played the systems game is of the intangible collective presence that arises: a larger, fleeting *something* emerging from the moment-to-moment interaction of the crowd's individual players.

The search for a theory that would explain these dynamics – and the emergence of that something – takes us all the way back to the nineteenth-century study of thermodynamics, with a handful of scientists and inventors struggling to improve the efficiency of the first generation of steam engines. Through slow trial and experimentation, they were stumbling towards some profound understandings. In his one and only publication, *Reflections on the Motive Power of Fire*, in 1824 French physicist Sadi Carnot put it like this: 'We may therefore state the following general principle: The amount of motive force in nature is unchanging. Properly speaking, it is never created and never destroyed; in reality it [merely] changes form, that is, assumes one or another form of motion, but never vanishes.' This observation ended up being formalised as the first law of thermodynamics, the law of conservation of energy. Energy in the universe is never created or destroyed; it merely changes form.

But changing form carries a cost that you never get back. This second law, flowing from the first, would be of more immediate use to the makers of these machines. Heat dissipates until everything is the same temperature; water flows downhill; friction bleeds energy out of moving machinery and disperses it as waste heat. You'll never see a cold object spontaneously transferring heat to a warmer object. The whole universe is falling inexorably towards thermal equilibrium – cold and dead and empty and pointless and dead, as though a Morrissey album has founded its own branch of physics.

The second law gave rise to the evocative concept of entropy. This term was coined by German mathematician Rudolf Clausius in 1865 as the measure of disorder in a closed system, which only ever goes up until equilibrium is reached. As energy dissipates, entropy increases, and this is always and forever a one-way ride. It means these bearded imperial nerds will never be able to build a steam engine with anything like 100 per cent efficiency. The moment they light up the coal in the furnace is the moment high-grade chemical energy begins its cascade into low-grade waste-heat, never to return. 'Reality is irreversible,' as Russian biophysicist Mikhail Volkenstein put it.

It is in the dissipation that everything interesting happens. Carnot and Clausius and the others may be laying the theoretical foundations for a world lit by coal-fired electricity, but they are writing their treatises by the light of gas mantles and candles. Look closer, at the dance of one of these small, perfect flames. Closer: to see what is happening as the superheated gas boils off the melting wax. The fastest, most efficient way for the candle to dissipate this energy is through a teardrop-shaped flame. Entropy is increasing, heat is flowing from a highly concentrated source to gently warm the surrounding air, and while it lasts, this ephemeral structure will float there, illuminating the room.

Heat a pan of water until it begins to boil, and the water will self-organise into bubbling convection cells – hot water rising, dissipating heated steam into the air, cooling and falling back towards the bottom of the pan. The same overturning convection structures can be observed on the surface of the sun, or in a bowl of hot miso soup. At the scale of the whole planet, slow-moving ocean currents and the largest-scale weather systems are in ceaseless overturn, dissipating equatorial heat towards the poles.

We may all be sliding towards the eventual heat-death of the universe, but the structures and standing waves that form as energy tumbles from high-grade to low have shaped everything we see around us. The study of such 'dissipative structures' is one of the tributaries that led, in the mid-twentieth century, to the development of what is known as general systems theory.

Austrian biologist Ludwig von Bertalanffy went looking for a unifying theory that would describe any complex system with constituent parts;

he probably would have enjoyed the swerve and flow of Joanna's game. In 1946 he wrote: 'It seems legitimate to ask for a theory, not of systems of a more or less special kind, but of universal principles applying to systems in general.'

A quick search turns up this definition of system: 'a regularly interacting or interdependent group of items forming a unified whole'. Any discipline that seeks to formalise the universal principles of 'systems in general' would seem to be hopelessly ambitious in scope. After all, we could be referring to the solar system, or the immune system, or an ecosystem. Or, for that matter, the phone system, the criminal justice system or the global financial system. This is a word that really gets around, and when it shows up it usually means things are getting complex.

Over the decades, this quest for simplicity has ramified into dozens of disciplines and sub-disciplines, elegant propositions and empty dead ends. The cybernetics people, with their feedback loops and ballistics tables. Game theory types, with their bounded rationality and prisoner's dilemmas. The chaos theory school, wielding strange attractors and infinitely self-similar fractal geometries. More than metaphor, it seemed the stirring of a butterfly's wings in the Amazon might really trigger a storm in the North Atlantic.

It's not immediately obvious why Joanna would invoke any of these abstractions at a civil disobedience workshop for a few dozen middle-class kids learning how to shut down logging operations. Or, for that matter, their relevance to people working any dimension of the larger struggle against a coin-doubling economy that has clearly lost its mind. Most of us don't have the time or the faintest flicker of interest in bringing graph theory or nonlinear dynamics into any part of our waking lives, so, as fascinating as these things might be to some, what is the pitch here, exactly?

By the 1990s, students of what would come to be termed 'complex adaptive systems' were turning their minds to questions that had previously been squarely in the domain of political philosophers and revolutionaries. Lines of inquiry that had begun with steam engine efficiency were somehow casting light on patterns of social contention, and the stratification of classes, and outbreaks of industrial action.

Across widely diverse contexts, some researchers clocked the recurrence of a fourfold cycle of innovation and conservation, collapse and renewal, operating at scales from local to global. Named it the 'adaptive cycle' and began to see it all over the place: the beginnings of a theory of how natural and social systems undergo regime changes. Ecologists put forward a name for the complex interplay of fast and slow adaptive cycles that sometimes collide with spectacular effect: they called it *panarchy*.

Thermodynamics won't help us find the people throwing children into the water: that's a political journey. But ever since I first played the systems game, I've wondered whether a theory of collapse and renewal might be valuable when we do finally meet our monsters face to face.

I can't shake the memory of the fossil gallery of Byblos, turning stone blocks carefully backwards through the oldest book in the world. On different terrains, these pages can be read all the way back into deep time, to spiral shells and track marks on seafloors made by beings that haven't existed for half a billion years. Deeper still, to rocks in the heart of the Pilbara in Western Australia, where chemical signatures hint at the presence of tiny lives making their way amid the late stages of the fiery bombardment that formed our world. Wondering what we'd see if we turned to the page before that —

cradle

We're adrift inside a giant molecular cloud, four and a half billion years ago. Everything in our story begins here, in an immense cloud chamber filled with soft light. This is deep space as no-one has ever seen it; slowly shifting veils of gas and dust, light-years wide, lit from within by fierce young suns.

Across the face of this vivid realm, a scatter of dark bubbles hang like ink blots. They are forming within the walls of the nebula, drawing the cloud matter inward to hide a growing warmth inside.

Move closer. One such bubble floats before us like a giant drop of oil against the floodlit backdrop. It envelopes a slowly turning hurricane of supernova rubble and drifting hydrogen. At the core, gravity is lighting a furnace as it pulls ever more mass into the collapsing eye of the storm.

In the blazing inner regions where the heaviest matter is falling, tiny planets are being built out of a tumbling hail of asteroids and dust. Countless hurtling pieces shatter and re-form in an orbiting demolition ballet that lasts a hundred million years. Only gravity and time can tell which of these worldlets will survive and which will be obliterated, but gradually, those lying in more stable orbits are sweeping up surrounding debris and collecting satellites. Further out, gas giants and ice giants are whirlpooling their own families of moons into existence.

The core of the solar cocoon is becoming a pressure cooker. Gravity is forcing a sea of hydrogen into a tight bomb lit by the immense pressure of its own collapsing weight. From the north and south poles of this giant electromagnet, vast plumes of ejected material flare into space. In these primal conditions, molecules are blown into their constituent parts. Then the individual atoms are themselves torn apart as pressure and temperature mounts. Stripped of their electrons, lone hydrogen nuclei in the core begin slam dancing at ten million degrees.

This is a protostar, a self-assembling thermonuclear power station that creates its archipelago of worlds even as it prepares to warm them for the next eleven billion years. It's hot enough now for our embryonic star to truly ignite, and a new kind of reaction takes over in the core. Hydrogen ions begin smashing into each other hard enough to overcome the electromagnetic repulsion between them. In this seething cauldron, a new element – helium – is being fused into existence, releasing a flood of heat and light.

This new star is passing into the main sequence, sullen red slowly yielding a clear yellow brilliance. It illuminates a scene of quite extraordinary carnage out in the solar wilds, the period of world-building named the Hadean eon, invoking the hell of ancient Greece.

Sunrise, Planet Earth. Three hundred million years have passed since we drifted into the cloud chamber; now a tortured landscape of coiled basalt lies under stormy skies, the pre-dawn temperature rising rapidly as the eastern skyline lights up like a furnace. Beneath a thin raft of recently cooled crust, the molten earth churns and shifts, convection currents bringing radioactive metals up from the deep and folding brittle terrain back into the depths. The dawn is brief – this battered world spins on its axis once every five hours.

The demolition ballet is delivering a fertile brew of hydrocarbons, silicates, metals and water to these burning lands. At least once, it seems, there is a collision that almost destroys the world. One afternoon, a body nearly the size of Mars smashes into our planet and catastrophically re-forms both worlds. Most of the heavy core of the impacting planet sinks and merges with ours, while an inconceivable spray of liquid stone arcs into space, spinning into a ring system that will slowly coalesce into the moon.

When we look at the scarred white face of our sister world, we can read ancient traces of the Hadean bombardment that formed our own planet. Impact craters and great flat seas of lava – the Maria – are visible from nearly four hundred thousand kilometres distant. Her surface is a mute, frozen mirror image of what our own world must have once looked like.

But four billion years ago, this new moon roars overhead as close as seventeen thousand kilometres, orbiting every few hours. This wild accelerated ride pulls both worlds into tidal turmoil, buckling the thin crusts that are slowly freezing into solid stone.

During the daylight hours, the surface is drenched in raw ultraviolet light that sears straight through the scanty atmosphere boiling out of the ground. As it thickens, this soup of nitrogen, carbon dioxide, and water vapour begins to lend protection from the sterilising torrent of solar radiation. It also serves to incinerate smaller meteors as they plough towards the ground, tearing larger missiles apart or at least buffering their impact.

Slowly, these racing clouds begin to have a cooling effect on the world's surface, reflecting some sunlight back into space while retaining a more evenly warmed layer of air close to the surface. Dissipative structures, the systems people will eventually call them; the first weather systems carrying equatorial heat pole-wards over these parched terrains. Awesome electrical storms scorch the air, each discharge creating a potent brew of novel hydrocarbons.

From deep within, water originating in the icy drift of space is carried upward in plumes of magma and blown into the sky along with great clouds of ash and sulphurous, carbon-rich gas. The surface temperature drops below the boiling point of water, and rain falls for the first time. As the clouds unleash titanic downpours across this torn wilderness, the first shallow seas collect in crater basins and volcanic caldera. For several thousand years, a worldwide deluge floods the restless, heaving earth and the great world ocean is born. Unevenly heated and drawn by colossal tides, great currents and eddies appear in this restless expanse of open water.

We're on our way home. Bathed in the filtered firelight of a pregnant star, this new world's formative circulatory systems have made a cradle.

abundance

I grew up in a home like this. Quiet street, trimmed lawns, neat fences. Drone of a lawnmower from somewhere, swish of the wind through dry palm leaves. Second-hand car in the driveway. Nice; nothing flash. Come in out of the heat and look around inside.

It's a fairly modest brick-and-tile, floor area about 170 square metres plus double carport. Built in the early years of the twenty-first century; recently enough to lack any obvious signs of its age. Four bedrooms, two bathrooms, a compact kitchen and dining area. Pergola and backyard lawn glimpsed through venetian blinds. Front room given over to a decent home-theatre set-up, curtains drawn against the blinding sun. Somewhere outer-metropolitan, Australia or North America or Germany maybe. Somewhere 'normal'.

See, this is not normal. This is miraculous. If you can, just for a moment, see this house through the eyes of someone from another age: someone from a Phoenician seaport, perhaps.

Look in the refrigerator. A bright tableau of fresh vegetables and fruit; firm strawberries the size of plums; leafy greens that look as crisp as the moment they were picked. Cold fried chicken, a side of ham, slabs of Atlantic salmon, all of it held in chilled suspended animation until you want it. Juices, craft beer, five different kinds of cheese. In the pantry, impermeable bags of pasta and rice, tinned foods, spices from all over the world.

There's more. So much more. Twist the kitchen tap and unlimited fresh drinking water flows. The mysterious sockets on the walls unlock narrow currents of pure energy into which you can charge anything from a power drill to a machine that makes perfect coffee. With the turn of a dial, these cooktop burners will ignite with rosettes of clear blue flame. After sunset, we'll hold back the night for as long as we want with low-wattage halogens.

That's just the kitchen. Wander the rest of the house now, this small world of internalised wonders. A bathroom, bright white, where waste is eliminated at the push of a button. In the living room, page through the channels on the television: a baseball game in Osaka, a newsreader in London, a field of nodding oil pumps in a desert somewhere. Gold up, brent crude down, Dow steady. There were three scheduled television channels when I was young; then four, then the first pay television channels, then a hundred, then quite suddenly a thousandfold proliferation on-demand, of everything, from everywhere.

Abundance. The simple existence of the gas line and a push-button bowl that makes your shit disappear would surely have impressed our ancestors. Imagine trying to explain that those little power sockets are holding back tightly constrained lightning. Or how, exactly, the newsreader can appear on the big flat screen even though she's sitting eight time zones away.

'Any sufficiently advanced technology is indistinguishable from magic,' Arthur C. Clarke famously proposed. But given enough time, even magic bleaches into the mundane, and it can take a trick of the light to see it again.

So, try something different. Look around the house again, but dial the walls and ceiling back until they're semi-transparent. We can see the bones of the place now; wooden trusses in the roof, and the forgotten concrete pad on which the whole structure sits. But we can also see behind the magician's curtain and get a sense of how some of the magic is done. A lacework of electrical cables connecting every socket and switch, bundled into a thickening conduit that tracks along the roof beams and down an outside wall into a compact switchbox. Pressurised water pipes, half of them emerging from a hot water heater you forgot was there, branching upwards from a feeder line emerging out of the ground. Thin strands of network cable patched into a router and a PC in the spare room, a landline socket nobody uses. A gas line feeding the hot-water heater and stove. Drainage pipes vanishing into the concrete beneath the bathrooms and kitchen.

Dial back the visibility of the concrete slab, and then the solid earth itself, to see what we're really dealing with. The delicate fingers of polypipe and copper that trace the outlines of the house are just the outermost branches of these heavy networks mapped out under our feet. Freshwater supply and sewerage pipes, thick power conduits nestled in with optical fibre cables, gas lines in their own trenches – all of it underlain with heavy concrete drainage mains sloping away under the street. A weird grammar of pods, pits and water meters break the surface to hint at the enmeshed assemblies below. We can't see the hubs of these networks; they lie far from view. But, as we step back into the quiet street, keep in mind the traceries of bright electrons, the underground transactions of water and gas, and the currents of data shimmering along glass fibre at the speed of light. Because while we're on the subject of form and flow, there's something else we need to see here.

Draw a square a hundred metres on each side. It encloses one hectare: twelve houses. At average occupancy rates out here, that's thirty-one people, but since nearly everyone is at work, or school, or sleeping off shiftwork, we won't trouble them to come out into the street. Imagine, instead, if we could see the annual throughput of this hectare's modest dwellings. One year's worth of all the stuff that makes this a place a quiet abundance for thirty-one people, all at once.

Immediately then, a cube of unsorted solid waste nearly six metres high dumps into the middle of the street. Rotting food, slabs of polystyrene, broken concrete, a mass of wet plastic and dead computers; a block of reeking trash that towers overhead. The people who live on this street are pretty good at recycling, but this is still what it looks like if you pile up 2.9 tonnes of uncompacted solid waste per person, for a year.

Four cows, ten pigs, eleven lambs and 720 chickens are suddenly loose in the street. So many chickens. In the course of the year, all of these bright and inquisitive beings will be raised, force-fed and killed in places most of us will never have to visit, or even think about. A heaving pile of fish and prawns weighing three-quarters of a tonne is asphyxiating on the front lawn.

Now a cube of water sixteen metres high blots out the sky behind us. All these houses have been designed to use drinking water to flush toilets, which seems odd; then add all the washing machines, dishwashers and groundwater abstraction to keep the lawns looking good. So that's what four thousand tonnes of water looks like.

Stack up 156 barrels of fuel for the cars. Because this is an outer-metropolitan area with only homeopathic traces of public transport, everything from school drop-off to buying a loaf of bread requires a drive. We need one car per working adult, so 156 barrels it is.

Roughly a third of a shipping container represents a year's worth of manufactured goods per person. This is a wild estimate that has to account for imports, exports and a huge number of empty container movements on our road and rail networks. So, for the sake of the exercise, there's now a stack of nine shipping containers out in the middle of the street.

Finally, the backdrop of this whole strange scene: a cube of pure carbon dioxide gas weighing eight hundred tonnes, nearly eighty metres high. That's the unseen output of an unregulated heavy emitter such as Australia or the United States – where, for some of us, this particular kind of abundance is normal.

There are chickens running everywhere, grateful to be momentarily free of the hideous cages they've been trapped in for their entire lives.

Fade to black.

show us the money

The quiet house in the quiet street is reassuringly solid: a thing of brick and tile and timber. It endures weather and the slow micro-erosions of wear and tear; it has a fixed address and it can be seen, with sufficiently powerful optics, from space.

But it also has another kind of existence, fluid and weirdly post-geographical, in which it is a construct entirely of mathematical agreements we refer to as 'money'. Sometimes, I wonder how it would look if we could see this money: not the coins and polymer notes and crumpled bills, but that imaginary place where tides of it shimmer and flow around the world like electric vapour.

Before it even existed as a floorplan, the house took the form of a million-dollar bank loan. Probably you don't have rich relatives or a million dollars. Possibly you don't want to spend the rest of your life paying rent. So you get a job, go to a bank and ask them to loan a million dollars into existence for you. The bank needs to factor in the curious reality that by the time you've paid it back, the million dollars won't be worth as much as it is today. It needs to pay all the people whose time and expertise will go into drawing up the loan. And because this isn't a charity, it needs to make a profit: as large a profit as it can squeeze out of you. And so, the bank charges a thing called compounding interest on the loan. The rate of interest will be expressed as a percentage – let's say 5 per cent. They give you maybe thirty years to pay it all back.

You sign the contract. Here, here, and here. Also, here, and here: congratulations, you can keep the pen.

You never actually get to see the million dollars; it has no physical existence. But over the course of the next few months, precise blocks of it will be metered out to conveyancing agents and quantity surveyors, truck drivers, bricklayers and roof tilers, electricians and plumbers, as a quadrangle of weedy sand is converted into a building site and – eventually – a residence. None of these people get to see physical money either; its existence is accurately tracked and completely immaterial.

It is hard to reconcile the intangibility of money with the gravity it exerts on nearly every aspect of our lives, and it gets harder the bigger the numbers get. But for the next thirty years, the physical form of the house and all those documents you signed assume an addressable mathematical shape on the balance sheet of the bank. And sometimes I wonder how it would look, and what would change, if we could see that.

Just as you go to make your first monthly repayment, the bank will add the interest charge – one-twelfth of 5 per cent of what you owe them – to the original amount you borrowed. Now you owe them an additional $4166.66. It means that your monthly payment of $5368 only knocks a tiny chip off the total amount you owe the bank. A month later, they do it again. And again, and again. Every month for the next thirty years you send them $5368. Three decades later, on taking full legal ownership of the house, you'll have actually sent them a shade under two million dollars.

Maybe the house has increased in value over that time, maybe it hasn't; either way, the bank has doubled its money.

Somewhere, the coin-doubling mathematician tilts back on his chair and grins.

There are even things called interest-only loans, which in this case would mean your monthly repayment is only $4167. At the end of twelve months of these payments, you've sent the bank $50,000 and you still owe them the entire original million dollars. It's the financial equivalent of running while standing still: you can imagine the banking industry straining to fellate itself on the day it first came up with this idea. And if you were, for some reason, to start regularly paying less than $4166.66, the amount you owe would gradually escalate, the magic of compounding interest driving it slowly but steadily upwards in the direction of Alpha Centauri.

There are loan calculators that show you what happens when you push and pull the repayment schedule and interest rates around, but the basic model is solid; in fact, the basic model is what underpins the global financial system. Maybe this sounds a touch melodramatic, but that's because the loan calculators don't have anywhere in their spreadsheets for the thing that holds it all together in the real world: coercion.

See what happens if you miss a repayment. At first, polite phone calls, a late fee, and this month's interest charges added to what you owe. Miss the next month, and the follow-up takes written form with a legalistic edge: offers to refinance, and also warnings that something called a collection agency is going to get involved. Miss another month, and it's on: this collection agency has sent some people to bang on your door, and they'll introduce you to the full range of state-backed legal sanctions being moved into position over your head. As cold as mathematics itself, the interest charges keep coming. Compounding.

You'll lose your credit rating, your car, maybe a mandatory proportion of your income, and eventually the house itself. A trustee will go through your stuff to see what they can sell to recover some of the money. A mesh of legal restrictions on your movements and financial activities will settle tightly upon you for as long as you smell of bankruptcy. In some places, you'll go to jail. For obvious reasons, the process is designed to be unpleasant: you promised the bank you'd double their money in the future in exchange for a house now, and even though this obligation exists only as a short sequence of code in a banking mainframe, there are very direct and tangible consequences for refusing to balance the books. There have to be: this kind of system couldn't exist otherwise.

People have lost whole countries to this twin dynamic of compounding interest and coercive force. In the 1970s, Western banks engorged with Middle Eastern oil money went on a bender across Asia, Africa and Latin America, lending vast sums at low rates of interest to dictators and democrats alike. When interest rates rose sharply in the 1980s at the same time as commodity prices were falling, many of these countries fell behind on their payments, and the debts began to rise on the coin-doubling path. When it became obvious that repayment would be impossible, the International Monetary Fund – acting as a kind of global collection agency – knocked on the door and introduced the people of Somalia, India, Chile and many other places to the full range of state-backed legal sanctions being moved into position over their heads. 'Structural adjustment' was the phrase they used. Instead of selling their cars, the IMF forced them to sell their healthcare systems, fisheries and mineral resources.

It's hard to overstate the influence of this simple leverage; this engine of debt ratcheting across scales of space and time like an imaginary force of gravity. In his epic treatise *Debt: The First 5,000 Years*, David Graeber traces this engine back as far as the formation of Mesopotamia's first cities. He notes that debt and its physical guarantor, coercion, are never seen far from each other: 'If history shows anything, it is that there's no better way to justify relations founded on violence, to make such relations seem moral, than by reframing them in the language of debt.' The cheque book and the cruise missile, to borrow Indian author Arundhati Roy's phrase.

What is the connection between the doubling coin economy and the doubling iron-ore-and-piles-of-wet-trash economy? And given the importance of these electric tides in shaping our world, doesn't it seem passing curious that there are so few maps of their extent?

hadean dance

On this sun-warmed bubble of molten rock, a nano-scale dance has begun. It is impossible to know for sure how it begins, or exactly when these early dancers take form. But for a moment, we can imagine how the fiery stage is set.

A lonely beach on Planet Earth, more than four billion years ago. Glittering black sand unmarked by any kind of footprint. An oceanic world ripped with volcanic island chains, still bearing the signs of heavy bombardment. The night sky is a shock; gauzy and red, alive with flashes and meteor trails, new moon riding close overhead with her impact scars still fresh. None of the constellations are familiar. On the near horizon, slow fountains of magma are heaving out of the ground, coughing millions of tonnes of ash into the bruised sky.

This seems an impossibly hostile place for our dance to begin. So step into the warm waters of the restless ocean and dip beneath the surface. The drenching torrent of ultraviolent radiation eases as we move into deeper water. Oceanic darkness, silence broken by subsonic creaks and groans from somewhere ahead. As we slip further from the shoreline, red illumination pulses from below. Way beneath us, the seafloor is alive with volcanic rifts. Rising steam boils through the heat shimmer. Down here, not far from the explosive meeting place of magma and seawater, we meet our dancers for the first time. Along fissures in the seafloor, mineral-rich plumes of superheated water are rising into the gloom. Let's dwell here a moment.

The world has inherited a wild melange of chemicals from the interstellar drift: not just the iron and silicates that comprise the bones of the landscape, but compounds of phosphorous and sulphur; subtle chains and loops of carbon, hydrogen, oxygen, nitrogen. Some of these have been forged into new combinations in electrical storms; some have come to be concentrated in tidal mud pools, and some have been enlivened by the intense conditions around these luminous oceanic vents. Suspended in the potent medium of liquid water, something weird is happening.

To see it, we have to become impossibly small, shrinking until we leave the familiar world far behind. As we shrink, a grain of ash a millimetre across drifts past us. Continue shrinking; now the grain of ash is the size of a boulder, then a skyscraper, expanding to fill half our field of vision as we plummet through orders of magnitude. The water begins to resolve into countless tumbling bubbles of pure force. Look closer and each bubble is an identical fusion of an oxygen atom with two hydrogen atoms: a water molecule. Dimly, above us, the grain of ash now seems to be a thousand kilometres wide.

Here, suspended in this surreal churn, a larger molecular construct bounces past like a bulbous assembly of electric Lego. It dances into another complex molecule; their watery chaperones make way and electromagnetic attraction glues them together in a novel form. This new compound is highly reactive, and if it chances across another very particular resident of this strange liquid world, it will snap it in half. By coincidence, one of the tumbling halves happens to work like a submicroscopic matchmaker: in its presence, unions of the two original molecules are accelerated a millionfold.

Fuelled by a steady source of heat, occurring only in the presence of liquid water, this tight little feedback loop will self-assemble countless identical copies, for as long as there is sufficient supply of ingredients.

There is a word for this cycle, and others like it: autocatalysis. The magic here isn't just within the assembly and disassembly of these little molecular clusters, but when the outputs of these reactions feed back into the inputs and they become self-reinforcing. Imagine a set of these small loops closing on themselves, such that through several steps networks of chemical reaction sequences begin to catalyse their own creation. Then you'd have something called an autocatalytic set.

A helps in the creation of B. B makes possible the assembly of C. C vastly increases the supply of A. Somehow, formations of these strange dancers are arising out of the background ferment, slowly increasing in complexity, flexibility, unpredictability.

One in particular catches our eye. A long, twisted strand, with dozens of daughter molecules pegged to it, is becoming oddly ubiquitous. Not only do snippets of this polymer dramatically accelerate certain reactions, but as we watch, it is assembling a copy of itself out of some of the fragments it helped create. And then another copy. And another.

Some of the copies are wobbly and imperfect, but those that are better suited to the ambient conditions are more likely to last long enough to make more copies.

Roll forward then, years blending into centuries, down through millennia. These looped reaction sequences wrap tighter around each other as ingredients become scarce. Some of them consume all available ingredients and collapse, some are wiped out by meteors, but on this planet, at least, some of them prevail. Entwined around fluxes of free energy and exotic chemistries, they are a form of accidental novelty and complexity pushing uphill against entropy's cold gradient. These fluid chemical circuits aren't alive in any meaningful sense, but exist in some liminal crossover between chemistry and life.

There is still no settled definition of what life even is, but here's one loose formulation. At its very simplest, life on this planet mostly shares three qualities: the ability to self-perpetuate, a metabolic flow-through of energy and materials, and some form of enclosure or boundary.

If these distinctions seem strangely arbitrary, it's because they are. We're looking back through an ocean of time, to a landscape that no longer exists, under geochemical conditions strikingly different to almost anything that exists on earth today. There are no fossils, no surviving geology, from this turbulent time. Traces and versions of this story have had to be reconstructed by several generations of patient geochemists, geneticists and microbiologists. There is little canonical certainty to be found here, just degrees of collective confidence or dispute over how well certain ideas and lines of argument fit with the afterimages of this lost time.

Perpetuation. Metabolism. Boundaries. As we float here, our autocatalytic dancers are perilously close to fulfilling all three. These ancient seas are adrift with particular flavours of lipid chemicals that can form semi-porous, water-repelling surfaces. One theory suggests these bubbles are closing over our self-amplifying loops, protecting them in waterproof vessels and enabling the next stage of their journey.

As more evidence is sought and assembled, details of the story will surely change. Maybe we'll never really know how it all got started, and that's okay. Hold here for as long as you like, rocked into a reverie on the tides of a Hadean sea.

in the shape of a city

Ten minutes walk from the quiet house in the quiet street, a concrete shopping mall bakes out on a tarmac plain. A scatter of parked cars shimmer in the afternoon sun, some scrawny trees signifying only the absence of shade. Sometimes old memories superimpose themselves over dreams from childhood, back when half the car park was scrappy bushland that we'd cross on our way to school. I didn't know this was originally someone else's country, didn't hear the old names spoken until I was in my early twenties. This was a place, once, but now it could be anywhere on the urban periphery of the industrialised world.

These structures always have their backs turned to the surroundings, blank and inward-facing. No windows, just eight-metre tilt-up walls indented by a shuttered loading dock and a queue of bins. Subliminal roar of rooftop air conditioners. Whoever built this thing was on a budget and in a hurry. Shading my eyes, stepping across the car park into the angled shadow cast by this monolith; anything to get out of the deadening sun.

Rounding the corner to discover that things are a little more active on the street frontage. A secondary arterial road and a feeder avenue intersect here; traffic banked up at the lights with the afternoon crush is slowing everything to a crawl. The opposite side of the intersection seems very far away. Aerial signage in primary colours, huge and simple enough to be read by drivers passing at speed. Global fast-food outlets with drive-through bays. Glass showroom of a car yard with bulked-up SUVs ramped against chain-link fencing. Familiar franchises on the kerb opposite: pawnbroker, service station, op-shop run by one of the big churches. More car parking. Roofline of a massive hardware store one block back. There's a bus stop here somewhere, a concrete bench and an orange post sticking out of the ground which gets visited by a bus every ninety minutes on alternate Wednesdays, maybe.

Under a vaguely faux-deco portico, a swish of automatic doors, into the freezing interior. A few of us tried to hold a low-key action in a place like this once, handing out leaflets and inviting people to sign a petition against a new uranium mine. Centre management's security contractors were onto us within minutes; it felt like we'd triggered a corporate immune system response, moving quickly to surround the suspected infectious agent, assessing it, dissolving it.

Not today. Today I just have a list of a couple of things I need. The anchor tenants are two ubiquitous shopping-centre chains; this one for groceries, that one for clothing and household items. A handful of smaller specialty stores are ranged around this enclosed simulacrum of a town square – a mobile phone shop, a newsagent, a cafe with pastries under glass. Without exception, all of these specialised outlets are copy-and-paste franchise operations, duplicated into existence and slotted into the power and telecoms sockets of the shopping centre.

From this concrete cube in the car park, the quiet house of abundance is restocked and provisioned. From here, the perfect vegetables and the five kinds of cheese and Atlantic salmon. This is where the circuit closes between vendor and customer: the Anthropocene's point-of-sale.

Today it has an atmosphere of transience and fatigue; something feels different. A swelling tide of commerce is routing around complexes like this now. The signs are everywhere; I'm pausing outside the little cafe to notice that the handful of patrons are all gazing into the depthless glow of mobile phones. These devices hybridised with credit cards within recent memory; now they pair with a fleet of delivery vans and bikes inbound from gargantuan fulfilment centres or the local Thai place.

Hiss and tap of an espresso machine.

Much like the playlist they have running unobtrusively over the sound system, this place is an artifact of the fast-receding twentieth century. It only works at a certain kind of scale. Even the greatest cities of antiquity were barely more than an hour's walk from side to side, fine-grained and human-scaled by necessity and design. In the industrial age, cities began to grow along the armatures of mechanised public transport, settlement archipelagos clustered around railway stations and along streetcar corridors. Each of these outposts, in turn, had to be pedestrian-scaled since only the very wealthy got around in horse-drawn carriages or motorised vehicles.

And then, in the shocked aftermath of World War II, came the coin-doubling surge of the great acceleration. A design template perfected in North America in the 1950s: oil refined in Texas, pumped into vehicles mass-produced in Detroit and parked in front of quiet houses in quiet streets on Long Island. Land-use plans rapidly evolving to accommodate the turning radii and stopping distances of two-tonne projectiles moving at eighty miles an hour, stretching the physical dimensions of human settlements out of all recognition. The city might still only be an hour's travel from side to side, but now you pass that hour in the comfort of a private rocket-cocoon with tail fins and wind-tunnel styling, and you traverse distances that would take five days on foot.

With the essential elements refined and market-tested by an advertising industry coming into its strength, it's time to put the show on the road. High streets and older urban cores will now be wiped out, erased for overpasses and car parks, bankrupted by self-reinforcing economies of scale. The streetcars and rail networks bought up and dismantled, bus services starved into obsolescence, Gulf wars and coups and assassinations, and blink through six decades to find that the explosive proliferation of the internal combustion engine has stranded us here, in a concrete cube in some edge suburb with the air conditioning turned up too high.

We should step along. Feels like it's nearly closing time here.

The consumer embryo begins to develop during the first year of existence. Children begin their consumer journey in infancy. And they certainly deserve consideration as consumers at that time.

JAMES U. McNEAL, PIONEERING YOUTH MARKETER

consumer

Rolling down the freezer aisle, wonky wheel on my shopping trolley, hurried list on a Post-it note. You can spend a lot of coins in here if your budget extends to artisanal herbs in plastic capsules or fancy cheeses that smell like spew, but for the most part the essentials are affordable. This is good, because right now I'm as broke as I've ever been.

Abundance, an absurdity of it. Down this aisle, gleaming pink treasures stripped of all signifiers of assembly-line slaughter. Wobbly ninety-degree turn into the fresh food department; the fruits of millennia of careful selective breeding by farmers whose names we'll never know. These lemons are from California, three for a dollar. Keep rolling. Plastic-wrapped toilet rolls from Sarawak, twelve for six dollars. Blocks of perfectly white copy paper from Vietnam. Everything in the cleaning aisle and the hardware and electrical goods section comes from the Pearl River Delta, cheap as hell. Clothes pegs on my list because every time I hang out a load of washing, more of them fall apart.

Another ninety-degree turn. Announcement over the shopping centre PA: 'People everywhere are today disobeying the law of obsolescence. They are using their old cars, their old tyres, their old radios and their old clothing much longer than statisticians had expected on the basis of earlier experience.' That's New York real estate broker Bernard London, sitting amid the catastrophe of the Great Depression in 1932. He is appalled that the Depression appears to be a crisis not of scarcity but of abundance: 'the fact that millions were suffering amidst glutted markets and surpluses'. His big idea is to reboot the stalled growth engine by making everyone throw things out faster.

'In the earlier period of prosperity, the American people did not wait until the last possible bit of use had been extracted from every commodity. They replaced old articles with new for reasons of fashion and up-to-dateness. They gave up old homes and old automobiles long before they were worn out, merely because they were obsolete.' Saying this like it's a good thing is how London makes the case for planned obsolescence. And if people can't be persuaded to throw things out fast enough, the things themselves can be designed to fall apart or start looking like shit just as the new season's goods are arriving in stores.

Now product cycles artificially accelerated by designer entropy and 'fashion and up-to-dateness' collide with the imperatives of least-cost waste disposal. The basic moving parts of the locust economy we're contending with today are already settling into place by the mid-1930s. All that remains is to weld it more tightly to the coin-doubling machine. In the aftermath of World War II, the focus won't be on extracting reparations from the shell-shocked populations of Germany and Japan, but on turning them into mass markets for US manufactured goods. The advertising industry goes to work on persuasion techniques for enforcing the law of obsolescence. The consumer age has arrived.

Hey – I've found the clothes pegs. For some reason they were next to the electric wine-openers and something called a salad spinner. Fifty pegs shrink-wrapped for two dollars. Amazing.

Like the man says, we begin our consumer journey in infancy. Even the word quietly sliming its way into our vocabulary: *consumer*. Apparently, this is me now: a helpless little chick in a soiled nest, beak desperately agape, screeching for someone to come along and regurgitate some goods and services into it. Consuming isn't something I do anymore – apparently it's what I am.

It's not like they didn't spell out what they were going to do to us. 'Advertising helps to keep the masses dissatisfied with their mode of life, discontented with ugly things around them,' announced Roy Dickinson in the US trade journal *Printers' Ink* in 1930. 'Satisfied customers are not as profitable as discontented ones.'

The mission here is to create both supply and demand, and to never, ever leave people contented. 'The future of business lay in its ability to manufacture customers as well as products,' according to one advertising journal. Manufacturing discontent not just with the ugly things around us, but inventing whole new insecurities within. Under this doctrine, we are now all the product of 'industry's conscious attempt to direct man's critical faculties against himself or his environment, to make him self-conscious about matters of coarse things such as enlarged nose pores, bad breath.'

If you're disturbed by what they're doing to man's critical faculties, wait till you see what they have in mind for women and people who don't slot into imaginary binaries. Soon you'll discover you are simultaneously too fat, too skinny, boobs too big, too small, hair's all wrong, those shoes don't match this skin condition we've just created.

Bastards.

In 1979, the US Federal Trade Commission considers prohibiting advertising targeted at children, since kids don't yet have the critical faculties to navigate the intense manipulation we're all being subjected to. Peggy Charren, the founder of Action for Children's Television, gives compelling evidence to one of their hearings: 'I think the child cannot bring enough information to bear not to be deceived and to have an unfair trade practice,' she tells the FTC.

How about no, say the Grocery Manufacturers Association, the Chocolate Manufacturers Association, the National Soft Drink Association, a whole slew of toy companies and advertising firms, and a creepy little outfit called FACT: Families Against Censored Television. This is the dawn of Reagan's America: shirt open at the collar, perfect hair slicked with pomade. The neoliberal tide is surging into the White House; Jimmy Carter and his solar panels and stupid cardigan are on the way out. Congress is open for business. In 1980, it passes the *Federal Trade Commission Improvements Act* – the first swing against the commission's existing mandate, starting the process of deregulating children's television advertising altogether. By 1984, it's a free-market free-fire zone. Any child old enough to be parked in front of a television can be made 'dissatisfied by their mode of life' by marketers employing an army of child psychologists and behaviourists.

And so here's where this leaves us: surrounded, democratic institutions hollowed out, paranoid about our nose pores. There is nowhere to hide. A marketing firm way back in 2007 estimated a person living in a US city saw 5000 commercial messages a day. 'We never know where the consumer is going to be at any point in time, so we have to find a way to be everywhere,' said the CEO of a New York ad agency. That's probably a severe undercount these days – commercial messaging on social media makes the ad world of 2007 seem as retro as those directives from the 1930s. Facebook retargeting now implants tiny tracking scripts on all your devices so that increasingly networked, adaptive and autonomous ads can be precision-guided into your desires and insecurities. If the scale of this marketing dystopia gives you anxiety, they'll likely know that well before your clinical diagnosis, and be pre-positioned to sell you a lifetime supply of anti-anxiety medication.

Thing is, I don't feel manipulated by advertising: quite the opposite. Economics textbooks say I'm a free-thinking individual who makes purchasing decisions based on rational needs and desires, and I find the suggestion that I could be swayed by something as crass as a browser pop-up a bit insulting. But globally, advertising was a US$532-billion-dollar industry in 2019. Why are they doing that if all of us are free-thinking individuals who make purchasing decisions based on rational needs and desires? Half a trillion dollars. Someone out there must be buying it.

Anyway, nose-pore tape was the last item on my shopping list: time to make my way to the checkout. Front wheel of the trolley spinning in desperate little circles. Right before closing time, nobody is working the checkouts but here's a bank of automated checkout machines blinking ominously. Doing my bit to prevent mass extinction and collapse, I'll spend an extra two bucks on a heavy polythene bag to join the twenty others at home that I keep forgetting to bring with me.

Placing the bag in the bagging area, eyeless face of the machine immediately flashing a panicked red. 'UNEXPECTED ITEM IN THE BAGGING AREA.'

I don't know if it's referring to me or the bag. Blood-pressure rising, trying to attract the attention of the shopping centre's sole living employee, and surely I can't be the only one in here who also feels like a misaligned wheel spinning in desperate little circles.

tumble and run

Anchored to the rocks not far from a simmering hydrothermal fissure, see what the Hadean dancers have wrought, given favourable circumstance and breathtaking spans of time.

She is maybe a micrometre from end to end – a capsule one-thousandth of a millimetre long – a giant compared to the simple constructs we were tracing earlier. Those protean molecular chains and grids have been copied and stacked, repeated, woven by trial and error into something so remarkable that it may never be possible to figure out how she did it. From the outside, a pleated, semi-permeable membrane allows the passage of valuable substances and energy-bearing chemicals into the tumble of activity within. In the psychedelic interior, we're suspended in a whirl of movement: reaction and construction and decomposition. Recognising some of those ancient autocatalytic cycles we met on the seafloor, stylised and streamlined, but familiar. Those primary loops of assembly and disassembly have been formalised somehow; metered out and synchronised.

At the centre of this effort lies a descendant of that self-copying helical polymer we met millions of years ago. In the intervening time, it has become paired with a mirror image of itself, in a characteristic double helix formation containing thousands of the daughter molecules, or nucleotides, like rungs on a twisted ladder. Deoxyribonucleic acid, or DNA, as it will eventually be known. The cell's means of perpetuation, transcribed in a self-authoring genetic cuneiform emerging at the intersection of chemistry and code. This is what the dancers have made.

Something else is also stored here: a library of molecular fragments hacked from parasitic viruses. These seas are saturated with them – mindless little hijackers that invade living cells and force them to replicate the virus. This tiny being has been forced to establish what microbiologists dryly refer to as 'a distinct self–non-self recognition mechanism'. In developing a form of adaptive immunity to viral attack, she has had to learn to recognise the difference between her own genetic material and that of the viral parasites she swims with. Even at this formative, ancient stage, she has learnt to cope with harmful attackers, and to distinguish self from other. All those that didn't are long gone.

47

Her world is drenched in radiation, heaving with volcanism, shocked by meteor bombardment, seething with viruses. This is Luca – the last universal common ancestor of all life on earth. Ancient, steadfast, delicate, and metal as fuck.

Her lineage takes in all the countless experiments and accidents and dark evolutionary alleys stumbled down, the tangled roots of life's tree sunk deep in shadow. This rock surface is coated with her sisters, daughters, near and distant relatives. They share loops and strands of DNA freely, in a world where the boundary between life and non-life is porous and ambiguous. Their metabolism is so tightly coupled with chemical fluxes within the environment it's hard to discern a boundary. None of them could have come into being without the collective existence of the whole, and each of them is subtly different from the others. As the world turns, these differences will be tested by time and temperature, contingency and luck. The slight but important differences between Luca's daughters are magnifying, diversifying over time. So while the world of the prochlorophytes and halobacteria might seem impossibly remote and irrelevant in our own chaotic age, these tiny beings seem to have quietly set about building the foundations of everything.

An ancestral *Escherichia coli* glides towards us out of the gloom, pushed along by whip-like propellers. She pauses, then abruptly her rotors begin spinning in reverse, cork-screwing in all directions and sending her tumbling away randomly. She pauses again in the middle distance and then, propellers aligned, jets off in a straight line, out of our field of view.

She's trying to find food. Be careful not to anthropomorphise – there's no point attributing human qualities or consciousness to a tiny shell of cytoplasm one-thousandth of a millimetre long. She has no brain or nervous system of any kind, no eyes, no sense of touch. And yet . . . she's trying to find food.

E. coli has no real sense of direction either, and only two modes of travel: swim in a straight line or tumble around at random. She is attracted to particular flavours in the seawater, and can detect them via chemical receptors arrayed along her flanks. This doesn't tell her which direction to swim in, just that it's out there somewhere. This existential dilemma is solved by comparing how strong the flavour is now compared to how strong it was a few moments ago. If it's stronger, tumbling behaviour is suppressed. If its weaker, she'll throw herself into a spin and try a different direction, testing the water against how it was a moment before. This process works just as well if she's trying to avoid toxins: if the water tastes worse than it did a moment ago, try a different direction. If it tastes better, keep going. Bacterial chemotaxis, they call it. Not all bacteria do it – if your kink is being anchored to the seafloor, slowly dissolving the ground, or just inhaling what's floating past, this doesn't apply to you in quite the same way. But if your search for food has taken you out into the wilds of the water column, you need a bigger behavioural repertoire if you're to survive. And if food has become scarce, that repertoire will be tested against that of your bacterial peers.

Here we glimpse the simplest origins of perception, memory and agency. Way back here at the very base of the evolutionary tree, these tiny cells are already able to perceive beneficial or harmful conditions in their environment, compare them with their states in an earlier time, and take action accordingly.

In the crossover between autocatalytic chemistry and the earliest life forms, we encountered metabolism, boundaries and perpetuation. Almost immediately, some of life's progeny have formed subtle new capabilities in pursuance of these primary imperatives – capabilities that will shape everything to come. These loops, too, are self-reinforcing. The creatures with slightly sharper senses, a slightly better memory, a more responsive set of behaviours will be fractionally more likely to survive and reproduce. Repeat. And repeat, and repeat, as the young planet swings around its home star through the galactic drift, year after year.

Metabolism, boundaries, perpetuation. Memory, perception, agency. Propellers whirring back into motion again and you can see, perhaps, where this tiny creature might be heading.

Just make sure you never anthropomorphise an *E. coli*. They hate it when you do that.

get a job

'Get a job,' the guy screams out the car window as he steers past us, and I've lost count of how many times I've heard that bawled at a demonstration. I can follow the logic, though. There's a mining industry conference happening over the road: if we're out here on a traffic island during office hours holding a banner demanding an alternative to coin-doubling collapse, then it looks like we're unemployed. Actually, some of us are. Tonight, on the television, a wax-faced politician will call us a drain on society, leaching on a welfare system funded by other people's taxes. If drive-by guy has to work ten hours a day on a 12/9 fly-in-fly-out roster at a job he hates, so should we.

The banner reads 'no jobs on a dead planet' because we were in a hurry and couldn't think of something more original, but that's not why he's angry at the sight of us. He works as a truck driver for a mining contractor, and he's just spent the morning reading about how the next generation of haul trucks are going to be driverless. His only real asset – a quiet house in a quiet street – is sliding in value in this queasy market, even though the real-estate pages keep saying things are about to pick up. They better, because he's on the hook for a million-dollar mortgage, and just the interest on that loan is consuming a third of his take-home pay. So, yeah: a stressful morning for our guy, who can honestly do without these fucking hippies obstructing traffic outside the conference.

Persuading him to make common cause with us seems a long way out of reach.

That's the basic picture of the economy, though: if I sell forty hours a week of my time, I'll be paid well enough to afford a roof over my head and a life of consumer abundance unthinkable to my grandparents, to look after the people I love, and to put something away for a rainy day or a holiday or whatever. On the other side of the equation, companies of all shapes and sizes will do the heavy lifting, producing the goods and services we could never produce alone, harnessing our collective labour and a steady flow of investment. The magic medium that makes the whole thing go round is state-backed currency, stacks of Anthropocene coinage seamlessly converting hours behind the wheel of a haul truck into interest payments on a house.

Economics textbooks from the late 1940s onwards illustrate this basic agreement as an eternal loop, a simple plumbing diagram, with money cycling between companies on one side and workers on the other. 'Henry Ford said he paid his workers $5 a day so that they could afford to buy the cars that they produced. Workers are depicted as paying their wages to buy what they make,' economic historian Michael Hudson explains. In the diagram, personal savings drain some of the flow away, and business investment recharges it. It's practically Taoist. From somewhere in this near-distant history emerges the phrase 'time is money' and that's the deal here: you exchange your time for money. You never get the time back, but the money can be converted into the things that keep you alive. On one side, firms investing and making stuff; on the other side, workers earning and consuming stuff – and all around this perpetual motion machine, unstated but implied, things getting basically better. Progress.

Let's add another loop to the diagram then, for the sake of completeness. About a fifth of what the truck driver earns never reaches his pay packet, because the state taxes it, taxes everyone, and from that collective pool come the schools, the hospitals, the roads we're all driving around on, the military deployments far from here to ensure the oil keeps flowing. The more you earn, the more tax you pay. Some of that pool goes to support people outside the employer–employee loop: students, the aged, the sick and those unable to find paid work. That's the social safety net, the part of the agreement that says the system will look after you for a while even if you're not part of the main game of productive exchange between capital and labour.

So when some of those people not willing to find work and pay tax are seen holding up banners outside a conference of people who are, then one's natural reaction might be to suggest that they put the banner down and *get a job*.

Our driver is in good company; in fact, he is very close to being in the majority. At the start of the 2020s on Planet Earth, 3.4 billion people have got a job. There are another 174 million people who are unemployed but looking for work, so we have a total global workforce of more than three and a half billion people – about 45 per cent of the world's population.

Okay, stop: maybe all those numbers jumbled up in a sentence made your eyes glaze over like mine just did. We can do this a different way. Imagine the whole human population – about 7.8 billion of us in mid-2020 – is represented by just a hundred people.

That's better. It's easier to remember that we're one huge extended family when there's only a hundred of us in the village. So let's introduce ourselves, starting with the twenty-six children here under the age of fifteen. That's right – a quarter of the village population are children – hey, kids!

While that sinks in, let's meet the eight people here over the age of sixty-five – would you like some tea?

Now let's meet the people doing the work. In rough numbers, it looks like there are forty-three people in this village over the age of fifteen who have a job, and another two who are trying to find one. Twenty-three of these workers are like our haul-truck driver – they are employed by someone else. Another fifteen people in our planetary village are what the International Labor Organisation calls 'own account workers' – they're self-employed, or working in partnerships or co-ops. An additional four people are characterised by the ILO as 'contributing family workers' – they work for a relative living in the same household: a family business of some kind.

So far so good. So, what do we all do for a living? Well, twelve of us work in agriculture, producing the perfect vegetables and the five kinds of cheese and the Atlantic salmon. Ten of us work in industry – mining, manufacturing, construction, transport. Another twenty-one of us work in services – that's everything from hospitality to call centres, aged care to teaching, and collecting statistics about everybody else. Don't forget two of us are unemployed, maybe long-term, looking for paid work that just isn't there.

Forty-five villagers in total, trying to work in order to survive: a whole class of us. A working class. But notice the huge racial and gender skew at all levels. Nearly all the wealthy people here are white. Nearly all the impoverished people are not. Nearly all the wealthy people here are men. Nearly all the impoverished people are not. Men overwhelmingly dominate the high-value occupations, and, worldwide, for every dollar a man earns, someone who isn't a man earns seventy-seven cents for carrying out the equivalent work.

And fifty-five of us, including most of the kids, aren't in the paid workforce at all – more than half the world's population lives somewhere outside that plumbing diagram in the textbook. And here's something: while there are only nine working-aged men in this village outside the labour market, there are twenty women. What do we suppose they are doing? Working for nothing, of course. Together with the unpaid labour performed by those women who are in the paid workforce – estimated at two and a half times more hours per week than that carried out by men – this gigantic contribution to the household and care economy is simply invisible to that textbook model. Time is money, unless you're a woman, in which case it's a donation.

'It is peasants, mothers, fishers and gatherers working with natural thermodynamic processes who meet everyday needs for the majority of people on earth,' writes Australian sociologist Ariel Salleh of this enormous volunteer economy. 'Inhabiting the margins of capitalism – domestic and geographic peripheries – these workers are unspoken, as if "nowhere" in the world-system.'

Look around more closely at some of the people we're sharing this village with. Twelve of us are undernourished. Ten of us are living in extreme poverty, without access to basic services, sanitation or safe drinking water. A quarter of the population of the village has one or both feet in the informal economy, where job security and working conditions can range from precarious to life-threatening. Nineteen of us – a fifth of the whole village – are employed in low-income or industrialising countries. Rounding up, one of the villagers is a slave – forty million people, most of them trapped in corporate supply chains.

The fact that there are now more slaves than at any time in human history brings the enforced cruelty of the whole set-up into focus. All that's needed to make it work is cheap transport, fast telecommunications and strong borders. They call this 'global labour arbitrage', which is just an edgy-sounding way of hiring people in weak currency zones and forcing them to do the same work at a fraction of the cost. Alternatively, import strictly delimited cohorts of low-waged workers into strong currency zones and get them to pick fruit or be maids or pour concrete. The combination of precarity, aggressive policing and hard currency is mostly effective at discouraging people from holding up banners at intersections.

The diagram in the textbook didn't say anything about this. It didn't say that money itself would tilt the terrain on which this interchange between workers and companies was occurring; that some would be playing the game with dollars backed by the US Federal Reserve, while others played with ringgit and rial and rupees.

Which leaves us with the 1 per cent – the only villager we've not heard from yet. The ILO classifies his employment status as 'employer', which means everyone else here works for him. With an inheritance from his parents and the profits he's skimmed off everyone else's work, he's been able to buy up 45 per cent of all the land, 45 per cent of the village infrastructure, 45 per cent of the farm animals in their feedlots and the chickens smashed into their little cages. This one white guy owns 45 per cent of everything. Clearly, being the only employer is a pretty good deal, because the poorest sixty-four adults in this village, nearly all of them people of colour, have only managed to hold onto 2 per cent of the village's wealth between them. Maybe they should get a job!

Our village metaphor gets shaky here, partly because dividing the world's population by 100 is too low-resolution a model to really convey these steeply engineered gradients of wealth and poverty. There are around twenty million millionaires in the world, so they make up only a quarter of a villager. Billionaires are much rarer: according to a thing that actually exists called the Wealth-X Billionaire Census, there are 2604 billionaires on the planet, or 0.003 per cent of a villager.

Here's the most important thing, the part they leave out of that economics textbook altogether. Our 1-per-cent villager doesn't have a 'job' in the same way the rest of us do. Because he's the sole employer, his job is to bank those profits. Because he owns 45 per cent of the village, his job is to bank the rent we pay him. Because he also owns the bank, his job is to loan this surplus to people who need money to buy a house, or a mine, or a squad of riot police. He loans it at competitive rates of interest, unless people are desperate, in which case he loans it for a lot more.

It feels like that stage midway through a game of Monopoly when you realise exactly which player's going to clean you all out. So maybe you and me and the angry truck driver are no closer to making common cause, but while we've been out here yelling at each other to get a job, our 1-per-cent villager just doubled his coins again.

Life did not take over the globe by combat,
but by networking.

LYNN MARGULIS AND DORION SAGAN, *MICROCOSMOS*

symbiogenesis

The world belongs to Luca's daughters. The Archaeans and the bacteria, their daughters and granddaughters will have the run of the place for the next one and a half billion years. The sun and its archipelago of worlds will complete six slow orbits around the galactic core, constellations shifting imperceptibly across this unthinkable span of time. Volcanic island chains outline the great tectonic seams of the simmering inner earth, buoyant cores of the earliest continents welded gradually together out of these early landforms.

Roll the clock forward and we'll witness the slow proliferation of these creatures into every habitable corner of the world ocean – anywhere there are fluxes of energy and raw materials to feed the ancient autocatalytic loops they've long since embodied. There is no agenda here, no intention, no purpose. Whoever is best at reading the oceanic room is rewarded with the possibility of continuity, and whoever falls out of sync with this slow-motion global dance is lost.

This is a collective endeavour – with the stakes so high, no-one can afford to be an island. Our ancestral *Escherichia coli* is able to tumble and run because she is a perceptive creature, reading chemical gradients in the seawater. Some of those chemicals are put there by her relatives and peers: even in these earliest of days, this sisterhood is alive with communication, and that's helping them survive. 'Quorum sensing,' we'll call it in billions of years' time – she's emitting specialised molecules called pheromones that help trigger behavioural changes in those around her. Perception and expression, entwined in a tight feedback loop.

There's more: hold here a moment to watch as two of these miraculous beings extend tiny drawbridges to each other, now passing segments of DNA back and forth like mixtapes. They are swimming in a sea of information; chemical and genetic innovations diffusing between wildly diverse branches of evolution's gradually spreading tree.

Already, three distinct lifestyles seem to be emerging. A diverse ensemble working as the primary producers, providing for their needs by consuming energy-rich chemicals wherever they find them. Methanogens, halophiles, sulphate reducers, take a squishy little bow.

They've done the hard work in building up complex organic chemistries, but the falling rain of their tiny corpses is far too rich a resource to just leave lying around on the seafloor. Enter the saprophytes – the decomposers – who make their living breaking down and consuming the bodies of the dead.

It doesn't take a huge leap of imagination to visualise these scavengers tucking into a meal that hadn't quite got around to dying; and so, the third great domain of cellular predation emerges. From the beginning, life is having to pay attention to the emergence and shifting behaviours of other life.

Even here, in the earliest times, these creatures are shaping their own conditions, widening the collective comfort zone. And now some have begun to experiment with the greatest energy source of all. The upper reaches of the oceans are drenched in sunlight, a radiant source of energy that has lain out of reach of their metabolic networks until now. There is no clear evidence who figured this out first or exactly when, but these early Archaean oceans are almost certainly home to the first photosynthesisers. The ability to convert solar energy into chemical energy and store it for when you need it: this will change everything. Freed from terrestrial energy sources, swarms of innovators proliferate across the sunlit upper reaches of the ocean, unaware of what they've set in motion.

By maybe three and a half billion years ago, one of them, the cyanobacteria, perfects a version of this trick that consumes carbon dioxide and emits oxygen as a waste gas. Alone or glued together in long spindles, now they begin to reshape the face of the planet. Immense algal blooms paint the open waters. In shallow tidal bays, untold billions of them create great

domed colonies – stromatolites – providing habitat for other bacterial deni-
zens and leaving behind some of the earliest fossil evidence of life in these
warm Archean seas. For several hundred million years, their fiercely reactive waste oxygen reacts with other chemicals in the seawater and out in the
desert uplands, oxidising them to create a wild array of new minerals. Tiny
particles of iron suspended in the ocean begin to rust, falling to the seafloor
and forming the first thick layers of what will eventually become banded
ironstone formations. Still the oxygen keeps coming. When everything that
can rust has rusted – around two and a half billion years ago – free oxygen
starts piling up in the oceans and atmosphere.

The cyanobacteria have accidentally kicked over an inconceivably
huge domino. The delicate organic fabrics of Archean cells have evolved
in a world without oxygen; many of them now begin to succumb to the
presence of this atomic-scale explosive. They begin their epochal retreat
into places oxygen can't reach: deep marine sediments, pools of mud,
hydrothermal vents. It is imagined that many, many cell lines vanish into
extinction as the oxygen crisis gains pace, but the next dominos have only
just begun to fall.

Even as this vast catastrophe is laying waste to the Archaeans, new
cell strains are adapting to the presence of oxygen in the ocean and folding it into their metabolic cycles, unlocking enormous energy potential.
Not only have living systems thoroughly intercepted global fluxes of carbon, nitrogen, phosphorous and sulphur for their own ends, they are now
introducing entirely new loops and pathways in a cascade of unintended
consequences.

As the Archean passes into the Proterozoic eon, one of these consequences almost kills our story dead. Oxygen produced by the runaway
proliferation of solar cyanobacteria has been seeping into the planet's
methane-dominated atmosphere. Methane is a potent heat-trapping gas
and until now has been largely responsible for keeping surface temperatures within a range tolerable for life. Now, traces of free oxygen are
soaking up huge quantities of it, oxidising it away into carbon dioxide
and water. Around 2.4 billion years ago, temperatures begin to fall, and
the world plunges into a forbidding ice age. For three hundred million
years, Planet Earth is an ice world, freezing most of the oceans over, nearly

shutting down photosynthesis and ending the whole show. For brief spells the planet lurches into warmer phases, before falling back into the deep freeze known now as the Huronian glaciation.

It's not clear how the world manages to pull out of this long winter, and it's not the last time the place will experience sudden wild swings into very different climate regimes. But as the oceans defrost and the glaciers withdraw, Luca's daughters bounce back, improvising something that will set the stage for the next great revolution of life on earth. It's unknown exactly when this experimentation begins, or how they pull it off, but sometime between 2.1 and 1.9 billion years ago, a bacterium starts living inside an Archean without either killing the host or being digested. Now considered one of the most significant leaps in evolution's long history, this 'symbiogenesis' transition probably reflects long relationships between bacterial strains slowly formalising in the most intimate way imaginable.

Most of the DNA of these hybrid creatures withdraws into its own specialised cocoon within the cell – the nucleus. Its operations are by now astonishingly complex and subtle. It encodes significant traces of the history of life within itself, such that the ghosts of its lineage can still be read in nucleotide molecules strung along its length. The presence of this nucleus gives these cells their name: the eukaryotes, or true seeds, to distinguish them from their Archean and bacterial ancestors the prokaryotes, or pre-seeds. In contrast to the wild genetic promiscuity of the prokaryotes, eukaryotes mostly hold their genetic cards close. Rather than passing mixtape DNA bundles between themselves, at the earliest branch point in their history, for reasons that may have to do with stripping out maladaptive mutations, keeping pace with parasites, or maybe just because it's so great, eukaryotes invent sex, and like it so much they stick with it for the next billion years.

The possibilities seem suddenly enormous: as we swing into the Neoproterozoic era around a billion years ago, evolution's tempo quickens as a proliferation of new kinds of eukaryote cells emerge.

The foundations of a living global metabolism have been laid down: primary producers absorbing sunlight or feeding off chemical fluxes, carnivores emerging to take what they can, and an army of decomposers digesting and recycling the dead. Swarms of life in the oceans, bacterial collectives experimenting with life at the edge of the land, a trace of oxygen, and sex in the air.

Great work, everyone. Slowly it's beginning to feel like home.

The Australian people, clearly, voted at the last election on what everyone knew was a referendum on the carbon tax, to get rid of the carbon tax . . . I congratulate the Australian public for their decision, and I congratulate all the parliamentarians who have followed the dictates of the Australian public in having this bill passed today.

SENATOR IAN MACDONALD, 17 JULY 2014

39 – 33

'The question is that the bills be now read a third time.'

I got a job. It hasn't turned out how I hoped. The president confirms this will require a vote, calls it on. A murmur of conversation among a knot of ministers down the far end of the Senate. The bells will ring for four minutes so that anyone out of the chamber can make it back before the attendants lock the doors. With the numbers so finely balanced, this can sometimes be a tense wait. Not today. This vote has been two years, an election and ten months in the making. Everyone in the building knows what's about to happen.

When the bills cleared the House a few weeks ago, a gallery photographer snapped an image that will forever define the moment: five government frontbenchers in an ecstatic group hug, beaming at what they've managed to deliver. In the Senate, nothing, just this gaunt wait for the clock to run down. 'Lock the doors.'

We take our places. Government and opposition whips flank the clerk's table, counting the votes. Low-key barbs and heckling from the government benches; on our side, just numb, legislative shell shock. The press gallery is packed to watch the final vote; they're leaning in to watch the body language from behind a whir of high-speed camera shutters.

I feel sick. The president calls order, stands, reads it in. 'The result of the division being ayes 39, noes 33, the question is resolved in the affirmative.'

There might have been jeers and applause on the government side, I don't remember. All I know is: we're done. Coal-fired Australia has just voted to dismantle nearly the entirety of the *Clean Energy Act 2011*, a body of law that for two years has imposed a modest price on fossil industry pollution. The money raised was being invested in clean energy, biodiversity protection, industry restructuring and low-income compensation. Carbon emissions from the electricity sector were trending down. It was the turning of the ship that I had dreamt of being part of since I got here, and now suddenly we're being forced back into the path of the storm.

Traditional wisdom says if you don't bring the people with you, you'll keep losing like this. Seems right. The fragile political alliance that brought the *Clean Energy Act* into being was outmatched by a heavily amplified and disciplined anti-carbon tax campaign. As soon as an election rolled around and people were actually asked their opinion, more than half voted for parties that promised to make electricity cheaper. We'd all get cheques for $550. In this kind of democracy, so the thinking goes, if more than half the people vote for something, that's what should happen. So here we are.

Electoral politics seems to be the art of convergence towards a slender majority of this imagined political 'centre'. That idea even has a fancy name – the median voter theorem. If that sounds technical, it's not, really. On paper, draw the politics of the voting public like this: a handful of extremists on the left; a handful on the right; and most people in the comfortable, sensible centre. Right in the middle is the imaginary median voter. If you capture their vote, you win the election. And so you should, because it means slightly more than half the population has voted for you.

The median voter model 'can be regarded not only as a convenient method of discussing majoritarian politics and a fruitful engine of analysis, but also a fundamental property of democracy', writes professor of economics Roger Congleton. This search for the 'sensible centre' is like a force of gravity driving political parties to converge. They will agree on most things so as to neutralise attacks, and stake out opposing positions only on the questions they imagine will help capture a majority, no matter how slender.

Once refracted through the quirks and contingencies of electoral systems, this can result in breathtakingly small numbers of voters deciding the outcome of elections. Political parties devote enormous resources to persuade the handful of undecided voters who will actually carry them past the 50 per cent mark. The way the theory goes, this is a good thing – it means that extremists will rarely get their hands on the levers of state, and it means that the candidates who best reflect the interests of the majority are the ones who get elected.

If there's a downside to this model, it's that the convergence towards the interests of an imaginary median voter tends to wash out the differences between political parties, to the point where they become indistinguishable from each other. 'In the limit, both candidates adopt the same platforms, and both candidates receive essentially the same number of votes . . . it doesn't matter which candidate wins the election in this limiting case,' Congleton writes.

The theorem is laced with assumptions and exceptions, and most public choice scholars acknowledge that the real world is often too messy to be described by such a simple rule of thumb. 'The absence of a median voter equilibrium may also arise in models where candidates can manipulate information and voter turnout,' Congleton deadpans in his analysis of where the theorem seems to hold true and where it doesn't.

Other ways of thinking about these questions don't involve sensible centres or median anything theorems. Here's one alternative: 'Competition between blocs of major investors drives the system,' insists political scientist Thomas Ferguson, based on his study of a century of US politics. It's a thing called 'the investment theory of party competition', and it's really simple: 'blocs of major investors define the core of political parties and are responsible for most of the signals the party sends to the electorate.'

Try to contain your shock: the coins of the Anthropocene are used to buy decision-makers. When industry coalitions invest heavily in particular candidates and party factions, the pay-off is the ability to determine who occupies the legislature. Ferguson's recent research has focused on the two-party Congressional races that the US political system generates every two years. Add up the amount of money flowing to either side of a contest and compare it with the number of votes the candidates eventually win. The correlation is direct: whoever spends the most money nearly always wins. This 'golden rule' holds dead steady as far back as comparable records of US federal campaign finance extend – back to 1980.

'There is a strong, direct link between what the major political parties spend and the percentage of votes they win . . . when the Democrats spend more than Republicans, their candidates win. When Republicans spend more than Democrats, they win,' writes researcher Lynn Parramore. It's curiously rare to see any acknowledgement of this in the media, or in political science textbooks. Nearly the entire political and media class continues to pretend that voters determine the outcome of elections, rather than money.

In a virtually unregulated funding environment, this has driven the cost of running elections through the roof. Campaign spending by candidates and influence groups during the 2018 US congressional elections was around $5.7 billion. That's just the money you can see. 'Political money strongly resembles the electromagnetic spectrum: only slivers of it are visible to the naked eye,' Ferguson warns. Dark money, in-kind support, free media coverage offered to provocateurs, resource deployment by independently wealthy candidates – that's all harder to quantify.

Maybe this would all be fine if every voter was equally resourced to throw twenty bucks at their preferred candidate, but of course that's not what's happening here. Glancing back to the 2012 election between President Barack Obama and Republican nominee Mitt Romney, an analysis by Ferguson's team discovered that 'both major party presidential hopefuls relied on donors giving $1,000 or more for about 90 per cent of their funding'. Who can afford to throw a thousand bucks at a presidential election? Only the wealthy: 'This leads to a significant conclusion that both major party campaigns float their campaigns on the basis of appeals to the 1 per cent,' they write.

So that 1-per-cent villager appears to have a lock on who runs the place – sometimes by heavily backing a favoured candidate, but more commonly by placing a bet each way and writing cheques to both.

This isn't new. Their research tracks more than a century of this behaviour, identifying how shifting coalitions of investors and major industries have profoundly shaped the politics of the world's largest economy. 'Both parties, not just the Republicans, were essentially transformed into business parties, and national party leaders increasingly mounted campaigns by striking deals with blocs of major investors for enormous sums of money that fund highly stylized appeals on a few hot-button issues that promise to mobilize subsets of increasingly turned-off voters,' the Ferguson team concludes.

This also isn't just a problem for the United States. France, with a radically different electoral system and much tighter campaign finance laws, suffers from a similar deadening correlation between cash inputs and voter outputs. They've even been able to put a price on it: 'According to our estimations, the price of a vote is about 6 euros for the legislative elections, and 32 euros for the municipal ones,' write French economists Yasmine Bekkouch and Julia Cagé. In their study of French municipal and legislative elections between 1993 and 2014, they note: 'in particular, private donations represent a much higher share of funding for right-wing than for left-wing candidates in both municipal and legislative elections.'

The rightward tilt in French national politics isn't a reflection of some kind of organic shift in community values; it's being purchased, six euros at a time.

Polling shows that the median voter wants a healthcare system that won't prey on them, an end to perpetual resource wars and a job that pays a living wage. The median voter wants a climate where the coastlines stay where they are. But since this is mostly immaterial in deciding the outcome of elections, the median voter can suck it. They are going to get financial deregulation, bank bailouts, arms races, tax cuts for billionaires and a cascade of violent climate emergencies; whatever it takes, so long as they make the next interest repayment on those coins they borrowed.

The United States is a vast, diversified economy, and tracking the opaque and occasionally conflicting interests of its elites is more than a full-time job. Australia, by contrast, is more streamlined: its politics are shaped directly by offshore coalitions of extractive industries, their suppliers and their financiers. The Minerals Council of Australia – the peak body for many of these interests – has an impressive record of converting cash into political outcomes. Journalist Michael West documents how the MCA and its satellite entities spent well over half a billion dollars between 2006 and 2017, destroying the prime ministership of Kevin

Rudd over his introduction of a mining tax. Then they wrecked the tenure of his successor, Julia Gillard, over her introduction of the *Clean Energy Act* in partnership with the Australian Greens and two independent MPs. In shaping these and myriad other policies to the advantage of the industries it represents, the MCA and its gas industry counterparts have played a central part in leaving the country almost completely unprepared for the off-scale damage inflicted by a rapidly warming climate.

Two and a half thousand years ago, Aristotle wrote, 'Oligarchy is when men of property have the government in their hands; democracy, the opposite, when the indigent, and not the men of property, are the rulers. And here arises the first of our difficulties, and it relates to the distinction drawn. For democracy is said to be the government of the many. But what if the many are men of property and have the power in their hands?'

In Australia, the parties that spent the most money won the most seats in five out of the last five federal elections. And so here we sit, in a minority, while the Senate votes to abolish the *Clean Energy Act*. Nobody will ever see a cheque for $550 – power prices will instead rise steeply – but the industry's media channels will sweep that inconvenience down the memory hole.

I'm looking at the majority chatting away on the opposite benches, realising it's a delusion to imagine they've come here to 'follow the dictates of the Australian public'. They're not here as representatives. They're here as investments, and they have just provided a return for their investors, of 39 votes to 33.

election night

There is something about this collective ritual that I still find strangely compelling. Surrounded by quiet houses in quiet streets, the school has been repurposed into a polling booth for a day. Fences draped under long shrouds of plastic banners unrolled by volunteers before dawn; by the time voters arrive, every available sightline will be a jumble of corflutes and candidate posters and pennants. This last-minute shriek for attention is the perfect way to wrap up the superficial infotainment barrage of a modern election campaign, but behind it there are always art projects pinned to the walls, books about trilobites in the library, echoes of recess intrigues holding their breath until Monday.

Right now, mums and dads and kids and couples are filing slowly past to determine the balance of numbers in a parliament of their peers. That's what the politics section of the library says, at least: some of the most powerful people in the country could have whole categories of agency and privilege revoked tonight, depending on what the median voters in this queue are thinking. In case the weight of this responsibility has escaped them, there are teams of volunteers working the queue with how-to-vote cards and three-second pitches.

That's how it's done here, in this place and time. This booth and hundreds like it all over the country will open for ten hours under the sharp eyes of an independent electoral authority. Local P&C committees will sell soft drinks and jam democracy sausages into buns, an adorable variety of dogs will be posted to social media, and most people will show up and drop their votes into sealed boxes. There are no soldiers, no police, no militias. When they are sealed at 6pm, the ballot boxes will be subjected to an auditable chain of custody. The votes will be tipped out and counted in front of scrutineers from opposition parties and independent candidates. Claims of voting irregularities can be tested in court if you have the resources.

Election night parties are a whole different thing. In the wake of the colour and movement of a polling booth, the heaviness of consequence sets in, and you never know in advance what kind of party it's going to be. For the first hour, the panels of professional opinion-havers on TV are working solely on rumour and prejudice. With only traces of the vote counted, it's just televised wheel-spinning while our beautiful crowd reunites to share stories of the day and celebrate the endeavour no matter the outcome. The conversational volume rising as teams drift in from across the city, but always, one eye on the monitor, one ear on word from the breakout room, where people are staring into laptops, hitting refresh, speaking in numbers. Empty graphs are projected onto the walls, awaiting the aggregated collective will. If you're a candidate at one of these strange, taut crossovers between public and private worlds, you're caught within an additional, personal liminality. The whole course of your life is now in the hands of hundreds of thousands of people you'll never meet, and there's not a thing you can do about it now.

Consequence. All the election night parties I've ever been to, overlaid one atop the other, superimposed afterimages of tension and relief. One night we help break a deeply unpopular government, bundle a prime minister out of office, win a seat in the national parliament. One night we celebrate silencing the chainsaws in Wattle Forest. One night our state representation is cut in half; tears and disbelief, people spilling away without waiting for the concession speeches. Sometimes there is dancing, the kind that stops traffic. Sometimes, we find a corner out of the way and contend with last drinks to the sound of political debris splintering and crashing to the ground.

But that's how it's done here, in this place and time. On Capital Hill, bookshelves will be emptied into packing cases, sad stacks of archive boxes, locked bins with contents bound for industrial shredders. This is how executive power is passed from one set of hands to another, without a shot fired, without guillotines in the town square. A formalised process of regime collapse, invited once every couple of years, conducted with pencil and paper and a sausage in a bun.

In other places and other times, it looks nothing like this. Regime change in Egypt sometimes comes in the ecstatic wake of vast popular demonstrations: hundreds of thousands occupying Tahrir Square in 2011, many millions across the country in 2013. Regime change in Iraq is conducted with cruise missiles and an occupying army; in Chile, by CIA-backed death squads and economic strangulation. It is averted with mass killings and columns of tanks in Tiananmen Square, and by assassination of journalists and jailing of opposition figures in Moscow.

'A long view of human history reveals not regular change but spasmodic, catastrophic disruptions followed by long periods of reinvention and development . . . Modern democratic societies are clearly vulnerable to the same process, but they have invented ways to diffuse large episodes of creative destruction by creating smaller cycles of renewal and change through periodic political elections,' writes Crawford Stanley Holling. This makes a certain kind of sense: elections as a form of political pressure valve, channelling the wild and frequently violent energies of contending ambition into a process that can be almost banal in its formality. The kink here, though, is that Holling is no historian, nor is he a student of politics – he's an ecologist. His take on elections is presented, almost as a throwaway line, in a paper for the August 2001 edition of the scientific journal *Ecosystems*. Not somewhere I had imagined our search for the monsters throwing children into the river would bring us, but here we are.

Tonight doesn't feel like a cycle of renewal or change. Tonight, it's to be a 'corner out of the way with last drinks' kind of party. Not just because the investor blocs seem to have elected for regime continuity, regime consolidation, regime insufferable smugness. Moreso, that even if there had been a change of government, we all know the greater part of our society's deadly momentum would have remained in place, entrenched and barely questioned. At no time during the election campaign were the suicidal fundamentals of the coin-doubling game given serious consideration. The rising volume of extinction and collapse was adeptly drowned out again, forced to the margins for the whole duration of the campaign.

One in ten voters heard us, and for that I'm grateful. It means a dear friend got elected, gaining everything attendant on a seat in that place: the resources, talented staff, ability to travel. But nine out of ten voters heard something else, and the party that spent the most money won the most seats. Again.

'If voting changed anything, they'd make it illegal,' an anarchist friend told me a long time ago. I remember replying that in a lot of places they have made it illegal. But on nights like tonight, it runs close to the surface, that sense of the democratic wheels still turning but the gears disengaged from the actual machineries of state. What happens when Holling's cycles of renewal and change become simulacra, electoral theatre in which the people moving into those offices on Capital Hill look and sound exactly like the people they replaced? What happens when you get a job as part of the pressure valve and realise the whole mechanism has been jammed shut for years?

Perhaps counterintuitively, the ecologists seem to have answers for some of those questions too, but that's going to take us a long, strange way from this election night party. 'Hierarchies and adaptive cycles comprise the basis of ecosystems and social-ecological systems across scales,' Holling writes cryptically. 'Together they form a panarchy.'

Okay, together they what?

small solidarities

Life has stuck together since the very beginning. Methanogens clumped on Archean seafloors huffing each other's pheromones. Cyanobacteria glued together in long filaments in shallow Proterozoic seas. Massed stromatolite reefs dominating the shorelines from just after our story began. Living together works. But the eukaryotes are going to take cohabitation to another level, inventing multicellularity not just once, but again and again.

The origins of these transformations are lost in time – such soft and long-distant creatures rarely fossilise. In the late Proterozoic, volcanic activity from the break-up of the vast Rodinia landmass begins to change the face of the world. Life is tested in slow-motion convulsions – between the extremes of Cryogenian ice ages bringing glaciers all the way to the equator and scorching greenhouse heatwaves, in which vast deglaciations drown coastal ecosystems. Again and again, the balance between land and sea is redrawn. Out of these geological traumas, life replies with the emergence of truly multicellular creatures. They are glimpsed like dreams in rare fossils in places like the Ediacara Hills in South Australia, which give residents of this time their name. Strange quilted jellyfish beings and frond-like creations; threefold symmetries and body types that no longer exist. Questions about how they lived, how they relate to the creatures that came after them, remain a mystery. Something is clear, though: in at least some of these enigmatic beings, huge numbers of eukaryotic cells are working together to form something quite new.

This will change everything. Single cells rely on chemical diffusion to move nutrients and waste around inside themselves, which sets limits on how large they can get. Although there are some extreme outliers, this has kept the size of most of the largest eukaryote cells to no more than about a tenth of a millimetre long. Most of their prokaryote forebears are ten or a hundred times smaller. Now the brakes are off: in small solidarities clumping together in larger and larger formations, life begins its long swim out of the microscopic realm.

Time is moving on. Between 650 and 550 million years ago, the supercontinent of Gondwana is welded together out of the dispersed remnants of Rodinia. As east and west Gondwana crumple into each other in extreme slow motion, an epic mountain range is formed across what will one day be East Africa and Arabia. The Transgondwanan Supermountain – as formidable as the Himalayas, but eight thousand kilometres from end to end.

And then, 542 million years ago, nearly all traces of the Ediacarans vanish. In their place, whole branches and pathways of the tree of life suddenly become visible to the fossil record, as creatures begin producing shells and chitinous body parts that stand a better chance of being preserved. Rock sequences from the Cambrian period tell of sponges and forests of tubes anchored to shallow seafloors; imprints of burrowing creatures skittering across soft sediments; and then, increasing in diversity, a graveyard of hard shells.

Like a flashbulb going off half a billion years ago, these fossil traces illuminate the hardening continuities of much older, soft-bodied relationships. Armoured brachiopods with their fan-like shells, molluscs inhabiting slow-growing spirals, the alien 'hallucigenia' walking on eight pairs of clawed feet. In the background, schools of what will become the first jawless fish are circling in the water column. Annelid worms, roundworms, nemertean worms and now, gliding just above the seabed, we see a trilobite's iconic segmented form for the first time.

Follow this little being, small enough to fit comfortably in the palm of your hand, and realise that at the scales we've inhabited since life took hold, she is a giant. It's worth taking a moment to appreciate what she's done. Since long before Luca's time, cells communicated with each other via ever-more specialised pheromone chemicals and direct DNA transmission. In truly multicellular creatures such as this one, these channels of communication are turned inwards to synchronise the activities of billions of cells within the larger entity. Ancient affordances of perpetuation, metabolism and boundaries; perception and expression, memory and agency: all operating at the scale of the collective now.

And so here she is, our trilobite, coming to rest for a moment on the sand. Imagine we could see within: to the architecture of an unremarkable cellular neighbourhood. Recall, for a moment, all that it takes to make this creature possible. There is something oddly familiar about the compact array of cells lined up along narrow capillaries, all of them delicately enmeshed in networks of ducts and fibres connecting them with the rest of the organism. These neural and cardiovascular networks bring information, vital nutrients and oxygen-rich bloodflow within range of every cell, waste removal and maintenance coordinated in ways that its distant ancestors couldn't have dreamt of.

She sees us, antennae waving, and darts behind a thicket of fluted Archaeocyatha sponges. Hold here, for a moment – we'll be back before long. Blink forward half a billion years.

above the city

There's a story they tell in the West sometimes, one of the oldest stories there is. I don't speak for these places and they aren't my stories to tell, but long before it was the site of a concentration camp, the place they call Wadjemup was somewhere you could walk to, a range of limestone hills overlooking the wild ocean.

Wadjemup is an island eighteen kilometres west of the port of Fremantle now; people call it Rottnest Island and go there for holidays. It's seven thousand years since anyone last walked out there from the mainland; when sea levels began to rise at the close of the ice age, Wadjemup was gradually cut off. There are sites and artifacts out there dating back more than thirty thousand years, but while physical access was severed, the storylines were not.

Memory holds. An ice age story, from the last time the oceans came in, carried with the most extraordinary fidelity from voice to voice, until now I'm hearing it for the first time from dear Uncle Noel. The Nyiting, he calls it, the cold time. I'm shivering to even hear it spoken.

My history in this place is more recent: from the shallowest blink of time. My point of reference lies a short walk from Perth's main railway station. For a long while this space was just a blank concrete quadrangle linking the cultural precinct with the cheerful jumble of the Northbridge entertainment district. Then a few years ago the city commissioned an unusual transformation: the sharp geometry of a bleak modernist pond was broken up and planted in, with native reeds and paperbarks growing out between worn granite boulders. On a warm night after the rain, you'll see members of the local frog community checking each other out on the margins of this reimagined wetland. Even as the bustle of evening commuters flows past in a blur of conversation and studied attention to mobile devices, this place has a meditative quality. Pause here, briefly, and the city's forgotten geography of seasonal lakes can be recalled, even if we don't know their ancient names just yet.

Some form of memory holds here, too. It feels at once timeless and new, a tiny island resurfacing from a lost archipelago amid the concrete and glass towers of the resource companies and the banks. Like a seed lodged in the pavement, something here feels heraldic, bearing hopeful significance way beyond its limited scale; prefiguring revolution.

Half an hour's drive from here, at the end of the quiet street with the quiet house, a narrow laneway cuts between these two worlds. The far end opens into stands of gnarled banksia forest and dimly lit paperbark glades. I used to stop here sometimes, between the sleeping houses, just to listen – the place ringing gently with rich layers of sound.

The Beeliar Wetlands were the first place I'd lived long enough to properly appreciate the seasonal undertows of intact ecosystems. The millionfold unfurling of new growth after the first drenching; flowering, seeding; quiet waves of collapse and renewal under patient trees.

Soon they will be attacked, a billion-dollar freight highway proposal emerging from lines on an obsolete land-use plan to sever two of the largest lakes in the system and erase a meeting ground that has been there since the Nyiting, the cold time. It hurts to even think about it; I can't imagine how it must feel to the people who know the old names. We will rally by the thousands under sky-blue flags; dusty scuffles with police, dozens of arrests, a community forged anew at the point of collision.

We haven't paused in this laneway to farewell the place, but to try to understand why this shit keeps happening so that this is the last time we have to fight it. A change of perspective might help here; so drift gently upwards into the warm night air. Shadowed backyard pools and wilting fruit trees now visible over the neat fences; higher, above the mosaic of rooftops and streetlights, to get a sense of how the place is put together. Already, from just a few dozen metres above street level, it is clear that this is something immense. A shimmer of light from horizon to horizon; distant port and stick-figure container cranes under a blaze of floodlights that will burn until dawn. A cluster of commercial towers glittering to the north, lights winking in and out as cleaning crews move from floor to floor.

From up here, the deep histories of the old lakes read as negative space, lost in the black against the city's bright traceries. Glancing back towards the house of abundance where we were not so long ago, to see it as one rooftop among many.

If someone were to ask you to find parallels between the inner workings of a trilobite from the dawn of the world and the structure of this outer metropolitan streetscape, you'd wonder if they were high. But recall, for a moment, all that it takes to make this place possible. There is something oddly familiar about the compact array of houses lined up along the narrow cul-de-sac, all of them delicately enmeshed in networks of ducts and fibres connecting them with the rest of the city. These underground supply systems and road networks bringing data, water, freight and energy within range of every home, waste removal and maintenance coordinated in ways that our distant ancestors couldn't have dreamed of.

So – hold on. The street is an artifact of human drafting and engineering, informed by ten thousand years of custom and practice. And yet some convergence of physics and evolutionary pressure has drawn it into a strikingly similar form and flow to the way cellular tissues organise themselves in small solidarities.

In biological systems, 'metabolism' accounts for the material and energy flows that sustain life: the food and water and oxygen that go in, the processing that occurs within, and the wastes that come out. The resting metabolic rate of an adult human runs to about 90 watts – the equivalent of an old-fashioned incandescent globe. That's everything it takes to power the thirty-odd trillion cells in your body, and the additional forty trillion bacteria that make up the human microbiome. If 90 watts sounds like a remarkably faint pulse to power such an astonishing collective, maybe you should have a coffee.

And there's the kick: at a minimum, that will require some way of boiling water and an extended global supply chain reaching all the way to Costa Rica or Timor Leste, which is why the metabolic rate of a city such as this runs closer to 11,000 watts per person. This is an abstraction that varies widely from place to place, but it hints at the scale of the industrial life support systems we've woven around us. In search of the comforts that coffee and technology can bring, some of us have had our resource footprints magnified more than a hundredfold – thus the six-metre-high cube of unsorted waste we saw out in the quiet street.

Borrowing from biology, urban planners and industrial designers have long spoken of this vast industrial overhead as an 'urban metabolism'. Through this lens, our thriving cities and towns are organised to perform the same functions of ingestion, transport, processing and waste disposal that shape every other living creature. They are the tarmac and steel expressions of our collective biological metabolism, doing the same job at scales thousands of times larger than the organic metabolic processes they augment.

No-one sat down and consciously decided to design the city according to organic principles, and the place can hardly be considered 'alive' in any meaningful sense. The distinction misses the point – cities solve the same problems of form and flow, and have been swept up in the same evolutionary tide as everything else on the planet, at a scale that can be hard to apprehend if you've lived your whole life inside one.

Urban metabolism. In my mind's eye, I'm looking over the railing into a primary crusher at a mine site, on land taken by force in the timeless Pilbara. The crusher looks like a set of giant, rotating iron teeth, pulverising truckloads of broken stone. Driverless haul-trucks make their way back into the open-cut, while dusty conveyors speed the rubble into secondary and tertiary crushers, milling it into ever-finer gravel, down into powder. Liquefied slurry fed into chemical treatment and beneficiation plants resembling nothing so much as externalised digestive systems; leach tanks and centrifuges nested within stainless steel entrails. In here, target minerals are slowly concentrated into useable form: gold, copper, rare earths, uranium.

On the outskirts of our cities, industrial parks take in these precursor materials and assemble them from simple components into ever-more complex and specialised artifacts, which is more or less exactly what goes on inside the submicroscopic ribosomes fabricating proteins in each one of our cells. Over time, our collective biological metabolism has been augmented by industrial processes operating at vastly extended scales. Which is fine, except that these metabolic processes appear to have been hijacked by the coin-doubling game, and surely that can't end well.

Let's move higher. While we're up here, we might as well try to get a view of the whole thing.

From above, our quiet house of abundance is swallowed up in an organic tessellation of residential and industrial districts marked out in pinpricks of light, threaded with floodlit avenues and freeways. Traffic lights metering out time at silent intersections; that shopping centre like an island amid an oceanic expanse of empty tarmac.

Familiar points of reference are blending into bright abstractions, from which we can discern the nodes and terminal points that shape the lives of everyone below. Compressor stations and borefields, thermal power plants laced into switchyards and substations. Water treatment plants and server farms; an unknown and probably unknowable geography of trunk mains and fibre backhaul. Physical distribution points for every kind of freight, intangible floods of data washing between radio transmitters, mobile cell towers and the world's satellite fleet.

Way to the east, passenger jets are queued like fireflies on final approach, inbound from Sydney, Tokyo, Dubai. An airbus on climb-out, turning for Johannesburg. There are still people alive today who were born before the first powered flight, but on the eve of a pandemic that will ground some of this fleet, nearly 10,000 aircraft are carrying more than a million people aloft at any given time.

This airborne swarm is heaviest over North America, Europe and East Asia, an invisible spiderweb of flight paths for those with the cash and the paperwork to bypass earthbound topographies.

To the west, the old seaport is a gateway to the 10.7 billion tonnes of cargo shipped by sea in 2017, via everything from bulk-ore carriers to container ships to small local freighters. A Japanese passenger liner with a bright red funnel, tied up alongside the terminal, carries a more complex cargo. A map of this slow haulage paints a dense weave of shipping lanes, knotted choke points in the Singapore Strait and the Strait of Hormuz.

Float higher; the city's delicate armatures extending to neighbouring settlements further down the coast, horizon curving away beneath us. Imagine all that it takes to keep this globe-spanning machine in motion and light these cloudbanks from below. Fourteen and a half billion tonnes of fossil energy carriers mined and burned annually, half of it in the form of coal.

The largest oil refinery complexes in Gujarat, South Korea and Venezuela are uninhabited steelscapes of pipework and pressure vessels, a modern alchemy of petrochemical production for distribution into every time zone.

Rough numbers: we mined 6.5 billion tonnes of metal ores in 2015, with iron, copper and alumina making up the bulk. We quarried an additional forty-five billion tonnes of construction materials, including sand and rock and asphalt. Add twenty-three billion tonnes of biomass, including primary crops, residues, grazing roughage and forest products. In 2017, we slaughtered 302 million cattle, half a billion sheep, 1.4 billion pigs, three billion ducks and just under sixty-six billion chickens. In 2018, we caught and killed 178 million tonnes of fish; piled up, that immense volume would fill a cube standing higher than the One World Trade Center in New York.

By 2014, we were diverting and desalinating nearly four thousand cubic kilometres of fresh water. These quantities numb the senses: one cubic kilometre stands three times higher than the Eiffel Tower and weighs a billion tonnes.

It all comes together on the concrete banks of the Pearl River Delta in China. This global manufacturing hub absorbs this incoming torrent of water and iron ore and oil and wood pulp, spinning it into cars, and computers, and furniture, and toys. On bad days, the air over Shenzen and Guangzhou is a featureless shroud of fine grey powder exhaled from a million exhaust pipes and smokestacks. Out in the delta, silhouettes of barges and jack-up rigs are framed by endless rows of skeletal container cranes, loading restless shipping bound for every port on earth.

The material flow analysis people draw elegant diagrams of this 'material throughput' to try and build a systems picture. Sankey diagrams, they call them: one-way arrows from the point of extraction via the point of use to the point of dumping. The ones with more of a design sense use colour coding. Over here on the left, brightly coloured bands of ores and timber and coal; over here on the right, landfill middens and an ocean of plastic. In the middle, fresh coffee, two-dollar packs of clothes pegs and unexpected items in the bagging area.

If we drape this diagram over a map of the world, it makes a different kind of sense. Old colonial gradients from Global South to North; mine and factory and clearfell and dump, coloured arrows pouring into the shopping trolleys and fuel tanks of the North, before folding back on themselves to expel the wastes into places I've never even heard of.

Standing under sky-blue banners to block its advance works often enough to make the effort worthwhile – we did manage to stop that billion-dollar freight highway in the end. But it's too big, multiplying and advancing on too many fronts. At the far edges of everything, like an invisible gravity well driving this ceaseless expansion, the coins of the Anthropocene demanding to be repaid, with interest.

Miles above the earth's surface, the cities reduced to a twinkling lacework, we have completely lost contact with our battered village of a hundred people. Nor do we seem any closer to discovering who's throwing the children into the water.

Let's leave the quiet house behind for a while. It's time to get on the road.

new silk roads

beqaa

We're pulled over at a roadside stand, the lights of Beirut draping the folds of the mountains, tracing the arc of the eastern Mediterranean all the way to the horizon. Byblos is back there somewhere, layers of memory descending into deep time.

I got a job, lost it in the most careless way imaginable, brooded and moped around for months. Then came an offer too good to refuse: travel to Lebanon to meet with emerging Green Party activists planning their next election campaign. A mix of research, exchange and training – it kicks off an unexpected year on the road, unexpected invitations and opportunities and, eventually, an unexpected book.

Soon we'll find ourselves in the Gobi Desert, and Nairobi, and on a ship dedicated to the preservation of a different kind of memory. But our road trip starts here, with a hit of cardamom from heavy coffee ladled into tiny paper cups, trucks heaving slowly past in low gear.

Beqaa is the northernmost reach of a complex of rift valleys and fault lines stretching all the way into East Africa. The crumpled mountain ranges flanking this wide valley have been shuddering imperceptibly in opposite directions for untold millions of years. To the south, this same system cradles the Sea of Galilee and the Jordan Valley, down to the Gulf of Aqaba, where epic tectonic rifting is slowly opening the Red Sea. The upflung ramparts we crossed last night are dusted with snow this morning; far to the east, the angular profile of Mount Hermon marks the Syrian border.

'The concept of power for me personally means knowledge. When you have knowledge, you have power,' Najah tells me while we wait for the guests to arrive. She is one of two key organisers driving the Green Party of Lebanon's efforts in the Beqaa Valley. 'But coming to apply that in Lebanon, our dear Lebanon, power is different. Power is with authority. Inherited authority. Power is with the religious people, who tell you what to do and what not to do. Power is in the hands of the rich people, who can play with you, manoeuvre with your principles and buy your ideology. This is the power in effect in Lebanon.'

Her friend and colleague Vanda agrees, adding, 'The best thing about Lebanon [is that] even with all the corruption, even with having politicians who inherit their positions and who are not elected, I believe we have a very important margin of freedom.' She notes the relative safety within which they are forming a new political movement, and the raucous affordances of Lebanon's free press. In 2016, the restive sectarian cartel that runs the country made some grudging reforms to national electoral laws, potentially opening the way for independent candidates to win seats in the parliament. 'Now I feel that, with the change of the electoral law, we have a chance of breaking into the parliament, maybe getting a seat or two,' Vanda says.

Nothing about this will be easy. The first barrier they face is persuading supporters that it's even worth bothering. The electoral system is a tortuously complex stitch-up between the leadership of incumbent parties representing Lebanon's eighteen main religious denominations and sects. The law allocates key offices and blocs of seats in the single-chamber parliament to these sects in advance. The election – if it gets held at all – will merely determine which of the party nominees get to fill these allotments. Someone has done the numbers and realised that with the right candidate and some adept alliance-building, people from outside this cosy arrangement have a shot in a couple of districts, including here in Beqaa.

As the guests arrive for this organising meeting, it becomes even clearer that most of the heavy lifters in this insurgency are women. 'It was always a patriarchal society. It was always dominated by men. So when we introduced women, we started playing with the balance of our society,' Najah reflects. 'I believe that if women don't do something for themselves, enhancing the economic mind or the political mind, we will stay the same. They are the fulcrum of change. They can change the balance of everything.'

Only six of the 128 seats in the Lebanese parliament are held by women. Four times that number are now crowded into the living room. Coffee is poured. Another strand in this patient braid of movement-building begins to take shape: a conversation about how these women might help change the balance of everything.

Days later back in Beirut, Nada Zaarour has managed to grab us half an hour with a feisty opposition party leader, H.E. Ghassan Moukheiber. He doesn't seem to be in the mood for diplomacy. 'Anyone who says they understand Lebanon has had it explained to them very poorly,' he says, grinning at my evident bewilderment. 'Lebanon is a communitarian, systemically corrupt oligarchy.' His advice to Zaarour, the leader of the Greens and its highest-profile candidate, is to go for it, but to choose her allies with the greatest of care.

Zaarour is a seasoned environmental and social justice campaigner. She is well known for her grassroots advocacy, but her stepping into a leadership role within this upstart political movement has created a stir.

Later, from the party's small office a block from the militarised heart of Nejmeh Square, she is contemplative, and realistic about her chances. 'People trust us. We have many supporters on the ground, but they are waiting to see the seriousness of the Green Party: whether we are serious about running in this election.'

It's been raised at every planning meeting I've been to on this trip, from Beqaa to Shoef to Zgharta: doubts by sceptical allies as to whether the party has the resources to break through the watertight electoral armour of the establishment, and what it would mean even if they did. It costs staggering amounts of money to field candidates here. In this highly sectarian application of the investment theory of party competition, all the investors refract their ambitions through religious institutions with centuries of history behind them. The Greens have no such backers; in fact, the absence of this kind of influence is the whole point.

There is a deeper problem here, never far from the surface of conversation. Lebanon lies at the crossroads of contending regional powers, fractured by geopolitical tectonics that occasionally threaten to overwhelm this bruised and precious enclave. Israel and Palestine to the south, Syria to the east, a standing army of Iranian-backed militias on home soil; political rift valleys and fault lines pressurised by decisions made in Moscow and Washington. The longer I spend here, the less I understand the place, which is probably what Mr Moukheiber was trying to convey.

'Thirty-five per cent of the voters don't participate in elections at all, because they don't trust the electoral law, and they don't trust the candidates – the same figures, the same parties, they don't trust them,' Zaarour says. This non-participation has nothing to do with laziness or apathy, I realise – it's an adaptive response to life in a communitarian, systemically corrupt oligarchy.

Many people just leave this tormented country, try their luck with thriving diaspora communities from Sydney to São Paulo. Nada Zaarour is staying put, juggling phone calls and the next round of appointments. 'We can make the difference this time, we have a chance,' she says. 'And then: we have nothing to lose.'

I'm thinking of Holling's throwaway line about elections functioning as a pressure valve, a formalised ritual of peaceful regime collapse. That ritual feels halfway to simulacrum back home; here in Beirut, the establishment is barely even pretending. I'm wondering where all that pressure is going; realise the answer is standing guard in the street below Nada's window.

In 2005, assassins detonated a massive car bomb as prime minister Rafic Hariri's motorcade was making its way along the waterfront a few blocks from here. Twenty-two people were killed, including Hariri. More than a decade later, Nejmeh Square and the adjacent parliamentary precinct is still a fortified green zone of boom gates and blast barriers.

The line between life and death on the margins of these Mediterranean shorelines is razor-fine. In place of a pressure valve, a permanent cordon of watchful soldiers.

'The poor foreigner,' he said, 'has been acquainted with our grasslands but for four short days.'

'We must pity him,' said the old man with feeling.

'How hard it must be,' commented the woman, 'not to be born a Mongolian.'

'To be sure,' said the old man, 'the fellow is most unfortunate. But how blessed he is to have found his way to us!'

FRITZ MÜHLENWEG, *BIG TIGER AND CHRISTIAN: THEIR ADVENTURES IN MONGOLIA*

wellfields

The mountains are just a cut-out shape on the horizon now. Half an hour out of the southern Mongolian city of Sainshand we turned into a bumpy laneway on the edge of a township I didn't catch the name of, and there the road ended; tyre tracks fanning out onto the dusty steppe. There's no phone reception, and the GPS is blank, but a teenager sitting nearby had given Boldbayar the directions he needed, gesturing with an outstretched arm. Far behind us, sacred Khan Bayanzurkh Khairkhan mountain, bedecked with Buddhist spires and ragged strands of prayer flags, is now just a pyramidal silhouette receding against the sky.

And so now the four-wheel rolls south across the Gobi Desert, air still heavy with last night's dust storm. We're following a track half-imagined across a lunar terrain that looks like it might have been levelled with a laser. A smudge of smoke on the horizon ahead blends into the milky sky, and an hour after leaving the road we pass into an abandoned Soviet-era military base. Züünbayan, my companions confirm.

Boldbayar, the laconic deputy secretary of the Mongolian Green Party, spent years of his childhood here. We pause to find his old house, slowly disintegrating against a backdrop of empty concrete apartment blocks.

Steering past cars marooned up to their axles in fine sand, a handful of new vehicles are drawn up against buildings that look occupied. A derelict Soviet tank sits at the centre of the empty town square. We park the car, and duck into a brick building that seems newer than the rest. Children's voices, raised cheerfully in some kind of call and response. Later, I'll wonder if I imagined it: a brightly painted classroom, two dozen young kids and their beaming teacher welcoming the sudden interruption. Boldbayar introduces us, invites them to continue while we listen in for a brief time. I'm contending with the strangeness of the juxtaposition; the shock of the familiar so very far from home.

Their singing drifts out into the quadrangle where we left the car.

Taking instructions from a small work crew presiding over the desolation, we're directed southwards again. Barracks in a state of collapse, falling away behind. The horizon dissolves into a mean-looking haze, the sun just a diffuse glow in the dust shroud that's been drawn across the world.

Life still makes its way out here. The hard ground is spotted with a mosaic of tough grasses, and at one point we come across a family of horses standing with their backs to the gathering wind.

The track braids and diverges around low dunes, and suddenly off to our right, the heraldic form of a beam pump rising and falling. Steel assembly on a concrete pad, a motor driving rotating counterweights on one end of the beam, drawing the pump head up and down monotonously. Chinese characters on the safety signage. The track leads us through a field of them, a blank landscape punctuated with a robotic cuneiform of nodding oil pumps and powerlines.

Somewhere up ahead, a LandCruiser is parked by the side of the track, to guide us the rest of the way in. We bump and rattle along in silence, leaving the oil wells behind as the lead vehicle bears away. An hour deeper into the Gobi, we glimpse a communications mast above a compound of low sheds and shipping containers. A few kilometres beyond, a smaller complex lies fenced against the desert. Just outside the perimeter, earthmoving gear and drilling gantries stand against the monochrome sky. Here, the LandCruiser pulls over and we're instructed to put the camera equipment away.

We've arrived at a trial in-situ leach site owned by French nuclear giant Orano. A small cohort of construction workers and technicians are putting the finishing touches on the installation, which is due to begin leach trials in a matter of months. Several thousand tonnes of sulphuric acid and other chemicals will be pumped into the ground at high pressure, saturating the target geology and dissolving uranium and a cocktail of other radionuclides and heavy metals into the groundwater. Six extraction wells surround a central injection well, which will draw this radioactive liquor back to the surface and into a small treatment plant inside the chain-link fence. Here the uranium will be chemically separated and dried into a powder; the remaining slurry will be injected back into the ground.

Should a team of analysts in Courbevoie deem the trial a success against the world uranium price, the mine will move to full production. A grid of these giant industrial needles will be trucked into position across the landscape, feeding a commercial-scale treatment plant. The dusty half-trails we've followed out here will be graded and sealed for a fleet of tankers delivering process chemicals, road trains carrying away drums of uranium oxide.

Out here, hours beyond the edge of the world, a Chinese oilfield and a French uranium play. There is truly nowhere left on earth that our metabolic armatures can't reach.

To be sure, nothing here is completely new. Trade has existed in some form probably as long as human feet have walked the earth. We're not so far from the famed Silk Road, which provided an east–west trading corridor across Eurasia for more than two thousand years. But it's a long time since commerce only moved at the speed of a camel train. Now it moves at the speed of light, on doubling paths as urgent as Orano's glitchy stock price, as patient as a field of beam pumps in the desert.

The sense of remoteness that hit me outside the implausible schoolroom in Züünbayan collapses into a strange vertigo. To help me get my bearings, when we get back to the city Boldbayar wants to introduce me to the country's former president, so I can hear first-hand what happens when you stand in the path of the traffic bearing down on these new silk roads.

oyu tolgoi

We're onto our third coffee in a glass-walled cafe not far from the Mongolian parliament. Later, when the wind turns, an ashen fug of coal dust will fall across these chilly streets, but for now the city of Ulaanbaatar is beaming under an ice-blue sky.

Boldbayar is cheerful but focused as he gives me a fast-forward history of a place that spent seven decades as a Soviet satellite state before being cast into the global economy with the break-up of the USSR in the early 1990s. Landlocked between Russia to the north and China to the south, Mongolia's copper, coal, iron ore and gold provinces immediately caught the eye of global resource giants. What happened next sounds familiar enough. A surge of cash was injected at high pressure into the country's tight-knit political class, warping fragile regulatory structures to accommodate a rush of prospectors and surveyors jostling to claim title over prospective ground.

The Chinese beam pumps, the uranium site we visited: that's third or fourth tier. The South Gobi hosts the immense Oyu Tolgoi copper mine, which will be the third-largest copper mine in the world when it gets to full production. Nearby Tavan Tolgoi hosts one of the world's largest metallurgical coal deposits. Almost without warning, over the course of a decade, mining grew to become the country's largest industry. It only employs 4 per cent of the workforce, but generates a third of the country's GDP and nearly 90 per cent of its exports.

'The mining sector is dominated by the Oyu Tolgoi state- and privately owned copper mine and the Erdenet state-owned copper mine,' enthuses the European Bank for Reconstruction and Development, which has invested heavily in the industry. 'The sector also has substantial coal, gold, iron ore, uranium and other resources. Mining has been prominent in national politics in recent years. A recently-agreed IMF stability package bodes well for political and economic reform.'

Ah – there it is. The unmistakable signature of the investment theory of party competition, steppe style. 'Mining investors increasingly anticipate that the past populist pressure to pay higher taxes will ease and that important reforms tied to IMF lending will be carried through,' the EBRD nods approvingly.

Newly dependent on these global undercurrents, now the country's fortunes rest on their ebb and flow. The land rush has sparked fierce disputes over ownership, costs and benefits, which simmer like background radiation. One of the many projects Boldbayar has in the air – in addition to helping grow the presence of the Greens here – is supporting a diverse coalition pushing to amend the national constitution. 'Check it,' he says: 'In the current constitution, article 6.2, it says Mongolian land and its minerals belong to the Mongolian people, okay? But right now, people get nothing from the mining projects.'

The initiative to give the constitution teeth is getting traction – they have hundreds of thousands of signatures already, and the exercise is helping build trust and goodwill between disparate political and civil society movements. Door to door, at public events and street stalls, there's a groundswell of people demanding to know where all the money is going. Nationally, nearly one in three people live below the poverty line; in some regional areas it's closer to one in two, and nobody escapes the consequences.

'Ulaanbaatar is the worst city in the world for air pollution,' Boldbayar says. 'Children die, women [are] losing unborn babies because of the air pollution.' The highest points on the city skyline are the cooling towers and smokestacks of coal-fired power stations situated well inside the city limits, but that's not really what he's talking about. Six out of ten people in this city of a million and a half live in gers – traditional felt-lined tents heated by woodstoves. In the winters, when temperatures drop below freezing and stay there, the lucky ones stay warm by burning raw coal. Those who can't afford it burn whatever they can. 'They burn anything. Car tyres, plastics, any paper they can find. Just for heating,' Boldbayar explains. 'It's very cold in the winter, so it's just for survival. And it's very windy from the north. So all the ash, all the dust, comes into the town centre.'

We've been talking for a couple of hours; I glance outside to see that the weather is turning. The concrete and glass towers of the capital are softening, dematerialising behind an incoming tide of fine ash.

Night falls early; in this quiet little bar, Chinggis vodka is flowing freely. Boldbayar is juggling phone calls and trying to wedge us into the former president's diary.

'We have this word "democracy", "democratic society", but we've never experienced it.' Softly spoken, Saruul chooses her words carefully. 'It's totally new. At the beginning, in the 1990s, everyone was very excited. And then since that time, people realised they didn't have any idea about the new society. People didn't have time to do politics, actually. And now 70 per cent of the population are poor, and everywhere on Mongolian territory mining companies are exploring, or mining.'

Saruul Tovuusuren has one foot in the emerging Green party, the other in the world of traditional nomadic herders in Khövsgöl province in Mongolia's far north. 'So now people understand, okay, we must fight for our economy, for our life, and for our belief,' she says. 'People said we want to fight these terrible people; we want to keep our pasture. We want to live as we were for hundreds of years, but we don't know how to do that. We tried so many things – we wrote letters to the government politicians, but no results.'

Like most of us, the nomads have missed the memo that investors are the only people whose mail is getting opened these days. Short of armed struggle, they're running out of ideas. Saruul and other allies in the city help craft a campaign; they start with a video that goes viral in the province and begins to build movement structure, public meetings and a sense of hope. Not long afterwards, the local community joins forces to take legal action against the company. Everyone knows that fending off one miner, one project, does little to tip the overarching balance of power, but most people are too busy fighting local emergencies to ponder the larger structural forces that seem to have so rapidly turned against them.

Boldbayar comes off his call looking pleased, pours out another round. He's got us an appointment with someone who has seen those larger structural forces at work from very close range.

Nambaryn Enkhbayar is a rare politician, and not just because he's the only person in Mongolian public life who at different times has served as prime

minister, speaker of the parliament and president. I'm familiar enough
with people going into politics fired up and radicalised only to become
an obedient cog in the institutional machinery over time. It's much more
unusual to find someone who has walked that path in the other direction.

'In the beginning I was very much a pro-market-oriented prime minister,' he tells me. 'I was thinking that foreign investment is good. We have to
invite foreign investors, give them the best conditions and they will come
here, create a lot of jobs, pay a lot of taxes. The country will develop rapidly, and Mongolia will be a success story.'

Enkhbayar rode that line of argument all the way into the prime minister's office, a block away from this quiet meeting room overlooking a
frosty streetscape. From opposition, he had watched as international con-
sultants were hired to draft the highly permissive national mining laws
that sparked an avalanche of miners, explorers and opportunists. Now he
was responsible for keeping the rollercoaster on the rails.

I'm listening as he turns three decades of Mongolian history over in
his hands. This place is a geographical crossroads; I ask to what degree
he thinks other countries' interests are at play here. His answer takes us
right back to the early years of Mongolian democracy, after the break-up
of the Soviet Union. 'Americans were setting up so-called NGOs to directly
influence people's choice, under the mask of explaining democratic values,
of explaining about Western democracy. Russians, they were supporting
mainly the Mongolian People's Party but also some candidates from the
Democratic Party. And now Chinese are very actively supporting MPP
and some candidates from DP. So we have the three largest countries in the
world directly influencing Mongolian democracy.'

It's the investment theory of party competition, with superpowers the
largest investors of all. And now, the reality is hitting home. 'The so-called
foreign investors don't pay a lot of taxes,' Enkhbayar says. 'They find different ways of going through offshore schemes to hide their income.'

In the regions, the herders are losing their lands to expanding moon-
scapes of coal and copper mines. Wells are running dry. Roads fragment
the landscape and haul trucks frequently collide with livestock. Wealth
inequality is skyrocketing. BMWs have begun to clog the broken roads
while coal-burning shantytowns swell the population of Ulaanbaatar.

'INVESTMENT CLIMATE IN MONGOLIA'S MINING SECTOR DETERIORATED SHARPLY IN 2006' bawls the headline of a diplomatic cable from the US embassy, briefing allies on the country's volatile turn. It is a needle in the immense haystack of US State Department cables published by WikiLeaks in 2011. 'A proliferating set of relatively small new civil society movements have often further pushed the public discussion of the issue in nationalist directions . . . Those politicians who do not agree with the nationalist tenor of debate and legislation on the mining sector find it politically unwise to voice such reservations in public.'

Enkhbayar and his allies begin introducing laws to take a greater stake in the industry, start talking about nationalising things. In 2006 they introduce a mining super-profits tax to claim a greater revenue share from Oyu Tolgoi and other top-tier mines.

Enkhbayar may have read the mood on the streets, but he's made powerful enemies in the boardrooms and embassies. The investors make their move: he loses the presidential elections in 2009 and shortly afterwards his replacement announces the mining tax will be scrapped. 'This is an incredibly important milestone in bringing on-stream one of the finest undeveloped copper-gold projects in the world,' Rio Tinto chief executive Tom Albanese ejaculates.

The rest of Enkhbayar's former colleagues fall in line. With rivers of cash about to flow through the capital, there will be no further loose talk about nationalisation or new taxes. Unbowed, he forms a new party, brings the whole membership base with him, and hits the campaign trail with his eye on the 2012 elections.

The investors have different ideas. In a massive police operation, Enkhbayar is arrested and jailed on charges of corruption that materialise from nowhere. Thousands of his supporters take to the streets; he goes on hunger strike and begins to rapidly lose weight. Amnesty International demands that the authorities release him, pending trial, 'unless evidence has been presented to a court in a manner allowing for his lawyers to challenge that evidence.'

The indignity of a show trial ignites public fury, international alarm and calls from the UN secretary-general. The government caves and releases him. Shortly afterwards he is banned from standing as a candidate in the

2012 elections. He turns to the meticulously indexed State Department cables to help make sense of the predatory crosscurrents overtaking the country.

'It is interesting to observe how Americans, Canadians, especially and other countries were trying to get behind Oyu Tolgoi, and Rio Tinto and the big companies,' he says. 'The ambassador was writing about Mongolian politicians: who is in favour of Rio Tinto, who is not in favour of Rio Tinto, whom they support directly or indirectly. So this is the reality.' He pauses in the telling. 'The writer Aldous Huxley said, "The perfect dictatorship would have the appearance of a democracy." So we have a mask of democracy here.'

He knows now, better than anyone, what's behind the mask. With Boldbayar and their other allies he is spearheading the movement for constitutional reform and planning the next election. 'If we wait until the election campaign starts, we will one hundred per cent lose. So our strategy is, we work every day. We go to the countryside, we go to the ordinary people, we meet with the people. So that before the election campaign starts, we have good support among the voters, even if they are paid with a huge amount of money.'

Yes, I've heard that correctly – incumbent politicians are paying people in exchange for a commitment to vote for them. How does he plan to combat that? He gives me a wry smile. 'I tell them this money they paid to you is only a thousandth of the money they stole from you.'

I'm thinking on the last thing Boldbayar says to me before we farewell: 'Next time you see me I'll either be in parliament or in jail.' He's only half-joking.

Outside the cafe, the morning air is heavy with ashfall. 'Miners ready for new Mongolia boom with one-fifth of the country to be opened for digging', reads the CNBC headline. I'm scrolling through the news to the cheerful hiss and clatter of a coffee machine. Outside the cafe, the hulking form of Chinggis Khan looks out across Sükhbaatar Square from the parliament's colonnade, flanked by his sons on horseback. He looks pissed. Keep scrolling. A Sant Maral poll is recording 70 per cent of Mongolians would feel favourable towards 'a strong leader who does not have to bother with the parliament or elections'.

So the electoral pressure valve is being deactivated here too. No prime minister has served a full term in Mongolia since 2004. Mining investors publicly destroyed a government over a mining tax, then took ownership of both major political parties. A green insurgency simmers at the margins, its potential as yet unrealised. Rising temperatures and a bruising drought are reshaping landscapes and economies, silently pushing things towards a place of no return. Far to the south, a column of coal trucks twenty kilometres from end to end is backed up at a checkpoint, haulage from Tavan Tolgoi on its way to blast furnaces on the other side of the Chinese border.

Ulaanbaatar is probably as far from home as I've ever been, but there are symmetries here that feel legible. Coffee's ready. Realising I know the song filling the cafe; cheerful kitch from some long-distant Australian summer; humming, 'Do you come from a land down under'.

Stepping out into filtered light of ashfall; the shock of the familiar so very far from home.

jharkhand

Crammed into a sleeper bunk on an overnight coach, I'm waking to flicker-ing sun through the curtains without having really slept. Half-remembered din of the Kolkata bus terminal, a 3 am truck-stop somewhere outside the steel city of Jamshedpur. Four hundred kilometres of potholes and airhorn blasts, bucketing across West Bengal while the moon rides over-head unseen. Drawing the curtains back a little to see the dawn landscape flowing past; liquid orange sun balanced on the horizon, framed by steep-sided volcanic cores. I remember this place now; sometimes it comes back to me in dreams. Twenty years since my last visit, I'm back in Jharkhand.

Shriprakash meets me sandy-eyed and quite deliriously happy a few hours later. We've not seen each other since the World Social Forum in 2004, and we have some catching up to do. Swinging into Ranchi's early morning scramble, electric rickshaws and bikes dodging past taxicabs and heavy freight.

We find Dayamani Barla in her roadside teashop on one of the main feeder roads out of Ranchi. Ducking into the shady interior, place seems part teashop, part information exchange, part organising hub. Shri has worded me up on the way – this is someone worth meeting. She beams at us, good morning, eyes dancing behind wire-rimmed spectacles, serves tea. We hold up here for a time while a couple of visitors transit through for chai and documents, gossip and fresh intelligence.

She's ready; so now the three of us are southbound, an hour bouncing down rural laneways through a dry-season landscape of farm forestry and small landholdings. At the direction of Dayamani Di we're pulling into a tree-lined village to an enthusiastic welcome; she's greeted like royalty as we're ushered into a small community hall. Tea on wooden trays and two dozen people seated in a circle, keen to relive that time this community linked arms and kicked the world's largest steel corporation out on its arse.

Jharkhand is mineral-rich, dirt-poor and achingly beautiful. Memories from my last visit are a pastiche of smog-shrouded steel towns and underground coal fires that no-one knows how to put out. Forty per cent of India's mineral resources are concentrated in this state alone: nearly 30 per cent of its coal, a quarter of its iron ore and most of its uranium. Economic growth was a phenomenal 10.2 per cent in 2017–18, coin-doubling every seven years.

The blazing pace of extraction and combustion has spawned political instability, burning through five chief ministers in thirteen years. Somehow this immense wealth extraction is also causing absolute destitution. Four out of ten people live below the poverty line, and nearly 60 per cent of children below the age of five are underweight.

Jharkhand is distinctive for another reason. A quarter of the population are Adivasi – Indigenous tribal people with deep ancestral ties to *jal, jungle aur jameen* – water, forest and land. Land-rights struggles have shaped the politics of this area for centuries, waves of conflict and dispossession that recent decades have hurled into fast forward.

Through Shri's adept interpretation, Dayamani Di is describing the arrival of ArcelorMittal, which calls itself the world's leading steel and mining company, committed to a promise of 'transforming tomorrow.' In 2005, they announced a plan to transform fifty square kilometres of the Manoharpur area into Mordor, with one of the largest steel mills in the world. Adivasi opposition is highly visible and effective, and the company is sent on its way. They try it on again in nearby Karra block in 2006, cutting a deal with local landholding elites, only to retreat in the face of even greater opposition. Two years later, they're back, targeting the district right where we're sitting.

In 2006, Manoharpur locals had pitched in to support Karra block communities and share their experiences, joined by local anti-dam organisers with decades of experience. Dayamani Di recalls a delegation of these seasoned campaigners arriving to raise the alarm. 'They came to this area and they went village to village. Most of the villagers were not aware that the government had any plan to displace them. So these people went to the villages and held meetings, and talked about their experience. The villagers said yes: we will fight, but we have no experience. So you can lead us, or you can support us, but we will fight.'

It's an asymmetrical conflict. Luxembourg-based ArcelorMittal has a lock on local politics and seemingly unlimited amounts of money.

The villagers have only themselves. They set to work, but this is something more than an awareness campaign; they're building community as they go. In some villages, the absence of kerosene oil means kids can't study in the evenings, so the organisers pitch in to buy them solar lamps. The campaigners take on village oligarchs, advocate for fairer distribution of rations and resources with the local authorities, and challenge the thousandfold small injustices and torments of village life. 'It is not that some people are coming and talking about the steel plant and then going away,' Dayamani Di insists. 'The strategy of the movement was at various levels. You have to understand that this area is very, very poor, and now the company and government is coming with very lucrative options and promises. "We'll provide you with jobs, we'll provide you with football fields." There's a lot of confusion and conflicting information.'

All of this has happened before. The region is disfigured with mega-projects from decades past: mines, dams, steel mills, power plants. One dam alone displaced eighty-four villages. So the organisers form a delegation of volunteers to meet with villagers and see how things have worked out for them. 'We took forty people from this area and went to all these megaproject areas, went to the people the government had promised that "after displacement you will have a very nice kind of life. You'll have a good housing system, you'll have running water." Let's go and see.'

She describes this as a turning point: meeting face to face with the dispossessed, people with less than nothing. The moment the government got them out of the way, the promises of jobs and housing evaporated. Without their land, the ancestral structures of tribal communities simply disintegrated.

Shriprakash is a documentary filmmaker who specialises in recording and reflecting these struggles back to the communities as a form of self-defence. He recalls three films showcasing successful local campaigns against an army base, two dams and a steel plant. 'These three films were massively screened in this area. They also had the firsthand experience on the trip to displaced people, and they had the knowledge of two successful movements against ArcelorMittal,' he says. 'They are determined now that whatever the government and this company is planning, it's false. They've said: we will not leave the land.'

They move from community building and information gathering to direct action, and the results are immediate. A planned demonstration at the Governor's House in Ranchi pulls in so many people that newspaper headlines claim the movement has seized the city. They've drawn enough support to expand the remit of the organisation: now it's not just representing the interests of the Adivasi but the broader community as well.

They are on a roll. They get hold of internal documents that disclose the vast mismatch between what the government is offering people in public and what it's actually planning. This gets converted into ten thousand information packs for distribution all over the region. Unified, the community begins rejecting government overtures of gifts and sweeteners and eventually bans government representatives from entering the villages altogether. The company sponsors regional soccer and hockey tournaments; the villagers tag all the team uniforms with eye-catching movement insignia. They've probably stitched in something culturally resonant and locally iconic, but in my mind's eye I'm picturing an embroidered middle finger.

Shri and Dayamani Di's storytelling has provoked gales of laughter by this point; they are simply running circles around this hapless corporate giant. Something important is happening along the way: their collective identity is strengthening. 'They wanted to promote their language, their culture and their history,' Shri says. 'They started celebrating the anniversary of a tribal leader who was martyred; they also re-started a festival related to the environment, forest and culture.'

They've made a decision to take no money from local NGOs or national organisations; they will stand or fall on their own terms. They face death threats, infiltrators, violence and intimidation from armed thugs. Dayamani Di recalls sitting with Shriprakash when she gets a phone call warning her, 'If you will not stop this activity, we will fill you with so many bullets they won't be able to count them.'

They hold the line. The intimidation has only strengthened their resolve. 'You can imagine in isolated village areas here, how much pressure, how much tension this powerful company and the government, the police, the militia, they can create in this area. So these people,' Shri gestures to this quiet circle of villagers who have done the impossible 'these people, with their organisation, with their unity, they were able to stop all those things.'

Dayamani Di smiles at the memory. By 2010, ArcelorMittal has had enough, retreating back over the horizon. The Adivasi are left with nothing but their land, their culture, their dignity and some flash new soccer uniforms.

dulsunum

Last time I came to Jadugoda, Shriprakash smuggled me in, hunkered all the way down in the back seat of a taxi while he kept an eye out for cops. In 1999, outsiders were a rarity and authorities were trying to keep a lock on this district in Jharkhand's south.

This time it's going to be different: they've organised an actual parade. We are elaborately garlanded with loops of bright orange marigold flowers and now we're taking to the streets, paying our respects to a statue of Santhal archers at the main intersection. Traditional drummers setting the tempo for a double file of women in brilliant green and magenta saris. Our noisy procession makes its way down the main street, and then under the eaves of a walled forest. Something catches my eye – there are bright murals on the concrete walls; pictures of trees, and birds, and smiling cooling towers standing next to cartoon nuclear reactors. A double-take. Our march has taken us beneath an overhead slurry conveyor; through the trees, glimpsing the rock-walled ramparts of a massive tailings dam. Shri nods, gesturing over the defiant racket of the demonstration – *that's the Jadugoda uranium mine. Welcome back.*

I don't realise how much the procession is a calculated 'fuck you' to the authorities until much later. We've made camp in the home of Ghanshyam Birulee and his family, a Santhal elder who has helped lead this people's struggle against the Uranium Corporation of India Limited for decades. It's uncanny; he hasn't aged a day, but he's sure enjoying relaying the phone conversation he's just concluded with the local police, who want to know if the foreign 'dignitary' staying with them needs anything, accommodation perhaps. I think my hosts have talked up the 'former senator' thing, maybe downplayed the 'semi-employed writer' elements of my CV to remind the state that the Santhal will invite whomever they please onto their own land. So no, accommodation is sorted, thanks anyway.

Jadugoda is a nightmare installation: a uranium complex that has slowly lurched and sprawled across the landscape for fifty years, consuming villages, rice paddies and grazing pastures under an expanding perimeter of rock walls and mine dumps. In addition to the heavy groundwater impacts, chemical run-off and dust plumes attendant on any active min-ing operation, this community has had to contend with something else, something invisible. This is the epicentre of India's uranium province; the deposits are low-grade and deep underground, but the country's long isolation from global markets has meant it has squeezed this landscape for every last kilogram. After extracting that faint trace of uranium, truly immense quantities of finely powdered radioactive tailings are left behind, pumped through those overhead pipeways out into waste dams the size of airfields. Most of the uranium may be gone, but the radioactive thorium, radium, radon and other isotopes now sit ticking imperceptibly within these mesas – all of them carcinogenic and chem-ically toxic. Thirty-five thousand people live within a five-kilometre radius of this plant.

The only thing worse than doing this to a traditional farming commu-nity is doing it and then bullshitting about the health impacts of chronic exposure to low levels of radiation. While the underground workforce was returning home with skin rashes and lung damage, a slow-moving epidemic of miscarriages and birth deformities began to engulf the vil-lages. Still the authorities insisted there was no risk of harm, blaming the health catastrophe on alcoholism. Spurred into action, Ghanshyam and his community faced not just a state-backed uranium monopoly with bottomless cash reserves, but a dead-eyed bureaucracy, compliant media and national security institutions unwilling to let a few disobedient Adivasis derail India's nuclear weapons ambitions. And then, a decade later, just as independent health experts had warned, the cancers began to emerge.

'They never told anyone about the danger of uranium mining or radi-ation or long-term effects or impacts,' Ghanshyam says. 'They only said that this industry will bring employment, your life will be better, your sons and daughters will become doctors and engineers, your hut will become a building. They never talked about health and radiation issues.'

This is a heavy place. Because they have nowhere else to go, the Santhals and their tribal neighbours have stayed and fought every expansion, every imposition, every distant deception. With the help of grassroots organisers and one of Shriprakash's superb, timely films, they have regrouped, found their strength, and done something more than just survive. The mine still festers at the heart of their homeland, but as the parade was intended to demonstrate, they are far from helpless.

We've talked until deep into the night, and now it's time to rest. Tomorrow we'll invite the spirits of the recently departed to join all those who've gone before them.

It's bright out here, and I'm gently lightheaded from the home-brewed rice beer everyone is sipping from artfully constructed palm-leaf bowls. What's left of Chatikotcha village is baked dry in the subtropical heat, but we're comfortable in the shade of bamboo pavilions constructed especially for this event. Numbers are swelling, families drifting in from all over the district, bearing food and gifts. Every family group has its place out of the sun; the shelters are subdivided into numbered quarters with straw-mat flooring and wood for cooking fires. Whatever is happening here, everyone's invited.

I ask how the state dealt with the most recent uprising mounted by the Jharkhandi Organisation Against Radiation. 'During that period, a lot of things happened,' Ghanshyam recalls. 'Protest marches, many of us went to jail. That was the hardest part, and the police brutality was extreme.'

Shriprakash pauses in his translation to note one key difference in the levels of repression faced here. 'The government says you are anti-national. They say you are working with the hands of foreign people who don't want India to be strong, or to have nuclear ambitions. Because uranium is a very political mineral, not just commercial like other kinds of materials.' People campaigning for clean water and radiation safety are placed a perilously short rhetorical distance from foreign-backed agitators trying to undermine national security.

Somehow, though, they are making ground. Like the communities targeted by ArcelorMittal, they've built enduring and supportive networks across a wide area, held on to traditional language, culture and economies, and resisted any kind of dependence on distant NGOs or tangentially supportive political parties.

'This ongoing struggle is very long, but it has resulted in some outcomes,' Ghanshyam says. 'It used to be that overburden[3] from the mine was used as a landfill. So, they are openly giving this overburden to the people to make their houses, make roads, make walls. That has been stopped.'

So has the practice of letting fleets of haul trucks loaded with uranium ore plough through narrow village laneways, shedding dust and rubble in their wake. Their organising has delayed the expansion of tailings dams, forced significant plant redesigns and won limited compensation and relocation packages for some displaced families. Tailings structures and other heavily contaminated areas have been fenced, and livestock are now mostly prevented from grazing in the radioactive ponds. That even these basic safety measures were only grudgingly undertaken after years of hard-fought and risky campaigning underscores the kind of institutional malice they're up against.

'Then, after pressure from JOAR, they started supplying water to three villages nearby,' Ghanshyam says. 'They provided water for drinking and other uses. If things had not been destroyed, why would they need to provide this water?'

I look to see what he's pointing at: an unhitched water trailer not that far from where we're sitting, surrounded by children in bright clothes; a scattering of older kids have water containers and jugs. Rising directly behind the pavilion opposite, a thirty-metre-high ramp of rock and weedy grasses. This whole ceremony ground is backed by a flat-topped wall too level to be the work of geology. This is tailings dam three: an armoured structure impounding millions of tonnes of powdered low-level radioactive waste. Half of Chatikotcha village is entombed under it.

'Most of the people who gather here, they have no idea what is the danger of this dam,' Ghanshyam says. 'There are some small boards there,' he points, and I can just make out what he's referring to in the fading light. A couple of sad little safety signs out in the weeds. 'So those words are saying it's dangerous – do not take photographs – but as to why it's dangerous, nothing is said.'

---

3   Overlying waste rock with uranium concentrations too low to be worth putting through the mill.

In the cool of the evening, this meeting place is aglow with campfires and woodsmoke, alive with music and quiet conversation. Some time ago, one of Chatikotcha's senior women passed away. Tonight, in the presence of people from miles around, she's being farewelled, reunited with her husband and everyone who has gone on before her.

'Why we are here is because his maternal uncle has invited Ghanshyam for Dulsunum,' Shriprakash tells me. 'This is a ceremony for inviting a spirit who has died in the recent past, inviting that spirit to a certain place where they can rest, for the rest of time.'

Faint stars hanging against a turquoise sky. Down here, life and death forever intertwined, flowing around this monstrous thing that has forced its way into all their lives. For this brief time by the light of the campfires, that's set aside; the Adivasi have come together to wish their beloved old one a safe passage home.

Just before sunrise, the air already heavy with humidity. Halfway up the hillside, Ashish Birulee pauses to let me catch up, taking in the view across the forested slopes. A landscape as seen from underwater, everything swimming in soft layers of mist blending mountains into sky.

Onwards, then, along the ridgeline towards the final climb. Ashish is young but already taking on leadership roles; even in my brief time here I've seen others looking up to him. Now he's working his way along a narrow path between domed granites at the crest of the hill, finding a perch and lending a hand up.

Way below us, laid out across four or five hectares, the Jadugoda uranium mill, township visible through the treeline behind. Battered sheds and water towers; a quarter of the plant looks like an abandoned construction site. The rest of it just looks hammered; covered conveyors and thickening ponds enmeshed in grids of pipework. Panning across it through the viewfinder of an SLR, I see a dozen or more day labourers waiting quietly under the safety signage at the front gates. Ghanshyam's voice comes back to me: 'The words are saying it's dangerous – do not take photographs – but as to why it's dangerous, nothing is said.'

While Ashish waits patiently, I take dozens of photographs: of the plant, of the people whose names I don't know, of the gathering dawn. They won't be as evocative or perfectly framed as local photographer Anupam Kar's work, but they will help hold the memory.

I've never seen anything quite so . . . parasitic. It sits on the landscape like a scab, a proboscis of unseen declines and elevator shafts injected six hundred metres into the landscape. It is an extraction machine, crushing and digesting and concentrating and then shitting its waste slurry into those cancerous terraces looming over last night's ceremony. It is slowly burning through and discarding a softer and more abundant resource: the young men now filing through the gates, who will spend the next twelve hours exposed to subliminal fluxes of radon gas and airborne dust laced with radionuclides.

It's very early in the morning to be feeling this angry, but Ashish isn't keen to stay up here too long now that it's getting light.

Scrambling back down through the granites; last look. This country is mesmerising. Liquid orange sun balanced on the horizon, framed by these ancient granites. I already miss Jharkhand and I haven't even left yet.

> It is ordained that there should be no brewhouses with seacoal within a mile of the King or Prince's house.

UK PARLIAMENT, HOUSE OF COMMONS, 8 MAY 1624

shit glitter

Some beaches really work at night. Copacabana isn't one of them. The terraced wall of white towers on Avenida Atlântica is floodlit and stark, giving nothing away. The beach shadowed and empty, the quiet sound of the breakers. Bass metronome of dance music from somewhere. The streetlights are catching something glittering in the sand, a thousand points reflecting back at me. Shock in realisation: plastic cups mostly; plastic bags; a scatter of bottles and wrappers and other debris. Probably many tonnes of it, distributed from one end of this famous stretch to the other, waiting for the wind and tide to bear it out into the South Atlantic. Miserably, I begin collecting a couple of handfuls; chance across an intact plastic bag, and set to this tiny pointless-adjacent task in earnest. A habit picked up years ago that's now following me around the world. For a moment I'm visualising all the plastic I've ever picked up and binned – probably a decent pile – dwarfed by a loose pyramid of all the plastic I've ever briefly used and then tossed. All of it still out there somewhere; most of it compressing down into landfill strata, some of it raining slowly towards the abyssal seafloor.

A plastic sandal. A big wad of shrink-wrap. Paper cup with the logo of some mall – hold on – this isn't paper, it's been laminated with indestructible polyethylene. Into the bag, mind drifting. Did you know that for the price of US$425 and an internet connection, you can order a designer pack of gel capsules filled with flakes of twenty-four-carat gold leaf? Wash them down maybe with some sparkling mineral water from Norway, and in a few hours' time your turds will be glittering with actual gold. Gold! Designed as an ironic take on consumerism by New York artist Tobias Wong, the shit glitter caused a minor stir a couple of years ago when of course people started buying and eating it for real.

Fifteen minutes into my Copacabana collection, I realise there are crews working the beach with gloves and proper garbage bags, assembling temporary middens of discarded trash every few hundred metres. I can't work out if this makes my solitary effort feel more worthwhile or next-level futile, but at least I'll have somewhere to dump what I've collected. I decide it does make me feel better, actually: even if I'm finding the concept of global metabolic waste flows completely intractable for the moment, this particular small haul of once-used champagne cups and chip wrappers isn't bound for the abyssal plain tonight. Subsonic thump as a long, perfect wave sends a sheet of foam surging up the beach in agreement. I'll take small significances where I can get them.

Every society that ever existed produced waste; honestly, so did every organism that ever lived. Billionfold swarms of Luca's tiny daughters helping someone digest that parma, farting tiny little quantities of hydrogen sulfide and dimethyl sulfide into their intestines; better out than in.[4] By the ancient grace of Archaen cyanobacteria, those trees on the Atlântica promenade are silently expelling the oxygen they can't use from networks of pores on their leaves. Wombats deposit stacks of perfectly cubic nuggets in highly visible places on the high side of rocks and logs, for other wombats to read as territorial signifiers. A narrow but important branch of palaeontology is concerned with the study of coprolites – fossilised shit – because of how much you can read into the remains. Amazing how much corn is still left in there! Waste is natural, and it's everywhere; the thermodynamics people reminding us that every physical and energetic process in the universe is shedding some kind of waste in the form of low-grade heat.

Our ancestors crafted technologies that faded away after use, or tossed away harmless materials which posed no threat in build-up. Metres-thick shell middens in the coastal Pilbara and Southern Africa tell of societies worlds apart whose collective waste streams left only the subtlest of traces across tens of thousands of years. In the Indus Valley, the eroded bones of one of the world's oldest cities at Mohenjo-daro feature well-preserved wastewater and sewage drainage networks that would be roughly familiar

---

4   Everyone should read the Wikipedia entry for farting at least once: https://en.wikipedia.org/wiki/Flatulence

to modern civil engineers. Collective human metabolism extending, shaping an emerging urban metabolism. Pollution at an industrial scale comes later. In the UK, when it began to offend the wealthy in 1624, a bill was brought before the parliament to 'prohibit . . . the burning of seacoal in brewhouses within a mile of any building in which the King's court, or the court of the Prince of Wales, should be held, or in any street west London Bridge'. The bill was explicitly not about reducing air pollution for everyone: 'It is ordained that there should be no brewhouses with seacoal within a mile of the King or Prince's house.' The bill sailed through the House of Lords but stalled in the Commons, where the London Brewers Company worked the numbers to prevent it ever coming on for a vote. Brewing being one of London's most lucrative industries at the time, MPs knew what they had to do, even with an actual king coughing into his handkerchief at them.

I'm paused on this great arc of sand with my sad plastic bag, wondering at that inflection point between the shell middens and the seacoal pollution; the conceptual distance not just between the technologies but the ubiquitous power dynamics that sustain them.

People on tight schedules, ambitious five-year plans and fine profit margins never, ever spend their own money containing or cleaning up their shit. They only do it when forced to; they are practically thermodynamic in their consistency. This forcing only ever happens through political collisions, and sometimes it seems you can even be the literal king and still lose out to the investment theory of party competition, seventeenth-century Westminster style.

Realising I have no idea if the beach where I'm standing is even going to exist in a few decades' time, because four hundred years on, the seacoal people still seem to have the numbers.

Moving along the beach collecting oversized pieces of shit glitter for another ten minutes and then making for the last metro home. Big day tomorrow.

> The economic logic behind dumping a load of toxic waste in the lowest wage country is impeccable and we should face up to that.

WORLD BANK CHIEF ECONOMIST LAWRENCE SUMMERS

samarco criminosa

The schoolroom in the dead village is on the second floor, child-sized chairs and tables askew and overturned, embedded a foot deep in mud set like concrete. That's when it hits me, I think, the scale of what happened to this place. Minas Gerais, Brazil: nearly three years after the November 2015 tsunami of mud that surged through this quiet river valley and wiped the village of Paracatu off the map. The high-tide line on the remaining building shells – including this school – is at least three metres above ground level.

In a hotel room in Belo Horizonte this morning, I've gone online to see if there's any record of the day it happened. It starts as a dusty haze billowing over the lush vegetation, shaky phone camera footage of something churning across the floor of the valley. And then they run. Panicked voices from out of shot. From higher ground, it's a catastrophe – a river of mud moving impossibly quickly downslope, carrying everything in front of it. In the background, I recognise a flat-topped mesa like the ones that loom over Chatikotcha village in Jharkhand, only this one has breached, disgorging forty-four million cubic metres of waste slurry and heavy metals into the valley. An entity called Samarco operates this iron ore mine – a shell company jointly owned by Australian mining giant BHP Billiton and Vale S.A., headquartered in Rio.

The people of Paracatu had a crucial margin of warning; everyone was able to get out before the mudtide hit. A few dozen kilometres upstream, it hit the village of Bento Rodrigues before anyone had time to evacuate. Nineteen people were buried alive. The plume sluiced down more than six hundred kilometres of waterways before disgorging into the South Atlantic, sterilising the river basin and wrecking local fishing grounds up and down the coast.

There are hundreds of schoolbooks baked into the mud that drowned this classroom. The walls are slashed with graffiti: *samarco criminosa* in angry red paint. I have no Portuguese, but the message still lands: what happened here wasn't an accident. This was a crime.

Letícia Aleixo is a lawyer working with affected peoples further down the river system – Indigenous communities who lived here for thousands of years before Portuguese occupation. We've caught up back in Belo and as she's speaking I feel like I know what she's about to say, nearly word for word. The template by now so familiar: 'As they are a traditional community, they were very linked to the river, to fish, to swim, but also they have spiritual links to the Doce River. Now the fisherman say that the fish are contaminated . . . their eyes are not the same. And of course there are no studies about the quality of water.'

'We do not see ourselves without the sea, without the river,' Rosetânia Ferreira tells the Incidence Project on the Mining Agenda, which Letícia coordinates. 'Because they are our identity. The sea is our life. The river is our life.'

For four years, Letícia has been part of a network representing the 1.9 million people affected by the disaster. They've been set against an army of commercial lawyers, a captive state bureaucracy and a national government that will flip from complicated to hostile with the election of Jair Bolsonaro in 2018. Now they wade through a swamp of litigation while thousands of the dispossessed await something resembling justice. 'The problem here in Brazil is that everybody thinks about compensation, but nobody thinks about prevention, and the next time,' Letícia says. 'In international law we call it "non-repetition measures" because this is a structural problem. In Minas Gerais, for example, we have almost a thousand dams and they are not secure at all.'

Non-repetition measures. When someone seriously hurts you, things get set in place preventing them from ever doing it again. In the precise language of law professor Naomi Roht-Arriaza, 'whatever measures are needed to prevent a recurrence of the serious human rights violations or international crimes committed in the past'.

Because this really is a structural problem. We glimpsed some of the structure high above the city not so long ago, the coastline marked out in bright sheets and grids of light. Not that the numbers mean much, but here's how high we'd stacked our Anthropocene coins by 2015: 'The annual material throughput of the world economy amounted to around 89 billion tonnes.'

Numbers too big to parse. Arrows on the sankey diagram moving from left to right, feeding everything into this thing we call the global economy and stacking it on the shelves of supermarkets on the urban periphery. Between 1900 and 2015, the economy captured 925 billion tonnes of this infalling torrent in what the diagrams describe as 'net additions to stock', which just means everything we hold onto for a while: the quiet house, the tilt-up supermarket, the car that brought me here.

Over that same span of time, the coloured arrows representing the other two and a half trillion tonnes of transient stuff: we're done with it. Vent it into the air, pipe it into the ocean, leave it lying around on Copacabana Beach. Here's some of it now, caked a foot deep on the second floor of an abandoned classroom.

I understood these diagrams intellectually before, but I'd never inter-nalised them. Now I can't look at them without seeing peoples' faces. The young woman in the half-buried car with her arm in the lock-on pipe. Dayamani Di organising an insurrection from a tea shop in Ranchi. Boldbayar working the phones trying to build a coalition strong enough to survive in unbreathable air. No faces will come to mind in Paracatu – this town is dead, because *samarco criminosa*.

The face I see in the middle of the diagram, the beneficiary of this planetary tide of clearfelling and landfilling, looks a lot like a middle-class white guy steering a shopping trolley with a wobbly wheel down the clothes pegs and salad spinners aisle. On that note, my laptop dies for no reason and never starts up again. Much later, I will be quoted $1500 to get it fixed. Maybe this is it. This is what the consumer age looks like.

In Accra, what the consumer age looks like is forty-foot shipping con-tainers full of 'recycled' appliances arriving from the Global North. They unload at least 6500 tonnes a year of it at Tema, Ghana's main seaport, and haul it into town for sorting and assessment by Accra's network of second-hand dealers. What can't be quickly on-sold ends up being carted out to the vast industrial middens of Agbogbloshie, where an informal work-force up to ten thousand strong sets about dismantling it. Everything from washing machines to gaming consoles, dead laptops, photocopiers and obsolete mobile phones find their final resting place here. There's nothing intrinsically wrong with a specialised waste recovery economy, but not a single one of the expired devices dumped here is designed to be recycled. Most of them are broken up and stripped by hand for whatever copper and iron and aluminium can be usefully recovered before they are pushed into piles and torched.

The fires of Agbogbloshie send plumes of smoke laced with cadmium, mercury, chromium and PCBs across the city. The site is a notorious hot zone of heavy metal pollution and burning plastic: one poisoned node in the network of cities across Africa and East Asia in receipt of almost fifty million tonnes of e-waste every year.

'The smoke is a very big problem for us, and you will sit down all day, you will not get up, you just sit at one place and dismantle, you know the hammer has weight. We are really suffering in this work,' one worker told a local panel of health researchers.

'I think the economic logic behind dumping a load of toxic waste in the lowest wage country is impeccable and we should face up to that . . . I've always thought that under-populated countries in Africa are vastly under-polluted, their air quality is probably vastly inefficiently low com-pared to Los Angeles or Mexico City.'

We should thank whoever leaked World Bank chief economist Lawrence Summers' notorious 1991 memo, because advocates of this 'impeccable economic logic' know how sociopathic it sounds when you say it out loud, and so they very rarely do. The memo betrays the basic asymmetry that runs across every dimension of the world's industrial metabolism. In Accra, the heavy metals are in the bloodstream, not in the gold-flecked floaters of the ironically wealthy.

The terrifying thing is that there must be worse things in the world than sitting amid a haze of toxic fallout smashing computer equipment to pieces with a hammer, or they wouldn't do it. 'The only thing worse than being exploited by capitalism is not being exploited by capitalism,' suggests British economist Joan Robinson, and imagine if she's right.

In January 2019, the tailings dam at Vale's Brumadinho mine collapses, spilling twelve million cubic metres of mine tailings into the watershed. Two hundred and fifty-six people are buried alive – non-repetition measures don't seem to be a priority for the Bolsonaro regime. The coloured stripes on the diagram will need to be twice as thick by 2050 to feed another doubling of the coins, nearly two hundred billion tonnes of iron ore and cement and chickens somehow pouring through the guy's shopping trolley every single year. That's a lot more tailings dams poised for collapse, a lot more toxic waste dumped in the lowest-wage countries. The present form of our global industrial metabolism feeling not merely extractive, but actively predatory. What the sankey stripes are describing isn't an accident. This is a crime.

If there's no economic plan for the unnecessariat,
there's certainly an abundance of plans to extract
value from them.

ANNE AMNESIA

unnecessariat

A day after standing in the ruins of the abandoned village, I'm on a mid-night street full of abandoned people. Parts of central São Paulo are open-air dystopian after dark, confronting in the way the city steps around the broken people as though they aren't there. It shows in the architecture, entropy driven hard into battered facades, every surface laced with strange runic graffiti. For some reason it feels very present tonight, that sense that one of those figures slumped in a doorway or lying out on the footpath could easily be me. Run of bad luck or bad decisions, it could be any of us.

'Surplus populations' the economics textbooks call them, if they mention them at all. We've met them, back when we were introduced to the village of a hundred people: the ones the economy doesn't need. Living out at the raggedy edge of an economy that forced them off their ances-tral lands, where they lived in self-sufficiency, because it needed someone to do the actual work. As long as the economy was growing in a certain kind of way, it inhaled people like this. But when growth stalled, it shed its workforce back onto the streets like garbage. The ancestral lands are gone now, lost under a mine dump or clearfelled for paper pulp; there's no going back. The social safety net, if it was ever there; that's being abolished too – this is capitalism, not a circus trapeze act.

The 1-per-cent villager who wrote these rules doesn't actually mind having a visible pool of the desperately impoverished who will do anything for work. The market has found a use for those of us it leaves discarded on these streets: we're there as a form of advertising collateral, to focus the minds of everyone else. Maybe hold off on that request for more regular hours, or a lunchbreak, or some safety equipment. Maybe avoid eye contact with that colleague when she asks if you've thought of joining the union.

This seems to be an intrinsic property of certain kinds of economy. In 'Estranged Labour' in 1844, Karl Marx wrote, 'The worker sinks to the level of a commodity and becomes indeed the most wretched of commodities.' Three years later, in *Wage Labour and Capital*, he was warming to the theme: 'He works that he may keep alive. He does not count the labour itself as a part of his life; it is rather a sacrifice of his life.'

That's the only commodity most global villagers have to offer: our time. Precious and irreplaceable hours of our one and only life. The 95 per cent of us who don't have big landholdings or a portfolio of investments doing the work for us, we have to mete out spans of our life in exchange for money. Through accidents of birth and circumstance, hard work and the generosity of others, maybe we get to do something we love: something creative, meaningful, worthwhile; maybe we're paid well for it. Or maybe we're risking our lives as slave-adjacent construction workers on Dubai high-rises, or stitching shoes together fourteen hours a day in Guangzhou. A lot of us increasingly find ourselves working at the tense intersection of labour and automation, places where people are expected to work like machines even as machines become more adept at doing the work of people.

Amazon's warehouse worker-tracking system surveils its human workforce at increasingly fine resolution, counting every second a worker spends 'off-task'. Overrun your allowance of time off-task, or miss production or fulfilment quotas, and the system begins issuing automated warnings. Cross enough of these thresholds, and the software will draw up termination paperwork and bring you to the attention of a supervisor. For the time being, it's the supervisor that legally does the terminating, not the worker-tracking system. But we can't be far from the day when a process-management algorithm with sufficiently human-like judgement fires a human being for lacking sufficiently machine-like discipline.

This is economy as automaton: a faceless thing we're told has no agency of its own, deploying technologies of human obsolescence the moment the cost–benefit analysis hits a critical threshold. It's not just a case of letting go of your ambition to be a haul-truck driver so you can 'learn to code'. The code is learning to code. Manufacturing industries are returning to China after their sojourn in Bangladesh and the Philippines, just as China records its seventh straight year as the world's largest market for industrial robotics.

Some of this feels familiar. Automation happens, so mostly we don't weave clothes or plant seeds by hand anymore. As the coin-doubling economy expands and inhales, more work opens up in more fields. There aren't many weavers or farmers left where I come from, but there are Enterprise Solutions Architects, Fintech Quantitative Developers and Business Intelligence Engineers, and even if nobody knows what the fuck it is these people actually do, some of them seem exceptionally well paid, and good on them. If automation were just a straight-line pathway to mass unemployment, industrialised societies would look very different to how they do.

But some of this feels unfamiliar. After every economic crash, it takes longer and longer for the jobs growth to catch up with the coin-doubling economy. There's a jobs lag, and it gets longer with every convulsion, a phenomenon of 'jobless recoveries' that has grown much more pronounced since the 1990s.

The jobs themselves are changing; with each successive shock, the work this thing wants us to do becomes more and more attenuated. Ride bikes delivering food to shiftworkers and single parents too exhausted to cook. Wait tables or sell shoes on a zero-hours contract; we'll call you if we need you; okay, we need you in an hour. Cut code for a developer at the bad end of a crunch: you'll work eighty hours straight, but help yourself to those cans of liquid speed in the fridge. All of us contractors and sub-subcontractors now, piece workers, micro-entrepreneurs isolated from each other, and from workplace protections that six generations of union organisers fought to win. It's not sitting in a haze of fallout smashing obsolete computers to pieces with a hammer, but you can see it from here.

In 2011, the Occupy movement kicked off a cascade of defiant occupations of public places, turning empty corporate plazas into temporary autonomous zones and introducing the concept of the 1 per cent to a global audience. They popularised economist Guy Standing's use of the word 'precariat' to describe people living contract-to-contract on the finest of margins between solvency and poverty. The term is a riff on 'proletariat', which Marx defined as anyone dependent on wage labour for survival, someone without land or assets who would be 'thrown into the street as soon as he becomes superfluous'.

But at least the precariat have jobs. Blogger Anne Amnesia coined the term 'unnecessariat' for those people the economy can't even be bothered to throw out into the street. 'From where I live, the world has drifted away. We aren't precarious, we're unnecessary,' she writes. Preyed on by payday lenders and opioid manufacturers, edged into the informal economy or the black market, whole generations end up walled into ghettoes of mental illness and addiction. 'The world of self-driving cars and global outsourcing doesn't want or need them,' Amnesia warns. 'Someday it won't want you either.'

These depredations are nearly always inflicted unevenly along fault lines of race and gender, and sometimes what privileged communities see as approaching dystopia is just the advancing edge of how many people in this village already live. As the ranks of the unnecessariat swell, states are increasingly turning to incarceration to manage them. Prisons have re-emerged as a bleak form of extractive industry, licenced by carceral states to mine forced labour from people overwhelmingly jailed for crimes of poverty. In the United States, people of colour make up 60 per cent of the two-million strong prison population, while making up only 30 per cent of the wider community. In Australia, Aboriginal and Torres Strait Islander people make up 27 per cent of the imprisoned, and 2 per cent of the population outside. Prominent US prison abolitionist Professor Angela Davis invites us to consider the grim continuities between 'convict leasing, peonage and the penitentiary system, all of which clearly were institutional descendents of slavery'.

The thing holding this bitter mess of stolen time and coercion together is the sense that it's inevitable and immovable, locked down by the dead hand of the market or even the laws of nature. And surely that's one crack in the dismal armour, because it just isn't true.

'Robots are not killing jobs,' Brian Merchant writes for *Gizmodo*. 'The managers who see a cost benefit to replacing a human role with an algorithmic one and choose to make the switch are killing jobs.'

Foreigners are not killing jobs either. Managers who see a cost benefit to evacuating your workplace to a weak currency zone are the ones killing jobs. Managers who contract a private prison workforce to stitch footwear are killing jobs. These managers are simply following the logic of the coin-doubling game, the whole thing diffused behind a fog of inevitability as though it's not the outcome of very specific decisions made by that 1 per cent guy in the village, the one who owns the whole thing.

From the out-of-work haul-truck driver to the homeless in São Paulo to the young men queueing at the gates of Jadugoda, all of us are subjected to an economic logic that makes it increasingly difficult to tell whether we are consumers or consumed. It's not just mine tailings and dead laptops caught up in this accelerating cascade of planned obsolescence. It's us.

tooth and claw

She is no more than three inches from nose to tail: a small armoured form skimming the seafloor in search of breakfast. Propelled along by two rows of feathery oars evolving midway between fins and legs, she is just one browser among many down here. Working her way between towering sponge complexes, antennae sensing chemical gradients in the seawater perhaps; glittering compound eyes scanning the dappled sand, looking for . . .

. . . that. An unwary annelid worm chooses exactly the wrong moment to shift in its burrow, and it's over – breakfast is served in a brief skirmish that sends a whorl of sediment into the water column. The trilobite pauses under the shelter of swaying algal fronds to dismantle the annelid, which itself had only just consumed its last breakfast of benthic detritus. The pause saves her life in turn – a marauding Anomalocaris has just passed overhead, shadow of a metre-long nightmare rippling across the sand. Hold still under the fronds for a moment. The line between life and death on the margins of these Cambrian shorelines is razor-fine.

She's here now, right here, where I'm sitting. A fossil trilobite no more than three inches from nose to tail, segmented imprint of a life still half-encased in the host rock. A gift from a precious friend on a bright day, this unexpected writing companion from deep time. She is perhaps four or five times older than those slender fish held in the oldest book in Byblos. These artifacts of geo-memory only exist because our trilobite and her contemporaries had begun producing armoured body parts robust enough to be carried forward in silt and sediment through these inconceivable spans of time.

The armour, the teeth, the claws, the bivalve shells with holes drilled into them by carnivorous gastropods: life on these long-vanished seafloors is dangerous. It's unlikely to be a coincidence that eyes and antennae are arriving around the same time in the evolutionary record. There are abundant fossil hints that other forms of perception, memory and agency are supplementing the sensory repertoires that carried our ancestors through from their Hadean inception. From viral replicators to motile bacterial hunters to Anomalocaris – staying alive down here means paying attention. And with every passing generation, there is a little more to pay attention to; faster predators, smarter prey.

In the 1850s, English naturalist Charles Darwin and his contemporaries begin placing their observations of the living world into the bottomless context of this fossil record, culminating in the publication of a five-hundred-page work titled *On the Origin of Species by Means of Natural Selection*. Within a few years, Darwin is persuaded by philosopher and biologist Herbert Spencer to adopt his phrase 'survival of the fittest'. 'This survival of the fittest, which I have here sought to express in mechanical terms, is that which Mr. Darwin has called "natural selection", or the preservation of favored races in the struggle for life,' Spencer writes in 1864. The struggle for life: nature as a seething, competitive bloodbath in which only the most finely honed killers will prevail; 'Nature red in tooth and claw', to borrow British poet Alfred, Lord Tennyson's phrase. Spencer's carefully reasoned analysis – and the fossil evidence of the competitive failures of past ages – is a powerful conceptual fit for European powers engaged in the ruthless extraction of labour and resources from their distant colonies. God's chosen people begin to cede intellectual ground to the preservation of scientifically favoured races.

Even Darwin – who chooses his words more carefully than some of his colleagues – concludes in 1871 that 'at some future period, not very distant as measured by centuries, the civilised races of man will almost certainly exterminate, and replace, the savage races throughout the world . . . The break between man and his nearest allies will then be wider, for it will intervene between man in a more civilised state, as we may hope, even than the Caucasian, and some ape as low as a baboon, instead of as now between the negro or Australian and the gorilla.'

Effortlessly, this white supremacist caricature of natural systems locked in endless competitive arms races is brought into the service of power. 'The professionalization of political science in the early 1900s would be marred by naturalistic fallacies that twisted Darwin's thinking into justifications of racism, eugenics, war, and genocide,' write Steven A. Peterson and Albert Somit in the gruesome introduction to their *Handbook of Biology and Politics*. We'll hear from the Nazis before long, but in the meantime, as for politics, so too for commerce. Well before the turn of the twentieth century, elevating ruthless competition to the status of a natural imperative is a huge hit with US oil monopolists and steel oligarchs.

'We accept and welcome, therefore, as conditions to which we must accommodate ourselves, great inequality of environment, the concentration of business, industrial and commercial, in the hands of a few, and the law of competition between these as being not only beneficial but essential for the future progress of the race,' Andrew Carnegie writes in an essay titled 'Survival of the Fittest' in 1889. I own all the steel mills, and all the iron ore, because science.

'The growth of a large business is merely a survival of the fittest . . . This is not an evil tendency in business. It is merely the working-out of a law of nature and a law of God,' John D. Rockefeller tells a Sunday School assembly. I own all the oil, because science, and also God.

If you think it takes audacity to stand before an audience of prey and openly describe your business model in terms of predator–prey relationships, wait until you hear about Ayn Rand.

There's a reason why industrialists and colonial administrators are comfortable quoting Darwin and Spencer but overlook people like Pyotr Alexeyevich Kropotkin. Two reasons, actually – first, they are unlikely to have many revolutionary anarchists on their bookshelves; second, his observations run directly counter to their carnivorous interpretations of the natural world. Kropotkin is a Russian philosopher and geographer who marries close study of Siberian and Scandinavian ecosystems with a nuanced reading of the literature his European contemporaries are producing. In his collection of essays titled *Mutual Aid*, published in 1902, he draws attention to the wider context in which the competitive 'struggle for existence' is taking place, realising that Darwin himself had warned his readers against 'overrating its narrow meaning'.

Darwin 'pointed out how, in numberless animal societies, the struggle between separate individuals for the means of existence disappears, how struggle is replaced by co-operation, and how that substitution results in the development of intellectual and moral faculties which secure to the species the best conditions for survival,' Kropotkin writes in Mutual Aid's first essay. 'He intimated that in such cases the fittest are not the physically strongest, nor the cunningest, but those who learn to combine so as mutually to support each other, strong and weak alike, for the welfare of the community.'

We've seen this already, at world-building scale. Luca's daughters, passing their DNA mixtapes back and forth in fluid exchange, working from a distributed library of genetic material vastly larger than the collections held by any individual cell. We see it in the quiet architectures of the stromatolite reefs that ornament the planet's shorelines for a billion years and more. We see it again when these ubiquitous creatures begin working together in the intimate partnership of symbiogenesis that brings forth the eukaryotes. We see it yet again when these complex cells in turn begin clustering together into multicellular life forms that bring forth the sponges, the annelid worms, the trilobites, the Anomalocaris.

Collaboration: struggle replaced by cooperation. Those who learn to combine so as to support each other. These are the alliances of collective benefit that have built the foundations of the world.

Now those foundations are being consumed by hole-drilling carnivores with monopolistic intent. Their target isn't some hapless bivalve evolving a harder shell as fast as it can; the coin-doubling investors have set their drilling platforms against the world system itself. Somehow, we're being called upon to develop profound new ways in which to combine so as mutually to support each other: a form of mutual aid at planetary scale.

The consequences of failure are written in the pages of the oldest book in the world, segmented imprints of long-vanished species still half-encased in the host rock. On the upside, as we're considering the nature and scale of such a transformation, maybe it's a comfort to know that every cell in our bodies has been through this before.

Deep breath. Maybe we got this.

captured states

Johannesburg, with a hint of summer in the air. The coffee shop in Rosebank is filled with sunlight and conversation as we pick through the mechanics of how South Africa's future was stolen.

'If it wasn't for the fact that we are quite free to report, this whole state capture decade would have gone for much longer,' Inge Willowmore observes. As the deputy editor of an Afrikaans-language newspaper, she's spent years reporting on the looting of post-apartheid South Africa. One of the things the ruling clique has done to keep themselves and their allies in power is to remove a key piece of accountability machinery. 'What [Jacob] Zuma and the government did is they destroyed the prosecuting authority. So the judiciary and the media was still up and functioning, but if anything got past the weakened police it got to the state prosecutors and just stopped there.'

Institutionalised patronage and graft multiplied on an epic scale; so embedded and systematic that people ceased referring to it as corruption and branded it state capture.

The phrase grabs me. Somewhere along the slide from corruption to full oligarchy, the phenomenon of state capture has been clocked everywhere from post-Soviet republics to Latin America to postcolonial Africa. The forms and institutions of democracy remain in place, but over time they get wormholed, hollowed out and repurposed. 'The classical definition of state capture calls attention to the way bureaucratic rule and formal procedures are manipulated by private firms in their attempt to influence state policies and laws in their favour,' according to one study.

This isn't about the kind of petty corruption that grabs headlines and provokes an occasional high-profile resignation. Well-orchestrated state capture generally ensures that no laws get broken at all, since it's the process of lawmaking itself that's the prize.

'Corruption tends to be an individual action that occurs in exceptional cases, facilitated by a loose network of corrupt players. It is informally organised, fragmented and opportunistic. State capture is systemic and well organised by people who have an established relationship with one another. It involves repeated transactions, often on an increasing scale,' write the authors of *Shadow State* about South Africa.

The state's metabolic flows of minerals and fresh water, timber and tourists expertly parasitised by a small handful of powerful families taking their places among the country's old colonial elites. So now Johannesburg is two separate cities, rifting in opposite directions. On a packed bus out to Soweto, I get a glimpse of life on one side of the rift, a place where unemployment is somewhere between a quarter and a half of the population. This storied township is backed by flat-topped mesas and slag heaps laced with cadmium, arsenic and uranium: mountainous residues of expired goldmines.

On the other side of the rift, the quiet streets of Randburg are lined with brilliant jacaranda, a hint of jasmine. The walls of every fortified house are topped with strands of electrified wire; placarded death threats from companies with names such as CSS Tactical and ADD Armed Response. To meet Inge for lunch, I've travelled from Sandton's inward-facing complex of office towers and malls, in a gold railcar on a private subway line, emerging into a functionally identical mall complex in Rosebank – a whirl of bright boutiques and polished nails and credit cards tapping on sensors. All global brand names and chain stores; maybe three I don't recognise. In these segmented alcoves, look: mobile phones, a newsagent, a cafe with pastries under glass. Copy-and-paste franchise operations; room-sized blocks of retail Lego. I swear these are the same units I saw in that faded tilt-up shopping centre on the periphery of my old home town.

All these places fusing into the same place somehow. At the points of extraction and dumping, from Soweto to the Gobi to the mineral fields of Jharkhand, the politics and the poverty and the mutilated landscapes all assume a crude form of symmetry. Something similar seems to be happening at the point-of-sale: retail replicators converging on an idealised form of maximum extraction and minimal cost.

Since leaving the quiet house, we've traced the perilous extent of our industrial metabolism. What began as an odd analogy between the streetscape's unseen architecture and the internal structure of a passing trilobite turned political almost immediately.

'Industrial metabolism' is a concept borrowed from the study of living systems, adapted into the language of urban planning because, at the macro level, the form taken by our settlements is shaped in part by the externalised metabolic demands of nearly eight billion people and our captive animals.

But living systems have always been more than just metabolism. All the way back at the dawn of the world, Luca had developed boundaries and the ability to reproduce. To survive, her daughters were establishing the ability to recall past conditions, perceive present conditions and act to shape their future conditions. Pausing to watch one of them tumble and run past us, we realised she'd already got to work on all three. She's never been alone: perception and expression emerging in a two-way feedback loop as millions of these creatures quorum-sensed their way to collective action.

Metabolism, boundaries, perpetuation. Memory, perception and agency. These are life's longest continuities: ramifying slowly into more complex and sophisticated forms with every generation; membranes hardening into chitinous exoskeletons; photosensitive cells resolving into compound eyes. My question, then, is: how far might this continuities metaphor extend? If metabolism has refracted seamlessly into human collectives, what then of boundaries, and perpetuation, and memory?

This isn't an academic question: in the course of their coin-doubling, those metabolic sankey stripes have somehow captured our institutions of collective agency, so much so that we now seem helpless to prevent them consuming the world itself. Captive states delivering gold trains to the few, mountains of gold tailings to the many. Those on whose land this vast extraction takes place are written out of the story altogether, lost to the collective memory.

When we blockaded Wattle Forest, our intervention was aimed directly at one strand of this metabolic flow: to block physical access to a targeted resource. But these holding actions are usually overwhelmed unless a wider political field is engaged. To silence the chainsaws, it took a massive campaign of community awareness-raising, changing the collective perception of native forest logging. This was artfully converted into policy change using the fulcrum of an election, until laws for new national parks were eventually proclaimed by our institutions of collective agency.

International buyers then hit other places a few million tonnes harder. Our efforts had effect only within the collective boundaries of our state, leaving the structural imperatives of the coin-doubling machine unmoved. One strand of the sankey diagram was shoved into a different configuration, but now there are plastic-wrapped toilet rolls from Sarawak in my shopping trolley.

Lifting our eyes from the clearfells and the mine dumps, then. It seems we can't make sense of industrial metabolism without understanding these other continuities, starting with the patchwork of boundaries and borders that someone has drawn across our global village. Suitcase packed in the corner of an empty room; compact blue passport on the bedside table.

Treading with real care now. Somewhere up ahead are monsters.

continuities

As Home Secretary at this defining moment in our country's history, I have a particular responsibility when it comes to taking back control. It is to end the free movement of people once and for all.

UK HOME SECRETARY PRITI PATEL, 2019

the map is not the territory

The coach rolls into the ferry terminal at fortress Calais at 2 am, the night air damp and heavy. We were hours late out of Dortmund; now dozens of us are disembarking onto floodlit tarmac, irritable and disoriented. We shuffle between plastic barriers with passports in hand, neither asleep nor awake. Metal detectors, fingerprint scanners, passport in the illuminated slot, sir what is the purpose of your visit to the UK. I snap out of my reverie: pay attention. They're pulling a tall young African man out of the queue behind me, uniformed customs agents surrounding him, drawing him off to one side. A heated argument in French; he's being led away and his luggage removed from the coach even as I'm waved through.

The border is open, until it's not.

On the ferry, ninety minutes of liminality with nothing to do but walk the decks or read. 'Open borders are already a reality, not some future utopian dream,' Parvathi Raman observes. She's the founding chair of the SOAS Centre for Migration and Diaspora Studies. 'But at the moment only some are afforded the luxury of being able to move safely, while others have to face making clandestine, expensive and dangerous journeys.' And now I know what she means. A year on the road is firmly imprinting the highly selective porosity of the world's borders.

Here's one now: a 33-kilometre expanse of fog and heavy weather, one of the world's busiest shipping lanes. Seen from the port we've just left, this moody stretch is the Pas de Calais. On the leeward side of the ferry out of the freezing wind, a line of white cliffs are resolving out of the dawn, signifying this same seaway as the Strait of Dover. At some unmarked moment on this sleepless passage, we crossed a line.

I've been fascinated by maps since I was a kid, but they have a way of flattening your perspective. National borders are traced with the same sense of object-permanence as coastlines and mountain ranges. Later this week, I'll make my way three levels below the cheerful hustle of the market at Camden Lock, to a cramped but excellent stall where you can find maps featuring Palestine, Tibet, Yugoslavia, the Union of Soviet Socialist Republics. On newer maps they draw newer lines: South Sudan, Timor-Leste. Then there are the lines on maps yet to be drawn, enclosing forms of collective yearning – Kashmir, Kurdistan, West Papua. Borders sit mostly static for decades, then whiplash across the terrain, blinking in and out of existence. When the Berlin Wall came down in 1989 there was even loose talk of a borderless world. With neoliberalism emerging supreme, history itself was coming to an end, they said. That turned out to be an illusion, as Michel Foucher pointed out in *Border Obsession*: 'Of the 248,000 kilometres of existing land borders, 26,000 have been established since 1991.'

The concept of nation-state borders is quite a recent idea. Exhausted by decades of war, in 1643 hundreds of European aristocrats and monarchs sent their envoys to a rolling series of negotiations in the Westphalia region of what would one day be northwestern Germany, to achieve a lasting peace. The treaties that would emerge in 1648 – while by no means ending the bloodshed and contention – would stabilise the European political order and signify the approaching dissolution of the Holy Roman Empire. Scholars of international relations trace back the foundational rules of the modern nation-state to this 'Peace of Westphalia', although the actual treaty documents were overwhelmingly concerned with settling more urgent contemporary disputes.

'Even to this day two principles of interstate relations codified in 1648 constitute the normative core of international law,' writes Seyom Brown, professor of international cooperation at Brandeis University. The principles read like this: '(1) the government of each country is unequivocally sovereign within its territorial jurisdiction, and (2) countries shall not interfere in each other's domestic affairs.'

In the aftermath of World War II, the drafters of the United Nations Charter made an attempt to subordinate these arbitrary sovereignties to the principle of collective security, and an ambitious human rights declaration.

Despite this extraordinary attempt, Westphalia remains deeply baked into international law. 'Nothing should authorise intervention in matters essentially within the domestic jurisdiction of any state,' says article 2(7) of the United Nations charter.

Decoded, that means within any territory enclosed by the lines on these maps, whoever can manage to stay in charge is allowed to do whatever they can get away with. Read that sentence again, maybe: it does sound like the kind of thing a bunch of aristocrats and monarchs would come up with.

'The map is not the territory,' mathematician Alfred Korzybski suggests. It's a reminder never to trust maps too absolutely, but it's also one of the reasons nation-states are often an unstable combination of nested and contested identities. Nations are groups of people bound together through common descent or affiliation, which may have existed for centuries before states got demarcated and superimposed over them by the aristocrats and monarchs.

Window seat on a bright red double-decker bus stop-starting towards Trafalgar Square at just under twenty kilometres an hour, I'm five years old again. This rainswept old town wrote the source code for the colonial cityscapes I grew up in – the original Hyde Park, the original Oxford Street; wrote it and then sent it outwards on prison ships to seed and take root amid the nations of the Eora, Yuin, Arrernte, Mirarr. Westphalian DNA coding for a certain kind of border, certain kinds of political identity to take form within them. For those of prior sovereignty fighting the violent enclosure of their lands, holding onto collective identity would soon become survival itself.

'The British and the French divided up the Middle East in accordance with two specific goals: the maximum weakening of each other's position and their shared aversion to the risk of an Arab alliance.' That's Italian scholar of geopolitics Manlio Graziano describing the colonial incision of new lines on some of the world's oldest maps in 1916. Borders drawn with the intention of 'harming competitors and preventing the creation of a coalition of local, prenational, protonational, or worse, national interest'.

Colonial possessions in contested parts of the world are thus born internally divided. While at home, nationalism gets cultivated and amplified into a polarising force, a solvent directed against older, more organic solidari-ties. 'Nationalism is founded on the idea that members of the cross-class "nation" can live harmoniously together,' says Nandita Sharma, an associ-ate professor of racism, migration and transnationalism. 'Nationalism tells us that the only reason we don't is because of the existence of "foreigners".

Ah. There it is.

Versions of this script are being executed simultaneously seemingly everywhere. There are more than seventy border walls already in existence, from the palisade barrier taking shape between the United States and Mexico to the barbed wire no-man's-land between India and Bangladesh to the complex of walls and checkpoints in the West Bank. When UK Home Secretary Priti Patel declares in 2019 that her mission is 'to end the free movement of people once and for all', I presume she's got polling data showing the Tories have managed to engineer substantial public support for the idea.

Alighting in Trafalgar Square with a dear friend; the demonstration is already well assembled and on the move. Not everybody agrees with Patel, it seems. Drummers and megaphones; a robust crowd, cheerful defi-ance echoing off timeless architecture. Hard to estimate the crowd size, but it fills these streets for as far as I can see – all ages, all ethnicities, bright blue placards, circles of yellow stars. One hundred thousand, organisers will announce over the PA later in the event, filing past Downing Street to demand a resolution to the torment of Brexit.

All of this, it occurs to me, over the status of that invisible line I crossed on the Dover Ferry.

the wall

Miranda has brought us to the welcome warmth of the Singer Cafe in Beit Sahour in Palestine. Time will move at a different speed in here; the front room homely and comfortable, alcoved windows overlooking the street below. Dozens of framed portraits on the wall: John Lennon, Ho Chi Minh, Rosa Luxemburg. Through the doors, the main bar is a dim and convivial place of chain-smoking and strong coffee; time in here doesn't move at all. This is where we find Baha. He's the principal driver behind a small collective called To Be There, who conduct tours of the history and daily reality of life in the occupied West Bank.

The lines on Baha's maps are etched in concrete and barbed wire. 'Here,' and he traces a red line that folds and doubles back across the topography. 'This is the most famous Israeli wall. It doesn't mean that's the only one – inside this locality, you're surrounded by walls. The West Bank has [one] 730 kilometres long, twice the length of the borders. About 65 per cent of it is completed. The rest is just like, you know, whenever they're ready to get money for the wall, they will just build more.'

We're on to about the fifth coffee, deep into the evening. It's my first night here and I'm struggling to get my mind around how this place even works. Walls, checkpoints, the thousand daily inconveniences and violent intrusions of a life under occupation. Fast-forward through the history of the Basel Congress of 1897, the Nakba, Oslo, Trump. 'The thing is, like, if there's nothing in common between me as a coloniser or settler, and you as a native person, then you don't exist,' Baha says. 'It's not that you're a lesser human being. You're just not there.'

Heart breaking gently on the walk back to the hotel. Crooked streets trace the topography of these storied hills, shopfronts decked with Christmas lights and blinking neon. The shopkeeper remembers Miranda from the last time she was here; greets her like family. If we walk this street another half-hour westwards, we'll pass into Bethlehem – the original one – so maybe that's why I'm finding the festive decorations unusually moving. Even at this late hour with a deep winter chill in the air, Beit Sahour feels alive.

Days later, the core of old Hebron feels dead. Baha's colleague Mohammad has sent me on alone. 'Last time I've been down the street that you're going to visit was 1999,' he tells me, working through a little more of the lunch his father has set out under the eaves of his shopfront. 'I can't go there now.'

So it's just me, walking this dead street from end to end. Faded green shutters welded closed, tattered awnings; one of the oldest markets in the world evacuated and silent. Blockhouses and barbed wire at the far end; a squad of soldiers. A dog observing me nervously from one crumbling section of wall.

'When they closed Shuhada Street, it killed the whole town,' Mohammad had explained. 'That's why we call it ghost town: 1829 shops were affected when 512 of them were closed by military orders.'

He knows he has allies on the other side of the wire, that there are people trying to build humanity and peace in all parts of this torn country. One frustration is the distorted lens through which the outside world is forced to view this place. 'I'm here only to tell people they have to come and see it. They must come and see it. Things you see on [the] media – it's not true.'

I leave ghost town with an armload of gifts and mementos; he offers to walk me back to the car. 'I have to believe that this cannot be going on forever this way. It can't go forever.'

In place of a pressure valve stands a concrete wall eight metres high. Anchored by dystopian watchtowers, it cuts this ancient district clean in half; pockmarked and scorched under layers of defiant graffiti. Borders may be social constructs, written in pen and ink on maps and treaty documents, but the walls that give them physical effect are clearly intended to convey the same sense of object-permanence as coastlines and mountain ranges. Now a handful of nervous tourists arrive to photograph this most ominous of landmarks.

'Our vision for the future is not to continue to document this reality for the next half-century, right? Like at some point, something has to give.' Hagai El-Ad is the director-general of B'Tselem, a Jerusalem-based human rights organisation that has worked for thirty years to end the fifty-year occupation. I've asked what he thinks that's going to take. 'We believe that the only nonviolent path for ending this reality is through international action. And since we have an absolute commitment to nonviolence, that's what we're calling for.'

El-Ad is someone who chooses his words with great care. 'We enjoy a bargain that we get mostly from the West,' he says. 'We have it both ways. We have military oppression of Palestinians for half a century and counting, constantly advancing Israeli interests over Palestinian lands. And at the same time, everyone keeps thinking of us as a Western democracy with all of the perks that go with that. That's the deal. Now put yourself in the shoes of voters for a minute. Why opt for something else? As long as you can have it both ways?'

'Now, imagine an alternative reality, a future I hope, a near future. In which the West would tell Israel in a variety of one or ten or a million different ways in which you can do it: that deal's off the table right now. You need to make up your mind – one thing or the other. Now, if that happens, then it will lend credibility to Israeli politicians who will tell Israeli voters that out of self-interest, we need to recalculate. And then we have a fighting chance.'

Jerusalem has turned me around completely with the shock of the familiar. I've never been here before but apart from the artfully scrambled alphabet, this could be a civic square in my old home town, or anywhere like it. Elegance of a restored heritage core, but also a pizza place next door to the hostel, busy alfresco cafes, mirrored windows of a light rail vehicle making its way down Jaffa Street. I'm adrift in a tide of people like me, just going about their lives in peace.

Stopping, trying not to stare. A young woman is perched on the edge of a bench in Zion Square, scrolling through her phone, cradling an assault rifle in her lap that looks as though it weighs more than she does.

An hour later, I'm describing this to Sahar Vardi, and she just nods. 'We don't see that anymore. It's transparent to us.'

Now in her twenties, she has already served three prison sentences for refusing conscription to military service when she was eighteen. Now she helps support other *sarvanim* – conscientious objectors – and works on Israeli arms exports and the broader project of demilitarisation of her society. 'It's just daily life for us. It's like – read a second-grade math textbook, one of the questions will be: you have forty squares of chocolate in five rows, how many squares? And then the question after that is: you have twenty-seven soldiers in three rows, how many soldiers? So it's normalised; you just stop seeing weapons. And you stop seeing them as threatening, which is, like, the main issue, right? Like, for us, weapons are completely connected to security. One of the core issues in Israeli society is how much our society is structured around fear on a very deep level,' she says. 'And it's constructed, like any narrative of the sort.'

The disconcerting flashbacks are only growing stronger, even though white Australia's rituals of collective identity are different from the ones implanted here. On Anzac Day, we'd get up very early and stand before sombre monoliths to people lost in distant horrors, lest we forget. On Australia Day, we'd just go to the beach or something, maybe climb up on the roof and watch the fireworks. Somehow, as the years turned, these occasions got engineered into harder, more instrumental forms. It's now mandatory for national leaders to maintain ten-hour Anzac Day erections for televised pageants sponsored by US military contractors. Australia Day got twisted into a flag-waving loyalty test and an exercise in collective amnesia.

We had a hundred-and-fifty-year headstart, and so it was possible to grow up as I did, without realising that the maps I was using were of occupied territories. In Zion Square, the occupation is so fresh it's open carry, but I'm again struck by the shock of the familiar. It always seems to come down to land, enclosed by lines on maps; whoever can manage to stay in charge within these walled enclosures is allowed to do whatever they can get away with.

How, exactly, is a set-up like this going to operate when the oceans rise?

Waking, disoriented, to a hit of turbulence, window seat on a 500-tonne double-decker bus skidding into the polar jetstream at just under a thousand kilometres an hour. Seatback screen says it's minus fifty degrees on the other side of this thin skin of aluminium and composites.

Compact blue passport in my pocket. An accident of birth placing me in the minority of villagers for whom open borders are already a reality, not some future utopian dream. I can still hear Baha, and Mohammad, and Sahar and Hagai El-Ad insisting that the map is not the territory; that these boundaries are constructed, like any narrative of the sort. We're a social species, so many of our boundaries are socially drawn. Even walls, with their pretence at object-permanence, rise and fall on the tides of social contention.

Out the window, an entirely different kind of liminality, so far above the world. No borders visible below, but above the bright horizon of a receding sunset the sky grades blue into deepest black. Ninety per cent of the volume of the planet's atmosphere lies below us. That's a border that feels real, suddenly. Above us, just a gradual attenuation into nothing at all.

thieves in the lifeboats

The air over Dhaka is deadening and heavy, skyline of the world's ninth-largest city lost in a humid shroud of fine particulates. At street level, the capital of Bangladesh feels like one of the most dynamic places I've ever been: an intense hustle of foot traffic and cycle rickshaws, street markets and packed laneways. Twenty-four hours before my coach is due to depart, I'm gleefully adrift in the megacity.

'In the past decade alone, nearly 700 million people, half of the region's population, have been affected by climate-related disasters,' Bangladeshi prime minister Sheikh Hasina declared in 2020. The country is already a case study in climate resilience, with 1 per cent of its GDP dedicated to adaptation since 2010. But with disasters multiplying on every front, surely local resilience will only stretch so far. So I'm stuck on that question of what's going to happen on these borders when the oceans rise.

'Borders are the environment's greatest ally; it is through them that we will save the planet.' Jordan Bardella's words to a journalist from *Le Figaro* hint at one answer. Bardella is speaking in his capacity as lead candidate for the far-right National Rally in the wake of European parliamentary elections in 2019. The party's manifesto is mostly composed of the usual ingredients: uncompromising cultural and economic nationalism, coded white supremacy and opposition to immigration. This time, as Bardella indicates, there is also something new in the platform: saving the planet. National Rally's president, Marine Le Pen, is proposing a 'Europe of Nations' to found the world's first 'ecological civilisation'.

In the United States and Australia, the hard-right political identity is so profoundly welded to dead-eyed climate denial that it's hard to imagine their messaging ever taking this kind of ecological turn. Staffed and funded by industry, backed by an integrated machinery of think tanks and broadcast platforms, the Republican establishment and their low-rent ciphers in Australia are wholly and proudly owned by fossil capital. In this political echo chamber, 'ecological civilisation' is just socialism with tofu.

As the skies darken with ashfall and falling leaves, this may become untenable. Blustering in denial while seawater inundates wealthy communities from Mandurah to Miami may eventually carry a heavy political penalty. If the powerful decide to do what they've always done – deflect blame onto others and hold onto power at all costs – hybrid forms of 'green' authoritarianism could scale rapidly.

'The climate crisis is the foundation on which the politics of the twenty-first century will be built,' organiser and freelance journalist Kate Aronoff writes. 'The xenophobic right is beginning to catch on to what an opportunity this crisis represents for them, and the potent political capital of promising to prevent the end of the world.'

Standing on a crowded street corner waiting for a break in Dhaka's intense traffic, I catch the eyes of a child on the pillion seat of an electric scooter, bouncing past in perfect silence. By the xenophobic right's cold calculus, she's on the wrong side of the border, her fate cast into the teeth of coming storms. It won't be incendiary coin-doubling to blame, of course: Bardella and others like him long ago decided that her very existence is the source of the problem.

'The power of population is so superior to the power of the earth to pro-duce subsistence for man, that premature death must in some shape or other visit the human race,' writes Thomas Malthus in England in 1798. He's observing the dawn of a population boom among major European powers and their colonies. The coin-doubling game is far enough advanced for him to project that in good times the human population will rise much faster than the capability of productive land to feed everyone. Although he underestimates the ability of scientists and farmers to dra-matically improve crop yields over time, his mathematical reasoning and arguments for population control make a profound impact on his con-temporaries, kicking off a debate about 'excess populations' which still reverberates today.

'With savages, the weak in body or mind are soon eliminated; and those that survive commonly exhibit a vigorous state of health. We civilised men, on the other hand, do our utmost to check the process of elimination; we build asylums for the imbecile, the maimed, and the sick; we institute poor-laws; and our medical men exert their utmost skill to save the life of every one to the last moment . . . excepting in the case of man itself, hardly any one is so ignorant as to allow his worst animals to breed.'

With these words, Charles Darwin's publication in 1871 of *The Descent of Man, and Selection in Relation to Sex*, brings questions of population growth and survival squarely into the domain of evolution by natural selection. Darwin clearly supports 'civilised men checking the process of elimination'. But he warns that such acts of compassion put them at an evolutionary disadvantage relative to more robust populations of 'savages' honed by nature's unyielding selection pressures.

Some of his intellectual descendants take a different view. By the early decades of the twentieth century, social-Darwinist thinking is lending scientific legitimacy to the intellectual flag-bearers of white supremacy, and the eugenics movement is born. Rather than lamenting the burden of humanity's 'worst animals', the eugenicists suggest breeding them out altogether.

This thinking is interwoven with strands of Romantic nationalism holding that states derive their identity not from divine or hereditary right but from the cultural and ethnic unity of those governed. By the late 1920s, this is mutating into the doctrine of 'blood and soil', and from there into the expansionist platform of the German Nazi Party.

'When people attempt to rebel against the iron logic of nature, they come into conflict with the very same principles to which they owe their existence as human beings. Their actions against nature must lead to their downfall,' Hitler writes from his prison cell in 1925. 'There cannot be a separate law for mankind in a world in which planets and suns follow their orbits, where moons and planets trace their destined paths, where the strong are always the masters of the weak and where those subject to such laws must obey them or be destroyed.'

Hans Schemm, head of Hitler's teachers' association, the National Socialist Teachers League, is more succinct: the program here is 'politically applied biology'.

The Nazis bring cold rigour to the pursuit of human perfection: their objective is the construction of the *Herrenrasse*, the master race. 'Just as in cancer the best treatment is to eradicate the parasitic growth as quickly as possible, the eugenic defense against the dysgenic social effects of afflicted subpopulations is of necessity limited to equally drastic measures,' writes

Konrad Lorenz, having been drafted as a military psychologist for the Nazis in 1941. Now politically applied biology unleashes a Holocaust.

The concept of welding 'the iron logic of nature' to a violent manifesto for human conduct doesn't die in a bunker in Berlin in 1945. It leaves seeds in the ground for others to harvest, awaiting, perhaps, just a change in the climate.

Sleeper bunk on an overnight coach somewhere out of Dhaka; midnight glimpses of rural Bangladesh through the curtain. Sleepless; I'm recalling a town hall meeting from my former life. That moment when a gentleman – always elderly, always white – takes the mic to ask why no-one has mentioned population.

This gentleman has kids, and grandkids. That's not the kind of population he's worried about. He's talking, not to put too fine a point on it, about foreigners, and that they seem very numerous. He hasn't quite come out and said, 'The power of population is so superior to the power of the earth to produce subsistence for man,' but you know it's back there somewhere. The prescription, without fail, is for lower rates of immigration. And because that seems like a sensible idea, people will nod, and sometimes applaud.

It's unlikely that this gentleman with the raised hand has ever heard of the ecologist Garrett Hardin or the concept of lifeboat ethics, so there's nothing automatically sinister about just asking the question. But the full title of Hardin's 1974 essay is 'Lifeboat Ethics: The Case Against Helping the Poor'. In it, he invites the reader to consider the fate of fifty people in a lifeboat adrift at sea, with room for maybe another ten in the boat. There are a hundred desperate people in the water. What should they do? To make himself clear, he identifies the lifeboat as North America, and the people in the water as Colombia and Morocco and Bangladesh and wherever. While they are drowning, they are also somehow reproducing much faster than the people in the lifeboat. In case the title of the essay doesn't give it away, one of the subheadings is 'Population Control the Crude Way'.

Hardin admits: 'we are all the descendants of thieves' – those in the lifeboat are only there because they stole it from Native Americans.

And then comes the rhetorical shrug that the whole colonial enterprise rests on: 'The law zealously defends property rights, but only relatively recent property rights.'

He now proposes that everyone in the water will have to drown in order to guarantee the survival of those in the lifeboat. If you find this repellent, he invites you to leap into the water to make a place for someone else.

Hardin's essay matters because this openly genocidal environmental ethic has wormed its way into more coded and reasonable-sounding forms over the intervening decades. It is a reinterpretation of 'politically applied biology', speaking not of blood and soil but of carbon cycles and carrying capacities. And that's why the gentleman at the public meeting wants to know how many more people we're planning on letting into the lifeboat.

'When the lifeboat is full, those who hate life will try to load it with more people and sink the lot. Those who love and respect life will take the ship's axe and sever the extra hands that cling to the sides of the boat,' says the Finnish deep ecologist Pentti Linkola. Linkola, who describes people as a cancer on the planet, worked for decades on a more lyrical, earth-centred rendition of lifeboat ethics, but somehow it always ends the same way for the people in the water. Linkola's misanthropic longing for a depopulated world was less racially selective than Hardin's. He describes, approvingly, the deaths of thousands of the 'wealthy, busy, environmentally damaging and world-devouring portion of mankind' in the carnage of the September 11 attacks in the United States.

Linkola and Hardin represent the extreme fringe of this kind of thinking, but there are strands of racism and misanthropy woven right through Western environmental thought. Sir David Attenborough, whose soothing voice and endless curiosity have delighted audiences for two generations, told *Radio Times* in 2013, 'We are a plague on the Earth . . . either we limit our population growth or the natural world will do it for us, and the natural world is doing it for us right now.'

Describing human beings as a plague is a dangerous way to run an argument, and it feeds a worldview that will be wide open to exploitation in the crises to come. Queensland Greens MP Michael Berkman, on announcing the arrival of the newest member of his family on social media, was informed by a commenter: 'Bringing unnecessary invasive pests into the world is not what environmentalists do. Population growth is worse than coal, fuckwit.'

Human beings as a plague, a cancer, an invasive pest. Canadian blogger Carol Linnit has coined the term 'Misanthropocene' to describe 'the phenomena of cultural misanthropy, including the desire for humanity's demise, in the age of the Anthropocene'. Disguised or out in the open, these beliefs leave campaigners hopelessly exposed to accusations of being anti-human – which are hard to defend against when they're true. The Attenborough quote and choice nuggets from Earth First! founder Dave Foreman's apocalyptic worldview are widely distributed on right-wing blogs and climate denial sites, arming their readers with ample evidence that environmentalists hate humankind.

Misanthropocene sentiment seems almost exclusively concentrated within the wealthy consumption powerhouses of the Global North. It is ripe for exploitation by emerging movements that will only need to tweak people's views on which human beings constitute a plague in order to weaponise environmental anxieties in service to true ecofascism.

All the pieces are in place: we already live with one foot in Hardin's lifeboat. Over two decades, Australia, the United States and parts of Europe have essentially normalised the practice of extrajudicial concentration camps for people fleeing the chaos of war and collapse. This infrastructure of detention and dehumanisation awaits only an environmental turn.

The old gentleman at the town hall is no Nazi. He's just asking an obvious question on the basis that the lifeboat seems to be perilously full. But Hardin's prescription for life and death on the high seas rests on a bullshit premise to ensure it delivers the conclusion he wants. Who says there are only ten places left on this thing? And why are those already in the lifeboat taking up such an extraordinary amount of space?

Jolted awake by the air horn on the coach; cramped and disoriented. Daylight through the curtains. We're pulling into Cox's Bazar, a hazy tourist township far down the coast on the Bay of Bengal. It's time to meet some of the children Hardin wants us to throw out of the boat.

trapped at the intersection

Two dozen of them follow us up the handmade steps to what passes for a lookout across the city of children; giggling, bright eyes and faded clothes, younger ones racing ahead or clutching at the hands of older siblings. 'How are you!' they call to the stranger with the camera, 'How are yoouu!' in a chorus that keeps dissolving into laughter. They want to know where I'm from. They want a go with the camera. The thing I least expected to find today was joy.

We're an hour's drive south of Cox's Bazar, Bangladesh. From the hilltop, Kutupalong is a mosaic of tarpaulin and bamboo all the way to the horizon. Under a milky sky, everything is the colour of dust. Eight hundred thousand people are sheltering here; more than a million including the satellite camps. Well over half the population of the world's newest and youngest city are children. The vista is what I had imagined the largest refugee camp in the world might look like: vast anonymity, improvised housing jigsawed across scrubby dunes, inhabited by faceless people passively awaiting their fate. Discovering, of course, the opposite. The camp is alive with preparations for the coming monsoon: construction, drainage works, pre-positioning of medical supplies. An edgy combination of Rohingya resilience, Bangladeshi generosity and a tightly coordinated surge of international emergency aid has provisioned the camp, forced infectious diseases to the margins, and is hardening the place against the coming storm. There is unthinkable trauma here, and somehow amid it, this raucous entourage is capering around us demanding to be in the photographs, and then to immediately see the photographs. 'How are yooooooouuu!'

The guy who wanted to talk about overpopulation at the public meeting? These are the children he was talking about. They have nothing – they were burned across the border from Myanmar into Bangladesh with little more than the clothes they were wearing. It's not clear to me what contribution we expect them to make in rapidly decarbonising the global economy. Maybe they should recycle more or something. But South Asia and Sub-Saharan Africa are the last two regions on earth with relatively high population growth, so this must be the 'population problem' he's so worried about.

This part of the world has long experience with men in distant cities exercising opinions and making decisions about how many children should exist here, and how those who bear them should be forced to make the numbers add up. 'From ancient times, women almost everywhere have known of methods and techniques of birth control; men, too, were aware of practices that precluded conception,' write Vandana Shiva and Maria Mies. 'The beginning of the "population explosion" dovetailed neatly with the expansion of British rule in India, when the people's resources, rights and livelihoods were confiscated.' The same phenomenon and timing can be tracked across Africa and Latin America.

In the 1970s, Paul Ehrlich's *The Population Bomb* ignited another round of Malthusiasm for population control aimed at the Global South. Techniques ranged from forced sterilisation to one-child policies to mass education programs, family planning and contraception provision. 'The population controllers . . . see women only as aggregated uteruses and prospective perpetrators of over-population,' write Shiva and Mies. 'Women of the South . . . are increasingly reduced to numbers, targets, wombs, tubes and other reproductive parts by the population controllers.'

One signal stands out from the population noise: educating women and girls is the most reliable way to slow rapid population growth. Family planning and access to safe contraception matter a lot, but broad-based education is the thing. 'Although also shown to be effective in reducing birth rates, family planning education for women is insufficient compared to comprehensive education through secondary school,' notes Beth Kinsella for the *Harvard College Global Health Review*. The Indian state of Kerala is often held up as an exemplar: the small southern state pursued a very different development path to the rest of the country post-independence, leaving it with among the lowest population growth and highest women's education and literacy standards in India. 'Unlike women in the rest of India, high educational and literacy attainments have fostered pride, autonomy and aspirations among women in Kerala, who find it difficult to adapt to the domination of males in the workplace and at home,' according to Aparna Mitra of the University of Oklahoma and Pooja Singh, an independent Indian researcher. 'This contradiction between the modern outlook of highly educated females and male dominance in all social and domestic spheres has contributed to high rates of family violence and female suicide rates in Kerala.'

So it's not just about education: it's also about power. In her manifesto *Women & Power*, Mary Beard invites us to listen in while Telemachus, son of Odysseus and Penelope, addresses his mother in Homer's *The Odyssey*, one of the oldest stories in the Western canon. Here he is now: 'Go, then, within the house and busy yourself with your daily duties, your loom, your distaff, and the ordering of your servants; for speech is man's matter, and mine above all others – for it is I who am master here.'

'The first recorded example of a man telling a woman to shut up,' Beard says, 'telling her that her voice was not to be heard in public'. Telemachus sounds like a real piece of work. But he was hardly alone: his assertion that 'speech is man's matter' is a thumbnail sketch of a society-wide division of labour that consigned women to child-rearing duties and household provisioning, while the men were out stacking coins and doing politics. 'The way Western culture understands and treats women is similar to and reinforces the way it understands and treats nature,' according to feminist scholar Dr Valerie Carroll. Somehow, after tens of thousands of years of dynamic balance between the sexes, men have 'seized control of the means of reproduction', to borrow a phrase.

Okay – hold it there.

Our journey began with accelerating torrents of collective metabolism, then traced the nested identities and borders of collective boundaries. Now, somehow, we've reached the crux of collective perpetuation. An unbroken sequence of childbirth receding back into deep time, delivering us immediately into the service of structures in which it is Telemachus who is master here. Fine-grained infrastructures of social conditioning await just outside the door: online, in peer networks, in schools; a bombardment of advertising and in-group rituals to perpetuate particular kinds of society.

Despite some postmodern flourishes, the basic architecture of a nineteenth-century factory-model education system remains in place across much of the world. It's a production line stamping students into pre-stressed components according to bank balance, postcode, caste and gender. For the kids up the back, here's Ellwood P. Cubberley, the dean of Stanford University School of Education, in 1929: 'Our schools are, in a sense, factories, in which the raw products (children) are to be shaped and fashioned into products to meet the various demands of life. The specifications for manufacturing come from the demands of twentieth-century civilization, and it is the business of the school to build its pupils according to the specifications laid down.'

Laid down by whom? Mostly by people with names such as Ellwood P. Cubberley.

Here's what these specifications have coded for: of all the heads of government recognised by the United Nations in January 2019, there were 183 men and ten women. The economic disparity is just as skewed as the political: more than 80 per cent of the world's land is owned by men, and 89 per cent of the world's billionaires in 2018 were men. It's not just your imagination: Telemachus and Cubberley have a lock on the world's resources and decision-making structures, from the traditional family unit to the world system itself. Entwined and embedded within these structures, violence is ubiquitous: from the global pandemic of intimate partner violence to rape used as a weapon of war.

Decades of exceedingly dull scholarship have attempted to prove that men are biologically better at property ownership, or have some kind of political gene that makes them more suited to being in charge of things. This whole intellectual dead-end could have been avoided by just going outside and talking to people from cultures with tens of thousands of years of profoundly different gender roles and expectations. For 95 per cent of human history – the 95 per cent that didn't trigger global mass extinctions or cross climate tipping points – gender expectations were very different. In many places, they still are. Within the five-nation Haudenosaunee Confederacy occupying what is now the northeastern United States and Canada, kinship ties were established through matrilineal descent. For hundreds of years, the Confederacy existed under a 'Great Law of Peace' which stated 'women shall be considered the progenitors of the Nation. They shall own the land and the soil.'

The Minangkabau people of Western Sumatra also pass land and property through matrilineal descent, and ceremonial life is organised through gendered spheres that are complementary rather than hierarchical. Palyku scholar Ambelin Kwaymullina points out that 'for thousands of years, the many diverse environments of Australia were sustained by the cultures of Aboriginal and Torres Strait Islander nations. Integral to these cultures are the law- and life-ways of Indigenous women. What is sometimes called Women's Business is separate to Men's Business across Indigenous nations but not inferior to it.'

For as long as the means of reproduction remain in Telemachus's grip, as long as Ellwood P. Cubberley's schools are stamping children into pre-stressed components, speech will remain man's matter, and these are the kinds of society that will be perpetuated. But if these roles are socially constructed and arbitrary, it means we can change them. It means the future can be different. We're not going up against fixed aspects of 'human nature' but foundational alignments of social and political power.

Working at this generative level changes everything. Every patient teacher passing on the tools of critical thinking; every student who chooses curiosity over compliance. Every parent who shields their child from destructive gender norms; every child determined to be themselves, even without such a shield. Every generation that rebels against the established order, or fights for reproductive autonomy, or wins a seat off some latter-day Telemachus: these things have far-reaching effect. Change at the level of collective perpetuation can be slow, but it transforms the kinds of society being reproduced. Remembering Najah's words in Beqaa: these people are the fulcrum of change. They can change the balance of everything.

For the ones with bright eyes and faded clothes capering along the endless terraces of Kutupalong, change has to come soon. They aren't a population problem; they're just kids. Knowing what Hardin and Linkola have in mind for them, I feel we've just made fleeting eye contact with the monsters throwing the children into the water.

bloom

Roll the clock slowly forward from the thriving seas of the Cambrian to the late Ordovician. Clouds are gathering, although the causes of what's about to happen are hard to read after such an immense lapse of time. The end of the long Ordovician greenhouse period is marked by a sudden sharp drop in global temperatures as the ice returns around four hundred and forty-five million years ago. Sea levels fall rapidly, wiping out a vast swathe of marine life as shallow warm water habitats retreat and then vanish entirely. A second wave of ecosystem collapse accompanies the sudden swing back to a warmer world a million years later. In total, 60 per cent of marine species are vanishing into the fossil record. This long-distant carnage will stand as the first of six global mass extinctions to have hit the living world since the advent of complex multicellular life.

Life continues, flows around, makes a way. Fish with jaws and teeth are swimming sleek and streamlined into the ecological space left vacant by these slow convulsions. Ancestral sharks make their appearance and settle in for the long haul. Giant sea-scorpions browse shallow seafloors still alive with trilobites and crinoids. Through the achingly long passage of time, marine food chains are reaching a form we'd find familiar today: coastlines laced with coral reefs and glittering webs of predation swimming atop the ancient base of life's pyramid: phytoplankton and tiny algae.

More than three and a half billion years have passed since we met Luca. Her extended family now inhabits every reach of the world ocean and is beginning, through slow experimentation, to try its luck out on the undiscovered country beyond the reach of the endless sea.

If we want to live on the land, we have to take the ocean with us. Life's chemistries evolved in liquid water; without it, we return to dust. Making our way out here, we'll be drenched in raw ultraviolent radiation, on the margins of unforgiving landscapes far from the sheltering sea. Testament to the scale of this challenge, for the first three and a half billion years of life's dominion, the pages of the terrestrial world's fossil record has remained almost entirely blank.

Almost entirely. For many millions of years, the tides and the seasons have been testing coastal communities with cycles of inundation and drying in shallow basins and lagoons. On longer timescales, slow changes in sea levels force marine creatures to adapt to drying environments, ready or not. Tentative lines of evidence hint at the existence a billion years ago of hardy microbes weathering bare rocks to form the first soils. Sealed against desiccation, almost unnoticed around four hundred and eighty million years ago, these ancient pioneers begin to work together with an unassuming freshwater algae, hybridising into the first land plants.

The world begins to bloom with the descendants of this remarkable partnership: photosynthesisers reaching for the sun, fungal threads seeking water and mineral nutrients in the soil. Together, they are unstoppable. They don't know it, of course, but they're about to take over the world. Mosses and liverworts range out in advance; centimetres high, they tower over the microbial communities and fungal decomposer networks that have occupied the damplands since the late Proterozoic. They still depend on the presence of liquid water in order to reproduce, and so their range will hold close to the humid margins of the world ocean for a time. But having gained this foothold, now the horizon is the limit.

The rewards for adapting to life under the open sky are huge: access to unfiltered sunlight, a greenhouse climate rich in carbon dioxide, and space to grow out of reach of predators. Evolutionary pressures nudge those a little more tolerant of dry spells and poorer soils; entire continents await those who can make their way out here. It is as though the endless crashing of the waves on these nameless shores has gathered into a strange, slow-moving surge, a wave of a different kind, carrying the ocean's descendants a millimetre at a time into the brittle landscapes above the high-tide line.

Pause, from within the margins of this damp moss forest, to see something quite new unfolding into the sky. These creatures stand taller than their mossy surrounds, with pendulous spore pods upraised at the end of outstretched green branches. This can only have happened with the advent of new structural innovations carrying water and nutrients up into the heights of these collectives. The first vascular plants have arrived, during the mid-Silurian, around four hundred and thirty million years ago. Their armoured spores are scattered on the breeze and into the fossil record, heralding another slow wave of the ocean's arrival.

Turn the geological page slowly into the Devonian, and watch their descendants reaching inland; taller, with more developed branching root systems, the first leaves unfurling, taller still.

Already, they have company. Where you find abundance, follow the opportunists. Soft velvet worms undulating along the ground on rows of stumpy legs. Ancestors of mites and spiders, a wild proliferation of millipedes; segmented arthropods working their generational way from the swamplands into the shady ecosystems created by the ramifying advance of the land plants. At some time in the Devonian, it seems likely that tiny Rhyniognatha insects take flight, opening the skies to Luca's great granddaughters for the first time.

Looking down, these pioneer aviators might have witnessed swamp-adapted lobe-finned fish dragging themselves cautiously onto the mudflats in search of something other than seafood. Their cousins the coelacanths remain behind, long-lived, patient.

By the late Devonian, tree ferns tower over the landscape, sheltering an understorey of horsetails and clubmosses. And then, taller yet, reaching thirty metres into the sky, Archaeopteris raises great fans of fern-like canopy aloft on a thick, woody trunk. Lost to the present, its fossils are scattered worldwide as a signifier of a branch point into the next great wave of plant evolution.

A mass of mycorrhizal fungi threads are woven through the ground, feeding, decomposing, reaching for water in a soil matrix teeming with land-adapted bacteria. In exchange, the sun-drenched upper tiers of these creatures are using sunlight to crack water and airborne carbon dioxide into energy-rich glucose molecules, some of which they can donate to their fungal partners working away below. In an echo of what their algal forebears had set in motion during the long-distant Archean, this planet-wide carbon inhalation will have consequences, with heat-trapping carbon dioxide in the atmosphere falling by more than two-thirds. This is still vastly higher than we're used to today, but combined with ever-increasing quantities of exhaled oxygen, the global climate is again being edged towards a tipping point.

The origins of the late Devonian mass extinctions are obscure and hard to decipher: some combination of climate and geology sending vast numbers of terrestrial and marine creatures over the edge. Soil weathering and the colossal impacts of land plants seem to be implicated, with evidence of algal blooms in shallow waters having a devastating effect on inshore ecosystems. The fossil record holds mute afterimages of widespread forest fires and cycles of rapid sea level rise and fall. Whatever the cause, the enormous abundance of Devonian reef ecosystems is hit hard, and browsing residents of shallow seafloors are hammered in successive extinction waves. The entire lineage of placoderms – armoured fish up to seven metres long – are going to the wall. Trilobite and brachiopod families dating back to the Cambrian are vanishing, ceding ecological space to those better suited to the planet's turmoil. At least 70 per cent of marine species are passing into extinction. The riot of land-dwelling millipedes and exotic arthropods fall silent; the swamp-dwelling fish with terrestrial ambitions vanish with their potential unrealised. The lush rainforests of the Devonian are in a state of collapse, as sea levels fall precipitously and a new ice age seizes the land.

The geo-memories written in these 375-million-year-old stone pages describe a planet frozen in the slow grip of the second mass extinction event.

> Language is survival.
>
> KARINA LESTER

memory holds

Somewhere forward, the bow of the ship is ploughing into oncoming weather. Voices outside the cabin, receding. I keep forgetting to breathe.

'No matter how hard I try, I cannot remember what I did after that,' Mr Miyake Nobuo tells Michi and I. 'I think I saw even more horrific sights. And I decided to erase them from my memory.' He will speak for nearly ninety minutes without pause, his voice even and measured. I'm listening through an earpiece as Michi translates from Japanese into English in real time, so that Mr Miyake can simply focus on the story without waiting for interpretation.

He is slight in appearance, a little stooped, his face alive with fierce intelligence and humour. Until this moment, his recollection has been pin-sharp. Born in 1929, he is a sixteen-year-old boy in August 1945, riding a crowded streetcar through town on the way to meet his mother. Glancing up, the ceiling of the carriage imprints with a blue-white flash. Fearing an electrical fault, he jumps into the street, and is blown off his feet by an immense blast wave. Somehow, he is alive. 'At that moment, I knew that we had been bombed. I thought it was all over and remained lying face-down on the ground.' He is sprawled, enveloped by a wall of dust and ash, 1.8 kilometres from the hypocentre of the atomic bombing of Hiroshima. Eighty thousand people are dead or dying. He describes moving through the city to find his mother's house as the firestorm gathers strength, recalls seeing ghostly survivors stumbling, flayed by the heat, begging for water. And then his memory blanks; hours gone missing, and I can only feel a kind of relief that he's been spared that, at least.

Three days later, a blink of white and thunder opens over the city of Nagasaki, killing seventy thousand people. Within days, Imperial Japan has surrendered, and the occupying administration moves rapidly to lock down information flowing from the stricken cities. 'The US did not want the world to know about the catastrophic humanitarian consequences it had caused by dropping atomic bombs on Hiroshima and Nagasaki,' Mr Miyake says.

The survivors begin to piece together what has been done to them, but for everyone else, rumour fills the void. In the absence of hard information, a slow-moving catastrophe of birth defects and radiation sickness twists into social discrimination. 'And so many people had no choice but to keep hidden the fact that they were from Hiroshima. They had to live lonely, secretive lives,' he recalls. The atomic bomb survivors come to be known as *hibakusha*, the explosion-affected people.

For decades he blocks out the terror of August 6, 1945: moves to Tokyo, gets a job, marries, visits his old city as little as possible. The nuclear establishment discovers how to use Hiroshima-type weapons as detonators to ignite hydrogen bombs with a thousand times the explosive yield. Now the fate of everything hangs in this balance of terror.

Thirty years after the bombing, something shifts, and he becomes aware of the grassroots advocacy of others like him. They speak firsthand of the unfathomable violence of a nuclear strike, but their testimony is given in service to something larger: to be the last *hibakusha*. Never again. Under the umbrella of the confederation Hidankyo, they form a network of abolitionists; in the 1980s, Mr Miyake joins them, to tell the story of the day the white flash and the blast of thunder took his city. He tells it to diplomats, to prime ministers, to activists, to students. Now he's telling it again, in a quiet cabin on the ship they call Peace Boat, cutting a slow path across the vast Southern Ocean.

In 1983, a group of students at Waseda University in Tokyo began resisting efforts by their government to whitewash the atrocities perpetrated by Imperial Japan. 'It was a big shock for me to see how history textbooks were completely manipulated by the government,' Yoshioka Tatsuya recalls in an interview many years later. 'We had to know what the Japanese had done in Asia. We had to know history well. The people who did it, the aggressors, could forget, but the victims would not, especially concerning rape and genocide.' Undeterred by the prohibitive costs of airfares, Mr Yoshioka and a hundred and fifty students chartered a ship instead, going heavily into debt to visit the places where their government had unleashed atrocities that it now sought to forget. Face to face, they sat and listened to the stories that had been removed from their textbooks. The following year, they ran the project again, this time sailing to Nanjing. The Peace Boat project was born: an uncensored political space designed for network building, direct exchange and the preservation of history; an organising platform that would grow over time into one of Japan's largest independent non-government organisations.

The joint influence of Peace Boat's interventions, lawsuits by respected historian Ienaga Saburō and international diplomatic pressure mean that today Japanese textbooks acknowledge the violence of the country's imperial past. Despite the ongoing efforts of ultranationalists and their allies in power, for the moment at least, memory holds.

We've been three days out of sight of land, our world confined to this floating steel island two hundred metres from end to end. Waking at first light to the rainswept blight of the port; rocky breakwaters gliding past, industrial architectures softened against a sepia sky. The ship turning slowly, decks hustling with activity. Thirty-five years after Mr Yoshioka and his friends sailed south on a much smaller ship, Peace Boat's ninety-sixth voyage makes landfall in Port Adelaide.

Hours later, I watch a small number of the *hibakusha* alight from a minibus. They are welcomed and assisted under the eaves of the old harbourside shed where the meeting will take place. Before the official proceedings get underway, something profound is happening. Through a small team of interpreters, the Japanese *hibakusha* are introduced to their counterparts on this ground: Yankunytjatjara and Pitjantjatjara elders and their families, who carry their own memories of atomic bombing of their homelands, not so far from here. A circle of chairs is drawn up for this exchange; a timeless sense of enclosure settling around them. Perhaps a hundred people will soon be here, drifting in in ones and twos to hear the testimony of the *hibakusha*, but I'm realising that the real purpose of the meeting is for this circle to be held, for the children and grandchildren present to hear these stories told against the day when responsibility for carrying these memories will pass to them.

Karina Lester remembers seeing her father Yami on the television in London back when she was a child, lobbying British MPs for compensation and recognition of what their nuclear weapons tests had done to the people under the fallout. Yami was just a child when the British government began its series of bomb tests across central Australia and the northwest, and they would shape the rest of his life. 'We heard the big bomb went off that morning, a loud noise and the ground shook,' he told the ABC in 2017. 'I don't know how long after we seen this quiet black smoke – oily and shiny – coming across from the south. Next time we had sore eyes, skin rash, diarrhoea and vomiting, everybody, old people too.'

Before long, with the whole community stricken with illness, Yami's eyesight failed. Despite a regime of strict government secrecy, his family began to organise, spreading the word about what had happened and building supportive networks further afield. In time, that work passed to Yami and now, in turn, it rests with Karina. 'I think the support from those people, his family, just made him want to go out there and do it and get the story out that Aboriginal people were impacted by those British nuclear tests,' she tells me. 'In particular, Walatina community had the highest radiation fallout; we saw the black mist rolling in, the ground shaking. We were living in the sand dune country, our people got sick; he really felt that that was a story that needed to be told.'

'The first step in liquidating a people is to erase its memory,' Milan Kundera wrote. 'Destroy its books, its culture, its history. Then have somebody write new books, manufacture a new culture, invent a new history. Before long that nation will begin to forget what it is and what it was. The world around it will forget even faster . . . The struggle of man against power is the struggle of memory against forgetting.'

Kundera was reflecting on the speed with which Soviet administrators set about erasing the history of his native Czechoslovakia after annexing it in 1948. He described the outcome of this cultural unmooring as a form of 'historical amnesia'. Discovering that you've been subjected to it hits you with a peculiar kind of force.

Reflecting on the struggles of Peace Boat and its allies to preserve an honest reckoning of their government's atrocities, I realise that at least they are prepared to admit there was a war. Here, on occupied Kaurna lands as the ship prepares to sail, there is only silence. The history textbooks I grew up with spoke of a great age of discovery opening vast empty lands for settlement and civilisation. The protagonists were fearless men of the British Navy: Captain James Cook, Captain Arthur Phillip, Admiral Charles Fremantle. The textbooks commence with their arrival; history's first page opening in 1788 with the founding of a penal colony at what they call Port Jackson. The prior sovereignty of the Gadigal people of the Eora Nation barely rates a mention; nor do Karina's ancestors, or the presence of Uncle Noel's people of the southwest.

And then, the mass killings begin: a hundred and fifty years of massacres coinciding with an almost seamless absence of cultural recall. Amid the bloodshed, forcible extraction of wool and wheat, gold and iron, gas and coal, from terrains described in legal terms as terra nullius: empty land. Even today, with the publication of detailed maps of colonial killing grounds, the Frontier Wars are almost completely absent from white Australia's formal collective memory. There are no official days of mourning, no flags at half-mast, nothing within the sombre enclosures of the National War Memorial to suggest anything untowards in the national origin story.

To zealously defend the relatively recent property rights of the occupation, our 1 per cent villager needs us to believe that none of this really happened. This is what Kundera observed at the hands of the Soviets; we see it in the work of Chinese Communist Party authorities, wiping out Tibetan culture or forensically erasing all memory of the massacre in Tiananmen Square.

This is an ancient continuity: the stewardship of collective memory becoming ever more a question of politics; oral histories condensing into written form, the collections of great libraries to be digitised in turn; statues and monuments and memorials to serve the persistence of particular kinds of memory, particular kinds of forgetting. 'Who controls the past . . . controls the future: who controls the present controls the past.' George Orwell's warning in *Nineteen Eighty-Four* speaks of a universal need to question, always, in whose interests memory serves.

There's a catch; simple enough to be understood by *Escherichia coli* bacteria. Memory loss is dangerous. The inability to recall past conditions makes it impossible to compare them with present conditions. Makes it formally impossible to learn, or adapt, or respond to threats. Protection of our collective memory from mutilation by the 1-per-cent villager isn't a luxury: when Mr Miyake speaks of his determination to prevent twenty-first-century atomic bombings, I realise the struggle of memory against forgetting is a species-wide obligation.

Karina speaks movingly at the meeting in Adelaide; a hundred more of us will now carry the story of her memories with us. This has become her life's work now – not just attending gatherings such as this, but as a linguistics researcher, working for the preservation of the medium in which these memories are held: language itself.

'One of our key goals was to really maintain our strong identity through language,' Karina says, 'and to keep those old ways alive and ongoing for the next generation to have the knowledge of our country, our lands, which is the Anangu Pitjantjatjara Yankunytjatjara lands, and to value it and respect it.' These are some of the oldest language groups in the world, reservoirs of deep cultural memory unlike anything else that exists, but her passion for their preservation isn't just about history. 'Language is survival,' she says, as her daughter bounds up to us, seeking news of dinner.

While we've been talking, the ship has begun making her way slowly between the breakwaters to meet the long swells of the Southern Ocean.

There must always be room for coincidence, Win had maintained. When there's not, you're probably well into apophenia, each thing then perceived as part of an overarching pattern of conspiracy. And while comforting yourself with the symmetry of it all, he'd believed, you stood all too real a chance of missing the genuine threat, which was invariably less symmetrical, less perfect.

WILLIAM GIBSON, *PATTERN RECOGNITION*

anglerfish

Slow passage across a silvery sea, the liner's foamy wake receding all the way to the edge of the world. I could lean on this railing for hours, mesmerised by the light glancing off the ocean in such a particular way. But I'm invited to join the *hibakusha* and some of the other guest speakers for a tour of the bridge, so I'll return to this quiet deck later tonight.

Wide bay windows with a panoramic view of the endless horizon; four duty officers in crisp white shirts on watch. The bridge is a fascinating jumble of instruments and monitors interspersed with phone handsets; a couple of high-backed chairs face a central console, joysticks in the place where a wheel might once have been.

Every duct and fibre of the ship's central nervous system converges here, along with two old-fashioned magnetic compasses resting within brass gimbals. For the moment, the ship sails in seamless exchange with a small constellation of satellites, but there's still a chart table on which someone periodically updates the ship's position with a pair of dividers and a pencil. Many layers of navigational technologies are superimposed: if twenty-first-century affordances fail, those of previous ages of sail are still here as back-up. In a real blackout, we'll rely on compasses first deployed by Chinese mariners two thousand years ago.

I'm taken by how much the design of the bridge has been driven by the need for accurate collective perception. From the panoramic views to the satellite downlink, much of this space has evolved in service to the crew's need for precise understanding of the ship's position relative to navigational hazards, shipping lanes, storms. So too for the vessel's internals: from here the duty officers can monitor fine details of engine performance and fire warnings. A large measure of our safety out here is owed to these modes of perception, the eyes and ears of the ship, attentive to the subliminal under-tow of the earth's magnetic field and those whispered signals from orbit.

That global satellite fleet serves a much wider purpose than keeping this ship from being torn open on a reef. It is only the most recent layer of augmentation woven atop the institutional eyes and ears of whole states.

In *Seeing Like a State*, political anthropologist James Scott describes how nations began to harden and change in the fifteenth century as they developed from the Middle Ages into the early modern period. His study queries why rulers seem so determined to forcibly settle 'people who move around . . . nomads and pastoralists (such as Berbers and Bedouins), hunter-gatherers, Gypsies, vagrants, homeless people, itinerants, runaway slaves, and serfs . . . the more I examined these efforts at sedentarization, the more I came to see them as a state's attempt to make a society legible, to arrange the population in ways that simplified the classic state functions of taxation, conscription, and prevention of rebellion.'

Scott argues that everything from the standardisation of weights and measures to the census to formalisation of a national language plays a part in making society legible to the people who would govern and control it: 'In each case, officials took exceptionally complex, illegible, and local social practices, such as land tenure customs or naming customs, and created a standard grid whereby it could be centrally recorded and monitored.'

These capabilities have come a long way since the fifteenth century, driven by military imperatives as much as those of tax administrators. Now the world's pre-eminent economic and military power just calls it the Global Information Grid: 'the globally interconnected, end-to-end set of information capabilities for collecting, processing, storing, disseminating, and managing information on demand to warfighters, policy makers, and support personnel.' In its appallingly designed presentation slides, the US Department of Defense visualises these capabilities as a pyramid, with the GIG at the base and 'full spectrum dominance' at the apex.

In a hotel room in Hong Kong in 2013, former CIA subcontractor Edward Snowden provided three journalists with a huge cache of source material detailing how the standard grid had evolved into a global mass surveillance network anchored by the US National Security Agency. 'When you think about what the NSA does, you are at least supposed to think that they spy on bad guys, right?' said Snowden, speaking on *Democracy Now!* in 2019. 'Define them how you will, but they are looking at particularized people that they have a suspicion they're engaged in some kind of wrong-doing. Well, the systems that I had built, the systems that my generation had built, had produced a system that instead spied on everyone.'

Other modes of collective perception work very differently to the dystopian platforms Snowden risked his life to disclose. If 'seeing like a state' requires a standard grid for recording and monitoring, 'seeing like a society' invokes a different set of tools. To understand the operations of power, specialised institutions of investigation and inquiry, publication and distribution have been developed, often at significant cost to their practitioners. When Snowden decided to disclose the extent of the grid in 2013, that's who he turned to: working journalists. Within a week, the stories were leading news bulletins globally, rapidly altering the world's collective perception of the US government's mass surveillance capabilities.

That's the principal purpose of the craft of journalism: to act as the eyes and ears of the public. It's right there in the name: publication. Since the map will never be the territory, we're not seeking the representation of some singular 'truth'. Rather, we need our media to act in the same overlapping, multi-modal way as the ship's sensory platforms, providing a composite picture of the workings of power.

On a good day, that looks like the Snowden publications: a lens of transparency directed into the heart of unaccountable power. On a bad day, it looks like journalism as stenography, a profession hollowed out and repurposed as a channel through which the 1-per-cent villager broadcasts his opinion to the rest of us. And on a very bad day, it recalls a decade-old memory of London: passports, phones, keys handed off at reception, to be ushered into one of the most intensively surveilled environments on earth.

✶

Something has gone hideously wrong here. A superpower has wrenched the lens of institutional transparency back and inverted it, now using it like a magnifying glass to burn a hole in an independent publisher. WikiLeaks had begun publishing the raw materials of US diplomacy and war-making – the very recently compiled source code of empire, working with media partners all over the world. Gunship footage of US war crimes in Baghdad, and a vast undercount of civilian dead in far-flung resource wars. Diplomatic bastardry at the United Nations; US embassy staff tasked with collecting the DNA of foreign leaders. Now, WikiLeaks editor-in-chief Julian Assange and his colleagues and sources have been targeted for public destruction; first their reputations, and then their lives. The Ecuadorian ambassador, on welcoming us into her besieged workplace, tells us in a low voice, 'They can hear our thoughts.'

At a public meeting before his long years of limbo in the embassy, Assange sets out his purpose: 'Until we know the basic structures of our institutions, how they operate in practice – these titanic organisations, how they behave inside; not just through stories but through vast amounts of internal documentation – until we know that, how can we possibly make a diagnosis? We don't even have a map of where we are. So our first task is to build up the intellectual heritage that describes where we are.'

Here's one important landmark: spy agencies routinely undertake commercial espionage dressed up in the solemn guise of 'national security'. Australian spies wiretapped the East Timorese cabinet rooms in 2004, not to fight terrorism but to give gas multinationals the upper hand in negotiations with the Timorese. Mongolian prime minister Nambaryn Enkhbayar turned to the WikiLeaks archive of diplomatic cable traffic, only to discover the US State Department acting as the intelligence-gathering eyes and ears of Rio Tinto.

The repurposing of public institutions to serve parasitic private extraction is a distinctive signature of state capture. So it shouldn't surprise us to see these modes of collective perception bent in service of expanding the flows of natural gas and marine diesel and metallurgical coal.

'Investigative journalism is the noble art of seizing reality back from the powerful,' Assange has said. That's how high the stakes are: our collective perception of reality itself. The forces at play in the pressure cooker of the embassy will soon be transferred into a freezing cell in Belmarsh

Prison, a warning to the rest of us that seizing reality back from the powerful sometimes comes at an appalling cost.

I'm back at my railing after nightfall, air heavy with marine diesel fallout drifting into the darkness with the wake of the ship. Five kilometres below us lies an unseen topography of seamounts and rift valleys at the very floor of the world.

Psychiatrists speak of a condition they call 'apophenia' – a tendency towards faulty pattern recognition that can develop into a pathology. Perception gone awry; pull together a few facts or sense impressions, go ahead and form a satisfying and completely false conclusion. We must all suffer from it to some degree; as Mark Twain may or may not have said, 'It ain't what you don't know that gets you into trouble; it's what you know for sure that just ain't so.'

If someone were to jam the ship's sensory platforms and feed them corrupted data, she risks being torn open on a reef. If someone lies to you persuasively enough about the social distinction between red and green, you'll die at the next set of traffic lights. So I'm imagining how it might feel to descend now, slowly sinking some intermediate depth into this cold, sunless ocean. Amid endless darkness, lights: tiny lights suspended. Drifting closer – we're not imagining it, something down here is aglow – maybe a food source, or a glimmer of sunlight, or —

Glistening distended jaws of an anglerfish. We've been fooled into lethal proximity by a bright fleshy lantern suspended in front of a face that's mostly teeth. For pandalid shrimp or small curious fish, accurately reading these spectral light sources may be the difference between life and death.

Leaning on the railing, wondering now at the vast expertise brought to bear in cultivating society-wide apophenia. Coin-doubling anglerfish jamming our collective eyes and ears; a bright fleshy lantern of commercial bombardment, race hate and angry nationalisms, disinformation and manufactured insecurities. Accurately reading these spectral light sources may now be the difference between life and death, an arms race between perception and deception as deep and old as the ocean itself.

thinking like a state

It's like a blast furnace on Capitol Hill in Washington, DC. A handful of families are attempting arduous-looking picnics under the trees, but otherwise the National Mall is empty of life. Monumental architectures; grand stairways, white colonnades and long sightlines designed to make us quail or feel part of something mighty, I can never remember which. It all feels strangely insubstantial today, the whole assemblage wilting under this unyielding sun. Sound of helicopters; from somewhere I can smell smoke.

Through several layers of security, I've made it into the public gallery of the United States Senate with my guidebook and floorplan. Telemachus is on his feet, delivering a speech on family values; a handful of other senators reading or conversing quietly. A strange hit of nostalgia for my old life; the procedures down there are different but the purpose is familiar. In the guidebook, here's constitutional drafter and slave-owner James Madison envisaging the Senate as 'a necessary fence' designed to protect 'the people against their rulers'. The guidebook says the job of the Senate is to watch over and amend the excesses of the executive government, and of the House of Representatives on the other side of Statuary Hall. A double-chambered legislature, issuing coded scripts and rhetorical directives that shape the form and function of the republic itself. The architecture that Madison and his revolutionary colleagues settled on says that power will be constitutionally fractured between legislative, executive and judicial branches of government so as to prevent the re-emergence of tyranny. Each of these grave responsibilities is hosted in separate structures laid out along the axis of the Mall.

If we were extending our continuities of life metaphor and thinking like a state, these buildings are one place we'd go looking for collective agency. Deliberative and executive and regulatory functions are hosted here, welded to dozens of auxiliary organs evolved to improve their operations and prevent the whole thing from chewing its own face off.

Jan Slaby of the Freie Universität Berlin and Shaun Gallagher of the University of Memphis propose the idea of 'cognitive institutions', structures that facilitate collective cognition. They don't constrain their study to parliaments and congresses; they draw on examples ranging from educational systems to museums to scientific organisations. But following the continuities-of-life metaphor, these chambers seem like a locus of collective agency at the scale of the nation-state. Through slow deliberation and majority vote, their job is to determine whether various armatures of the US government should tumble or run.

Every duct and fibre of the nation's central nervous system converges within a few miles of here. Monuments and museums, libraries and statues invested in preserving canonical forms of collective memory. Bureaus of investigation, press galleries, situation rooms and satellite feeds filtering the raw materials of collective perception. Office blocks housing Homeland Security and Immigration and Customs Enforcement functions, charged with maintaining ever-more militarised boundaries and borders. And just over the river, the vast pentagonal complex of the Department of Defense, coordinating the armed enforcement of a large part of the world's industrial metabolism, from shipping lanes in the Persian Gulf to lithium coups in Latin America.

On this uncomfortably warm afternoon, looking down into the Senate chamber, noticing the decision-makers mostly look like our 1-per-cent villager: old, white and male. Not all, but mostly. If I take my eye off the guidebook and look up who paid for their campaigns, it will be a list drawn mostly from the investment theory of party competition. Outwardly it looks as though 'We, the People' selected the occupants of these Congressional benches, but, apart from a few powerful exceptions, familiar blocs of coin-doubling investors control the numbers down there.

'It's the basic intellectual dynamic of parasitism,' economic historian Michael Hudson observes drily. 'In nature, parasites don't simply attach themselves to a host and suck out blood, or take the surplus in an economy. In order to do that, they have to numb the host. They need an anaesthetic so that the host doesn't realize it's being bitten . . . biological parasites in nature have an enzyme that they use to take over the brain.'

Huh.

'The brain of the host is tricked into thinking that the parasite is a part of its body, to be protected. That is what the parasitic sector, the FIRE – Finance, Insurance and Real Estate – sector has done in modern economies,' Hudson suggests.

Cognitive institutions, infected with a brain parasite playing a game of double or die. Listen to most of what passes for debate down there on the Senate floor; see how long it is before someone stands up to speak for the investors who elected them. Open a newspaper, watch the talkshows, skim the timeline; it seems to be everywhere. Glancing at the White House homepage for signs of it: 'The stock market has been unstoppable under the influence of President Trump,' it shrieks. Scrolling further, realising, with absolute certainty, that this thing has indeed begun chewing its own face off.

Exactly 895 days after my brief visit, guns will be drawn on the Senate floor; legislators evacuated as members of the ruling party's militia briefly occupy this chamber. The halls of the Capitol will churn with rioters bearing fascist insignia: tokens of a collapsed regime's twentieth-century attempt to enforce politically applied biology across a whole continent.

'Fascism should more appropriately be called corporatism because it is a merger of state and corporate power,' according to fascist philosopher Giovanni Gentile – although the quote is often attributed to his boss, war-time dictator Benito Mussolini.

FIRE sector, you say. Maybe that's why everything smells like smoke.

stumbling stones

There is an ache to Berlin, and they take care to ensure it never fades. Some of the wounds lie out in plain sight – remnants of the Wall, scars of small-arms fire in Mitte, the haunted concrete grid of the Holocaust Memorial. But some are more subtle. Hours adrift; I don't need to be at the cafe until noon, and so here, at the front door of some terrace house on a street I could never find again, I've come across three stumbling stones. *Stolpersteine* – raised brass plaques set into the pavement. Each one records a life: the names and dates of birth of a Jewish family. A man and woman in their sixties, their son in his thirties. The plaques record that they came for the young man first, deporting him to Auschwitz in February 1943. His death is undated. Then they came for his parents, deporting them to Theresienstadt, where they were murdered six months later. They were taken from this house, behind this door, where I'm standing seventy-five years, one month and twenty-five days later.

There are more than seventy thousand of these blocks emplaced right across Europe, from Spain to the Baltic, the work of German artist Gunter Demnig. They hold a profound resonance here, in the city from which this monumental crime was orchestrated. Berlin is laced with these stones, weatherproofed elements of a distributed collective memory. Implied in their placement, implied in all the memorials and museums, is that remembering the past is a form of protection against certain kinds of future.

It is stirring again; it never completely went away, the thing that took this family. For a long while it lay underground, hybridising with digital subcultures, dismissed as an ironic fringe. But then came the warning signs, from those who should know; when fascists feel safe enough or angry enough to occupy talkshows and Capitol buildings, maybe it means it's into the bones, like it was here in the 1930s. As it attempts to take institutional form again, one of the warning signs will be the fingerprints of erasure; subtle manipulations and deletions of this collective memory.

I check the time; it's much later than I realised.

body politic

I find Professor Peter Droege in the cosy recesses of the rambling old cafe. He's the general chairman of the World Council for Renewable Energy and the director of the Liechtenstein Institute for Strategic Development. He's known in policy circles as someone who was researching the interface between cities and climate long before it was cool. I ask him what he's working on these days. 'My priority is the so-called low-carbon agenda,' he deadpans. 'By low carbon I mean . . . really low carbon.' Not just zero emissions, but rapidly drawing down the overshoot that's already battering the world.

I want to catch up with Droege because he works with the urgency of someone who understands the lateness of the hour. Asked by a *EuropeNow* interviewer what he thought was the biggest challenge of our times, his answer was on point: 'Failed investment. Over a trillion dollars in fossil and nuclear energy subsidies, and a good portion of the two trillion dollars in global military budgets dedicated to protecting petroleum sources and markets, are essentially applied to make Earth uninhabitable to humans, as quickly and effectively as possible.'

He's not that interested in talking about solar megaprojects or high-profile prototypes. He wants to know what would happen if that investment was redirected into regional-scale adoption of softer, closed-loop systems that do multiple things at once. He thinks about energy, water, waste, transport, land restoration, manufacturing and food production not as separate problems needing separate experts, but different dimensions of the same problem.

As he speaks, I'm imagining the sankey stripes of collective metabolism folding back, the one-way consumption and dumping torrent closing into regenerative loops in which outputs from one process serve as inputs to others. It feels so similar to how natural systems function that I'm tempted to ask him whether he sees any merit in metaphors of industrial metabolism.

Hesitating, a little. The idea that human social organisation borrows significant characteristics from the natural world has a deep lineage, much of it self-serving and hideous. The intellectual distance between politically applied biology and the silence of the stumbling stones is short and direct. It was Darwinian survival of the fittest that required John D. Rockefeller to corner the nation's oil, according to John D. Rockefeller.

But that's just scratching the surface: at least three thousand years ago, the Rig Veda, one of the oldest texts in Hindu scripture, set out how the Indian caste system has a place for everyone, 'comparing the priesthood to the mouth, fighters to the arms, shepherds to the thighs, and peasants to the feet of mankind'. The priests issuing such texts seemed comfortable assigning themselves the role of mouthpiece; someone else would have to be the feet, sorry.

The metaphor drifts in and out of Western political philosophy more or less at random. Aesop's 'The Belly and the Members' describes various organs of the political 'body' going on strike against the stomach and immediately regretting it; this story even making its way into Livy's history of Rome. During one *secessio plebis* – a massive general strike where Rome's working people would abandon the city and leave the aristocrats to clean their own toilets – the senators delegated Menenius Agrippa to negotiate everyone back to their jobs. According to Livy, Agrippa led with this: 'the Senate-belly agreed that it received food from the plebs-body, but it did not go to waste. The Senate digested it and sent it back to blood and veins of the republic; hence, cooperation between all gave vitality to the republican body.' Apparently the plebians were persuaded by this wild ride of an argument and called off the strike.

The metaphor winds its way through Christian political thought, suffering partial dismantlement at the hands of Thomas Hobbes and other Enlightenment philosophers, who preferred mechanical analogies to organic ones. Nonetheless, 'for three centuries, concepts of the state have been animated by one of the most powerful metaphors in politics: the body politic, a claustrophobic and bounded image of sovereignty,' writes international relations scholar Stefanie Fishel. Claustrophobic, because the people who come up with these metaphors invariably cast themselves as the head, or the brain, or the mouth; if you've been assigned to the armpit, that's where you'll stay.

States, and human collectives more broadly, are clearly not just scaled-up humans, any more than humans are scaled-up cells. States don't seem like bodies of any kind; they feel more like entirely novel, colonial expressions of these ancient continuities of life. The notion of an urban metabolism – a concept lifted directly from biology – seems to exist out at right angles to these more literal conceptions of the body politic. For one thing, just like a chamber of parliament, the cities we construct are contentious environments shaped by human agency and a debatable form of self-awareness. It isn't some mysterious property of biological 'emergence' that delivers electric light rail to the inner city and cancels the bus service to the outer metropolitan shopping centre. It's politics.

So I ask Professor Droege what he thinks of the idea of cities as metabolic structures; whether life's long continuities might find expression at the scale of streets, or cities, or states. As it turns out, he's not quite buying it.

'The difference between economies and ecologies is that ecologies don't use money. Ecologies don't use an intermediate value system. Money drives certain dynamics which remove it from anything else that happens in nature. It punishes those that don't have enough money, and rewards those who have the ability to lend money,' he says. 'So it's a social destabliser; you don't have that in natural systems.'

And then, the kick. 'It has its own logic – particularly the role of interest rates – that drives an increasing requirement to accumulate more value to service the debt.'

A medium removed from anything else that happens in nature, driving runaway accumulation making earth uninhabitable to humans, as quickly and effectively as possible. In my mind's eye, the coin-doubling mathematician just pulled up a chair uninvited and helped himself to our coffee.

The dominant element in our financial oligarchy
is the investment banker . . . These bankers are, of
course, able men possessed of large fortunes; but the
most potent factor in their control of business is not
the possession of extraordinary ability or huge wealth.
The key to their power is Combination – concentration
intensive and comprehensive – advancing on three
distinct lines . . .

LOUIS DEMBITZ BRANDEIS, *OTHER PEOPLE'S MONEY
AND HOW THE BANKERS USE IT*

unmooring

They will call it the Great Depression, and the establishment won't see it coming.

'Stock prices have reached what looks like a permanently high plateau,' declares economist Irving Fisher, just before the US economy goes into cardiac arrest and dies. The tenfold speculative expansion of the Dow Jones Industrial Average during the Roaring Twenties shudders into reverse in September 1929. Traders oscillate between fear and greed for weeks until, in late October, the market hits the wall. The Federal Reserve Bank stands on the sidelines with its hands in its pockets, and banks begin to fall like dominos, triggering a feedback loop of panicked cash withdrawals and more collapses. President Herbert Hoover has faith the market will revive without intervention, and so by 1932 the Dow has lost nearly 90 per cent of its value, five thousand banks have gone into liquidation, and more than six hundred thousand properties have been foreclosed. The crash has broken the back of the world's largest economy.

When markets remember the mathematician's imaginary coins don't actually exist, the shock waves can be global and severe.

The gruelling deprivation – and the sense that the establishment that caused it now has no idea what to do – unleashes a wild cycle of rebellion and transgression, vividly sketched by writer Steve Fraser: 'Factory occupations, urban street battles, violent strikes in the South, mass marches of the unemployed, seizures of mines and public utilities by the freezing and desperate, squatting on vacant land and in unoccupied houses, and blocked foreclosures and evictions in big cities were all symptomatic of a more general readiness to trespass across lines of authority and private property that had long been verboten.'

That's the context which helps sweep Democratic presidential candidate Franklin Delano Roosevelt into the White House in the 1932 election. He has campaigned on a program of vast public works, employment protections, wage increases and direct government investment in industry and agriculture. 'I pledge you, I pledge myself, to a new deal for the American people,' he tells the Democratic National Convention.

In the first hundred days of his presidency, Roosevelt introduces an *Emergency Banking Act* that literally switches the surviving banks off and then on again, followed by the introduction of an Act forcibly separating commercial banks from investment banks in the hope of preventing future speculative self-destruction of the financial system.

Now Roosevelt announces emergency support for people in poverty. A Civilian Conservation Corps. A Public Works Administration funding billions of dollars' worth of new construction projects. A Securities and Exchange Commission to help police the unhinged excesses of the stock market.

By 1934, it's becoming clear that the brains of the operation is actually Roosevelt's Secretary of Labor, the formidable Frances Perkins. Serving as the first female cabinet secretary in US history, Perkins proceeds to work through an ambitious list, starting with a *Social Security Act* for 'federal old-age insurance, Federal–State public assistance and unemployment insurance programs, and extension of public health, maternal and child health, services for crippled children and child welfare services, and vocational rehabilitation.' The American Medical Association manages to kill her proposal for universal health insurance – slow clap – but otherwise, she's on a roll.

In 1938, Frances Perkins gets her *Fair Labor Standards Act*, which bans child labour, caps the maximum number of working hours and establishes a minimum wage for the first time. The president and his colleagues have successfully used the tools of central planning, labour empowerment and limited wealth redistribution to head off some of the far more egalitarian and revolutionary impulses that had begun to emerge in the winter of the Depression.

As the country lurches slowly out of recession, history takes a violent turn: fascism is ascendent in Europe and East Asia, and the overnight conversion to a planned economy now turbocharges the industrial might of the United States.

Six months before the fall of Berlin, the architects of an imagined postwar economic order gather at Bretton Woods in New Hampshire. They begin drafting a system of tightly controlled currency exchange rates backed by gold and the US dollar, and a set of institutions designed to prevent the catastrophic debt defaults and trade imbalances that scarred the first half of the twentieth century. The International Monetary Fund and the International Bank for Reconstruction and Development – which will eventually form the core of the World Bank – are born, both of them under the watchful control of the US government. The Bretton Woods agreements are the legal DNA coding for the coin-doubling acceleration that will punch a hole in the Holocene: a reconstruction boom powerful enough to begin tilting the planet's largest-scale climate feedbacks.

In the 1970s, a fourfold spike in oil prices and the vast cost of the carnage it is inflicting on the people of Vietnam spark an economic crisis in the United States. Unemployment spikes and coin-doubling stalls; now the coins themselves began rapidly losing value. It's the crisis a small handful of extremists calling themselves neoliberals have been gagging for. 'Only a crisis – actual or perceived – produces real change,' enthuses economist Milton Friedman. 'When that crisis occurs, the actions that are taken depend on the ideas that are lying around. That, I believe, is our basic function: to develop alternatives to existing policies, to keep them alive and available until the politically impossible becomes the politically inevitable.'

The 'alternative to existing policies', proposed by the men who own the coins, is simple: put the coins in charge. Let the free market decide. A compelling rebrand of a wearyingly old idea is hatched in closed discussions incubated within the Mont Pelerin Society. Now formalised as doctrine, the idea is forcibly injected into global economic policy via a network of think tanks and institutes. The investors, moving as one, invest in new advocates: Reagan and Thatcher, Trudeau and Mulroney, Hawke and Keating, all of them reading from the same script. They begin unmooring the coin-doubling game; deregulation, they call it. From that point until today, all you'll be able to see through this newly delimited Overton window is a contest over who can most effectively guarantee 3 per cent annually compounding growth, so that the owners of the coins get twice their money back in twenty-five years' time.

For some, this all seems terribly avant-garde. For others, it is business as usual, with interest. People newly freed from colonial domination are discovering neocolonialism – permanent entrapment within extraction and plantation economies – as an enforceable condition of IMF loans their regimes signed them up to. Uprisings and wayward socialist experiments will be repressed with death squads, capital flight and coups, and not a trace of this violence will make its way into the collective memory of the Global North.

Organised labour now comes under determined assault; public assets broken up and sold; social welfare systems eroded and curtailed. Manufacturing industries relocate down the cost gradient, from the Midwest to Nagoya, then the Pearl River Delta and on into Bangladesh and the Philippines. Service industries begin to follow them; what can't yet be automated is being offshored into gated free-trade zones with permissive tax regimes. At the margins, everywhere, emerging ranks of the unnecessariat.

To commemorate their deregulated unmooring by a compliant Congress, US mortgage lenders detonate a bruising global financial crisis in 2007. Banks are falling like dominos again: New Century, IndyMac, Lehmann Brothers.

Preventing another implosion of the coin-doubling game will require an upfront taxpayer bailout of just under a trillion US dollars in 2008 and 2009, and a total bailout commitment of $29 trillion by the US Federal Reserve in its role as lender of last resort.

The construction cranes swing back into action on the skyline of Manhattan. Oil-fuelled coin-doubling resumes; the oligarchs continue their long march out of Mont Pelerin, and the whole system begins winding the spring on the next crash.

crash habit

Show us the money, we suggested, long ago in the front yard of the quiet house in the quiet street. Turns out that's not as easy as it sounds. Because it exists only in the form of symbolic agreements, money can take whatever form we want it to. At different times thoughout history, it took the form of seashells, imprints on clay tablets, handwritten IOUs, gold coins and polymer banknotes.

The money that matters most right now is of a very particular kind. The electronic coins of the Anthropocene are mathematical agreements created in the form of interest-bearing debt: they are loaned into existence by private banking corporations and central banks, on the condition that they are repaid with interest. This runaway money is born with a singular obligation: within a fixed period of time, it demands to be returned as a bigger stack of imaginary coins.

We're standing out on the mathematician's chessboard once more, watching giant pieces of robotic earthmoving equipment piling the next stack of coins twice as high on the square in front of us. The air is heavy with smoke.

The coin-doubling game is a real-time example of what the systems theory people call 'positive feedback'. One dictionary defines the term as 'the enhancing or amplification of an effect by its own influence on the process which gives rise to it'. Even the definition is circular. Environmental scientist and author Donella Meadows puts it like this: 'A positive feedback loop is self-reinforcing. The more it works, the more it gains power to work some more.'

We witnessed this effect, in autocatalytic form, amid the fiery formation of the planet. But self-amplifying feedback loops aren't just for loose hydrocarbons flirting with each other on primordial seafloors:[5] they take transient form in many domains. Stock market rallies, nuclear

---

5   Did you expect to read that phrase today? No, you did not.

weapon detonations, rabbit plagues, pandemics: a wide spectrum of physical, ecological, technical and social phenomena can undergo runaway self-amplification. The larger they get, the larger it allows them to get.

And then they're gone. Here's Meadows again: 'Positive feedback loops drive growth, explosion, erosion and collapse in systems. A system with an unchecked positive loop ultimately will destroy itself. That's why there are so few of them.'

One accelerant of our malfunctioning economy's crash habit is just economies of scale. The way the 1 per cent villager has written these rules, the larger an economic entity gets, the more efficiently it can procure the next phase of its own growth. Economic thinkers at least as far back as Adam Smith and Karl Marx detailed how expanding the scale of operations allows firms to drive down unit costs through greater purchasing power across supply chains, access to cheaper credit, negotiating leverage with their workforce and ever-more specialised division of labour.

On the ground, this looks like a wave of bankruptcies and shop closures on the old High Street when they implant that concrete shopping centre on the edge of town. It looks like three decades of consolidation in the global agricultural, media, mining, engineering, finance, entertainment and defence sectors, as ever-larger corporate entities use their increasing scale to leverage further increases in scale.

US platform monopolist Amazon designed a positive feedback model to grow its way from a niche bookseller in 1995 to the world's largest online store, with a dominant presence extending into cloud computing, electronics, footwear and in-home consumer surveillance devices. They called their model the flywheel: 'Lower prices led to more customer visits. More customers increased the volume of sales and attracted more commission-paying third-party sellers to the site. That allowed Amazon to get more out of fixed costs like the fulfilment centres and the servers they needed to run the website. This greater efficiency then enabled it to lower prices further. Feed any part of this flywheel . . . and it should accelerate the loop.'

It works. Before the pandemic that would engorge him even further, Amazon CEO Jeff Bezos was already sitting on a stack of imaginary coins worth something north of $150 billion. Now analysts speak of him as having the potential to become the world's first trillionaire. 'The only way that I can see to deploy this much financial resource is by converting my Amazon winnings into space travel. That is basically it,' he says, sounding like the world's least interesting man walking out of a big night in a casino.

Because these accelerating loops continually run up against community opposition, labour rights and ecological reality, they long ago hybridised with another positive feedback phenomenon: the cultural and territorial flywheels that drive the accumulation of political power. At least since the time Telemachus's ancestors began enforcing patriarchal divisions of labour in settled agricultural societies, access to power has opened avenues to even greater access to power. This positive feedback problem has occupied political theorists and revolutionaries for millennia, while around them city-states were coagulating into nations and then into ever-larger empires; walls and borders writhing and whiplashing across the map.

Positive feedback loops end in explosion or collapse unless other feedbacks come into play, moderating their steep growth curves and drawing the system towards some kind of dynamic balance. A population of rabbits will proliferate wildly until all available food is gone, unless someone introduces a family of foxes into the picture. A pandemic will race out of control until it has infected the whole population, unless we all mask up and deploy a vaccination program. A revolutionary uprising will overthrow an illegitimate government, unless someone deploys troops and secret police to smash it. In systems parlance, these moderating influences – the fox, the vaccine and the secret police – are considered negative feedbacks.

Seen through this lens, democratic regulation of the economy, antitrust laws, transparent and progressive tax systems, collective workplace bargaining rights, environmental protections: all of these can be read as forms of negative feedback on the coin-doubling cascade. All of them have been subjected to five decades of neoliberal assault, in order that nothing get in the way of the next drop of the coins.

'At the point where debts can no longer be paid, you have a break in the chain of payments. That's what causes a crash,' says Michael Hudson. 'Usually, crashes result from a fraud or insolvency, or somebody makes a bad bet for a big bank, or an environment crisis causes a break in the chain of payments.'

The warped genius of the Mont Pelerin people was to put the coins in charge. So now, instead of democratised institutions of agency guided by tools of collective perception and cultural memory, our industrial metabolism's runaway accounting system has been put in charge.

I'm trying to imagine what would happen if the ribosomes inside a cell staged a coup and started behaving like that. Or if my liver somehow overthrew my body's delicate self-regulatory systems and forced every organ to produce bile, all the time, twice as much tomorrow as yesterday.

Our metaphor is by now perilously overextended, because the rest of the natural world would have immediately dispatched such a maladaptive experiment into the silence of geology.

if a tree falls

Breathe deep. The oxygen that fuels your body's cells was exhaled by a swampy rainforest of ferns and lycopods and scale trees that stretches halfway around the world. The supercontinent of Pangaea is in the late stages of formation, dominating the tropics and southern hemisphere while a single world ocean stretches over the horizon. With the ghosts of the Devonian extinction waves long gone, shallow seas on the continental margins are teeming with life again. The vanishing of the armoured placoderms has opened ecological space for the sharks to come into their own, and freshwater ecosystems now host giant rhizodont fish, topping out at seven metres long.

Stand under the lush verdance of tree-fern canopy in the late Carboniferous, more than three hundred million years before the present moment. An oxygen-rich atmosphere has supercharged a carnival of giants on the forest floor. Millipedes two and a half metres long are roving through the undergrowth, giant scorpions and spider-like creatures have taken up terrifying positions at the apex of terrestrial food chains. Above them float clouds of mayflies, and dragonflies with wingspans more than half a metre across.

This riot of arthropods is witnessing another wave of tetrapods hauling themselves out on the mudflats – a handful of survivors of the Devonian extinctions making another go of it. These opportunistic fish descendants have spent tens of millions of years fooling around with longer and longer periods out of water. By the slow trials and forgotten lives of generation after generation, they have diversified into true amphibians, fins morphing into articulated limbs as their paths take them ever further from the ancestral sea. Some are developing the ability to lay shelled eggs resistant to drying out, freeing these proto-reptilian pioneers to expand their range away from the damplands. The ocean is internalised for these land-dwellers; in salty bloodstreams and amniotic eggs, clad in suits of toughened skin and scaled armour against the unfiltered sun.

But it is the forest from which this distant age takes its name. This is a world of deep, trackless rainforest; giant tree ferns and the grandparents of conifers, but also the tall, unfamiliar forms of giant horsetails and club mosses thirty metres high. If a tree falls in this forest and no-one has evolved a way to digest the wood, it will lie there forever. As competition for sunlight drove the forest canopy skyward in the Devonian, the vascular plants borrowed an old trick from marine algae and turned it to a new purpose: lignin. This curious biopolymer comes in many varieties, but all share the common property of being as strong as hell when cross-woven into structural materials. As the increasing height of land plants places new demands on the cells working away within them, lignin is brought into service as a ubiquitous, flexible scaffolding.

The thing is, lignin is nearly indigestible. To anything. Even the slow-motion seethe of fungal threads on the forest floor doesn't know what to do with the stuff, and so dead wood simply piles up where it falls. Cycles of inundation and drying on meandering riverbeds are recorded in thick strata of buried and compressed plant matter from these ancient forests, some of them containing achingly well-preserved fern leaves and winged insects. The Carboniferous is an age of slow, planetary-scale inhalation of atmospheric carbon dioxide into the embodied form of a continental rainforest, with much of it buried rather than returned to the air by decomposers. This is stripping a blanket of heat-trapping gas out of the atmosphere, sequestering it beneath swamplands alive with a hum of insects. We know all about these rich, buried stockpiles of fossil carbon today. We call it coal.

One line of theory holds that these lush rainforests have helped set their own destruction in motion. By around 290 million years ago, white rot Agaricomycetes fungi have at last developed the ability to decompose lignin, and set to work on the backlog.[6] Forests of future ages will still leave coal formations behind, but never again in the enormous volumes of the Carboniferous.

It's too late, though; the climate is already cooling and drying sharply, with the rainforest having drawn down carbon dioxide levels as low as they've been since the formation of the planet. Abruptly, the world snaps into a bleak new ice age, and the global forest is broken into shrinking refuges sheltering diminishing populations of rainforest-adapted species. The long, damp dominion of the amphibians is coming to a close, drying

---

6   Just a lil' joke there.

conditions playing in favour of their reptilian cousins. Sea levels fall by a hundred metres as the glaciers return, exposing wide expanses of continental shelf and sending marine communities into retreat. Future geologists will refer to this episode as the Carboniferous rainforest collapse.

It's not as simple as just blaming the trees and the scandalously late arrival of the Agaricomycetes for their own demise. The close of the Carboniferous also coincides with widespread eruption of the Skagerrak-Centered Large Igneous Province in what will eventually be northern Europe. This magma blowtorch rising from the planet's molten interior is turning an area of half a million square kilometres into a volcanic hellscape, sending untold volumes of sulphuric ash into the sky. The weathering of these fresh silicate rocks acts as a giant carbon sponge, slowly drawing carbon dioxide out of the air and washing it into the ocean, where it ends up incorporated into the shells of a billionfold tiny marine creatures, eventually falling to the seafloor. Maybe we'll never know exactly what killed the rainforest, but the fingerprints of climate change seem smudged on the remains.

Three hundred million years before the present, the Carboniferous is over. One day we'll call this new chapter of the oldest book the Permian period. The Pangaea supercontinent spans half the planet, still carrying the polar icecaps of the late Carboniferous, with the immense continental interior dominated by wide, arid deserts. Veterans of the lost rainforest world survive in river valleys and coastal ecosystems, but this is the age of dryland-adapted reptiles as they diversify into fabulous new forms. Dimetrodon, a formidable fanged synapsid with a ridged sail on its back. Diadectid, a bulked-up herbivore several metres long whose descendants left fossil traces all over the world. The early Permian also sees a disturbing proliferation of cockroaches filling every conceivable ecological niche available to cockroaches, so let's keep moving.

For the long forty-five-million-year summer of the Permian, the drift towards a drying climate continues to favour creatures less dependent on the humid conditions of the distant past. Carbon dioxide levels are slowly rising again, and conifers, ginkgos and cycads are emerging to fill out the depleted ranks of Devonian tree ferns and lycopods. Breathe deep: catch the warm, unmistakable smell of pine needles for the first time.

Here's something: an ancestral cynodont maybe fifty centimetres long; a quick, sure-footed predator hunting the undergrowth in the shadow of her much larger reptilian cousins. While they remain clad in armoured scales and toughened hide, it seems likely that she's wearing fur.

Watch this one – she moves like quicksilver, and something about her feels familiar.

bomb

Unceded Yuin country on the south coast of New South Wales, sun hanging heavy and red in the burned air. The smoke gets to you after a while, into your hair, your eyes, your sleep. In the old shack this morning the air seemed tinted blue, but out here everything has a bruised orange cast to it. At Mystery Bay, the high-tide line was inscribed in long arcs of greasy ash and perfectly intact eucalyptus leaves, dead black. Our investor-nominated brain parasite salesman is posting holiday snaps from Hawai'i, while here on Australia's eastern seaboard, a land area the size of Belgium is on fire.

Scorched leaves have begun fluttering back to earth, brittle fallout from carbon bomb detonations only a few dozen kilometres from here. Evacuations are underway in East Gippsland and Shoalhaven and the Northern Rivers. Our turn will come; here it's tinder-dry but all quiet, just this slow rain of debris. Sirius can sense our agitation, I think, knows something isn't right. Checks to see if a lick on the face would help.

It kind of does, but still, it's overwhelming, if I'm honest. News has just come through that another volunteer firefighter has been killed at the fire front. Numbed edges of something glitching between rage and helplessness; perfect mindset for a paralysed scroll down the timeline, hoping someone smarter than me has found the one thing we should do that will fix this shit.

Here's one from a little while ago; still my favourite. 'The first step to reducing your emissions is to know where you stand', chirrups the official BP account. 'Find out your #carbonfootprint with our new calculator & share your pledge today!'

The purity of it. The flawless, crystalline audacity of a global oil and gas major helping me to find out where I stand. According to a recent quarterly report, this is where BP stands: 'Started up six major projects, making a significant contribution to the 900,000 barrels per day of expected new production from major projects start-ups between 2016 and 2021.'

Coin-doubling, all the way into ashfall and evacuations. Thank you, BP. This actually is helping me work out where I stand.

'There is evidence that the amount of carbon dioxide in the earth's atmosphere is increasing rapidly as a result of the combustion of fossil fuels, wrote James R. Garvey, president of Bituminous Coal Research Inc. in the August 1966 edition of *The Mining Congress Journal*.

'If the future rate of increase continues as it is at the present . . . the temperature of the earth's atmosphere will increase and . . . vast changes in the climates of the earth will result,' he warned. In 1966.

The oil men knew too; Exxon executives had climate models in front of them in 1979 that forecast 'dramatic climatic changes' within the next seventy-five years. The company responded with a ten-year research program that produced chillingly accurate predictions of what would happen if it continued burning oil and gas. Exxon shut the program down, lit up an anglerfish lantern of denial and disinformation, and continued burning oil and gas.

They knew what they were doing. They had some of the best scientists in the world working for them, who told them, in detail, what would happen. They knew. And they did it anyway. Designed it, armed it, lit the fuse. And then rolled it down the hill towards us, towards the future, gathering speed and political power and fearsome momentum. And now that future is here, hanging heavy and red in the burned air.

Sometime between this coin-doubling and the next, the chess game ends, because the board is on fire. If we're to have any hope of disarming it, we need to be honest about how it's rigged, and why so many previous attempts to defuse it have failed.

The rigging is beyond diabolical. They've hitched the planet's temperature regulation to the coin-doubling game. Unearthed that immense reservoir of carbon inhaled by a vanished global rainforest in the long-distant Carboniferous. And all the oil. And all the gas. Geology's entire inventory of buried carbon: this thing has been designed to combust all of it, doubling and doubling again until it's gone. While in Sarawak and Wattle Forest and the Amazon Basin, the coins have sent machines with tank-tracks and tungsten saws against forest ecosystems that should have been the first line of defence in a crisis like this. Seabed trawlers commandeered to similar effect on the continental shelves: the unseen clearfelling of the planet's oceanic lungs.

Look how viciously this thing is wired. Even the briefest pause in the doubling cascade will send coin-operated broadcasters into high-volume hyperventilations. The entire economic dashboard will light up red: RECESSION. Governments fall, supply chains sag, businesses close, thousands of us evicted into the ranks of unnecessariat. A really bad one they call a depression; the whole business ecosystem goes into cardiac arrest. Watch now as the investor blocs again bend the combined resources of government and industry to focus everything on getting back on the chessboard in time for the next round of double or die.

This is the part that really gets me: these people honestly thought that their imaginary coins would win an argument with a planet. Bet themselves against the atmosphere – and the ocean – geology itself. Even by their own stunted and one-dimensional frame of reference, burning an asset to the ground and expecting it to still repay the money you lent it seems like something their insurers should have flagged. But no. 'At the point where debts can no longer be paid, you have a break in the chain of payments,' Hudson reminds us. 'That's what causes a crash.'

We need to brace ourselves, then. The weather forecast is for a geological break in the chain of payments unlike anything any previous generation has experienced.

The coin-doubling game is over, the investors just don't seem to know it yet. It's doing the thing that cartoon coyote used to do after racing off a clifftop; legs still churning the air, but all that matters now is the timing and manner of the fall. We'll know precisely the moment the coyote looks down and realises how far above the ground it is, because around four trillion dollars' worth of its coins will suddenly blink and vanish as though they were never there.

This is the fuse the investors have lit. Other people, working to older imperatives, have begun gathering the numbers we'll need to disarm the carbon bomb once and for all.

power laws and dragon kings

We are in the beginning of a mass extinction and all
you can talk about is money and fairy tales of eternal
economic growth.

GRETA THUNBERG,
TO THE UN CLIMATE SUMMIT, SEPTEMBER 2019

runaway

It's not the largest demonstration I've been to, but it's unlike any I've attended before.

There's plenty here that's familiar – improvised sound system, hand-made placards, speeches read from prepared notes and directly from the heart. But the organisers, and all the speakers, are children. When they speak, some of them standing in front of a crowd for the first time, it is mesmerising. A few are confident, already accomplished public speakers. Others are visibly shaking but determined to do their best.

We are far from the bright centres of power and capital; this is a dairy town on Yuin country hundreds of kilometres from the nearest city. Afterwards, organisers of the youth climate movement will tally 2598 events in 134 countries across a twenty-four-hour period: two in Bangladesh, 229 in France, 37 in Mexico, 165 in Sweden. One right here in Bega, New South Wales: attendance approximately two hundred people and some good dogs.

The School Strike 4 Climate movement is a living example of the protest cascade phenomenon. It is unusual in that we know the moment the avalanche begins: the decision of fifteen-year-old Swedish student Greta Thunberg to go on strike in August 2018. Instead of sitting in class, she sits on the steps of the Swedish parliament with a placard, announcing she'll continue striking on Fridays until her government's actions to defuse the carbon bomb are brought into line with its rhetoric. She has a very direct way of cutting through complexity: 'Why should we study for a future that may not exist anymore?'

It takes effort to imagine an intervention less threatening to the Anthropocene status quo than a teenager with a cardboard placard taking a day off school. She wasn't even the first: in 2015, the UN Climate Change Conference in Paris provoked a widespread school strike. But for some reason, this time something sparks: Thunberg's quiet act of defiance catches the moment.

'When we start to act, hope is everywhere. So instead of looking for hope – look for action. Then the hope will come,' she tweets in October 2018. The following month, a handful of students in Australia take up her call. Thousands walk out of class in support, leaving conservative politicians frothing. With the COP24 climate conference as a focal point that December, the movement begins to smoulder around the industrialised world, rebounding back into Europe, Japan and the United States, with around forty-five thousand students participating. Three months later, more than two million people answer the students' call to events in every time zone on earth.

School strikes take place from Ghana to Kashmir, but the big numbers are still largely concentrated in the Global North, the consumption power-houses that drive the coin-doubling game ever onwards. This fact isn't lost on the strikers, as Melbourne-based organiser Nyah Shahab tells me.

'What keeps me going? The privilege of knowing that I'm the least impacted. While I'm scared for my future, and I know that we're causing irreversible damage, I get the privilege to strike. The people who are the most impacted usually don't have that opportunity, because their voices are the ones that are ignored the most by politicians; the voices of minorities that are facing those impacts every day.'

Some of the school strikers are aware that their movement is just one expression of a much older conflict. 'The amount of civil disobedience that has taken place over 231 years – it's extraordinary,' says Jai Allan Wright, a young Yugambeh striker from southeast Queensland. 'I wouldn't be here today unless my own family, my own mob had been engaged for that long.'

In September 2019, there's another surge, and this time the numbers have tripled. Over two consecutive Fridays, more than seven million take to the streets, making it the largest climate demonstration in history. 'Sea levels are rising. So are we,' reads the placard held by a tiny kid who can't be more than ten years old, marching at the head of a climate justice rally in Kolkata. In Moscow's Pushkin Square, Arshak Makichyan stands alone, with a #FridaysForFuture poster. 'One person holds a poster for five minutes, then hands over to the next person who is waiting nearby,' he tells *The Guardian*. 'That way, we don't have any problems because it is a series of solo strikes rather than a group gathering.' He will later spend a week in prison for the action.

In China, where the Communist Party's brittle grip on civil society has prevented widespread organising thus far, courage finds a way through cracks in the concrete. Back in May, Howey Ou had undertaken a solo climate strike in front of a government office in her home city of Guilin. She kept at it for seven days until the police bundled her away and threatened her parents. A nuclear-armed regime commanding the world's second-largest economy, 1.4 billion people strong, fully aware of the power of a sixteen-year-old girl with a cardboard placard. For the September strike, Howey adapts, avoiding government offices. Organises a tree-planting action on a supportive relative's land, posts it to social media. 'I feel planting trees is a way to spread the message in China,' she says. This time, a friend joins her. Her strike has doubled its numbers too.

I'm adrift in a sea of people at the Melbourne school strike, which has overflowed Treasury Gardens and closed the top end of the city. Bourke Street at a standstill as the march forms up: a sea of banners and pennants and cardboard signs, joyful acoustics of a hundred thousand voices raised. I'm momentarily overwhelmed by the numbers these children have brought together, and by the wild courage of Howey and Makichyan and others like them, defiant even without the safety of numbers. Now the movement rolls across the time zones like a wave, lighting up cities and towns one by one. This must be how it feels to live on one planet, dull nationalisms slipping as we glimpse each other, recognising allies even if we can't always read the script on the handmade signs. Children. Children have done this.

The leading edge of the march has rounded the corner of Flinders Street and is making its way back towards Treasury Gardens before the tail-end of the rally has even finished leaving.

I've paused on the steps of parliament to wonder at the symbolism of that; trying to work out if it feels like a self-sustaining loop or a sign of futility. The state long ago figured out that we were no threat as long as we just marched around in circles. They know that sooner or later we always go home, with no real concessions sought or given. So they keep track of our numbers and divide by three for the evening news, photograph and tag as many of us as possible for the file, but basically leave us alone. We feel like we've made a difference, they know we haven't really; everyone's happy.

Something about this feels different. These must be powerful and formative experiences for the organisers and for everyone who has taken part. I was still working my way through *The Hobbit* when I was ten; these kids have brought seven million marchers onto the streets. Confirmation that none of us are alone in this is also reward in itself. But mostly, it feels different because it's genuinely new. The future generations we've been taking about for decades; they're here, and they're building an escalating series of global strikes. This isn't just a demonstration, it's a synchronised act of refusal. Finding their feet and their organising tempo; the potential, if they can find ways to keep escalating, is profound.

Scanning the evening news and the radio grabs, coverage is almost overwhelmingly positive. This demonstration, I realise, is a raucous collective signifier of a million quiet conversations around the kitchen table, children's tears and trauma newly radicalising two generations of parents and grandparents.

The carbon investors and their nominees in government are floundering, still working out their attack lines. 'The children should be at school. They should be learning about Australian history,' deputy prime minister Michael McCormack tells Greens MP Adam Bandt in the Australian House of Representatives. It's like being attacked by a wet paper bag.

Others have gone in much harder. US podcaster and commentator Michael Knowles tells a Fox News panel that Thunberg is a 'mentally ill Swedish child who is being exploited by her parents'. 'I have never seen a girl so young and with so many mental disorders treated by so many adults as a guru,' seethes Murdoch columnist Andrew Bolt in one of a series of tabloid hit pieces.

Some of this horrific provocation is just for hate-clicks; you'll still see the ads even if it was disgust that brought you to the *Herald Sun*'s trashfire of a site. But some of it is genuine alarm. Thunberg at the epicentre of a mass movement of future voters, workers and leaders is simply beyond the ability of these people to parse. The only way she makes sense is if she is exploited and mentally ill. But they all recognise the danger this movement poses to their fragile world. 'Tase and arrest her,' suggests US blogger Stephen Miller.

Something deeper is in motion here, and perhaps that's what has them so rattled. The coin-doubling parasite has a very narrow rhetorical range, which is partly what gives it power. Adults with jobs and resources can be derided as latte drinkers, hypocrites, elites. Adults without jobs and resources are designated as hippies, bludgers, anarchists and ferals. But attacking children on your TV panel show just makes you look like a malignant bully; it's only a persuasive line of argument for online bot swarms and other malignant bullies. So although it may sound compelling to Bolt and Miller, it's tanking out here in the real world.

From lone striker to seven million strong. Runaway positive feedback, but for social movements.

'Their denial has gone on for far too long,' writes Izzy Raj-Sepping as the east coast burns. She's just been threatened with arrest at a demonstration outside the absentee prime minister's official residence. 'I'm tired, tired of the lies and misdirection. I'm tired of watching my future, my friends' and family's futures, all of our futures, burn before our very eyes.'

Izzy is thirteen years old. The placard she holds high as the police escort her and her father away from the front line reads, 'Look at what you've left us. Watch us fight it. Watch us win.'

The writing is on the wall, and it's in a child's handwriting. Momentarily, the brain parasite is at a loss.

This is not a protest. It is not a campaign. It is a rebellion. We are in active rebellion against our government. The social contract is broken, the governments aren't protecting us and it's down to us now.

Dr Gail Bradbrook, Extinction Rebellion

emergency

Two young people are lying across central Brisbane's busiest street, stretched out on a zebra crossing in the morning humidity. Hands chained together, encased in a steel lock-on pipe, glued to the road. They are refusing to move. Police are in attendance. Motorised traffic is at a standstill, backing up rapidly as morning peak hour funnels a tide of vehicles into a city with a protest clot in a key artery. Drivers fuming at the front of the queue at least get to see the message on the banner held by a handful of supporters: 'Business as Usual = Death'. On patches stitched into their clothing, the symbol of an angular hourglass in a circle.

On the far side of the world, Europe lies in the grip of a slow-moving heatwave. Hundreds of demonstrators, many of them students, occupy the Pont de Sully in central Paris. Mostly seated, linked arms, unmoving. Even under blowtorch skies, the mood is heady with defiance and transgression. And then black-shirted riot police stride into the knots of young people sitting on the bridge, attacking them with handheld chemical weapons, directing jets of teargas directly into their faces. Jumpy footage of the incident ricochets around the internet, setting out the stark terms of coming confrontations. On the flags flying behind this one-sided melee, an hourglass in a circle.

The hourglass symbol was designed by London artist ESP in 2011 as an open-source 'extinction symbol' conveying time running out on a finite earth. Seven years later, 1500 people assemble under the hourglass banner in London's Parliament Square to declare an extinction rebellion: 'a non-violent rebellion on behalf of life itself and against our criminally negligent government.' In a move that will become a signature of XR actions, immediately following the speeches a large number of people take to the road in front of Parliament Square and lock it down. Skirmishes, arrests, interviews, a blaze of social media posts. The fuse is lit.

Over the next fortnight, the movement steps up a rolling series of actions, culminating in mass civil disobedience in mid-November. Six thousand people swamp London's five major bridges, closing them to traffic. By now, actions are sparking elsewhere across the UK like embers fanning out ahead of a forest fire; jumping the Channel into Berlin, Copenhagen, across the Atlantic to New York City.

Extinction Rebellion's explicit intention is to spin up a positive feedback cycle of training, action, recruitment, training: a flywheel of rebellion. Borrowing from decades of movement experience, the organising model is an artful mix of structure and fluidity designed to invoke what US writer and community organiser Nicholas von Hoffman describes as 'the moment of the whirlwind'. In the movement handbook *This Is an Uprising*, Mark and Paul Engler explain that 'the defining attribute of a moment of the whirlwind is that it involves a dramatic public event or series of events that sets off a flurry of activity . . . this activity quickly spreads beyond the institutional control of any one organization. It inspires a rash of decentralized action, drawing in people previously unconnected to established movement groups.'

By some combination of planning, circumstance and fortune, now XR begins to take on the characteristics of a movement cascade. In April 2019 comes the surge: a vast ten-day carnival of defiance across central London, thousands of rebels holding down the city's most storied intersections. With authorities reeling, organisers use the blockaded intersections as temporary autonomous spaces to strike against oil company headquarters, the London Stock Exchange and major financial institutions. The whirlwind has arrived, bringing more than a thousand arrests.

As suddenly as they had arrived, they are gone. As they cheerfully clean up behind themselves, it suddenly becomes clear that this won't be an Occupy-style endurance test, but something more agile. In an early sign of the movement's strength, a week after the carnival dissolves, XR delegations are invited to meet with the mayor of London, the environment secretary and the shadow chancellor. By early May, the UK House of Commons has passed a resolution by the Labour opposition to declare a climate emergency, the first national legislature in the world to do so.

The motion is non-binding: it exists, thus far, as no more than a statement of intent on the Commons Hansard, a written testament to the power of collective organising. But it forces us to ask, in the spirit of being careful what we wish for, what the real-world declaration of a climate emergency might deliver.

The concept of a climate emergency has been on a slow burn within advocacy and movement circles for years. In 2007, during a scientific tour of Antarctica, then UN secretary-general Ban Ki-moon tells accompanying journalists: 'I need a political answer. This is an emergency, and for emergency situations we need emergency action.' In 2008, Australians David Spratt and Philip Sutton describe what this would look like in *Climate Code Red*. Under emergency conditions, governments would take direct control over key sectors of the economy, essential resources would be rationed, and industries would be focused and directed towards the singular goal of survival. These recommendations read in stark contrast to the denial and numbing incrementalism that have paralysed international climate negotiations for decades.

In response to determined local organisers, at the end of 2016 Darebin council in Melbourne's north becomes the first local government authority in the world to declare a climate emergency. A few months later, the council lays out detailed proposals for heavy cuts to carbon pollution within the city's catchment area, and a divestment plan to pull funds from entities invested in fossil energy. Other local councils follow: in ones and twos, then dozens, and then into the hundreds.

But demanding wartime measures at a national level carries risks that people living on the wrong side of unaccountable emergency powers understand intimately. Authoritarians throughout history have used the cover of crisis and emergency declarations to suppress opposition and suspend political checks and balances. There is nothing to guarantee that governments responding to threats of climate change won't use such powers for wearyingly predictable ends.

As Australian writer Jeff Sparrow points out, the declaration of a wartime emergency 'allowed governments to ban strikes, implement censorship, prosecute pacifists and do whatever else they deemed necessary to win the war. Is that what we want today?'

There's nothing hypothetical about the question. In September 2020 the Australian government introduced legislation making it easier to call in the military for the purposes – among other things – of 'policing the population under exaggerated stresses such as food and water security'. It's right there in the name: the *Defence Legislation Amendment (Enhancement of Defence Force Response to Emergencies) Bill 2020*.

Extinction Rebellion's call for a climate emergency sits embedded within the other demands: principally, for the establishment of citizens assemblies, which would represent a radical extension of democracy, rather than its curtailment. Insisting that these demands are indivisible, rather than allowing the rising urgency to be hijacked by authoritarians, might end up being the most significant challenge the movement faces as it scales. Down some of the darker timelines ahead of us, that hourglass flag is raised by white supremacists over border walls and loops of razor wire, and looking these possibilities in the face now might help us avoid them later. Skyler Simmons, writing for *Earth First!* website, is blunt: 'We have no choice but to be explicitly antifascist environmentalists. Knowing that the far-right is using the human collateral damage from ecological crises to whip up their racist base, there must be no ambiguity when it comes to our message of collective liberation.'

The whirlwind has touched down in Belmore Park, clock tower of Sydney's Central railway station rising through the treeline behind. Maybe five hundred of us; passionate speeches recalling Eora resistance and the blood already shed in defence of this ancient ground. We are so very far from Parliament Square in old London: here the rebellion is in the process of decolonising, remembering, adapting. Drums keeping time as we form up into a noisy procession; bright hourglass flags streaming in the breeze. Realising it's the first time I've marched under this symbol, feeling again an almost cellular sense of contact with thousands of friends and allies I'll never meet, raising this same defiant banner in every time zone. I can't remember feeling happier.

The police are on edge, sensing this is going to go off-script at some point. Halfway up Broadway, the signal goes out and the march transforms into a roadblock carnival, hundreds suddenly seated. Drummers pick up the tempo. From a covered flatbed truck just ahead, a small team is heaving at a huge pink water tank; before the police can react, it's out into the middle of the road with four people locked down inside it. From somewhere, a choir is raising its voice.

For a moment, Broadway belongs to the Extinction Rebellion. That's when I realise where we are. Immediately up ahead, the angular geometries of a high-rise building have been softened by a vertical alpine forest – a riot of runaway species well into the process of overgrowing the architecture. Someone has invited the planet back into the city. I'm momentarily reminded of that tiny wetland they made a short walk from Perth's main railway station. Like a seed lodged in the pavement, a narrow window opening into a different kind of future.

A firm gloved hand on the shoulder now, closing it again sharply.

intolerable dissent

'This government will tolerate dissent only while it remains ineffective.' Australian prime minister John Gorton's warning in 1969 to anti-apartheid campaigners has a timeless blend of menace and condescension. Fifty years later, the only thing that's changed is the elegance of the phrasing.

'Everyone has the right to conduct a peaceful protest, but the activities of some are not. Blocking roads is dangerous, reckless, irresponsible, selfish and stupid.' That's Annastacia Palaszczuk, premier of Queensland, in August 2019. On behalf of her coal and gas investors, she's announcing punitive new anti-protest laws in response to extinction rebels gluing themselves to a road in Brisbane. A 'peaceful protest' in the city square can be safely ignored, just how the investors like it. Gluing yourself to a street and bringing a city's central business district to a standstill cannot.

The basic dynamic here is a microcosm of 'contentious politics', a set of analytical tools developed by US political sociologists to explain why some social movements succeed and others fail. One of the leading scholars in the field, Sidney Tarrow, describes it like this: 'Contentious politics emerges when ordinary citizens, sometimes encouraged by leaders, perceive opportunities that lower the costs of collective action, reveal potential allies, show where elites and authorities are most vulnerable, and trigger social networks and collective identities into action around common themes.'

'Action' is the key word in this dense description. Contentious politics involves direct challenge to powerholders and deliberate attempts to shift the status quo. The political opportunities perceived by these extraordinary citizens were summarised by Charles Tilley – another big name in the field – like this: 'openness of the regime, coherence of its elite, stability of political alignments, availability of allies for potential actors, repression or facilitation, and pace of change'. Each of these six factors shapes the context of what's possible. Now tilt the political table with floods and firestorms to focus the minds of all involved.

The basic idea is clear: social movements exist in dynamic tension with the people and structures they're making claims on. We act, they react; we react in turn. A dance, like Joanna Macy's systems game. All sides have institutional and collective memories, which manifest as 'repertoires of contention', a phrase coined by Tilley in 1978.

'Particular groups have a particular history – and memory – of contention. Workers know how to strike because generations of workers struck before them; Parisians build barricades because barricades are inscribed in the history of Parisian contention; peasants seize the land carrying the symbols that their fathers and grandfathers used in the past', Tarrow writes.

Crucially, these repertoires are unstable, composed in a kind of shifting grammar of discontent and repression. The process is fundamentally adaptive: change can happen when people improvise and shake up the repertoire. Instead of holding a transient demonstration and then heading home, in 2011 the Occupy movement brings tents, digs in and begins prefiguring a post-capitalist society. The idea rebounds around the world, with states at a loss for what to do. Instead of getting a permit and marching around in a circle, rebellious climate campaigners lock down urban centres and make their actions impossible to ignore. Suddenly, they're everywhere, forcing politicians into awkward press conferences to threaten new kinds of repression. Students who know their future is on fire go on strike; the next thing you know there are seven million of them.

Novel actions outside the range of accepted practice, or old ideas in new contexts, sometimes open brief, beautiful moments of runaway possibility. Moments when we can see, for real, glimpses of the world that comes next. For the existing order, these moments are usually intolerable; they must be shut down, bought off, bargained with, smashed. The idea that things could be different is the most dangerous idea of all.

Sometimes they offer a concession so we feel like we've won. Sometimes they apply police violence so we feel like we've lost. Sometimes they wait us out or poison our relationships with bots and infiltrators until we lose cohesion and go home.

John Gorton is long gone. So is the formal regime of South African apartheid. Along with a broad-based, increasingly militant uprising in South Africa, something new entered the repertoire: cultural and sporting boycotts, trade sanctions, an arms embargo and a global divestment campaign. The tactics were bitterly contested by the regime, but they caught on, spread, took their place within the wider movement ecosystem.

Nelson Mandela was released from prison in 1990 as the regime began to come apart and seek a negotiated settlement. 'It always seems impossible until it's done,' he reminds us.

Among Tilley's extensive study of contentious politics through history, one understated phase jumps off the page: 'rising threats to collective survival tend to incite increases in collective action by well-connected groups, at least in the short run'.

Gorton and Palaszczuk are trying to tell us something: when they stop tolerating our dissent, it's because they fear what we're doing is working. Makes me wonder what other kinds of dissent they might find intolerable.

death / rebirth

We've reached one of the darkest chapters of the oldest book in the world: rock sequences from 252 million years ago, on the brink of the catastrophe that closes the Permian. There are no rebels here to block roads or go on strike, just a sombre reminder of how deadly extinction cascades can get.

Some interpretations of the story implicate an asteroid strike, ozone depletion, a volcanic winter or a catastrophic release of seabed methane, or all of them, tangled up in recondite climate feedbacks. Three extinction waves come hard, one after another. Coinciding with the sharp geological boundary dividing rocks of the Permian from those of Triassic age, one feature stands out. Seven million square kilometres of what will one day be Siberia are being inundated with flood basalts, the surface expression of magma plumes rising from the earth's deep interior. This is one of the largest volcanic provinces the world has ever seen. Over the course of two million years, an area nearly the size of Australia is burned back into the Hadean, a volcanic wasteland pouring billions of tonnes of carbon and sulphuric ash into the air. Atmospheric carbon dioxide spikes, perhaps tenfold in the quiet years of the late Permian. The oceans are turning acidic as they draw down this atmospheric carbon, but while this slow process unfolds the world wilts in the grip of an unbearable heatwave.

More than 90 per cent of all species are dying. In oceans overheated and starved of oxygen we farewell the last of the trilobites, their dominion having spanned an astonishing 269 million years. Corals are decimated; brachiopods and bivalves and bryozoans from the Cambrian dawn are almost completely wiped out. Acidic seas are laying waste to anything whose shells are made from calcium carbonate; seafloors are now thick graveyards of these tiny creatures. Oxygen starvation cuts down nearly everyone else, with the shallow continental margins hardest hit.

The damage on land is almost as bad as the collapse in the oceans. Seed ferns and pioneering conifer and cycad species are hammered, woodlands retreating into isolated pockets, fragmenting and vanishing. Amphibian lineages are crashing; two-thirds of all terrestrial vertebrate species will be lost. The hum and scuttle of arthropods is nearly silenced in the only known mass extinction of insects. The world is being emptied.

In rare sheltered refuges and cooler waters, survivors from the deeper past manage to cling to life as everything around them slowly falls apart. In the intertidal zones, bulletproof microconchid worms are clustered in batteries of armoured shells. Lingula bivalves are dug into abandoned shallow seafloors. On land, weedy lycophytes and a scrappy assemblage of hardy survivors are rallying: mosses and lichens from the Silurian, stress-tested arthropod families that refuse to die. Within and beneath them all, Luca's microbial granddaughters keep the ancient foundations of life in motion without pause.

For five million years, shattered and simplified ecosystems are rebuilt slowly by those who made it through the planet's near-death experience. It will take thirty million years for the world to recover anything like the diversity and ecosystem structure that was lost, but as we move deeper into the Triassic it seems that through unbearably long passage of time even savage ecological wounds can heal.

Roll the geological clock slowly forward with relief, as planetary temperatures begin to ease. The supercontinent of Pangaea is rifting east to west, with Gondwana dominating the southern hemisphere and Laurasia the north. Slow incursions of the Tethys Sea into the widening rift valley will eventually divide the terrestrial world in two, but for now the globe is still defined by this single landmass stretching pole to pole. Far from the moderating influence of the world ocean, the continental interior is mostly arid in the Triassic, with coastal ecosystems in slow recovery under a fearsome tropical monsoon. The icecaps of the mid-Carboniferous are just a memory now: temperate woodlands grow at the poles, and reptiles forage under the midnight sun.

About those reptiles. The handful of families that made it through the Permian catastrophe now set about taking over the world. Dog-sized *Lystrosaurus* is a tusked and beaked herbivore, first out of the gate and pleasantly surprised by the near total absence of predators in the shell-shocked aftermath of the Permian. Blink and these little friends are everywhere – they are by far the most abundant land vertebrates in the early Triassic. They begin to munch their way across the undivided continent, leaving fossils from Antarctica to South Africa to Siberia.

Where we find abundance, follow the opportunists. In a world dominated by slow-moving, burrowing herbivores, it's only a matter of time before fast-moving innovators on strict paleo diets appear to end the lystrosaurs' brief dominion. The archosaurs are the ones to watch; among them, some species of Rauisuchia will grow into fearsome apex predators four to six metres long. In the damplands, their relatives the phytosaurs streamline into long-snouted, muscular hunters, while aquatic ecosystems host equally uncompromising amphibious carnivores. Sometime in the late Triassic, the pterosaurs take flight, launching into the updrafts on great leathery wings. Out in the open ocean, a foretaste of the reptilian gigantism that's about to sweep the world: long-necked plesiosaurs and fish-like ichthyosaur predators have come full circle, their reptilian ancestors having returned to the oceans in the distant past. They swim amid a rich ensemble of ray-finned fishes and sharks diversifying out from the handful of species that made it through into the Triassic.

Not everything in this age will be toothy and terrifying, although ecosystems are being increasingly shaped by those that are. Pause in the shade of new kinds of cycad, and welcome the arrival of ancestral frogs into the world. Frogs! Wait until after dark to see who else might be about. *Trirachodon*, distant grandchildren of the fur-clad cynodonts we met in the twilight of the Permian. Venturing out only in the relative safety of the evening, by day these sleek creatures live communally in vaulted tunnel complexes that hint at emergent social organisation. They and their small insectivorous cousins subsist at the periphery of this archosaur-dominated age. There they will remain for many millions of years, crunching furtively on arthropods and trying to stay out of the way of the murderous reptiles slowly bulking up around them.

The sharp close of the Triassic period 201 million years ago is marked by another brutal extinction event, the fourth of the 'big five'. As with the end of the Permian, the fingerprints of volcanic flood basalts are all over the crime scene, this time in an igneous province more than eleven million square kilometres in extent that heralds the break-up of Pangaea. As with all the world's major extinction waves, the real causes are complex and contested, but the fallout is clear: marine reptiles are decimated, and major changes to terrestrial plant species accompany a rapid collapse of large amphibian lineages. Much of the archosaur diversity of the Triassic is snuffed out. Those who remain to see in the dawn of the Jurassic period seem absolutely pissed, and set about evolving into the most formidable creatures ever to walk the earth.

The slow dance of the continents moves to a new tempo now. Rifting is opening the Tethys seaway between east and west for the first time, breaking Pangea into two unequal pieces and allowing the verdant return of the rainforest to the continental interiors. The volcanic province that may have helped end the Triassic is opening into what will become the North Atlantic, sending Europe and North America their slow, separate ways. Within each of these landscapes, conifers come into their own, towering above lush tiers of tree ferns and cycads humming with insects.

Giants walk these forests. Sauropod herbivores the size of suspension bridges browse slowly through the wetlands. They are stalked by allosauroids and others like them: powerful killers hunting on their hind legs, smaller forearms equipped with lacerating claws, jaws like a vice. Wheeling pterosaurs own the skies, their distant relatives the plesiosaurs and ichthyosaurs still marauding freely in the oceans.

While the terrestrial dinosaurs mesmerise with the sheer audacity of their presence, many others are also making their way. Turtles quietly enter the fossil record, finding a niche in riverine ecosystems. Feathered avialans take to the air late in the Jurassic, dinosaur cries modulating into birdsong as continental drift slowly redraws the map. As we pass into the Cretaceous period 145 million years ago, global temperatures cool and snowpack returns to the polar regions. The break-up of the great southern land of Gondwana has begun, with the cores of South America, Africa, Australia and Antarctica slowly rifting and calving away from each other. On land, the dinosaurs continue their wearying arms race. Spiked and armoured herbivores face off against ever larger and more cunning predators, culminating in the monstrous tyrannosauroids of the late Cretaceous.

In the midst of this bloodshed and body armour, it seems passing curious that a change of greater consequence has been unfolding humbly in plain sight, with the entwined evolution of flowering plants and their attendant pollinators. They arise in the tropics and begin their long march into higher latitudes, diversifying and growing taller as they go. Oak and maple begin to crowd out conifers as the dominant canopy trees in tall forests. The hum of bees arises in a haze of pollen on the warm afternoon air; from somewhere, the scent of magnolia.

We are still deep in a greenhouse world, with high sea levels inundating the continental margins and hosting a riot of life in the shallow seas. On the eastern shores of the Tethys, a quicksilver flash of small fish shoaling in a shallow embayment. A coelacanth moves among them; unbroken memories of the Devonian. Delicate crustaceans observe the ebb and flow with twitching antennae.

And then, death takes them all, an algal bloom lacing the water with toxins. Buried in silence, out of reach of oxygen or the busywork of Luca's decomposers, they will lie here as soft rains of silt are pressed into limestone over the course of a hundred million years. Light won't touch them again until the moment their entombing strata are cracked open by a careful geologist's chisel, blocks set to rest in a steel rack like the pages of the oldest book in the world.

That's a story yet to be told. For another forty million years the dinosaurs will rule this age, armed to the teeth and doomed, while the continents recede from each other and life takes its own unique course on each island raft. The first ants are exploring the forest floor; millions of them somehow working as one. Snakes glide past their busy endeavours, and at night, wide-eyed placental mammals pause on the edge of their burrows to test the breeze. Above the canopy, a bright ocean of stars.

Somewhere out there, inconceivably far from this forest ringing with every kind of life, some orbital undertow has drawn a small island of orphaned stone onto a subtly different path. Brace yourself. Gravity will take it from here.

friday night in nagatacho

Tokyo, 2012. The sidewalks are so jammed it's difficult to move; stretched police lines holding the roads open through social convention alone as the crowds heave and flow. The humid August evening simmers with joy and rage, last of the light fading behind the pyramidal rooftop of the Parliament of Japan.

It's Friday night in Nagatacho, and two hundred thousand people have come.

In the aftermath of unthinkable disaster, the country's most powerful industry is on its knees. It has been more than a year since 3/11, the Great Tōhoku earthquake and tsunami that claimed more than nineteen thousand lives and wrecked the nuclear reactor complex at Fukushima Daiichi. Deep political ley lines are shifting even as the ruined reactors boil and smoulder into the Pacific. For the first time since the Tōkai plant started up in 1966, Japan's entire fleet of nuclear reactors stands idle. And now, demands by the industry to begin restarting them have brought this immense crowd to the gates of the parliament.

Something subliminal runs through the massed assembly and without premeditation we take the road, police lines dissolving in the surge. Anything seems possible in such a moment; the parliament surrounded now, an island in this euphoric ocean of banners and pennants. This is the culmination of eighteen months of organising, sit-ins, shareholder activism and deep institutional turmoil.

In a month's time, prime minister Yoshihiko Noda will declare a nuclear phaseout by 2030, with new renewable energy to make up the electricity shortfall. The proposal doesn't meet the demands of the demonstrators, but it still represents an unprecedented rupture in national energy policy. Then comes a harsh lesson in Japanese realpolitik: four months on from the demonstration, the investor blocs elect nationalist hardliner Shinzō Abe to the prime ministership. The nuclear industry has installed a crucial ally in its push to restart the nation's fleet of shuttered reactors.

Blink forward, then, to a frosty night in March 2018.

Drums echoing from somewhere, blending uneasily with the thump of an unseen helicopter. Tokyo at its most alienating: ponderous blocks of glass and steel sharply outlined against the fading sky. No familiar landmarks; low-resolution cut-and-paste towers across the whole field of view. A small knot of uniformed police stand at the far end of the avenue, so maybe I'm getting close. Check the phone. I'm a small blue dot edging across a grid that feels as though it's rendered in the same polygons as this cold quarter of town.

Here, at an intersection not far from the national parliament, the source of the racket. Forty or so people rugged up against the evening chill, ranged along a narrow kerb with banners and pennants. Drummers belt out a metronomic backing beat for the young man leading a call-and-response chant. What they lack in numbers, they make up for in volume and energy, but surely this can't be it. The three dozen people hemmed in behind plastic safety barriers are nearly outnumbered by a watchful detachment of police. Apart from the demonstrators themselves, no-one has come to hear the chant.

Momentarily wishing my broken Japanese extended further than buying beer and apologising for being in the way, I'm stepping along down the empty boulevard. More protesters are straggled in ones and twos under streetlights, hand-painted banners a jumble of kanji and trauma, smiles and thumbs up as I pass.

Thud of the helicopter, running lights blinking as it passes overhead. Rounding the corner, glimpsing the familiar outline of the national parliament building, recalling vivid memories of that night back in 2012. Tonight, columns of police vans and rows of white-gloved officers; further back, the hulking forms of riot vehicles. A restive crowd, ranks of tall yellow flags catching the breeze. A young woman stands astride a temporary stage before a bank of cameras on tripods, her amplified voice rolling across the assembly.

It's Friday night in Nagatacho, and a thousand people have come. They have come every Friday night for seven years since the giant waves overwhelmed the reactor buildings at Daiichi. The event is feisty but transient. Energies nearly smothered by the overwhelming police cordon and circling *uyoku dantai* ultranationalists in black vans, blasting the assembly with the Japanese national anthem. Between the frozen wind and intense police presence, I can't help feeling dismayed by the contrast with last time I was here.

When the activists pack it in later in the evening, there will be no visible trace of the gathering. The national government, the nuclear utility corporations that own whole towns, the TV stations: all of them are unified against these people. They have unlimited amounts of money and a cold institutional patience that is wearing everyone down. It feels so very familiar.

When thousands of us rallied under sky-blue flags to stop the billion-dollar freight highway through the wetlands, we succeeded. When we buried cars up to their axles in cement across the logging roads, we succeeded, mostly. But when thirty-six million of us tried to stop an avoidable war in Iraq, we failed totally, and more than a million people were killed.

If a demonstration is held in a city and no-one hears it, does it make a sound? Are we better off working for gradual reform or wholesale rebellion? Are there common patterns to simmering campaigns that suddenly explode into public consciousness, removing dictators and reshaping whole societies? Or are these events simply random, as stochastic and senseless as white noise?

Generations of historians have gone looking for orderly patterns in the bloody churn of long-term human behaviour, returning instead with tales of quasi-cycles and resonances unfolding amid endless surprises and unpredictability. Philosopher and essayist George Santayana's warning that 'those who cannot remember the past are condemned to repeat it' speaks to these cycles, but even people who well remember the past are sometimes blindsided by the abruptness of unexpected futures.

These questions are of enduring concern to historians and philosophers. They are also heavy with consequence for people trying to defuse a carbon bomb in the face of concentrated institutional power. The school strikers and rebels, the divestment movements, the global resistance networks and First Nations warriors holding the oldest of front lines: how will history read us? Are we the ones who stopped the freeway and the machines with tank-tracks and tungsten saws? Or are we the ones who tried, and failed, to prevent an avoidable war on the earth itself?

When Joanna taught us the systems game, she was doing it not just because it was entertaining but because it was potentially actionable. The systems people are with us not just because feedback loops and butterfly wings are interesting, but to see if they can help us guide decisions. After all, some of them have promised us theories of how regimes change; this kaleidoscope of collapse and renewal they call panarchy.

I leave Nagatacho via a subway station that feels like the emptiest place I've ever been in Tokyo. Let's get off these cold streets: somewhere in this endless, fascinating city, we'll find a warm place where we can understand these questions better. Or at the very least, be bewildered in a more interesting way.

sand pile

Warmth of a small dining bar not far from the owls of Ikebukuro, two narrow flights of stairs below street level. A cosy wooden booth; sound of running water from somewhere. Two bowls of hot miso soup; if you look closely, fluid overturn of miniature convection cells dissipating heat into the air.

Ready? Okay – close your eyes.

A grain of imaginary sand falls from nowhere, hits a sand pile directly in front of us, comes to rest. Another grain is falling, just behind it, and then another, and another.

Zoom in on the impact area so we can see exactly what's happening. Mostly, friction brings the impacting grains to a stop straightaway. Sometimes they dislodge another grain, or a few. As the pile grows, there are occasional small sand-slides, as if the falling grain had hit a patch of instability that we couldn't see. More specks keep falling, until the sand pile can't get any steeper. With the slope of the pile at this critical angle, it's impossible to predict whether the next infalling grain will roll to a stop without consequence, or set off an avalanche that reconfigures the whole pile. Or anything in between.

A sheet of imaginary graph paper will help here. Along the bottom axis, we'll keep track of how many grains shift with each impact: that's the 'size' axis. Along the left, we'll make a note of how often a shift of that size occurs – the 'frequency' axis.

Because they exist only in our imagination, we can roll the sand grains faster and faster. Drop a thousand grains, a million, and put a dot on the graph noting exactly how many other grains shift with each tiny impact.

What our graph will show is that small tumbles and sand-slides are much more frequent than big ones. It's going to look a bit like this: a large number of minor disturbances on the left, a declining frequency of larger sand-slides, and very occasionally, over on the right, a handful of cascades that escalate into full-blown avalanches.

Okay – big things happen less often than small things – that's not really a mystery. But we might be puzzled why the slope of the graph falls away so smoothly. There is no sign of a familiar 'bell curve' that would tell us the

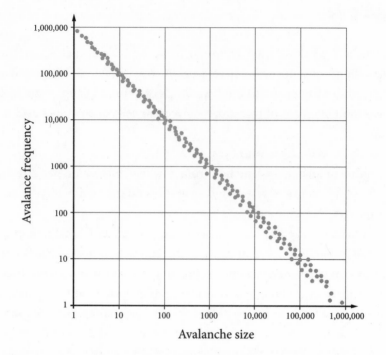

avalanches are clustering around a certain average size. If we were expecting a patternless zigzag of random white noise, that's not there either. Instead, the slope tells us that no matter what the impact of the last grain that hit, an avalanche twice the size is half as likely to happen.

Stop the falling grains for a moment: leave the next one suspended in space just before impact. There is no possible way of knowing how many grains it will dislodge when it hits, and yet this unpredictability seems to be nested somehow within a deeper order.

Imaginary sand piles first came to prominence in a scientific paper published in 1987 by Danish theoretical physicist Per Bak and his colleagues. It demonstrated a highly stylised instance of a relationship referred to as a 'power law': when a difference in one variable (size of the avalanche) implies a proportional difference in another (frequency of the avalanche). Their one-dimensional mathematical pile is an example of a system in a critical state, they proposed: 'As the pile is built up, the characteristic size of the largest avalanches grows, until at the critical point there are avalanches of all sizes up to the size of the system.'

'Critical state' is the state at which the sand pile can't get any steeper. With so many of the grains pressed together in chains and networks of instability, the whole pile could collapse on the next impact. It probably won't. But it could. In this and subsequent papers, the authors proposed that for any system perched on the edge of this kind of criticality, the intensity of the avalanches will be smoothly and predictably distributed through an enormous range of scales.

There are some subtle but important implications here.

First, that on the sand pile tiny tumbles of a handful of grains have the same causes as the epic landslides. The giants aren't freaks or outliers needing special explanation but an expected consequence of systems driven into this state of criticality. Second, if you know in advance that the model is in a state of self-organised criticality – and nothing else is happening to tilt the table – you'll only need to know a little of its history to be able to guess the frequency, and the size, of the really big events. You'll have no idea when they're coming exactly, but you'll know they're out there.

And third, events in systems such as this don't occur at random, but nor do they come in predictable cycles. They arise from somewhere in between and depend crucially on the entire history of the system in question. What happens next on the sand pile depends on everything that has happened before.

It's a big jump from mathematical abstractions to suggesting that any fine-grained system where tension builds up over time will display this behaviour. But over the last few decades, researchers went looking for the fingerprints of power laws in systems balanced at the critical state – and found them all over the place.

One study, which analysed long-run data on dangerous natural processes, concluded that 'three natural hazards – earthquakes, forest fires, and landslides – are complex phenomena that self-organize under a wide variety of conditions. In each case the frequency-area statistics are power law over a wide range of scales.'

It had been known for many years that the frequency and intensity of earthquakes bears out this relationship. It even has its own name: the Gutenberg–Richter law. Each increase on the old scale derived from this law – the Richter scale – represents a tenfold increase in earthquake size. For most active seismic zones, earthquakes become ten times less frequent with each increment on the scale. Real graphs of earthquake frequency and intensity – with important local variations – look pretty similar to the one on our imaginary graph paper. The distribution across orders of magnitude is fairly steady, from the billionfold tiny tremors that go unnoticed every day to a once-a-century Tōhoku catastrophe.

Pressed into contention by ponderous tectonic forces, earthquake zones appear to be self-organised at the critical state. This means that once an earthquake gets going, there is no way of predicting how big it will get. It depends on the entire history of the fault line, and the disposition of an essentially unknowable number of stress fractures and tensions that have evolved over time. No supercomputer on earth will ever be able to predict which tiny microquake will set off a neighbouring fracture, tremors proliferating outwards with increasing intensity as forces are triggered across a wider and wider area. But once it's rolling, the probability of the earthquake doubling in size is constant, no matter how large it already is.

In his elegant study of power-law relationships, *Ubiquity*, Mark Buchanan summarises the reason why generations of researchers searching for ways to predict earthquakes have come up empty-handed: 'An earthquake when it begins doesn't itself know how big it is going to be. And if the earthquake doesn't know, we aren't likely to know either.'

Wildfires, landslides and stress fractures on fault lines may be one thing, but do these relationships and properties extend into the human system? On reflection, it would be weird if they didn't. Look carefully enough, and the signature of power-law ratios can be found all around us. The frequency and magnitude of stock-market fluctuations. Income distribution. The popularity of web pages. The population distribution of the world's cities. It's right there in the title of Buchanan's book: *Ubiquity*. Per Bak's 1996 summary of a decade studying the phenomenon was just called *How Nature Works*, indicating the degree of significance that power laws and self-organised criticality had come to assume.

The proliferation of research and articles on the sudden manifestation of power laws everywhere – look, we even found one behind the couch! – sparked a rear-guard action by sceptics, including statisticians irritated at the sight of data being forced to fit foregone conclusions. In a blog post titled 'So you think you have a power law – Well isn't that special?' physicist and statistician Cosma Shalizi bursts the bubble on some of the loose claims being thrown about: 'Unfortunately, the detection and characterization of power laws is complicated by the large fluctuations that occur in the tail of the distribution – the part of the distribution representing large but rare events – and by the difficulty of identifying the range over which power-law behavior holds.' He is particularly critical of the tendency of some researchers to clip their data, omitting giant outliers that don't fit the picture.

Just as importantly, correlation is not the same as causality. One study into the frequency of violent events within insurgent conflicts warned that 'finding common statistical distributions (for example, power laws) in sociological data is not the same as understanding their origin'.

The map is not the territory, and lines on graph paper are rarely the safest guide to the world's messy contingencies. All the same, some maps are more accurate than others. Usually, when reality doesn't fit the model, she's trying to tell us something. Researchers studying the application of power laws to income distribution, stock-market fluctuations and industrial accidents kept finding outliers; giants at the extreme end of the spectrum that seemed much too large, breaking the smoothly proportional symmetry of the rest of the data. We won't see this behaviour on the imaginary sand pile, even if we drop a billion grains. But in systems undergoing certain kinds of stress, self-amplifying positive feedbacks can sometimes take over, turning big events into real giants. Past certain thresholds, 'extreme behaviors emerge due to an underlying mechanism that is fundamentally different from the mechanisms driving smaller changes. In this regime, dragon-kings occur as system-wide events representing the tendency of the system to globally synchronize'.

The staff in the izakaya are closing up shop. Up the stairs into dawn; Tokyo's majestic hush inhabited only by robotic-looking street sweepers and people like us who missed the last train home.

What does any of this mean for people trying to defuse a carbon bomb? If we go looking for power laws within social collisions, will we find them, and what will it mean if we do? And what the shit is a dragon king?

dragon kings

15:42 local time, March 11, 2011. The wave height at the Fukushima Daiichi nuclear power plant is 14 metres. A wall of water surges over the concrete seawall, inundating a reactor complex already severely compromised by the immense force of the Great Tōhoku earthquake. Debris-laden seawater cascades through the site and the back-up generators go down. Two of the operators are killed in the impact; the rest of them are on their own. They will have to manage the emergency without power for more than a week.

As designed, the operating reactors scrammed an hour earlier, shut down immediately on detection of the earthquake. Now heat is the enemy; with the reactor cooling systems unpowered, the decay heat of the fission reactions begins to melt the fuel assemblies. Zirconium in the fuel cladding reacts with the water cooking inside the pressure vessels, forming a build-up of explosive hydrogen gas. Horrifying and compelling, the images will shortly beam around the planet: the outer containment buildings of three out of the four reactors blown apart in sequential hydrogen explosions. In the three units operating at the time of the quake, molten nuclear fuel slumps to the floor of the pressure vessels and a plume of carcinogenic fission products begins to boil into the Pacific Ocean.

Within days, TEPCO – the plant's owner – proposes cutting its losses and abandoning the site. They have a point: their staff are suffering terrible radiation exposures as they improvise to keep the cores immersed in the seawater that churns out of the wrecked complex as fast as they can pump it in. Continued aftershocks threaten to ignite the huge bank of irradiated spent fuel perched in Unit 4. Prime minister Naoto Kan demands they stay on site and get the place back under control. He too has a point: if the utility pulls its staff out and lets the accident run its course, the exposed cores will burn through what remains of the containment structures, releasing uncontrolled amounts of radiation and forcing the abandonment of another nuclear plant further down the coast.

It is later revealed that against this possibility, senior officials have briefed the prime minister on the logistics of abandoning the northern half of Honshū island, including Greater Tokyo, population thirty million.

'It was a crucial moment when I wasn't sure whether Japan could continue to function as a state,' he told journalists in September 2011.

For decades, the nuclear industry around the world has declared its technology to be safe, backing the claim with detailed probabilistic safety assessment (PSA)[7] documents. The purpose of these painstaking and highly technical assessments, as the International Atomic Energy Agency puts it, is 'to determine all significant contributing factors to the radiation risks arising from a facility or activity, and to evaluate the extent to which the overall design is well balanced and meets probabilistic safety criteria where these have been defined'.

This is language designed to tranquilise rather than inform: as long ago as the year 2000, the Union of Concerned Scientists pointed out that PSA manuals are wormholed with breathtakingly naive assumptions. Plant operators will always comply with safety requirements. Plant ageing poses no risk to safety. Reactor pressure vessels are fail-proof. Such PSA documents are, in fact, a bullshit waste of paper: the confident risk curves they display bear no resemblance to the real-world operational history of the technology.

Five decades of operating experience show that accident frequencies and intensities at nuclear plants, measured either by cost or by radiation release, largely follow power-law distributions. This implies, as it does for other systems displaying these properties, that once a nuclear emergency is underway, the probability of it doubling in severity is constant, no matter how bad it already is. Research published in 2017 combined three different datasets documenting 216 nuclear accidents occurring between 1950 and 2014. The conclusion – a power law prevails across the whole time series, with one important caveat: the disasters at Three Mile Island, Chernobyl and Fukushima are off-scale, too damaging and expensive to be a good fit with the rest of the accident history. 'We . . . document a significant runaway disaster regime in both radiation release and cost data, which we associate with the "dragon-king" phenomenon,' the authors of the study write. Half a century of spills, fires, leaks, breakdowns and unforgivable contamination fit the profile of a technology balanced at the point

---

7   Sometimes abbreviated as probabilistic risk assessment (PRA).

of criticality. Three monstrous exceptions – dragon kings – lie out at the edge of probability, pulling plant operators, emergency service personnel and fleeing civilians into territories where there are no maps.

Three, so far. The study concludes with a cold prediction that won't be found in any industry PSA: 'there is a 50 per cent chance that (i) a Fukushima event (or larger) occurs in 62 years, and (ii) a TMI [Three Mile Island] event (or larger) occurs in 15 years.'

Whatever the nature of the energy transition that's unfolding around the globe, we have to do it without inviting another Fukushima.

And so they gather, every Friday night, in Nagatacho.

The enduring determination of Japanese organisers is a large part of the reason why the country's nuclear industry is still on its knees. While the nuclear powerbrokers contend with a catastrophe of their own making, the solar industry has stolen a march. In 2012, not long before the demonstration that brought that vast assembly to the gates of the parliament, the Japanese government introduced a feed-in tariff, compelling electricity companies to pay for electricity supplied by household or commercial solar power systems. It upended the century-old balance of power between energy producers and consumers. And now, combined with a national energy efficiency drive, solar farms and distributed solar-battery installations are eating their damaged competitor's lunch.

Because of the actions of the demonstrators and their allies around the country, all but nine of Japan's reactors still lie idle a decade after the nightmare of 3/11.

This movement has delayed plant restarts to such a degree that the world uranium price has collapsed, boosting the campaigns of people trying to protect lands far from here. Against daunting odds and the most powerful institutions in the country, it's working.

Here's something, then. In a purely physical system like a pile of sand or an earthquake, the tremors can only get so large; they are limited by the size of the pile or the geography of the fault zone. But in systems of considerably greater complexity, where some of the actors are learning and adapting through affordances of memory, perception and agency, the possibility of a new behaviour emerges. What the statisticians were charting in nuclear disasters and stock market convulsions – the dragon kings – they described as 'system-wide events representing the tendency of the system to globally synchronize'. A runaway change from one system state to another, as they put it; a change of regime. A regime change.

Enough about fault lines, then. We need to know whether these concepts have anything to tell us about picket lines.

strike wave

A concept so old it comes to us in a dead language: *divide et impera*. The original phrase is attributed to Phillip II of Macedon as he played Greek city-states off against one other in the fourth century BC. In ancient Greek, διαίρει καὶ βασίλευε; in English, divide and rule. A favoured tactic of emperors and dictators from Caesar to Bonaparte to Mao, it is also a staple of the modern workplace.

When workers organise to collectively withhold their labour while they negotiate with entities vastly more powerful than they are, it makes the news. Records are kept of the costs, duration, magnitude and extent of strike actions: in some cases, in great detail. Using exceptionally fine-grained records of strikes and strike waves from the US Bureau of Labor Statistics in the 1880s and the French Office du Travail in the 1890s, sociologists and historians have built a vivid picture of the dynamics of these class collisions.

'Transgressive contention occurs in waves. People suddenly shift from quiescence to defiance; they strike, sit in, demonstrate, or riot en masse; protest spreads across social networks and from place to place,' writes sociologist Michael Biggs in one such study. 'Positive feedback is implied by the metaphors employed by historically minded observers to describe the dynamics of large strike waves: metaphors of wildfire, avalanche, and epidemic . . . for strikes and strike waves alike, I find that the size distribution follows a power law spanning two or three orders of magnitude.'

Odd. Just like on the sand pile, the line on the graph is a smooth slope all the way from the smallest outbreak of industrial action through to strike waves involving thousands of people.

Positive feedback – we've seen this: in the school strike, in the Extinction Rebellion: the moment of the whirlwind where the flywheel spins up and up until the state pulls some negative feedback out of its repertoire to disrupt its rise. For every worker who decides that the best way to negotiate is collectively, the chances of more workers joining the strike goes up. With every visible public action and show of defiance, the chance that more will follow increases. Every organiser knows this, but there is still nothing quite like the rush of a campaign that suddenly gets traction, pulling in waves of new supporters, strengthening belief in the possibility of success and sending powerholders scrambling for a response.

On the sand pile, the tension is between gravity working to flatten the pile and friction between individual grains working to hold it up. On the fault line, the tension is between continent-sized blocks of terrain trying to move past each other. Neither of these systems is an adaptive learning structure, and so their tremors remain forever constrained to particular scales and behaviours. But in human societies, the pressure is built up through raw inequalities and injustice, class polarities of wealth and power. These are vastly higher-dimensional collisions, with whole repertoires of contention, perceiving, remembering, adapting and learning. Under certain kinds of synchrony, these systems are capable of wholesale transformations unavailable to simpler physical systems.

Researchers aggregating strikes, anti-government demonstrations and riots worldwide between 1919 and 2008 summarised this line of thinking: 'Civil unrest contagion occurs when social, economic, and political stress accumulate slowly, and is released spontaneously in the form of social unrest on short time scales to nearest and long range neighboring regions that are susceptible to social, economic, and political stress.'

In systems jammed into a state of self-organising criticality by slow build-up of pressure, every single action matters. 'What happens next depends directly on all of the events that have happened before,' as one study found. No act of resistance or creativity is too small to count, because every powerful movement is driven by cascades of small events and reactions. Even actions that appear to have failed or made no difference to the disposition of power still shape the ground for the cascades and landslides yet to come.

All this tells us is there is no upper limit on how outrageously successful a social movement can become. 'The probability of an (unfinished) event doubling in size is constant, no matter how large it has become already,' confirms Biggs.

It's as though the movement, when it begins, doesn't itself know how big it is going to be.

point of balance

A couple of the regular crew can't make it to the weekly organising meeting tonight, but our little campaign group has advertised it, so we've decided to go ahead. We've got an agreement with the manager at one of the rambling old local bars to use one of their rooms for planning meetings, so here I am, in dear Fremantle, with a beer and a notebook. Cheerful racket of music and conversation and flirting and football from the next room. I'm in my early thirties, naive as hell: I still believe we'll stop the invasion of Iraq. We could use some help, though. When the carrier battle group makes its stopover, the crew will take over the whole town. Most of the escort ships will come alongside in the harbour, but the nuclear-powered aircraft carrier will sit a few miles offshore, a 100,000-tonne steel signifier balanced on the horizon. We want to time our demonstration for maximum media coverage, just as the ships arrive: a noisy and highly visible reminder that some in this old port oppose their mission.

Soon we will be part of a worldwide mobilisation: hundreds of thousands in the streets, UN resolutions, whistleblowers sacrificing their careers to confirm that the whole rationale for this thing is bullshit. Surely they won't be so reckless as to launch an invasion.

It's half-past. Still just me here. Stare at the notebook, finish the beer. No-one's coming.

We make some phone calls. At the next meeting, there are seven of us. Anything from three to a dozen is good; *The Citizen's Handbook* says about nine is ideal, since that's the size of what sociologists call a 'primary group', in which trust and group identity can flourish.

Seven is enough to get started, but it won't stop the war, or overthrow the government, or defuse a carbon bomb. So how many do we need?

Political science professor Erica Chenoweth studied more than three hundred civil uprisings between 1900 and 2006, and reckons there's a number: 'Researchers used to say that no government could survive if five percent of its population mobilized against it. But our data reveal that the threshold is probably lower. In fact, no campaigns failed once they'd achieved the active and sustained participation of just 3.5 per cent of the population.'

Fine. We're not trying to overthrow a dictatorship, we just want to stop an invasion, so for the moment we'll ignore that Chenoweth's co-author is a strategic planner with the US State Department and just do the numbers. The population of Australia at the end of 2002 is about 19,700,000 people. Three and a half per cent of that is 689,500: so let's get them out onto the streets.

What happens next depends on whether or not we can shift a very particular point of balance. Whether we can trigger a cascade from seven to nearly seven hundred thousand depends on a rule that's almost appallingly simple. If everyone who joins us is able to persuade more than one other person to join, the movement will grow. Not the kind of sedate, linear growth that means there are fourteen people at the next meeting, and twenty-one the one after that. Runaway growth. And if everyone who joins us can persuade, on average, slightly *more* than one new person to join, we have a flywheel. A positive feedback loop that will rise out of the background noise until it reaches everyone – or until something significant happens to disrupt it and pull the critical number back below that threshold. People who fight epidemics for a living refer to this point of balance as the R_0 number – the basic reproduction number. Any pathogen with an R_0 number even a fraction above 1 will eventually escalate into a runaway pandemic unless interventions haul it back below that critical threshold.

Because this point of balance is the crucial determinant of whether a phenomenon will escalate or fade away, it's worth staying with it for a moment. If everyone in our little group of seven manages to persuade exactly one new person to come next week, there will be fourteen people at the next meeting. If each of the new seven feels inspired enough to persuade one new person in turn, then in week three there will be twenty-one attendees. Our R_0 number is exactly 1: roll this forward, and by the end of the year there will be 364 people in attendance. Okay. Won't stop the war, but at least there will be plenty of people at the debrief.

What happens if only six out of seven of us are able to persuade a newcomer to join us next week, and our recruitment holds steady at that rate? It means next week there will be thirteen in the room, which still feels like progress. But in weeks three and four, only five newcomers will join us each week, and only four will join us the week after that. In week twenty, one new member will join, bringing our total membership to fifty-three people. After that, nobody new turns up. Unless it figures out why it's not inspiring people, this little group will never grow again; one by one the regulars will probably stop coming until it's just some loser alone with a notebook.

Roll this thought experiment one last time. Now imagine that our recruitment is a touch more inspiring and the original seven of us manage to inspire eight new people to come to the next meeting. Now we are fifteen strong. If this rate of recruitment remains steady, next week there will be twenty-four of us, then thirty-five, then forty-seven. The growth curve is inflecting ever so slightly upwards; in fact, our membership is doubling roughly once every five weeks. By the end of the year, we'll need a stadium, because there will be 51,021 of us. By week 72, we will have passed the 3.5 per cent mark; by week 142, our movement will be larger than the number of people on earth.

The difference between a movement that plateaus and one that roars into mass consciousness depends entirely on whether each new recruit is empowered to inspire more than one new member.

Of course, social movements are far more volatile and interesting than these smooth abstractions, principally because we don't exist as isolated social particles waiting to be invited to meetings – we're embedded in complex social networks with highly variable access to power and information. But from school strikers to extinction rebels, the #MeToo phenomenon to the Black Lives Matter uprising, this is how runaway social earthquakes send tremors into institutions of power.

We're lifting this thing against the drag of hard and soft repression, and against ordinary social inertia that acts to dampen what we're trying to do. Absent a direct and personal threat, most people will stay at home. For those who do join the cascade, states are supremely adept at tracking these positive feedback loops and puncturing or diverting them.

And there, in that contention and puncturing, we glimpse the signature form of the power-law distribution.

Put five sand-pile graphs on the table side by side. Earthquake frequencies on Japan's Pacific Coast; forest fire outbreaks in New South Wales; influenza epidemics in Europe; industrial disputes in nineteenth-century Chicago; and global civil society uprisings over a ninety-year period. Close your eyes while we shuffle them. Okay: in all five cases, you'll see a lot of small events, a few medium-sized ones, a handful of big ones and, rarely, real giants. Amid all the disorder, a freakishly smooth power-law distribution of frequency and magnitude. It's impossible to tell which graph is which.

Why? The simplest answer – 'because big things happen less often than small things' – doesn't explain why the distribution is so smooth, nor why it looks so similar across such widely different domains. The fault line is a purely physical system. The forest fire is a complex interplay of physical, ecological and institutional processes. The epidemic spans biological, social and biomedical domains. The strikes and uprisings are political and class collisions involving thousands of human beings. Three of these systems – the epidemics, strikes and uprisings – are adaptive; the players learn from previous episodes and bring those memories to bear when the next ones arise.

On closer reading, all five phenomena have something in common. They are all slowly driven complex systems forced into contention. Pressure – whether seismic pressure, or fuel load in the forest, or resentment at injustice – slowly builds, and it has to go somewhere. Mostly it releases in small zigzags – a spot fire that goes out, a handful of people with the sneezes, a meeting that only one person attends. But a proposal to start a pointless and catastrophic war will pressurise a social system. Power structures laced with sexual violence and predation will pressurise a social system. Captive states wilfully triggering a for-profit mass-extinction will pressurise a social system.

How this pressure gets bottled up is dependent on the unique local context – the whole history of everything that has happened up to that moment. How this energy is transmitted, released, concentrated or co-opted depends sensitively on the structure of the network that's doing the transmitting. And because these structures are being pressured towards the critical state, tiny actions can have cascading consequences: a sand grain, a dropped match, a high-school student striking on the steps of the Swedish parliament.

A thousand people join us in the harbour on the morning the battle group arrives. We get good television coverage, donations, some fierce and fired-up new members. We're emboldened. I feel like the next thing we pull off is going to be bigger again. The flywheel is spinning. We are now in the midst of the largest civil society uprising on earth.

Two months later, cruise missiles begin slamming into night-time Baghdad. Columns of armoured vehicles roll down empty desert highways; serious-looking men safe in television studios tell us how well it's going. Some families don't get to watch the bombardment on television; they're under it, trying to survive until morning. We never did get to our 3.5 per cent, and so we'll never know if it would have been enough. The way they chose to collapse our momentum was by committing an unspeakably vast and unpunished war crime.

It felt like shouting through a megaphone at a wall of mirrored glass. Every whistleblower and insider leak told us the internal power structures were unstable, restive, divided internally. But the centre held, and so the cruise missiles rained down. Those on the other side of the glass were sufficiently unmoved. The only people jailed for this crime thus far are the handful of whistleblowers and publishers who broke cover and told the truth.

'Numbers may matter, but they are insufficient to guarantee success,' write Chenoweth and Stephan. 'This is because the quality of the participation – including the diversity of the resistance participants, strategic and tactical choices made by the opposition, and its ability to adapt and innovate – may be as important as the quantity of participants.'

So on the subject of the for-profit mass extinction: yes, we'll be needing numbers. But numbers are not enough.

Them old people used to look after it, that's the main thing, they've gotta listen to the elders. Go to your elders, *tjilpi tjuta* we call them, old people.

EMILY MUNYUNGKA AUSTIN,
OF THE KUPA PITI KUNGKA TJUTA

campfire

Crackling campfire in an old steel drum; conversation and laughter that will ebb and flow while the stars turn far above. The old people in camp chairs with mugs of tea, holding not just the memory of the twenty years we're celebrating tonight, but the whole history of this thing right back to the beginning. Tobacco passed hand to hand with story, and laughter, and loss. A couple of empty chairs; imagining them occupied by the ones we miss from campfires past.

I adore these people. Uncle is stirring at the fire with a stick and recalling the time they retrieved a coat of arms featuring their stolen emu and kangaroo from the Old Parliament House portico, prising it off with a crowbar and delivering it to the Tent Embassy. I don't think they have any idea how much they've taught me around circles like this. Thinking about what it's going to take to break the political grip of entrenched corporate power always brings me back here, because that's what these people have been forced to do, over and over again.

In the west, Robert Eggington and the Nyoongah warriors from Dumbartung have a saying: 'may your campfires burn forever'. Kids darting in and out of the circle, their earliest memories forming up around this constellation of fires in different landscapes, different campaigns, different nations.

'This organisation is not colour-based, it's not gender-based, it's based on the future for our unborn grandchildren.' That's Mitch, from a press conference back in 2014. She has a manner of speaking that makes you stop whatever you're doing so you can listen. 'We've beaten the government in Western Australia, South Australia and four sites in the Northern Territory. This little band of warriors has beaten the federal government as well as state governments and the Territory government. They didn't do it with selfish intentions, they didn't do it for themselves, they did it for the future.'

Once you'd call a fluke. Twice could still be good luck. But this extended family is starting to lose track of how much harm and destruction it has seen off. Radioactive waste dumps, domestic and international, from the Barkly to the Flinders Ranges. Persistent and increasingly shrill gambits for new Fukushimas. Uranium mines from Arkaroola to the Gulf Country to the goldfields. The background radiation to this whole story is the time the colonisers bombed them off their lands with actual nuclear weapons. The Commonwealth government, with unlimited access to broadcast networks, lawyers, cops. Multinational mining corporations with eleven-digit market capitalisation. Footloose junior explorers awash with careless investors' cash. Again and again, the most powerful entities in the country have trespassed on these peoples' traditional lands, seeking to poison and dump, extract and destroy. More often than the odds should favour, they end up retreating in humiliation. I would never, ever bet against these people.

Flashback to 1996: the spark that lights this network into existence comes when the incoming conservative government lifts the partial ban on uranium mining and begins aggressively facilitating a land rush, just as the world uranium price is surging. The sharp end of this invasive wedge of hi-vis and helipads is aimed at one of the world's largest remaining high-grade orebodies at a place called Jabiluka, on Mirarr country in Kakadu National Park. In 1997, a delegation of Mirarr and their representative body's firebrand CEO, Jacqui Katona, travel to Alice Springs to meet with affected communities and campaign groups from all over the country, to plan a way forward. The Alliance Against Uranium is born: a raggedy but robust accord of black, red and green, with confrontation at Jabiluka as the first item of business.

Now Jabiluka Action Groups begin forming around the country – rallies, concerts, office occupations, a community feeling its way towards a full-scale movement cascade. I am swept up in it, starstruck to be learning this craft from people like Jo Vallentine and Robin Chapple. Within a year, thousands of people are on their way to an improvised blockade camp a few kilometres from the mineral lease in Kakadu. In May 1998, Mirarr senior Traditional Owner Yvonne Margarula is arrested for trespassing on ground her ancestors have held for more than sixty-five thousand years.

This is the whirlwind that has picked up an unhappy, mostly out-of-work graphic designer and dropped him here, on a bush track leading out to a handmade village on this warm Kakadu evening. On my arrival, they've given me a passport that is both invitation and warning. The passport says you're on Country now; you always have been, but here you'll be invited to think about what that actually means. Screw up and you can hop on the next coach back down south. For the first time in my life, I glimpse what it might feel like to be at home in this country.

For eight months the camp stands at the fulcrum of a bruising collision between the coin-doubling game and the oldest system of law in the world. Half an hour down the road, the Ranger uranium mine has been slowly gouging immense terraced voids into the landscape since its coercive imposition in 1981. This malignant fenced-off moonscape of rock dumps and radioactive tailings dams is the principal reason Mirarr have tried to jam a spanner into Jabiluka. Now the clock is running down on this ageing monster. Without access to the Jabiluka orebody, the Ranger mill will begin to starve by about 2017. Two monsters, one spanner.

The campaign now reaches from the gates of the mineral lease to the World Heritage Committee in Paris, from sit-ins to Senate inquiries, lawyers to lock-on pipes. On some days, a thirty-foot tripod hung with flags and pennants is the tallest thing in camp; I've drifted over to see what it's for. An agile young woman is teaching others how to haul themselves into the apex of this formidable-looking structure; with these things you can block a road or a construction site for hours or days if you know what you're doing. In the cool of the evening, this place is something else: up to five hundred people prefiguring a revolution that seems so tangibly close. On the edge of camp at two in the morning, silhouettes move against showers of falling sparks, welded constructions and obstructions taking shape in a corrugated iron workshop that nobody talks about.

The campaign has hit critical mass. Dave Sweeney has spent thirty years working on these campaigns, twenty of them as the Australian Conservation Foundation's nuclear campaigns coordinator. I ask what he thinks the secret is. 'There's a bit of craft, there's a bit of leverage, there's a bit of pressure, and there's a bit of magic,' he observes. 'And things always look impossible just before they become self-evident.'

There will be more than five hundred arrests at actions ranging from tactical monkeywrenching to roadblocks to mass trespass. By the onset of the wet season, with Jabiluka by a wide margin the most prominent campaign in the country, the focus shifts to driving the spanner into the project's delicate financing and supply chains, working the World Heritage process and dialling up the political temperature by mainstreaming the protection of Kakadu. The blockade is dissolved over the course of a couple of weeks, its tensions and triumphs passing into folklore for the campfires to come.

For Mirarr, the campaign is hitting its most critical phase. A corporate takeover has delivered this conflict into the arms of Rio Tinto, bringing unwanted intrusions into their AGMs and risk advisories. A clause buried in the Ranger agreement says Jabiluka ore can't be milled there without Mirarr consent: if Rio wants Jabiluka, it's going to have to spend hundreds of millions of dollars on a new mill. Yvonne stares them down, and the company finally blinks. In 2005, Rio signs an agreement preventing any future development of Jabiluka without Mirarr signatures. Stalemate, with time now on Yvonne's side: the impossible slowly becoming self-evident.

'We have won many friends and our supporters are strong and stand with us,' Yvonne says. 'We have travelled a long road . . . We will continue to resist more mining on Mirarr country. We have no choice – this is our land and our life, we can never leave, we must protect it.' With the threat of Jabiluka receding, thoughts turn to the possibilities of life beyond mining.

While the spotlight is on Kakadu, the land rush across the rest of the country is hitting the wall. The uranium bonanza turns out to be a halluci-nation: two small, poisonous in-situ leach mines are forced into operation at Beverley and Honeymoon on Adnyamathanha land in northeast-ern South Australia; otherwise, the industry is turning into a bottomless money suck. The gargantuan open-cut expansion of the Olympic Dam copper/uranium mine at Roxby Downs gets quietly cancelled in favour of less ambitious underground options, maybe. A surreal disconnect has opened up between the shiny PowerPoint slides at numbingly dull industry conferences and the defiant reality on the ground. The social licence to operate has taken a battering, and even with the world uranium price spiking to record highs, the industry hits fierce opposition everywhere it turns. A change of government in Western Australia sparks another delusional land rush, and a new generation of campaigners are forced onto the front line or step up in support. Yeelirrie, the site of Western Australia's largest deposit, means 'death' in the old language. A succession of companies has been trying unsuccessfully to violate this place for nearly fifty years. The industry is terminal; it just doesn't seem to know it yet.

In 2005, the federal government opens another front, targeting three sites in the Northern Territory for a national radioactive waste dump. This is the most hazardous industrial waste the Anthropocene knows how to produce. Apparently it's safe enough to be left in a shed on Mitch's ancestral Country, but not safe enough to stay where it is under armed guard in 'Australia's centre of nuclear excellence' on the outskirts of Sydney. A year later, the feds are back with a fourth suggested site: a cattle station north of Tennant Creek called Muckaty.

The Alliance Against Uranium marks its tenth year, pivots to combating the waste dump – with a name change to the Australian Nuclear Free Alliance (ANFA) and a new lease of energy. This fight brings the Kupa Piti Kungka Tjuta out of retirement: a posse of formidable old ladies who drove the dump's earlier South Australian incarnation back onto Canberra's drawing boards in the late 1990s. Now they've arrived around the campfire to help orient the Territorians to their new reality. Together they set out on an eight-year campaign to push the dump dominos over one by one. Prime ministers come and go; industry ministers indistinguishable from industry lobbyists selling dreams of prosperity built on a bullshit mirage. In 2014, lawyers acting for the Muckaty Traditional Owners are closing in on a win in the Federal Court when suddenly it's over; the government caves and these powerful desert women can finally rest.

The press conferences and the demonstrations and public meetings happen out in the open. The bitterness of divided families and chequebook colonialism happens out of sight; the consent by attrition, the exhaustion, the funerals. There is nothing glamorous about these unsought conflicts, the endless meetings and weeks away from home and family.

Tonight, around this campfire with sparks twirling upwards into the stars, I can feel the edge of everything this work has cost them; the weight of twenty years fighting repetitive acts of deadening stupidity amid all the other Interventions they've been forced to contend with.

The Honeymoon mine is long since closed; a Beverley extension is stumbling toward expiry. People have nearly forgotten the Pangea waste dump campaign ever happened. Jabiluka is finished, and Ranger starved without it. While Rio Tinto draws up a budget for the ten-thousand-year obligation of tailings isolation and mine rehabilitation, Mirarr are now well into the process of master-planning the township of Jabiru as a cultural hub and regional services centre. 'We look forward to welcoming more people to Jabiru and Kakadu to share our country and cultural heritage,' says Mirarr Traditional Owner Simon Nabanardi. 'As the town changes, we hope Jabiru will be recognised around the world as a significant Australian cultural destination, a place where learning about living culture is accessible in a meaningful way.'

The Santhal Adivasi have said it. Rosetânia Ferreira and the downstream communities on the Doce River in Brazil have said it. Yvonne has said it. *We have no choice – this is our land and our life.* These are the people grounded enough to know there is nowhere else to go. The movements they inspire function like ecosystems: decentralised, diverse, powerfully resilient. I know I'll never find anything that explains their improbable effectiveness in any movement textbook, but something about resistance grounded in the original law of the land lends this work an almost geological immovability.

'Not only is there Aboriginal and non-Aboriginal people, we've got churches, we've got unions, we've got a whole lot of organisations standing up with us to say this is wrong and it will not happen,' says Mitch. Organisations anchored by the oldest living culture on the planet, somewhere between craft, leverage, pressure and magic. Bet against these people if you want, but you're likely to end up one of Uncle's punchlines around a constellation of campfires that I'm certain now will burn forever.

after chicxulub

Rest on this steep, shady riverbank for a moment. We're not far from the coastline of a warm inland sea that has gently inundated the future United States. Appalachia lies far to the east; this place, Laramidia, enfolds a quiet river in what will one day be North Dakota. Freshwater sturgeon, the long-lived descendants of streamlined Triassic forebears, are circling close to shore. It is the last day of the Cretaceous period, sixty-six million years ago.

Look to the south at exactly the right moment to see the sun catch an infalling shard. It is moving impossibly quickly. A block of stone or dirty ice half the size of Manhattan slams into the upper atmosphere at 72,000 kilometres an hour. A fraction of a second later it blasts a crater 180 kilometres wide into what will become the Gulf of Mexico, far over the horizon.

An immense front of pulverised rock is hurled into the stratosphere, some of it moving fast enough to be thrown into orbit. A shroud swallows the sun, sending the world into twilight just as the first shockwaves from the earthquake arrive. Standing waves ten metres high arise out in the seaway, sending walls of water surging upriver. Whole ecosystems are scoured and smashed up on the riverbank, marine ammonites and riparian vegetation bulldozed into the quiet world of the sturgeon without warning. The air seethes with an alien rain of tiny glass spherules melted in the heat of impact. Everything in sight is dead. A blizzard of shocked quartz and heavier rubble begins to shower the wreckage; later will come a fine haze of iridium and exotic elements from deep space, falling out with the dusty aftermath of this ruinous collision.

One of the great ages of the earth is ended. The debris cloud has been injected into the upper atmosphere with ash from continental firestorms, far above the rain belts that would otherwise wash it out. Photosynthesis collapses under a decades-long impact winter. Worldwide, the complex food webs and ecosystems making up the richness of the Cretaceous are shattered. The marine reptiles and soaring pterosaur lineages are finished. Terrestrial dinosaurs are wiped out save for a handful of ground-dwelling bird species.

Silence. A fibrous army of fungal decomposers work through the long night, dissolving the wreckage of whole forests. In the deep ocean and in places far from the devastation, ecological refugia hold their precious cargo close once again. Days will come when the sun makes its slow return, glowing red through the high-altitude haze. In these aftermath years, the world briefly belongs again to the ferns; low-light adapted and growing out from tiny armoured spores to soften broken landscapes. Mosses and molluscs and arthropods, seasoned and unstoppable, emerge from shelter into a world changed forever.

We have arrived, after a journey of nearly four billion years, in the dawning warmth of the Paleocene epoch. The thunderous, fanged nightmares that ruled the past are gone, and ecological fortune awaits those who remain. Look who has inherited the earth: frogs, rodents, ground-dwelling birds, adorable turtles, small apologetic reptiles of the emphatically non-dinosaur variety. Mammals – the humble trash of the Cretaceous – and all the other veterans of planetary catastrophes fast and slow.

Now, there is a new world to be made. Flowering plants and their propagators herald the change to come, overgrowing the endless ferns into newly structured ecosystems that begin to look tantalisingly familiar. They bring a rich banquet of pollen, seeds and fruits to the table, enlisting the whole world in their reproduction and dispersal strategies.

Day upon day, night upon night, we traverse an immensity of long, quiet years. The great wound of the Chicxulub crater softens and smooths over in time, filling in with marine sediments as the world turns and gradually recomposes. Island continents are drifting into new configurations: Gondwanaland is no more. Africa is slowly turning, coasting northward towards Europe, narrowing the Tethys Sea. India is well into its epic journey towards South Asia; Australia and Antarctica are still holding together, their cargoes of unique creatures soon bound for strikingly different fates. The Americas form a hemispheric archipelago, huge islands converging, inland seas in retreat. The poles are ice-free and sea levels are high in this humid greenhouse world, reef communities rebuilding as the horror of the impact winter recedes into geological memory.

Pause, at the dawn of the Eocene era, to see what the survivors of Chicxulub have created through all the uncounted moments that make up ten million years. Hot, like a sauna: a planet of forests. Vast stands of conifers grow in the high Arctic; Antarctica is fringed with verdant woodlands, and the tropics are alive with unmapped tracts of humid rainforest.

The planet is running a high fever: a weird temperature spike that may be correlated with a flare-up of volcanic rifting in the North Atlantic. East Greenland and Western Europe are tearing slowly apart, opening the Northeast Atlantic seaway. The rifting dumps huge volumes of invisible carbon dioxide into the air, piling an extra thermal blanket onto a world already warmer than at any time since the Permian extinction. Carbon dioxide levels in the air will more than double during the spike, possibly triggering the runaway release of buried seabed methane. Global temperatures jump between five and nine degrees. A cascade of climate changes and realignments follow; vast swathes of single-celled foraminifera living on shallow seafloors are wiped out, and widespread turnover of marine species follows the rapid acidifying of the oceans. In the far distant future, this hothouse world will be dubbed the Palaeocene–Eocene Thermal Maximum. It will take more than a hundred thousand years for the planet's forests and oceanic photosynthesisers to inhale this sudden carbon surge, but while this is unfolding, something of quiet significance has been happening under the endless canopy.

The humble trash are making their move. The mammals survived the long summer of the dinosaurs through stealth and smarts and fearsome attrition. Dodged the Chicxulub bullet through dumb luck and a diet of insects in the dark. And they are done with it. Rodents head for the hills, diversifying as they go. Eocene fossil strata contain the earliest forms of *Eohippus*, the dawn horse, and their cousins, dwarf rhinoceroses and tapirs. Well met, ancestral sheep and deer and cows, miniature great-grandparents of the elephant, and the first bats. Some of these gentle herbivores are stalked by *Miacis*, a fleet-footed carnivore the size of a weasel who may be the common ancestor of all the felines and canines and, eventually, Sirius. Some creatures have even returned to the timeless ocean, with the founding of cetacean and sirenian lineages that will give rise to manatees, dolphins and whales.

These foundational mammals don't have the world to themselves: giant snakes and hooved crocodiles hunt in these jungles. Flightless birds have returned to the apex of some food chains, dinosaur cousins forever keeping watch. A little off-brand, but already wonderful, penguins roost on the southern margins of what was once Gondwanaland.

So, this one would be easy to miss. She's small, weighing only a few kilograms, arboreal. Probably cute as hell, like a tarsier, with big eyes and clever hands; tail curled around a tree branch while she checks us out. A primate, new into the world. Moving along the branch to keep pace with us; agile, and curious, and pregnant.

> Six degrees of separation between us and everyone
> else on this planet. The President of the United States,
> a gondolier in Venice, just fill in the names. I find it
> extremely comforting that we're so close. I also find it
> like Chinese water torture, that we're so close because
> you have to find the right six people to make the right
> connection.

OUISA KITTRIDGE, SIX DEGREES OF SEPARATION

small worlds

The graph paper is limitless, horizon to hazy horizon under a blank sky. We're not graphing sand grains today, but ourselves, which is why we're standing on this grid rather than looking down at it.

Populate the grid with everyone you know. I'm imagining myself here, now, with a line drawn to my family and my closest friends. Everyone here has a cat's cradle of lines drawn between them too. Those close to me are fairly tightly woven together, because we've all been travelling in the same social network for years – it's like a small village, where most of the people I'm close to also know each other.

Some of them in turn are linked to people I've never met, people further afield. Two degrees of separation away, as the saying goes. Each of them, ranged out in the far distance, linked to more people, and now, because our piece of graph paper is very large, feel free to imagine all of us out here; the whole world's population, linked by lines of association. It feels like a higher-dimensional version of Joanna Macy's systems game, but instead of being constrained to only two influences in this strange dance, we're woven into dozens, hundreds.

It has long been reckoned that each of us only has the capacity to maintain about a hundred and fifty social relationships: the so-called 'Dunbar number', named after the British anthropologist who first did the maths. Very roughly, that's five close family members, another ten close friends, thirty-five people we know pretty well, and another hundred or so more distant friends. And then a penumbra of fainter links; maybe a few hundred associates, people you've lost touch with, can just recall from a party years ago. These numbers have held approximately true from Neolithic village life to a more recent study of mobile phone records.

The proposition is that this immense social network, heading north of eight billion people, is only about six links in diameter. That's the theory: that each of us is linked to every other individual on Planet Earth by no more than six associations – not just you and me, but everyone.

The secret to this astonishing connectivity isn't in our immediate ties to family and friends. If the whole world were just a collection of close-knit villages, the social distance between people on opposite sides of the world would be huge – millions of degrees of separation. Simply wiring up the whole planet at random would give you very short social distances from anyone to anyone,[8] but would not remotely resemble real social networks.

The real-world six-degrees magic lies in the combination of social clustering and the much weaker associations and distant friendships with people ranged much further across the network – people I might only have met a few times, but who connect me with other villages, and all their connections in turn. This so-called 'small world' network effect arises from these weak ties linking very different social networks together, ultimately bringing everyone alive within six friendly hugs of everyone else.

Nodes and edges, strong ties and weak, drawn on an infinitely large grid. The technical term for this kind of thing is a sociogram. It is, without doubt, a cold and bloodless way to visualise the warmth and richness of human social interaction. There are no campfires here. Lines and nodes on graph paper can't even begin to capture the endless nuance of our shifting relationships as we move through life, yet they do appear to have their purposes. Facebook's Mark Zuckerberg introduced the notion of the 'social graph' to an industry audience back in 2007 as a simplified representation

---

8   If I know 150 random people, and each of them knows 150 random people, that's already 22,500 people at two degrees of separation. 3,375,000 people three degrees out. 506,250,000 at four degrees. Just under 76 billion people at five degrees – ten times the actual population of the world.

of how his platform sought to map and commodify human relationships. Police and intelligence agencies use similar graphs to build profiles of networks of interest. Despite – or because of – their simplicity, patterns emerge when everything else is stripped away, and some of these patterns have bearing on sharply political questions. Why do some social trends die out while others cascade into unstoppable movements? Why does repression sometimes collapse a social movement and sometimes enrage it? And how, exactly, has the 1-per-cent villager managed to structure his affairs in such a way as to hold dominion over so many others?

The modern study of networks didn't begin with people, but with questions quite at home on graph paper. In 1736, Swiss mathematician Leonhard Euler accidentally founded the discipline of graph theory while attempting to work out whether he could walk all seven bridges of the Prussian city of Königsberg without crossing any of them twice. As it turns out, you can't – who cares – but in reducing the topology of the city to a diagram of nodes representing islands and riverbanks, and lines representing bridges, Euler had eliminated everything except the bare minimum that mattered for the purposes of proving up an answer. In the two hundred and fifty years that followed, students of pure mathematics, engineering, chemistry, ecology, genetics and sociology would use similar tools of abstraction to resolve increasingly complex problems. The curious thing is the degree to which discoveries in one field were readily transferable to others.

The peculiar phenomenon of small world networks was formalised during the latter part of the twentieth century, and these scholars brought a political curiosity to their task. One of the foundational research papers – Mark Granovetter's 'The Strength of Weak Ties' – sought to put questions of network structure to work in establishing 'why some communities organise for common goals easily and effectively whereas others seem unable to mobilise resources, even against dire threats'.

In 1967, US psychologist Stanley Milgram decided to test some of these ideas with a series of experiments that have since passed into folklore.

Milgram sent packages to hundreds of random people in the US Midwest, asking them to forward the package on to a friend or acquaintance whom they thought would bring the package closer to a named stockbroker half-way across the continent in Boston, Massachusetts. As you'd imagine, most of the packages were never heard of again, but those that did arrive had passed through an average of only five pairs of hands before reaching their destination. Not only was the social distance between random pairs of two hundred million Americans vanishingly small, but individuals were able to navigate that distance collectively to solve the problem, despite each of them knowing no more than a few hundred people.

By the time sociologist Duncan Watts and mathematician Steven Strogatz had set out the 'collective dynamics of small-world networks' in 1998, the concept had already swerved way out of its lane. They built a computer model to unpack the maths behind the 'six degrees of Kevin Bacon' game, using the IMDB database. They showed the electrical grid of the western United States, and the nervous system of the tiny nematode worm *Caenorhabditis elegans*, to have been constructed or evolved into a small world configuration. Combine a high degree of clustering with a handful of long-distance interconnections, and you'll have a small world.

Networks of this type arise in so many different places that it's tempting to assign them a kind of ubiquity. Not simply nervous systems and power grids but also the physical architecture of the internet, links between web pages, ecological food webs and the relationships between different biochemicals in cellular metabolism. For our immediate purpose – to understand whether any of these odd symmetries are politically actionable – we need to step back and look at the fact that not all of these networks are created equal.

Here's the first thing: some nodes in these networks are more connected than others.

Studies of the internet's physical architecture during its explosive growth in the 1990s showed data traffic making its way from one 'side' of the net to the other via an average of only about four hops as it bounced from router to router. To keep pace with its blazing growth, engineers had built hubs of outsized importance through which torrents of this data were flowing. One such study demonstrated that the number of these hubs, and their degree of connectivity, follows our old friend the power-law distribution. For any given node in the network, a node with twice as many links will be roughly five times less common.

In his succinct traverse of the science of small world networks, *Nexus*, Mark Buchanan describes how this subtle combination of small world networks and power-law scaling occurs within the cellular metabolism of the ancestral *Escherichia coli* bacteria we met tumbling and running billions of years ago. A couple of specific molecules act as metabolic 'hubs', participating in hundreds of chemical reactions, while many thousands of other molecules get to participate in only a couple of reactions. 'No more than four reactions link any two molecules,' he notes, the signature of a small world. Food webs in natural ecosystems display the same properties: the 'distance' in influence between any two species in a given ecosystem is vanishingly short in this ecological small world, and a handful of species play perilously important keystone roles.

Now we're getting warmer. In human social networks some people have a great deal more influence than others. We all know people who play key roles in our social networks: people who seem to know everybody, or act as a centre of social gravity. (If you don't know someone like this, possibly you are that person?) Institutionally, it is self-evident that social influence is distributed asymmetrically. Politicians, celebrities, religious figures and media oligarchs exercise undue influence over large numbers of people, which we could choose to visualise on our graph paper as a vast fan of weak ties running only in one direction.

This brings us to the second degree to which not all networks are created equal: differing forms of network structure have an outsized impact on how information and influence is propagated, concentrated or curtailed.

While it's mathematically true that you're probably less than six degrees of separation from the president of the United States, that doesn't mean you're going to be able to get a meeting with them. The maths may be elegant, but the clustering realities of geography and class impose significant barriers to seamless access. Milgram put it like this in 1976: 'We should think of the two points as being not five persons apart but "five circles of acquaintances" apart – five "structures" apart. This helps to set it in its proper perspective.'

States and corporations seem very intent on mapping all of us into their high-resolution sociograms. So what happens when we flip the camera around and look back at them through the same lens?

The idea itself, even if it is not made visual,
is as much of a work of art as any finished product.

Sol LeWitt

interlocked

At first glance the huge maps exhibited in gallery spaces in Soho and Chelsea – narrative structures, the artist calls them – only hint at the gravity of their content. In the 1990s, New York writer and conceptual artist Mark Lombardi begins making immensely detailed network maps of how the 1-per-cent villager has structured his relationships. So take a glass of wine or fresh juice and wander the gallery on opening night. Survey these fluid diagrams that look like weather patterns, magnetic fields, ocean currents. On closer inspection, they resolve as meticulous illustrations of America's interpenetrated corporate and political elite, mafia figures, intelligence agencies, armed insurgencies.

Here are senior Reagan administration officials organising illegal weapons sales to Iran and using the proceeds to fund an armed coup in Nicaragua. There's nowhere to hide here; these graceful sociograms don't lie. Here's George W. Bush only two degrees of separation away from the bin Laden family, via Texas businessman James Bath, who represented Osama's half-brother Salem in multiple real estate and banking deals. Nothing untoward alleged, obviously. Another wine?

With the exception of family trees, most human social networks throughout history went undocumented. Corporate directorships are different. They carry legal liabilities and reporting obligations; they come with start and end dates, and in public companies at least they are required to be disclosed to shareholders. They form a remarkable and almost unique time series of the shifting patterns of professional relationships within an elite tier of society.

Researchers have long sought to bring the tools of graph theory and network analysis to bear on corporate board interlocks – when one director sits on multiple boards. Immediately, they identified the classic fingerprints of small world networks: a dense network, highly clustered, with short average path-lengths between nearly all individuals. A rough power-law distribution of connectedness prevails, with one study noting 'thousands of directors served on only one board, and hundreds on two or three, a few dozen sat on five or more, and a handful on eight or more'. Within the dense core of this small, white, male world, everyone knows everyone, and even here, some are more equal than others.

The same pattern emerges when you shift focus to the interlocking relationships between corporations: if Halliburton has a board member who also sits on the board of General Motors, then those two corporations can be considered only one degree of separation apart. Some corporations lie in the more densely connected parts of the network, some are more peripheral. An Escher-like tangle of commercial relationships, cross-ownership and overlapping shareholdings reveals other dimensions of this tight weave. These aren't really separate entities at all.

'A handful of corporations maintained large boards staffed with well connected directors that gave them a distinct status as hubs of the network. As a result of these two features, the average geodesic, or shortest network distance, between any pair of directors or any pair of companies was remarkably short; that is, the network was a small world,' US researchers Johan Chu and Gerald Davis confirmed in 2016.

And then something weird happens around the turn of the century: directors overloaded with multiple board responsibilities fall out of favour with institutional investors and the representatives of smaller shareholders. Companies start appointing people with more time to dedicate to maximising shareholder returns, and the composition of this elite network loosens. Nobody gets to sit on seven or eight boards anymore, and that increases the social distance between people and boards. The sociogram is showing that corporate America is measurably less connected than it was at the turn of the twenty-first century, an elite network slipping and unravelling amid the quite rapid disappearance of its overcommitted superconnectors.

Board interlock isn't just an American phenomenon: a quick search turns up the same structure in Germany, Brazil, Singapore and elsewhere. In Australia, a densely enmeshed 2020 map of directorships was described as 'an invitation-only club' by one fund manager. However many decimal places the degrees of separation, this corporate inner circle exists around the world, flexing and warping and re-weaving with the changing composition of the economy.

Formal studies long ago confirmed that these people are drawn principally from privileged classes: this is how the village's 1 per cent are composed. They come from the same elite schools, they live in the same postcodes, they're overwhelmingly men; in the Global North, white men. They come from a small world and then the system they built condenses them into an even smaller one.

Of course, just drawing diagrams of interlocking boards on graph paper doesn't tell us how these people interact with each other, or the degree to which relationships are predominantly competitive or collaborative. 'Does a unified corporate elite dominate the political process to such an extent that state policy reflects business interests, or are capitalist interests diverse and contradictory such that there is no unified corporate elite and state policy reflects a plurality of interests?' asks Joshua Murray of Vanderbilt University. On the face of it, this is a fair question. In theory, it's possible they're all too busy fiercely competing with each other in the free market to have time to form a 'unified corporate elite'. In theory, it's also possible a unicorn will float past and shower you with fifty-dollar notes.

'Interlocks are considered an expression of class cohesion, integrating potentially contradictory interests (financial, industrial, commercial) of the richest families, whose investments span across sectors,' write William Carroll and J.P. Sapinski, in the fun-sounding *Handbook of the International Political Economy of the Corporation*. The really dense small world networks are excellent at diffusing information and enforcing norms, because the people in them get to hear what's happening from multiple directions at the same time. When it comes to feedback loops of expression and perception, small world networks are unparalleled. 'For individuals, interlocking directorships enable participation in the governance of multiple firms, enhancing contacts, influence and prestige; for firms, interlocking directorates put boards in contact, and may enable coordination of business strategies within an interlocked group.'

Back in 1956, Columbia University sociologist Charles Wright Mills had already named it: 'We must remember that these men of the power elite now occupy the strategic places in the structure of American society; that they command the dominant institutions of a dominant nation; that, as a set of men, they are in a position to make decisions with terrible consequences for the underlying populations of the world.' It's nothing Marx hadn't said a hundred years earlier, but it must have stung a little to hear it spoken from the heart of the US academic establishment. Mills charted the convergence of elite networks within a tightening knot of three institutions: the federal government, the military and a few hundred tightly interlocked corporations. On his way out the door, President Dwight D. Eisenhower christened this unholy intersection the 'military-industrial complex' during his farewell address in 1961.

The history of democracy, looked at from this angle, is partly a history of popular attempts to impose air gaps between these elite networks, to legally mandate social, commercial and political distance between people in control of powerful institutions. For states, that leads to the concept of separation of powers: 'where the constant aim is to divide and arrange the several offices in such a manner as that each may be a check on the other', as James Madison proposed in 1788.

For US corporations, it meant – for example – the introduction in 1890 of the landmark *Sherman Antitrust Act*, empowering the justice department or third parties to sue corporations for abusing monopoly power or forming cartels. The Act didn't just provide for fines, it permitted the department to break coagulated monopolies into dozens of smaller pieces. Smashing monopolies into competing fragments represented a new phase in the legislative arms race between private and public power in the United States, but it's hard to legislate against old friends having quiet drinks in wood-panelled bars.

Corporate boards aren't where policy work gets done, and what we've charted here catches only the most superficial layer of how these networks are coordinated and driven. So add another dimension of interlock, and draw the lines from those in the room when economist Friedrich Hayek founds the neoliberal Mont Pelerin Society in 1948 to those attending the re-energised meetings of the International Chamber of Commerce. Weave in the membership of the World Economic Forum, the Bilderberg Group and the acronym salad of think tanks, institutes, peak bodies, foundations and policy shops proliferating under the aegis of the Atlas Foundation. Shrug, and grab another plate of delicious crunchy snacks and more wine if you want – this diagram is now many metres from side to side, and it's changing very rapidly. At a network level, something is happening that will go part of the way to explaining the curious loosening and fragmentation of US corporate networks noticed by Chu and Davis and others: interlock is going global.

'Since the mid-1990s transnational corporate interlocking has increased while national corporate networks have waned,' write Carroll and Sapinski. Starting in 1996, their study tracks a decade's evolution of the interlock between the world's five hundred largest corporations and a selection of high-level international policy and planning institutes, headquartered mostly in the United States and Western Europe. These newly energised transnational corporate hubs aren't corporations at all: they're the World Economic Forum, the Trilateral Commission, the World Business Council for Sustainable Development and a proliferating splatter of other nodes and acronyms.

'What the fractured elite thesis observes is not an American corporate elite unable to reach consensus but a corporate elite unified by a different set of mechanisms – a change from domestic financial institutions and a national inner circle of elites as the primary factors mediating intercorporate disputes to a network of information that transcends borders and creates a leading edge of business politics that is transnational in nature,' summarises Josh Murray of Vanderbilt University.

Yes, that sentence reads like wet cement, but it's important enough to read again.

Interlock has overtopped the jigsaw map of Westphalian nation-states. We now have 'a corporate elite unified by a different set of mechanisms', mechanisms that span every time zone and which are truly planetary in scale. Corporations controlling a substantial faction of the world's industrial metabolism, synchronising their actions through industry peak bodies which in turn make up the membership of these elite global fora. We can fill out the picture with a handful of centralised media giants, four huge and diversified professional services companies, and some smaller entities specialising in lobbying and public relations, all of them seamlessly exchanging personnel with public interest regulators and political parties whose main job seems to be maintaining an illusion of legitimacy. Which invites the question: who air-gaps them now? Who separates these powers? Who swings the anti-trust hammer at this fluid mass of quicksilver operating way above the jurisdiction of any national parliament or congress on earth?

The global network is fractal in formation; it assumes miniature versions of its architecture within domestic boundaries. Scale the sociogram so it only displays Australia, and it's going to look a lot like the work independent journalist Michael West undertook with Greenpeace in 2019 to map the structures through which coal corporations captured Australia's national politics. Lombardi would probably have appreciated the elegance of their map.

Three tiers, with the mining giants at the top. Sometimes they get hands-on in the public square, but mostly they stay in the background and work through the middle tier. This is where we find peak bodies such as the Minerals Council of Australia and the Australian Petroleum Production & Exploration Association, where policies and laws are drafted for governments to present to parliament. This tier is home to the specialised lobbying firms tasked with shifting votes and shaping opinions behind the scenes. It is also where we find the public-facing media firepower of the News Corp mastheads and their digital platforms.

The third tier – the one at the bottom of the map – is the one we're invited to pay attention to. This is the governance tier, featuring the prime minister and his colleagues. When he steps up to a press conference podium flanked by the national flag, he looks like a democratically elected leader responsive to the will of the people who voted for him. But this graceful sociogram doesn't lie: the point of laying out the network diagram is to notice how it now functions as a single fused entity, with the democratically elected tier manipulated like a marionette. Staff move seamlessly between mining, media, lobbying and political offices; what looks like quite a complex articulated structure is actually behaving with considerable unity. The top-tier mining conglomerates drive this local network, writing every word that tumbles out of the mouths of these hollowest of men. Every part of the network performs a specialised role, including the empty suit at the prime minister's podium. While we're watching him, mocking him with spicy memes on social media, we've taken our eyes off the people who wrote the legislation he just introduced into the House of Representatives.

Mark Lombardi never got the opportunity to draw these narrative structures for us. In early 2000, with his work in multiple galleries and a major exhibition featuring time-series illustrations of the shadow banking industry about to open, his artistic career was 'on the verge of very major success', according to his biographer. And then, on 22 March, he apparently locked himself in his apartment and hanged himself from a sprinkler pipe.

Nothing untoward alleged, obviously. Another wine?

> When we lose our fear, they lose their power.
>
> JULIET WANJIRA

repression paradox

We don't know the name of the young man with the shopping bags standing before the column of tanks in Tiananmen Square in June 1989. But he will forever remind the world of the million student-led demonstrators occupying the Square in a carnival of defiance, demanding civil and political rights and basic democratic reforms. By the time footage of him was beamed around the world, hundreds – perhaps thousands – of those demonstrators were already dead at the hands of the People's Liberation Army.

A decade of slow but significant expansions of the rule of law and personal and collective freedoms slams into reverse immediately following the massacres in Beijing. The Beijing Students Autonomous Federation is banned and police begin a ruthless crackdown. 'Any student could be arrested. No one knows who is on the blacklist,' one student tells a journalist in the aftermath. Even as Communist Party leadership structures are consolidated and centralised, hardliners undertake a deep purge of moderates and 'counterrevolutionary thugs'. Officials from the most senior levels of the Party are removed from office, jailed or expelled. According to transcripts of tapes covertly recorded by former Communist Party general secretary Zhao Ziyang while under house arrest, upwards of four million members are put under investigation.

No uprising approaching this scale has occurred in China since then. In place of a pressure valve, saturation surveillance, mass arrests and executions.

'Repression is the process by which powerful actors attempt to deter a population from participating in a collective action that threatens them, such as protest, dissent, or rebellion,' writes political science professor David Siegel. 'The literature provides no consensus on its functioning. Studies indicate that repression can increase, decrease, or have no effect on levels of dissent.'

In 2011, he draws up four archetypal social graphs, in pursuit of a question rebels and dictators alike have grappled with for years. The title of his paper: 'When Does Repression Work?'

One graph he draws as a classic small world: a high degree of social clustering where most people know each other's friends and family, with a healthy degree of weak connections to more socially distant people in different clusters of profession or location. Two: a collection of tight-knit village networks, where everybody knows everybody intimately, but has almost no contact with the outside world. The only 'weak ties' across to other villages are held by elders who meet with each other occasionally. Three: an opinion-leader network, where most people have almost no connections with each other but are strongly influenced by charismatic or well-placed individuals who have hundreds of connections each. And four: a regimented hierarchy, where influence is heavily centralised and a tiny handful of people delegate authority and influence to an increasingly large population of otherwise disconnected individuals.

In Siegel's model, every actor is assigned an 'internal motivation' to rise up and take some kind of risky collective action. Some people are assumed to be firebrands who will almost always go out and participate; others are more risk-averse and will almost always stay home. Most people are comfortably somewhere in the middle, just getting on with life. When the model runs, each of the actors finds out how many others within their social networks have joined the action. This creates an 'external motivation' to rise up. If the combination of internal and external motivations crosses a certain threshold, the actor paints a banner and gets out into the village square.

We can see what's being modelled here. Each of us has a threshold for participating in risky collective action, but we're also influenced by how many of our friends and family are caught up in the moment. Depending on the starting assumptions Siegel feeds into his model, sometimes participation proliferates wildly on a positive feedback cascade as more participants encourage more participants until even the truly risk-averse feel safe to come out. We've seen this: that point of balance that determines whether you have a runaway social movement or not. With only marginally different starting assumptions, a few of the usual suspects will get out into

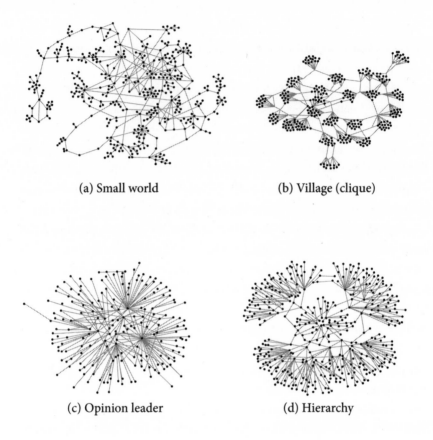

(a) Small world   (b) Village (clique)

(c) Opinion leader   (d) Hierarchy

the village square with placards but will be unsuccessful in inspiring any kind of mass turnout; eventually it falls back to being just one guy in a bar.

At this point, Siegel introduces the element of repression. Without warning, individuals are removed from the network by some external actor: assumed arrested or killed. Their participation in public action is prevented, along with their influence on those they are connected to. The model provides for either targeted repression, where people with the most links are snatched first, or random repression, where people anywhere in the network could go missing at any time. Siegel then adds a final variable to the model: allowing each actor connected to a fallen comrade to have their 'internal motivation' modified either through fear – which reduces the likelihood of future participation – or anger, which inflames it.

Siegel wants to know whether the four different kinds of network have much influence on how movements grow or are snuffed out. Some of the findings are as you'd expect: social networks in hierarchical or opinion-leader forms are far more vulnerable to targeted repression than village or small-world networks. As Siegel writes, 'exactly who gets repressed is very important in such networks'. Take out the leadership, and the sparsely connected masses at the outer tiers of the network fall back and stay home. Similarly, tight-knit village networks propagate the collective will fairly rapidly – whether in favour of participation or against it – because people get nudges and influences from many directions at once.

But other results of the simulation are less intuitive, highlighting the importance of those weaker, long-distance ties between people. In the village archetype, if the rabble-rousers succeed in setting off a movement cascade, they radicalise the whole village, since even the late adopters are soon getting incitements from everyone around them. But the lack of many weak ties to neighbouring villages is often their downfall, making it much harder for the uprising to propagate and spread the risk. The repression model repeatedly wipes these rebellious villages off the map, while the remaining villages stand by unmoved.

Under nearly all circumstances, the archetype most resilient to repression is the small world: the one combining clusters of strong relationships with many long-distance ties to other parts of the network. Without densely networked leaders to target, growing tides of collective action were able to survive the removal of many individuals, while a healthy network of weak ties was able to propagate waves of rage and activation widely, spreading the risk and igniting uprisings elsewhere.

The model is little more than a toy – a construct on graph paper – but it has enough resonance with real-world dynamics to point us in useful directions. As Siegel writes, 'answers to the question "When Does Repression Work?" depend fundamentally on the structure of the social network that connects the population.'

Crucially, he warns that under very high degrees of repression, network structure ceases to matter: 'Increase the intensity of repression enough by ramping up the rate of removal and not only will participation be squashed, it won't matter what network is in place'. And in the graph-paper model, the repressive state has to work with the network as it finds it. In the real world, authoritarians know that social networks can be actively deformed to impede the transmission of unwanted ideas or suppress them altogether.

Whole tracts of history can be rendered as the outcome of repression silencing movements or blowing up in the faces of the people orchestrating it. Gandhi was one of the first to recognise that deliberately provoking repression – and meeting it nonviolently and with dignity – was one way of pouring fuel on the fire of an uprising. Since then, some modern social movements have embedded the anticipation of repression into their theory of change, a strategy formalised by movement scholar Gene Sharp in the concept of 'political jiu-jitsu', a technique for turning the abuse of coercive power into an attack on the legitimacy of the state itself. 'In this process the stark brutality of the regime against the clearly nonviolent actionists politically rebounds against the dictators' position, causing dissention in their own ranks as well as fomenting support for the resisters among the general population, the regime's usual supporters, and third parties', Sharp writes in *From Dictatorship to Democracy* in 1994. The idea has been put into action so frequently it has become part of activist canon, from Gandhi's India to the US civil rights movement to Extinction Rebellion.

Standing firm in the face of baton charges, teargas and bullets can exact an appalling cost, and as the students of that lost Beijing summer discovered, it's no guarantee of success. But somehow, more than thirty years after the slaughter in the Square, the spirit of dissent and disobedience remains alive behind the Great Firewall. 'It's about believing that what you are doing is about justice, then you will have no fear,' says labour organiser Yue Xin. In August 2018, she and fifty of her fellow organisers are arrested by riot police in Shenzen and detained. Her only public appearance since then is in a forced confession video screened to other students early in 2019.

On the graph paper, salting the models with rage acts as an accelerant. Siegel noted that, 'If anger is strong enough, participation levels can be higher under repression than absent it.' Fear was modelled to have the opposite effect.

No matter how thin-skinned, violent and monstrous the regime's forces, deep down they know there will always be people with a spark of defiance: ignition sources for runaway waves of rage and activation. Their job is to suppress them; our job is to protect them, and to nurture that spark within ourselves.

When we lose our fear, they lose their power.

naming the monsters

In Mathare, they plant a tree for each of the ones they have lost, and it begins to change everything. In the teeth of repression, they are building something beautiful. They've done it from right here: a crowded organising space with second-hand furniture and posters on the walls. And I believe them when they say they're only just getting started.

Mathare is the oldest of Nairobi's slum districts, emerging more than a century ago amid riverside quarries where the stones for the grand colonial buildings of Kenya's capital were cut. At the core, a quarter of a million people make a home, in three square kilometres of concrete and corrugated iron terraces jammed along the contours of the Mathare River. There is no rubbish collection and no sewer system; power and fresh water are patched in by local syndicates working on the margins of the law. As with most settlements of the unnecessariat, it rarely makes the news, and when it does it's painted in the lurid brush strokes of gang violence and illegal chang'aa distilleries.

This caricature seems at odds with the high-energy racket echoing in from the walled yard: dozens of kids of all ages are playing at full volume, shouts and shrieks of laughter softening the bleeding edges of the story the Mathare crew are telling.

By far the most dangerous armed gang haunting these laneways is the one the city's wealthier classes call upon for protection: the National Police Service. Between 2013 and 2015, there were 803 reported cases of police executions across Kenya. In Mathare alone, police killed 156 people between January 2013 and December 2016, murdering someone on average every nine days. The slain are mostly young men in their twenties, teenagers, boys as young as thirteen years old.

'Before 2015 – before we started documenting it – the media had already normalised the killings. When it happens, they portray in the newspaper that seven more criminals, seven suspected gangsters are killed; that's the way they put it,' says Kennedy 'J.J.' Chindi. He's one of the lead community organisers with the Mathare Social Justice Centre, describing how the culture of impunity was justified in the absence of anyone to raise a voice for those in the firing line. Juliet Wanjira, one of the centre's energetic co-founders, explains, 'We'd always meet as friends and we'd find that in their hood a couple of boys were killed, and in our hood, and all over. So we formed Mathare Social Justice Centre.'

She lost her older brother to the police, and has no illusions about why the killing continues. Among Nairobi's middle classes, the spectre of gang violence and poverty renders the people of Mathare as something less than human. So the highest priority of this crew is to humanise the carnage, cracking the mask of normalisation that had settled across its face. Working from personal testimony, grassroots organising and a media audit, in 2017 they publish the first accurate account of this violent epidemic: 'For now, this is our small barefoot contribution to memory and justice. This is equally a "cry from the ghetto" but, above all, a demand,' the report says. 'It should not be illegal to be young and poor in any of our homes.'

Their report – the first of its kind in Kenya – is titled 'Who Is Next?'. On every page are the faces and names of their young men and boys, the stories of their lives and the circumstances of their abduction and murder.

Publication of the report opens up support within establishment media and larger non-government organisations and forces the police onto the defensive. The national conversation is changed forever.

'People are beginning to speak up more. Every time you switch on the news you will see extrajudicial killings: it's a national conversation now,' Juliet says. 'We had the secretary-general of Amnesty International visiting women who had lost their sons. For me, that was quite impactful, because at least people out there are beginning to see and notice that, hey, there's actually a crisis in Mathare.'

For the most part, the MSJC crew have steered clear of the swamp of electoral politics; they are up against the kind of financial firepower that can just walk these laneways buying votes. 'There's no way of ensuring that people we elect into power, even though they were activists before, remain connected to the grassroots,' says Juliet.

So, they build their own power. Gacheke Gachihi is one of the co-founders of the centre; someone who seems at ease working at the heart of the whirlwind he helped create. Now he steps through how what they've built in parallel with the police killings report: education and a dance program for the settlement's kids, reports on water and sanitation, work on disability justice, classes in political education and community organising. And then they began planting trees.

'The planting of the trees gave us an opportunity to softly connect to the people, with those who were opposed to extrajudicial killing,' he says. 'When we plant a tree for memory, it also is part of an ecological justice campaign, because in Mathare there were no trees. It's also like a healing; when you plant a tree with the family of the victim of an extrajudicial killing, it is very powerful.'

They plant trees for food, trees for shade and trees for remembering.

In the sunlit courtyard where the children cheerfully revel, what they're building here comes into sharper focus. Protected, in neat rows, each holding the memory of one of the informal settlement's executed young people. Behind them on the wall, a huge mural: Mathare in an urban forest under a bright blue sky. This, like everything here, has an organising story.

'The futuristic part of the Mathare Green Movement is intended to imagine the possible positive outcomes of our society if all of us were involved in the struggle and were involved in making Mathare a better place,' says Micko. He's the coordinator of the Art for Social Change project, working with a network of artists to put the defiant dreams of this place into public view. 'Art has become a basic need to the community,' he says.

'Art is a mirror of the injustices happening in the community,' says Juliet. 'But we also have these murals of the future Mathare: leafy, green, clean river. That's the Mathare we want.'

We walk, and I can almost see it; above and behind the corroded tin and besser block architecture of this shantytown right at the edge of possibility. The main artery of Mau Mau Road is unpaved, alive with cross-currents of music and commerce: stacks of firewood, charcoal, fresh fruit for sale. Heavily laden scooters and curious kids on bikes weave through the crowd. A strange flashback to the beaming faces of Kutupalong a lifetime ago; it seems this too is a city of children. Before long we have attracted attention, not just to assess the provenance of this out-of-context *mzungu*, but to pay respects to those I'm walking with. The Mathare organisers are treated with a warmth that approaches reverence, unable to step a dozen metres without a greeting or an acknowledgement.

Under a heavy afternoon sky, we stop by the river bridge: battered spans of concrete across a wounded drift of plastic and untreated sewage. The crew have plans for this river. They have plans for schools. They have plans for a library, and for reproductive health. 'The whole hood doesn't have a forest. When I was a kid, this place used to be a forest,' Micko says, gesturing up the hill towards a stand of hardy trees. 'So we are thinking about this place as a bird park – planting trees that will attract birds.'

I believe him; I believe all of them – this is a group of people who don't waste words. When they say they're going to do something, it happens. One of the murals in the compound is just a stylised raised fist. They're done waiting for someone else to deliver the Mathare they want; they are organising it themselves.

By September 2018, the campaign against extrajudicial killings has prompted President Uhuru Kenyatta to convene a series of national security conferences and police reform dialogues. Gacheke is at the table, with more than just Mathare behind him. Based on the model pioneered at the MSJC, social justice centres have sprung up in informal settlements across the country, dozens of them; now, as a co-chair of the working group networking these centres together, he and the others can look the justice minister in the face.

Our walk has brought us back towards the main road, to another huge piece of street art: a proud young boy, maybe eight years old, whose eyes follow you up the street. 'Nothing about us without us', it reads. Gacheke grins hugely; invites us to join him in a smoky little corrugated iron bar for beer and a heads-up on the next phase of the quiet revolution they are building in Mathare.

Dr Wandia Njoya takes the stage, and a hush falls over the auditorium. 'Okay, I am here to name the monsters that are responsible for our problems,' she declares.

'The reason we need to name these monsters is because I know some people from government are here; they are going to adopt what we are saying here, and speak it on the news media and then the rest of the Kenyans will say, wow, our politicians really know our problems. But they're just plagiarising and copying what we are saying.'

Dr Njoya is a senior lecturer and head of department at Daystar University, and she's not here to waste words.

The Mathare crew have invited me to sit in on an organising meeting of Kenya Tuitakayo – an emerging network of social movements demanding 'the Kenya we Want'. The auditorium is packed to standing room only, and I'm browsing their charter looking for familiar points of reference. 'The Kenyan state and public finance are under capture by a small but powerful group of individuals, who have directed public planning and development towards their own primitive greed and accumulation to the detriment of everyone else,' it says.

Without exaggeration, you could substitute the word 'Kenya' for 'Australia' and that sentence still lands. Or Mongolia for that matter, or Jharkhand, or Brazil, or the United States. Primitive greed and accumulation to the detriment of everyone else: she's speaking the language of state capture. Seems we've found our point of reference.

'The monster, for Kenya, is the comprador elite, whose job is to promote and protect the interests of international capital,' says Dr Njoya, to applause. That's a word she invites us to go and look up. Comprador: 'an agent for foreign organisations engaged in investment, trade, or economic or political exploitation.'

'The politicians behave as if we don't exist. We are a last resort; the only use we are to them is to give them power to negotiate with each other,' she says.

The comprador are born in Kenya; they wrap themselves in the flag, and they are very skilled at defining and delimiting the Kenyan national identity as a weapon against specified others. But that's not who they serve. They serve the same people the Australian comprador class serve: the investor blocs that finance their hold on power in exchange for land access and a pool of human beings desperate for a job.

Amazing. I'm nine thousand kilometres from home, and yet her monsters are somehow the same as mine. The same as Boldbayar's, and Letícia's, and Dayamani Barla's.

'The Kenya we want is the Kenya that cares for people. It is a Kenya that cares for the sick, supports the challenged, and educates the public. We have great ideas, and we have great skills, and we want to work to contribute to this economy. We get dignity from having influence in the world where we live,' Dr Njoya says, with the same energy as Micko, in his invocation of the bird park in Mathare.

She demands land reform. Taxation of obscene wealth. Channelling collective resources to the greatest collective benefit. She gets a standing ovation.

Out in the yard where the children play, the trees are just a little taller, a little stronger than they were yesterday. So raise a fist: with organisation and determination, Mathare's families are rescuing their children from the river, and now stand eye to eye with the monsters throwing them in.

PART 5

full circle

the lyrebirds

We looked back towards home last night, glimpsing mountainous Gulaga's reclining profile backlit under the plume. Somewhere in there behind her, a handful of friends have made the decision to stay and defend their homes and farms. I'm thinking of them and the army of sleepless volunteers deployed into the teeth of this thing. I'm thinking of Yuin mob losing places and story the rest of us never even knew were there. I'm thinking of the graceful pair of lyrebirds who have adopted us, scratching away at the garden mulch; when they run, it's as though they are flowing along the ground. Thinking of the family of magpies who sing to us, and the laconic kookaburras who keep watch from the fenceposts. The wombats who come and go mostly unseen, the eastern grey kangaroos who gather in the evenings. The valley full of graceful tree ferns invoking the long-distant Devonian: what happens for them. What happens for all of us.

Power is still out. Phones are still down. Our information field has contracted to car-park gossip, AM radio and an emergency briefing at the evacuation centre in an hour's time.

The fire was started by a lightning strike and a furnace wind from the northwest. The fire was started by an unyielding drought that wrenched every drop of moisture from these hillsides. It was started by a global temperature spike accurately predicted by the industries that ignited it. It was started by the forced dispossession of skilled custodians with a 65,000-year lineage of landscape-scale fire management.

The fire was started by a coin-doubling virus that is mining the world into mass extinction.

This mess of causality doesn't fit neatly onto a bumper sticker or into a one-page manifesto. Any theory of change that hopes to apprehend it will need to be as open-ended and multi-scaled as the thing itself.

I remember how, when I began making changes at a personal, individual level, at first the barriers seemed mostly internal. A lazy inertia, the lack of any real social penalty for continuing to do things I knew intellectually were part of the problem. I am, after all, an unthinking beneficiary of that forced dispossession; all the maps I read from are of occupied territories.

So the plant-based diet, flying less, making stuff last longer – tangible actions within the domains we have some control over – are surely worth it, for the faint ripples they send through supply chains, and for the influence we have on others. Everyone dancing Joanna's systems game with us will see another individual in their social field walking the talk and making an effort; we'll learn from each other, and the dance will shift just a little.

Catching movement out of the corner of my eye; silhouette of a young woman pushing her child on the playground swing under a nightmare sky. Time slows for a moment, stops. Both of them are wearing P2 masks in the sepia gloom; the child can't be more than four years old. A wave of grief hits me, that this is where we live now. My patchy but commendable record of recycling hasn't prevented the incineration of nearly the entire eastern seaboard. Personal action is necessary, certainly, but insufficient. The very existence of BP's bullshit carbon footprint calculator keeps reminding me of that.

So let's take a fast traverse through the scales of what we're up against, see if it's even possible to get its measure.

Say I accept this community noticeboard invitation to join a grassroots campaign for our local council to create a community garden or go 100 per cent solar. This endeavour will take a few months, in common cause with a handful of key organisers and a wider periphery of friendly supporters. When we succeed – and we probably will – it will affect thousands of people, make the cover of the local paper, and send ripples outwards that are greater than anything I could have achieved alone. Our friendship network will be measurably stronger, ready for a new challenge. But if I look up from this work . . .

She's taken the little one by the hand, helped him off the swing; they're walking slowly back to sit in the car and maybe take a rest from this shitful air.

While we were painstakingly building support for our community garden, the government just approved a massive new coalmine on the sovereign lands of the Wangan and Jagalingou people in Queensland's Galilee Basin.

Shift the scale of our focus, then. Now we are working with thousands of others on a national campaign that will probably take years. We're locked in contention with a well-connected megacorporation gouging the benefits of state capture. When we win – and maybe we will – it will send shockwaves through the investment community and the political class. It will inspire a generation of campaigners, and millions of tonnes of carbon will stay in the ground.

I've lost sight of the woman with the young child, all of us now joining the drift towards the evacuation centre to get a briefing on what the next twenty-four hours might bring.

Having started this thought experiment, best we see it through.

We beat the mine, but the power industry finds someone's else's country to loot for coal – someone in a weaker governance zone, or a place where extinction rebels can just be killed. The Minerals Council ragewanks into the Murdoch platforms for months, demanding its politicians introduce repressive new laws branding us economic terrorists. We'll have stopped the project, and that will matter. But we won't have changed the political economy of our energy system. That lies at different scale again.

So let's go there. Changing a system is a different proposition to stopping a single project. For this higher ambition, we finally take our lead from the global scientific community and commit to rapidly decarbonising the energy system, defusing the carbon bomb in the decade we maybe have left. To succeed, it needs to be an international project: an alignment of globally networked civil society movements from Traditional Owners and trade unions to school strikers, extinction rebels, greens of every denomination and all the friends of the earth. A newly aligned movement of movements making common cause with the clean technology sector and allied national governments working the UN system for all it's worth.

In my mind's eye, an energy ecosystem two hundred years in the making has been overturned. Yet something is still deeply wrong with this picture. Maybe a dismal little nuclear resurgence, Russia and China tempting dragon-king catastrophes. Mountains of expired photovoltaics going into landfill. A lithium coup in Bolivia – we need it for the batteries, sorry. Shortages of tellurium and rare earths; gunfire in exchange for cobalt in the DRC. Some communities get to leapfrog the fossil age altogether; others are walled into energy poverty for the greater good. Oceans still awash with plastic, forests still falling. Traffic jams, but quiet electric ones. To pull it off, we form alliances with fascist-adjacent hardliners, averting our eyes from the detention camps because at least they are good on energy policy. Most of the same monsters still seem to have a lock on this 500-year-old Monopoly game. Somehow, impossibly, they are trying to get solar-powered sankey stripes to double themselves again.

Feeling suddenly powerless under this burned sky. The bigger our project gets, the smaller and more remote I feel within it. The larger our frame of reference, the heavier it is to lift. Maybe it's not possible to get its measure; maybe it's just too big and too far gone.

Coin-doubling neoliberalism with solar panels is still a collapse scenario. And in the null hours of News Corp's televised fever swamps, they're onto us.

'The real issue we've got, is some of the people out there who claim to be very concerned about climate change, who want to reduce carbon emissions, their actual goal is not to do that,' says Senator Matt Canavan, Australia's former minister for coal. The interviewer nods eagerly, his body language vibrating at an unpleasant frequency. Canavan delivers his world-weary mic-drop. 'Their actual goal is to upend society . . . to move away from capitalism, to take down power structures.'

Upend society, you say.

An indoor basketball court transformed into a dormitory, muffled hammer of a generator running temporary lights that make it feel darker somehow. The air is swimming with fine ash. Swags and mattresses laid out in the gloom, families on the floor, elderly people on camp chairs with nowhere else to go. Some of them have already lost everything, some of them are about to. Eye contact, smiles behind these awful masks, rumours shorting out like static electricity. They are evacuating Bermagui to here. Mogo has burned. Batemans Bay has burned. Four thousand people are stranded on the beach at Mallacoota, backs to the sea with the town on fire. The largest evacuation in Australian history is underway.

I've seen this place before, in footage of the Fukushima aftermath and New Orleans and every single disaster movie ever made: monochrome dreamscape of an upended society.

Phones are up briefly: two new things to note in the timeline. Item one: a bot swarm is propagating a News Corp front page that is just straight-up disinformation. The fire was started by the Greens; by my colleagues and friends somehow, and an imaginary epidemic of arsonists. Item two: the reason our prime minister took an early holiday in Hawai'i while his country burned was so he could lead a coal industry delegation to India in January.

Move away from capitalism, you say.

For the first time in his political career, Canavan may be right about something. It's not just the energy system that needs to change; this heartless predation is interlocked all the way to the top.

What's emerging to replace it doesn't have a name yet, and maybe that's important. The world that comes next: post-capitalism built at the intersection of radical democracy, regenerative economics and First Nations sovereignty. A world come full circle. Everyone's vision of it is different, and that's important. But there's comfort knowing there's a chance that place will be there if we can make our way to it. How it might look when we swing the post-fossil transition beautifully. Looking back not on a terrible crash or some cobbled-together emergency landing laced with barbed wire, but having actually made it, with grace and determination. Arriving home safely, to find the lyrebirds have left a feather in the forest to let us know they made it too.

Taking down power structures, you say.

Individual empowerment and mass collective action. Shared strategy and gleeful improv. Multilateral diplomacy and a global strike wave. Creative world-building, and defiant monkey-wrenching hard into the gears. Recalling the words of ecologist C.S. Holling on election night: 'A long view of human history reveals not regular change but spasmodic, catastrophic disruptions followed by long periods of reinvention and development . . . hierarchies and adaptive cycles comprise the basis of ecosystems and social-ecological systems across scales. Together they form a panarchy.'

Social-ecological systems across scales – that sounds like a concept we could use. It sounds like something that could accommodate a theory of change that has to stretch from the personal to the planetary and all the scales in between; from a coal blockade in the Galilee to the shade trees someone is planting, even now, in the front yard of the quiet house in the quiet street.

> Bats can hear shapes. Plants can eat light. Bees can
> dance maps. We can hold all these ideas at once and
> feel both heavy and weightless with the absurd beauty
> of it all.
>
> @CryptoNature

miocene summer

The cloud forest is alive with humidity and birdsong: a dense chorus of call-and-response in dozens of unfamiliar languages. Fourteen million years from now, people will call this the Western Cordillera, will imagine back to this time and call it the Miocene epoch. We arrived here this morning, still deep in the time before names; forty-two million years since the day we made eye contact with an ancestor with big eyes and clever hands.

The canopy hangs in the mist above us like a dream. We're descending through dense tiers of understorey, buttressed columns of great old ones standing astride a riot of ferns and heliconia. Drift lower, beneath the outstretched arms of the ferns, until we can survey the soft gloom of the forest floor and catch sight of the improvised freight highway for the first time.

An intense hustle of attine ants are marching along a fallen log, following a switchback down into the jumble of decomposing mulch. Each of them carries an enormous wedge of green clenched in her mandibles, emerald arcs and slabs sawed away from the leaves of a stricken canopy tree somewhere far above. The majors have gone on ahead and cleared the path of debris so this column of mediae workers can do the heavy haulage, and on either side of the foraging line, aggressive little minors prowl the forest floor poised to hurl themselves at intruders. We're on the outskirts now, this hectic cargo procession bobbing and dragging by distributed force of will towards home. A garrison of majors stand guard at one of the outflung portals into the colony beneath their feet, antennae alive to news from the incoming workforce.

This place is home to many millions of residents; an underground ant metropolis that never sleeps. Descending surefooted into purest darkness, the inbound mediae bear their cargo into the care of cohorts of little minim ants who may never have known sunlight. In these busy chambers, armies of minims are scissoring the leaf fragments into smaller pieces; cleaning and perforating them, and then stacking them within a dense honeycomb of Lepiotaceae fungus. The fungus slowly overgrows this carefully tended compost with a haze of white threads, producing nutritious fruiting clusters, which the ants collect and distribute to all points of their city. This fungal harvest is principally for the benefit of the queen and her developing larvae nested deep within the honeycomb, tomorrow's army of foragers and farmers and bodyguards taking form within the gardens their forebears have made.

This arrangement is forever: the ants would die without the fungus, which would die without the ants. Watch these nervy little mimims dosing the leaf compost with a specific strain of bacteria. They do this to fight the growth of an invasive *Escovopsis* fungus, which will wipe out their crops within days if it gets out of hand. These sprawling collectives seem to have invented not only agriculture, but also antibiotics. Ants. Ants are doing this.

Theirs is a world tantalisingly familiar to our eyes, but if we lift away from the perpetual rolling mists of the cloud forest, we'll see that these territories still invoke unfamiliar maps. Although the planet has cooled significantly since the long-distant heatstroke of the Palaeocene–Eocene Thermal Maximum, we are nonetheless coming to the end of a three-million-year greenhouse phase that will later be known as the Mid-Miocene Climate Optimum. Something kicked the planet's long-term cooling trend into a high fever; likely a combination of orbital dynamics and the familiar culprit of immense volumes of carbon dioxide dumped into the air from volcanic upwelling. This time the hot zone was the northwest of what will eventually be North America, where a new flood basalt province began reshaping the landscape at about the same time as temperatures spiked. This surge pushed atmospheric carbon dioxide into the four hundred to five hundred parts per million range, lifting the world's average surface temperature by four to six degrees. In turn, that stripped Greenland and the Arctic largely free of ice and sent the glacial sheets of Antarctica into sharp retreat. A slow-moving, three-million-year blowtorch of cause and effect has raised sea levels somewhere between forty and fifty metres.

If some of these numbers seem ominously familiar, none of this is of concern to the attine. They take their world as they find it, and these geological convulsions are taking place at scales far outside their frame of reference.

The birdsong enlivening the air speaks in different dimensions to the chemical marching orders of the ants, but both are reminders that while we were watching sand grains and small worlds and shipping lanes, a deeply significant transition has been unfolding. The ants use pheromone signalling to synchronise their actions and make decisions, a communications medium that has served these ends since the first bacteria learned to tumble and run. The birds have retained this sense of smell, but deep geological time has brought forth new affordances of sound and sight.

Listen, for a moment, to this place. Every conceivable frequency carries a different voice. The whole acoustic field of the forest has been partitioned so that every species of cricket, frog, mammal and bird can speak and be heard amid the others. Countless layers of conversation; seductions, territorial advice, invitations, warnings. Some of these dialects are tens or hundreds of millions of years old, but all of them signify an underlying truth: for a long time now we've been living in a world of societies. Only a handful of these collectives orchestrate their affairs as rigidly as the attines, with caste specialisation and individuals dependent on the working of the whole colony for survival. Most of the birds we can hear exist within more fluid relationships, bonded by family or species-wide affiliation. The youngest ones are learning to fly, learning to fend for themselves, and learning the meaning of the ambient crosscurrents of song and signifier that fill the air.

In fourteen million years' time, Pyotr Kropotkin will muse that 'the fittest are not the physically strongest, nor the cunningest, but those who learn to combine so as mutually to support each other, strong and weak alike, for the welfare of the community'.

Mutual aid, for attine and aviators alike.

The world will continue to cool through the latter part of the Miocene; ice is slowly returning to the Arctic, and Antarctica is beginning its long journey into the deep freeze. There's still a place for loners and iconoclasts here, and yet everywhere we turn, there is music and conversation.

Bees dancing their maps. Spiders courting potential dates with drumming routines. Elephants with complex vocabularies and subcultures. Turtle hatchlings calling for parental assistance as they emerge from their nests, cetaceans roaming the world ocean with regional dialects evolving as they go: the world has somehow become alive with language and significance. Without fanfare, and at widely divergent places and times, another of life's great transitions has taken place.

> When you want to know how things really work,
> study them when they're coming apart.
>
> WILLIAM GIBSON, *ZERO HISTORY*

panarchy

On foot some hours before midnight, with the streetlights dead and the night air seething with ash: it's hard to imagine it, but the rain will come. I have to believe it, holding to the image of rain sweeping across grieving hillsides, under shrouds of steam and smoke. Light veils at first, then settling in heavier. It will come. And then, within mere hours, something unbelievable will have begun: a billionfold germination of microscopic seeds and spores and underground rhizomes embedded within every fold of the landscape. Luca's daughters whirring into motion post-catastrophe, as they have done so many times before. Days later it will be visible from the highway: faint shimmer of brilliant green amid the char.

Ecologists call them 'adaptive cycles' and draw them like a sideways figure eight: a möbius strip against a four-quartered backdrop that describes what the system is doing.

Let's take a turn around the adaptive cycle, imagining ecosystem succession in fast-forward. Upstart grasses emerging; amid the green shimmer, pioneering brackens unfurling, small herbaceous plants invoking attentive pollinators. This first phase of the adaptive cycle they call the erploitation phase; it is dominated by fast-moving species dispersing rapidly into open landscapes. Runaway opportunists on a positive feedback bender, seizing their moment in the sun to rapidly occupy the fireground. Insects and small mammals follow them in now that there's something to eat; call them weeds and pests if you want, but in the coming weeks they will rebuild the foundational tiers of the ecosystem amid the ruins.

The species that dominate this phase are prolific and often short-lived. In the 1960s, ecologists began referring to them as r-selected species, due to the fast rate of reproduction. So on the adaptive cycle diagram, call this the r phase.

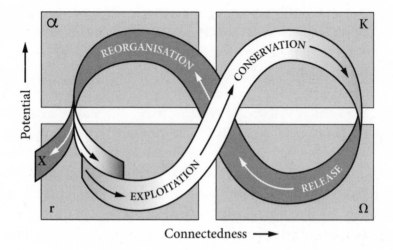

Connectedness ⟶

A stepwise transition is underway, with these fast-moving pioneers ceding ground to a more complex array of specialists. We're leaving the r phase now as the ecosystem begins accumulating structure, biomass and biodiversity. As the months slip quietly into a passage of years, we're moving slowly up the slope of the diagram into the K phase – borrowing from the German expression *Kapazitätsgrenze*, capacity limit. The K phase, or conservation phase, of the adaptive cycle favours creatures adapted to living closer to the edge of the ecosystem's carrying capacity, where it pays to invest in smaller numbers of offspring and stick around to look after them. If the r phase favoured fast and loose opportunists, the K phase is the home of longer-lived specialists at ease in a more complex and stratified world.

'During the slow sequence from exploitation to conservation, connectedness and stability increase and capital is accumulated. Ecosystem capital, for example, includes nutrients, biomass, and physical structure,' writes C.S. Holling, who helped develop the concept of the adaptive cycle during the 1990s. What he means is that in the decades after the burn, the ecosystem becomes rich and complex enough to support wombats in their underworlds of burrows and tunnels. Mature trees hosting whole communities of different creatures; lyrebirds moving through the undergrowth.

It looks as though we're halfway around the möbius strip, but time moves at different speeds depending on where you are in the adaptive cycle. Exploitation was fast: weeks or months, a couple of years for the wattles to get properly established. The conservation phase is slow: it can run for decades in these woodlands, centuries for the giant fire-tolerant eucalypts.

This part of the adaptive cycle, building slowly from r phase to K phase, is reasonably well studied by ecologists; Holling and his colleagues call it the 'front loop'. But the whole time we've been watching this ecosystem reassemble, fuel has slowly been building up on the forest floor: leaf litter, fallen wattles, long strips of bark from the silvertop ash and the stringybark trees. One night a lightning strike is going to hit this patch and send it over the edge into the most spectacular quadrant of Holling's diagram: the release phase, drawn with the Greek letter for omega, Ω. Here, the omega release will be as fast as a blowtorch westerly can push a ladder fire into the canopy and destroy everything that can't flee.

The release phase hurls us swiftly into the final stage of the cycle: the reorganisation phase, tagged with the Greek letter for alpha, α. This is a place where lasting change sometimes takes hold. 'It is a fertile environment for experiments, for the appearance and initial establishment of entities that would otherwise be out-competed,' writes Holling, 'many will fail, but in the process, the survivors will accumulate the fruits of change. It is a time of both crisis and opportunity.' Hit a system hard enough, and the omega phase will kill it. But for those who make it, the alpha phase is wide open.

While processes driving the front loop were familiar to the ecologists, this turbulent transition from an omega crash to alpha reorganisation – the back loop – was more mysterious. What happens next depends on how much has survived the cataclysm, the composition of the seedbank left behind, and proximity to nearby refuges from which enterprising survivors can move in and stake their claim on the open ground. When it emerges, that shimmer of brilliant green will be pregnant with possibility. What arises might be very similar to what has just been torched, or it might be something quite different. The only way to find out is to abide here and see how these creatures shape the next turn of the wheel.

Snapping out of my reverie of rains yet to come. I don't know what day it is.
The air is the colour of shit. I'm sick of wearing this mask; we've been breathing this hot mess for weeks now and my lungs are heavy with it. A hundred
thousand square kilometres have burned across four states: a land area four
times the size of Turkey. My mind rejects the scale of it, maintaining a ragged
emotional distance from the deaths, the places that no longer exist, the creatures emerging burned and disoriented into a newsfeed inconceivably far
from their frame of reference. It is easier somehow to grasp the dimensions
of political failure at play than the magnitude of what's being lost.

These are climate fires, with the fingerprints of the resources sector all
over them. The investor blocs know they are vulnerable to the backlash
they've been holding off for decades, and so the startled paralysis of that
sucking vacuum in the prime minister's office is now giving way to something more menacing. I'd caught hints of it a few days ago, but now the
anglerfish has fully deployed its lantern. The collective apophenia they are
orchestrating is simple: the fires are to be blamed on arsonists, and on the
Greens. They've made the prime minister a snappy little infomercial; here
he is striding onto the fireground like an erect penis, backed by helicopters and the army and millions of dollars they've ripped out of disability
funding. The bot swarm and clique of ideologically damaged News Corp
commentators take this direction and run with it, with the coordinated
backing of the US hard right.

On the ground, volunteers are trying to contain the fires. Online, the
messaging people are trying to contain this: 'Tell the prime minister to
go and get fucked, from Nelligen,' yells volunteer firefighter Paul Parker
directly into the camera lens of a startled news crew.

The prime minister's tumescent rallying cry is being broadcast as a party-
political advertisement to try and drown out this overnight folk hero. There's
even a donate button: click here to send your cash into the bank account of
a party captured by the same industries that unleashed this inferno —

Somewhere in my back-brain, a fuse blows. I have never been this
angry in my whole life.

Deep breath. And another.

The adaptive cycle möbius was drawn by ecologists to serve as a metaphor rather than a unifying theory, but once they'd begun sketching them, they started seeing them all over the place. A phase of accumulation, increasing connectivity and growing predictability, followed by a sharp regime change into deep uncertainty and then whatever comes next.

Holling and his colleagues were explicitly not trying to craft a unified theory of everything. Most ecologists have moved on from the oversimplified schema of r species and K species since there are so many forms of life that refuse to fit neatly into a category. There are also any number of ecosystems that clearly don't roll through adaptive cycles – open oceans and arid steppes being obvious examples.

But much of the rest of the biosphere seems to be weaving through this fourfold möbius dance of proliferation and consolidation, collapse and renewal. Crucially, this is happening at multiple scales simultaneously; smaller, faster cycles turning inside larger, slower ones. 'Each level is allowed to operate at its own pace, protected from above by slower, larger levels but invigorated from below by faster, smaller cycles of innovation,' writes Holling. 'The whole panarchy is therefore both creative and conserving.'

Panarchy. The word they've coined to invoke this fractal kaleidoscope of creatures and living systems making their way at all scales, from the ceaseless endeavours of Luca's daughters to the lives of the flowing lyrebirds, through to the forest weaving itself back into the fabric of the biosphere.

'Because the word "hierarchy" is so burdened by the rigid, top-down nature of its common meaning, we decided to look for another term,' explains Holling. 'These transformational cycles take place in nested sets at scales ranging from a leaf to the biosphere over periods from days to geologic epochs, and from the scales of a family to a sociopolitical region over periods from years to centuries.'

The panarchy metaphor gets provocative when we begin mapping human contention and collective behaviour onto it. Footloose insurgencies gentrifying into tradition-bound bureaucracies – now that feels like an invocation of the front loop. Fiery revolutions and crashes and great depressions spawning new footloose insurgencies – these feel like expressions of the back loop.

We'll tread with care, since this is only metaphor, but if these times of crisis are really also moments of opportunity, then this is the best possible time to tell the prime minister to go and get fucked, from all of us. What arises next might be very similar to what just burned to the ground, or it could be a window into something quite different. Now's the moment to lean in and help shape the next turn of the wheel.

recurrence

'When states have arrived at their greatest perfection, they soon begin to decline,' writes Niccolò Machiavelli. 'In the same manner, having been reduced by disorder and sunk to their utmost state of depression, unable to descend lower, they, of necessity, reascend, and thus from good they gradually decline to evil and from evil mount up to good.'

He's seemingly describing the Florentine adaptive cycle back in 1517 – the intuition that human institutions roll through cycles of consolidation and collapse goes back a long way. In his epic *Kitab al-'Ibar*, or *Book of Lessons*, fourteenth-century Tunisian scholar Ibn Khaldun is preoccupied with how the spread of institutional corruption and brittleness predictably heralds the downfall of even the mightiest of regimes. He popularises the concept of Asabiyyah, عصبية: group loyalty, unity and solidarity, which increasingly distant elites violate and exploit on their way up the conservation phase before falling to internal division or external depredation. Ancient Chinese political thinkers clocked the same patterns of overturn in dynastic cycles – Cháodài Xúnhuán, 朝代循環 – driven by the cultivation and squandering of the Mandate of Heaven. Han dynasty Chinese historian Sima Qian writes, sometime before 94 BC, 'We may see that the rulers at the beginning of each new dynasty never failed to conduct themselves with awe and reverence, but that their descendants little by little sank into indolence and vain pride.'

Sounds familiar. 'The eternal struggles between aristocracy and democracy . . . have never been anything more than struggles between an old minority, defending its actual predominance, and a new and ambitious minority, intent upon the conquest of power, desiring either to fuse with the former or to dethrone and replace it.'

That's German sociologist Robert Michels, introducing his 'iron law of oligarchy'. 'On this theory, these class struggles consist merely of struggles between successively dominant minorities.' He proposes the iron law in 1911, at the inflection point on his own political journey from German anarcho-syndicalism to Italian fascism. Direct democracy and worker self-management simply couldn't scale, he argues. 'The principle of division of labor coming more and more into operation, executive authority undergoes division and subdivision. There is thus constituted a rigorously defined and hierarchical bureaucracy.'

Shades of revolutionary r-strategists moving helplessly up the front loop into K-phase bureaucratic gridlock, another generation of jaded revolutionaries squandering the Mandate of Heaven. According to this bleak view, you either live in an oligarchy or you're somewhere on the slide towards one.

Cycles inside cycles, dharma wheels inside wheels. One step removed from the turmoil and tragedy of deep history, the systems theorists went looking for the symmetries and resonances driving these cycles, and what happens when the fast and the slow collide.

Trying to map history's turbulence and contingency within any kind of systems schema is fraught, but they propose two broad patterns underlying the evolution of human societies. 'The first is an overall increase in the hierarchical differentiation and complexity of societies,' writes Holling. 'That is, levels in the panarchy are added over time. If enough potential accumulates at one level, it can pass a threshold and establish another, slower and larger level.'

We witnessed this transition phenomenon several times during our four-billion-year journey from the Hadean; now here it is refracting into increasingly complex human societies.

'The second trend is defined by the occurrence of rapid discontinuous shifts . . . political breakdown occurs when there are simultaneous crises at several different organizational levels in society. In other words, adaptive cycles at different levels in a panarchy become aligned at the same phase of vulnerability [leading to] a cascading, panarchical collapse.'

Slow variables of climate and drought and fuel load and land degradation turning in the background. Fast variables of weather and electrical storms and blowtorch westerlies churning in the foreground. Line them up, and a century-old forest can be blasted into a moonscape within half an hour. Now the omega crash of an unnatural disaster collides with slow political variables of capital accumulation, state capture and civil society unrest. This catastrophe hasn't aligned with the electoral cycle, so it won't immediately bring down the government, but it has thrown ruling party factions out of alignment with each other, and kicked off an unforeseeable cascade of consequences.

So now we see a government moving, fast, to limit the damage, contain the turmoil to the most superficial layers. Quick, look busy. Force people to shake your hand on television. Make shitty infomercials, do scattershot cash handouts, propagate a disinformation swarm. Oil companies make out performative cheques to charity but mostly stay out of sight. The nuclear industry begins pushing hastily drafted opinion pieces into the field. The forestry industry steps into the breach with some helpful ideas for logging in national parks, volunteering to destroy the forest in order to save it.

Anything, it seems, to distract and misdirect from this momentary conjunction of hazard and vulnerability.

hazard reduction burn

In a car park with two hundred evacuees under mustard skies, I'm scrolling through my phone while waiting for the briefing. Volunteers in hi-vis are setting up a PA system on a flatbed truck; free water bottles and face masks if you need them; friendly chatter in the dinner queue.

Scrolling, scrolling. On the timeline, commodification of this miserable experience is already well underway: here are some ads featuring attractive models in designer P2 masks, styles ranging from K-pop to art nouveau. Mind drifting sideways, wondering what to do with Holling's observation of elections as a form of pressure valve: a ritualised mechanism to 'diffuse large episodes of creative destruction by creating smaller cycles of renewal and change'.

On the adaptive cycle, as systems climb higher into the conservation phase, they become conservative, inflexible and increasingly brittle. Holling puts it like this: 'The system's connectedness increases, eventually becoming overconnected and increasingly rigid in its control. It becomes an accident waiting to happen.'

Invisibly, the resilience of the whole structure is eroding even as it appears to be moving at the peak of its strength.

That's the phenomenon that fascinated Machiavelli, Ibn Khaldun and Sima Qian. Regimes at the brittle end of the K-phase become increasingly paranoid and differentiated from their host population, deploying police and surveillance powers while withdrawing their operations behind firewalls of secrecy and propaganda. Out on the social graph, classes become sharply stratified, separated and polarised, all in the service of locking in the current regime's inflexibility even as the world flows and tilts around it.

The Soviet Union and its satellite states provide the classic example of K-phase embrittlement. It took a combination of courageous internal dissidence and external pressure from more efficient market-based coin-doublers to bring it crashing into the omega phase. But these cycles never sleep; each of the great powers of Russia, China and the United States show deep symptoms of institutional embrittlement and will have to face reality at some point.

In the meantime, modern history is awash with examples of predator capitalism surging through the breach to colonise and exploit post-crash alpha-phase societies, from South Africa to Greece to Haiti to the wreckage of the Soviet Union. Described by Naomi Klein as the 'shock doctrine,' already there is abundant evidence of investors moving to profit from climate collapse, everything from designer P2 masks to freshwater arbitrage and privatised disaster recovery.

Holling and his colleagues imagined elections as a potentially effective way to avoid deep crashes and disruptions by empowering the populace to formally evict a rotten executive before it could bring down the whole structure: a sort of pressure-release valve. Standing at the evacuation shelter, I can't help but imagine a change of government as the political equivalent of a hazard-reduction burn: a low-intensity fire deliberately lit at an opportune time to make way for fresh growth without taking out the habitat trees.

In a hypothetical healthy democracy, a well-informed and fully enfranchised population can peacefully burn down a regime and install a new one without having to wheel guillotines into the town square. But under a regime of state capture, it may look like we have elections, but the deeper layers are untouched by the surface churn. Elections are fought out over confected moral panics and niche tinkering with tax and transfer systems, but the investors have culled any possibility of real contention getting within striking distance of executive government.

The thing is, parliaments are only one narrow forum for exercise of collective agency. The wisest and most adept decision-making I've ever experienced happened around campfires; old people with mugs of tea sitting with activists and researchers, making high-pressure judgement calls on the fate of whole landscapes.

So when we argue over whether it's better to be working for reform or rebellion, it may be that we have our eyes fixed on different levels of the panarchy. What can look like a promise of meaningful change may be nothing more than a concession offered by investors to shelter deeper layers from disruption. But as the organisers of whirlwind moments know, even a sand grain impacting at the right time can set off an unstoppable movement cascade.

A shriek of feedback from the PA breaks my reverie. The briefing is starting. Weather's turning against us again, they are saying.

And so the political fuel piles up on the forest floor, tinder-dry, a bomb of consequences awaiting an alignment of weather conditions and an opportune spark.

It is difficult to make a set of rules that will cover all contingencies since no two games are alike.

Lizzie J. Magie

do not pass go

I used to love the board game Monopoly as a kid, but only if I was winning. Being a precocious, competitive little shit, I used to win a fair bit. Now, while I'm stuck in jail with the other tokens tapping around the board past me, Jeff has gone on a bit of a spree, picking up a swag of properties down the valuable end of the board. Surveying everyone's holdings while I wait to get out. I can see what's happening here. It'll take another hour, but it looks like Jeff's going to clean us all out.

'The rallying and chaffing of the others when one player finds himself an inmate of the jail, and the expressions of mock sympathy and condolences when one is obliged to betake himself to the poor house, make a large part of the fun and merriment of the game,' writes the game's inventor, Lizzie J. Magie, in 1902. She clearly has a sharp sense of humour, but she's invented the game for a serious purpose: 'It is a practical demonstration of the present system of land-grabbing with all its usual outcomes and consequences . . . It was the original intention . . . simply to work out a demonstration of how the landlord gets his money and keeps it.'

Right. As a real-estate simulator, it's wearyingly accurate: once someone has started to win, they'll probably keep winning.

At last I'm out of jail, my little pewter hat skipping along, but now the board is perilously empty of friendly places to land. Fine – I can buy a railway station, even though the revenue is mediocre and I'll be teased for being the public transport guy.

In case this wasn't part of your childhood, the basic deal is you're rolling dice to get around a board subdivided into vacant properties; land on them, buy sets of them, develop them with little houses, and then the next time another player lands on one you own, they have to pay you rent. Around this end of the board, the properties are cheap and the rents are affordable; around that end, they can be game-ending if you're short of cash. You'll end up selling stuff, maybe trading with other players, just to stay on the board, but it's only a matter of time: you're screwed.

The game begins with everyone equal: same amount of starting cash, same starting position. The opposite of real life, but even so, watch what happens as it goes: the way the rules are structured, even with the levellest of playing fields and everyone using the same set of dice, whoever gets lucky and plays their cards right in that initial scramble is going to find themselves on a positive feedback escalator. The more property you have, the more rent you can charge, which allows you to buy more property and charge even more rent, breaking your fellow players one after another. Exactly like real life.

'A positive feedback loop is self-reinforcing. The more it works, the more it gains power to work some more' observes Donella, tapping a little pewter car five steps along and handing over a bunch of money to Jeff. Dr Njoya rolls the dice; bad luck for her too. The two of them exchange a long glance.

Back in 1904, when Magie takes out her patent on what she called the 'Landlord's Game', there are two sets of rules. One set – the one we play by today – is designed to demonstrate how capitalism works to impoverish the many and enrich the few. 'In a short time, I hope a very short time, men and women will discover that they are poor because Carnegie and Rockefeller, maybe, have more than they know what to do with,' she tells a journalist in 1906.

In her other, more egalitarian, set of rules, players sensing their impending destitution can vote to switch to a system of public ownership of utilities and land taxes to capture the profits of the wealthy. Then when you land on a property, the rent is paid into a common pool, and the game ends when even the poorest player has doubled their money and been rescued from poverty.

Magie based these rules on the work of nineteenth-century economic philosopher Henry George, who argues that 'what has destroyed every previous civilization has been the tendency to the unequal distribution of wealth and power'. His solution – one of them, anyway – is a broad-based land tax accruing to the public good. 'It is not necessary to confiscate land; it is only necessary to confiscate rent,' he suggests.

Those aren't the rules we're playing by today. Pyotr has just landed on one of Jeff's more lavish properties and is handing over what looks like half of everything he has left. The mood is darkening around the table as Jeff sorts his cash into piles, jokes about being able to afford to build properties in space.

Okay, I'm realising he's not joking.

Copies of the original game, with its politics intact, are passed around for thirty years; handmade boards, names on the properties localising into new home towns, rulesets diverging slowly. The game has become a freely shared piece of the commons, like chess or hopscotch. In that form it passes into the hands of one Charles Darrow, an unemployed radiator repair man from Philadelphia. Darrow simply claims to have invented it whole and complete out of his own brain. He sells the idea to Parker Brothers in 1935 and becomes fabulously wealthy when the game sells two million copies in the first two years. It's now the world's best-selling proprietary board game.

Darrow is credited as the game's creator; Magie is given $500 for her patent and invited to vanish from history. The rule that lets you work together to stop the monopolist from bankrupting everyone has been deleted. Most people have no idea it was ever there.

Your move, Karl.

Watching him roll, and land right on Jeff's most exclusive property, a web services business that controls 30 per cent of the cloud. That's going to ruin Karl, surely, and I'm only just getting to know him. This is awful; I lend him a chunk of money and Frances chips in the rest, but things are getting desperate.

I'm not even sure whose turn it is; nobody wants to roll. There is an almost palpable sigh of relief when Dr Njoya breaks the silence. 'Okay, I am here to name the monsters that are responsible for our problems,' she says, staring right at Jeff. It's the opportune spark the rest of us have been waiting for.

Now, the movement cascade. Pyotr passes me a handwritten note. 'The fittest are not the physically strongest, nor the cunningest, but those who learn to combine so as mutually to support each other, strong and weak alike, for the welfare of the community,' it reads.

I'm in. Passing the note around until everyone's on board; not you, Jeff.

The only way this is going to end differently is if we work together. Swap cards to strengthen each other's position. Forgive each other's debts. Pay each other's fines. Pool the income when Jeff lands on one of our collective holdings. Try and loosen the coins' cold transactional grip on our psyches and relationships. It's only going to work if we trust each other, and trust can be slow to build. The rules had us set against each other in Darwinian competition until moments ago, but unless we're ready to link arms and trust our lives to one other, we're all going to end up in the ranks of the unnecessariat.

Jeff has worked out what's happening. He's trying to buy off Frances, who is having none of it. Offers me a trip to his space station. Tells everyone he's actually the victim here, that if he goes down he's taking all of us with him, that Karl is a communist.

Fuck you, Jeff.

Unlucky roll: he's just landed on Donella's most important asset, a book called *The Limits to Growth*. He's not liking this at all, and Donella is now sitting on a lot of cash. Just for a moment we can feel the balance shifting, and that makes this the most perilous time of all. With Jeff's domination suddenly faltering, our solidarity loosens. The alliance risks fragmenting as each of us wonders whether we're well positioned to make a run for it and be the next Jeff.

Karl's just shaking his head. Some of his best ideas rely on us being smarter than that.

'People who manage to intervene in systems at the level of paradigm hit a leverage point that totally transforms systems,' says Donella. Taming runaway positive feedback cascades is something of a specialty of hers; she's even written a list called 'Places to intervene in a system, in increasing order of effectiveness'. If you could change anything for maximum leverage, she says, the most important point of all is 'the mindset or paradigm out of which the goals, rules, feedback structure arise'.

So she's sharing the proceeds around, and in the breathing space she's given us, we're coming up with better feedback structures so this thing doesn't keep ending the same way. Karl has some ideas. So do Pyotr and Dr Njoya; Frances has done this kind of thing at the highest levels. We got this.

Dear Lizzie J. Magie, whose own story somehow perfectly captures the dull menace of the very thing she was trying to warn us against, has dropped by to see how our game is going. She's brought an army of school strikers with her.

'Let the children once see clearly the gross injustice of our present land system and when they grow up, if they are allowed to develop naturally, the evil will soon be remedied,' she says. 'And fuck you, Jeff.'

new maps

After weeks of it, it becomes a blur, a discontinuous scramble of preparation and evacuation, boredom and intensity. A sleeping dragon, one of our neighbours calls it. It awakes on high winds, a thousand smouldering hotspots roaring back to life when the weather kicks up. The grey polygon on the map, unrecognisable now, lashing across the landscape in new directions, triggering new confrontations and evacuations, two thousand kilometres from end to end. Ashen silences shattered by a waterbombing helicopter drawing from the farm dam immediately down the hill. A wave from the co-pilot as this thunderous apparition turns and wheels back towards the firefront, returning again, and again. Convoys of tankers and strike vehicles pound the roads; bulldozers arrive at dawn to smash containment lines into these wounded hills. While the dragon sleeps, they backburn – anything to starve and contain its next flight.

We've come to that stage of the Monopoly game where Dr Njoya clears her throat and names the monsters. Systems language provides valuable metaphors and analytical tools, but abstractions have a way of diffusing things just when they need to be looked right in the eye.

We've watched sand piles and played systems games, drawn ourselves on graph paper, spoken of adaptive cycles and anglerfish and continuities, but always, at the heart of this thing, are people. People with names and addresses, making decisions from which consequences flow. They stay quite deliberately indeterminate, safely out of shot. Their maps of us are vastly more accurate than our maps of them, and that might be something we want to change.

The rigorous simplicities of the coin-doubling game and the power-law gradients of social contention don't get the oligarchs or the investor blocs off the hook. Different regimes, different rules or different economies would leave different statistical shapes on the graph paper. Regimes are the product of human decisions and exercises of coercive power, not eternal expressions of some natural law. 'The growth of a large business is merely survival of the fittest' was bullshit when Rockefeller pitched it, and it's bullshit now.

Neoliberalism, as a particularly aggressive strain of capitalism, arguably isn't a regime as such; it's something that infects regimes and reprograms them from the inside out. So we'll learn the systems game because these metaphors are useful, but before we get to the permaculture workshop there needs to be a bar-room brawl, the kind where the gas companies and their banks get hurled through the windows at the end. The time for negotiation has passed.

Capitalism is the problem. Capitalism in service to colonial, white supremacist patriarchy. We found the monsters throwing the children into the water, named them. Now we make them stop.

Three proposed agreements flow from here.

One: the fossil industries setting everything on fire need to be shut down now, as a matter of existential priority. We have to disarm the carbon bomb. Fossil is over. Focus on how.

Two: we may all be facing the same storm, but we're not all in the same boat. Garrett Hardin doesn't get to throw the children of Kutupalong into the water anymore: our work is for global, cross-border climate justice, not some kind of solar-powered green nationalism.

Three: we use the shockwaves from the collapse of the fossil investors to end the coin-doubling game before the planet ends it for us. Human dignity and survival should never have been made dependent on waged labour, and so the endgame is in sight either way. The biosphere absolutely will not tolerate another coin-doubling; the coyote's legs are churning the air, so far above the ground. It's time for the architects and cultivators of soft landings to seize the moment: there are other kinds of economy, other modes of production, other ways of relating to one other. It's time to remember, rebuild, and reinvent them, at scale.

Our quiet refuge is besieged on three sides now. From high on the hill, with the wind tearing in from five different directions, we can see it making a run. The dragon, stirring. Screened by tiers of weary eucalypts to the south, plumes of smoke are tumbling into the tormented air; the light changing even as we scramble back down the hill. A new front is bearing in on the southern end of the valley as we bounce down the road towards the highway, hypnotised by its proximity. It looks so different this close to hand; walls of filthy smoke boiling towards us, angry and uncompromising, racing on the strengthening wind. At the end of the world, an emergency vehicle parked across the highway with dome lights flashing, directing us northwards. Doomed stringybarks catch the last of the light before this advancing front takes the sun.

The urgency of the first agreement – that we have to end fossil burning – has been evident for decades. It is nothing more than accepting what the atmosphere, the ocean, the Arctic, the reef, the fireground and every relevant scientific discipline on earth is screaming at us: to have any reasonable chance of avoiding the hell-plunge into a five- or six-degree world, fossil burners have to come out of the system today, now, immediately. We also have to plant as though our lives depend on it and do a thousand other beautiful things, but unless all of the heavy emitters are coming out at the same time, it may barely even register.

It sounds easy when you say it quick. It isn't easy, and it won't be quick, but this is what climate organisers and scientists have been insisting for years. We are out of time.

We'll be needing new maps.

A global map of the monster's structure, its financial arteries, its weaknesses and chokepoints. It's going to look like one of Mark Lombardi's mesmerising sociograms, with the resources sector laced to the media entities and governments it has captured, its peak bodies, policy shops and public relations firms.

For petrostates and pollution exporters such as Australia, our map takes in the big engineering companies and accounting firms and ratings agencies who show up again and again. At the very top tier, draw the investor blocs driving the whole thing: the investment banks, the superannuation funds, the pools of capital desperately seeking a rate of return. The map will show us the carbon, but it will also, finally, show us the money.

The map illuminates which of the politicians fronting the cameras are just placeholders, political shock absorbers reading scripts written by their investors. Float logos above their heads so we can keep track of who owns them. And then put them on mute for a moment and look behind the curtain.

Scale the map according to carbon impact, and we'll see who the real monsters are. Just one hundred global entities are responsible for 70 per cent of the pollution that is burning down the world. Learn their names. Saudi Aramco. Gazprom. Shenhua. ExxonMobil. BP, Chevron, BHP. Some of them might have offices in your home town. You might work for one of them. Maybe one of them sponsored your arts festival or donated a prize to your school. One of the purposes of the map is to help us pick the most vulnerable ones and pull them into the foreground, where they least want to be.

In quiet and compliant parts of the world, they are not used to being attacked or humiliated; they are used to being invited to gala dinners and sporting events. Now, with ash on the breeze, it is time to name names. Who leads them? Who insures them? Who owns them? Who are the most nervous links in their supply chains? Which of those bloated investment banks is going down with this ship, and which ones, given a sufficiently vigorous shove, will jump?

The map is high-dimensional, like the system it approximates. Turn it one way to expose the relationship interlock. Turn it another to see the sankey diagram we visualised in the dead village of Paracatu, flow pathways of global industrial metabolism. Highlight the energy sector. Turn it sideways again to show us the money. This map is not the territory, but surely this is better than driving blind.

We're going up against a powerful set of interests, it's true. They control media, police, spies, banks and courts, but let's be clear: this is a vanishingly tiny number of people, with huge tides moving against them. They are not gods, not masters of the universe, just people. They are experts in the art of *divide et impera*, masters at gaming the repression paradox and dumping cold-water feedbacks on runaway social movements. And yet, the cascade of coal bankruptcies has begun. The power station closures have begun. The legal sanctions have begun. Their own children are looking at them differently. Nervous capital is shifting; unity fragmenting, fragile, restive. Sandcastle oligarchs realising, too late, the immensity of the incoming tide.

They are few, and we are very, very many. We have the wind at our backs now, and it is full of embers.

attack surface

'We ask you to make sure that every audience you have at Fringe World this festival season knows where you stand on climate and partnering with any dirty fossil fuel corporations.' Ash Traylia, in a glorious hoop dress and white Renaissance wig, has just crashed the stage at Perth's Fringe Festival and grabbed the mic. It takes the audience a moment to realise this isn't part of the official program. 'Our art [is being] tarnished and exploited as a multipurpose billboard for this corporation.'

They came to see art; this is art. Woodside clearly hasn't thought this through: in plastering its logo all over the festival, they've painted a target on themselves, and the city's feisty arts community doesn't miss. The climate emergency just crashed the party, and looked magnificent while doing it. Now a loosely coordinated guerrilla troupe of performers and rebels turn the gas industry's financial corruption of the festival into a vivid backdrop for climate action.

Investopedia defines 'social licence to operate' as 'the ongoing acceptance of a company or industry's standard business practices and operating procedures by its employees, stakeholders, and the general public'.

Fossil capital has an absolutely enormous attack surface, and 'social licence' is a crucial part of it. So turn it up to eleven: no office unoccupied, no billboard left free of public interest enhancements and replacements; a thousand stickers, paste-ups, stencils and murals. When we're done, offers of fossil sponsorship need to be treated like offers of a turd in the punchbowl.

Our first agreement – that fossil is over – simplifies life enormously. It means we no longer need to treat this as a negotiation, a journey or a respectful dialogue. Fossil fuel corporations and their financiers and their political proxies are not partners, stakeholders or 'part of the solution'. We don't have to worry about hurting their feelings, and we don't have to fight fair. We have to break them.

Sometimes, highly disruptive direct action gets the goods: not just in shoving the Overton window open, but in physically preventing destruction. That's the reason Woodside never got to build its thirty-square-kilometre onshore gas complex at Walmadan on Western Australia's Kimberley coast.

'Goolarabooloo always said no!' reads the banner on the beach, held up by the ragged but ecstatic blockade crew who have just thrown themselves into its path. 'As you know, every country has laws. Here we have our own Traditional Laws. Our Laws come from Bugarregarre, the Dreamtime,' reads the campaign handbook. Thus grounded, the defence of this place is immovable. An experience nobody present will ever forget: rich red pindan sand, under a bright blue sky, on the only road into the project site. Ranks of uniformed police jog alongside a convoy of commercial drilling equipment; state coercion in service to fossil capital, same as it ever was.

'The campaign was not won by political pressure, but through corporate pressure relating to direct actions, legal tactics and investor lobbying that cost the company money, time and social license,' writes Nicola Paris, founder of activist training organisation CounterAct. The campaign is complex and multilayered, but the direct action is what draws the cameras and costs the company time and money: dusty, bruising and spectacular collisions between community will and corporate power. In 2013, the Walmadan crew push the company past its pain threshold.

'Direct action can also confer political influence on the anti-fracking movement, as the imposition of moratoriums in France, Bulgaria, South Africa, Czech Republic and elsewhere has demonstrated.' That's Jonathan Wood, a global issues analyst with industry consultancy Control Risks, trying to help his clients work out why fierce-looking young people are locking their arms into forty-four-gallon drums on their construction sites. They are doing it, he explains, because it works. 'Blockades are a favoured non-violent direct-action tactic across the environmental activist movement, particularly for rural gas drilling projects . . . while the costs to activists of blockades are extremely low – both in terms of organisation and penalties – the potential for disruption to the target can be significant in terms of lost productivity and extra operating costs.'

The costs to activists aren't low at all, but otherwise this analysis stacks up. Amid dreamlike mists, imagine thirty-foot tripods at dawn, cabled to a formidable infrastructure of concrete barricades and buried cars; fortifications occupied by First Nations warriors, farmers and thousands of supporters from near and far. On unceded Githabul lands in the Northern Rivers region of New South Wales, the day before Metgasco's despised gas fracking proposal is due to run this blockade, the state government pulls their licence and the project collapses.

The Bentley blockade is an astounding case study in grassroots movement building, with direct action embedded in a wider field of capability and care. 'This was not a top-down community organising model, rather, local communities were assisted to conduct their own meetings and processes. It morphed into a form of civil defence networking, based upon the frames of local democracy and mutual aid,' write Annie Kia and Aidan Ricketts in their study of how the campaign was structured.

It doesn't always work. Blockaders at the site of the Beverley uranium mine in South Australia were beaten by riot police, locked in a shipping container and sprayed with chemical weapons. The mine went ahead. Direct action is met with gunfire from Colombia to Mathare; what works in one context is a repression nightmare in others.

But in the right place at the right time, the sites of transaction, extraction and pollution can all form part of the attack surface. News of a port shutdown when a citizens' flotilla blocks the shipping lane hits the CEO's desk, the stock market and the evening news, all at about the same time. Disruption at mines, ports and gasfields take planning and care, but as the Control Risks people point out, the payoffs can be immense. Disruption at banks, brokerages and corporate headquarters; that brings it all the way home.

Now, a silent line of Red Rebels stands before a cordon of armoured police, neither side speaking, neither side breaking eye contact. Like an island in shifting tides, on terrains as diverse as Walmadan and Bentley, Wattle Forest and Jabiluka, one central principle stands. It holds true at the decade-long occupation at La ZAD de Notre-Dame-des-Landes in France, on the Standing Rock Reservation in the United States, and on the mineral fields of Jharkhand. Legal proclamations written by investor blocs and issued by compliant politicians will be backed by state violence, but that's not a social contract, it's more like a form of organised crime. For as long as our states remain captive to the investors, none of us are under any obligation to obey their laws.

burn the money

Rain, endless walls of it. Dragon expiring on the forest floor in fuming middens of ash and fallen giants. More rain will fall in the next forty-eight hours than has fallen all year; this seems to be where we live now. Not so far from here, flooding is closing intersections, metro lines, elevator shafts and whole city blocks. All of it in a country with the wealth and resilience to send in rescue teams and reconnect the power; the safe side of collapse, for now. Just sitting with this for the moment, the roar of real rain on a tin roof, and the deeper thunder of this exhausted forest inhaling the drenching like life itself. Twelve hours in, streamflow for the first time in almost a year, dry gullies suddenly alive with churn and flow. A million frogs calling it in, arising from unseen refuges to fill the teeming air with a chorus as old as the Triassic.

'I'm done with fossil fuels. We're done.' Returning cautiously home to unpack after weeks of evacuations, I've had to turn up the volume to hear Jim Cramer over the rain. The host of CNBC's 'Mad Money' is dropping truth bombs while a startled interviewer tries to rein him in. He's not speaking to an audience of rebels or strikers; his segment is targeted at the investor community. 'We're starting to see divestment all over the world. Big pension funds saying we're just not going to own them anymore. The world's changed – we're in the death knell phase . . . the world has turned on them.'

Scan fossil capital's attack surface for points of intervention; notice that when we take aim directly at the coins, it draws the investors' full and undivided attention.

Picture this: an unlikely alliance of farmers, family and raggedy-looking blockaders are holding a vigil on the steps of the Supreme Court of New South Wales. TV news crews have got their cutaway footage; now scrolling through their phones waiting for an outcome. It is July 2014, and Jon Moylan is about to be sentenced. The twenty-four-year-old has been charged under the *Corporations Act*; he's facing up to a decade in prison and a $765,000 fine.

'I announced on behalf of the bank that the ANZ bank had pulled their loan for Whitehaven's Maules Creek coal project,' Moylan tells the

ABC a couple of years later. His hoax press release announcing the coal company had lost its financier was picked up by the national media, sparking a fleeting panic on the stock market. Whitehaven's share price fell 9 per cent within minutes, wiping $314 million off the value of the company. The prank was revealed immediately and the price bounced back, but that's not the point. Moylan had attacked the 'integrity of financial markets . . . and caused untold harm to investors who sold amid the panic', seethed a *Sydney Morning Herald* editorial. Commentary on the News Corp platforms was burst-blood-vessel unhinged. Moylan had crossed a line, caused a tremor in the sacred stack of coins – an apostasy for which he should face 'the full force of the regulatory hammer', according to one commercial lawyer. Major party politicians fell over each other to condemn this unthinkable obscenity on behalf of imaginary 'mum-and-dad investors' whose lives had been so callously destroyed.

Financial campaigning is an area of dissent for which the system has very low tolerance – it much prefers social movements taking the fight up to politicians. Ministers' offices are amply resourced with comms staff and campaign strategists to handle such contests; some of them appear to thrive on it. Using elected officials as shock absorbers for social discontent is one of the ways investors manage to stay in the background, letting their political investments draw the fire for a few years and then hiring them as lobbyists when they get worn out.

Short-circuiting this dismal circus is one of the organising principles of divestment campaigns run by groups such as 350.org. Adapting the anti-apartheid tactic of financial divestment to fossil industry supply chains has proven a runaway success, partly because it illuminates legible points of intervention everywhere from university campuses to the United Nations. 'The logic of divestment couldn't be simpler: if it's wrong to wreck the climate, it's wrong to profit from that wreckage,' writes US environmentalist Bill McKibben, one of the founders of 350.org. 'The fossil fuel industry . . . has five times as much carbon in its reserves as even the most conservative governments on earth say is safe to burn. The hope is that divestment is one way to weaken those companies – financially, but even more politically.'

It's working. As of early 2020 the campaign has provoked more than US$12 trillion in divestments, with churches, philanthropic foundations, colleges, banks and pension funds all selling up – well over a thousand institutions and more than fifty-eight thousand individuals. The European Investment Bank will have completely phased out financing oil, gas and coal projects by 2021, with EIB president Werner Hoyer announcing, 'Climate is the top issue on the political agenda of our time.' Late in 2019, Sweden's central bank announced it was dumping bonds issued by the carbon-intensive states of Queensland, Western Australia and Alberta. 'Australia and Canada are countries that are not known for good climate work,' explained the bank's deputy governor, Martin Floden. When central banks join your divestment campaign, you know you've hit a nerve. Big blocs of capital have begun distancing themselves from this network of industries that already have the smell of death about them.

Top-tier banks and gas corporations retain public relations and issues management teams to help deflect this kind of reputational damage, but even the largest players have a pain threshold. The deeper you work back into the supply chains of really big projects, the more you come across mid-tier engineering companies and, eventually, family-run haulage businesses and specialist suppliers. These are not campaigning organisations in the least; they are just people trying to do a job, and their pain threshold for being on the evening news in the middle of a demonstration is close to zero.

But if the job involves helping Indian billionaire Gautam Adani build one of the largest coalmines in the world, then the likelihood of ending up on the evening news rises significantly. #StopAdani campaigners have had a remarkable effect on the company's attempts to assemble its extended supply chain. Sixty-one companies – from small suppliers to major engineering and professional services companies such as GHD – have taken a pass. When campaigners put the blowtorch to Australia's four big banks, one by one they refused to finance the project. Adani put its hand out to Chinese state banks, which began slamming the shutters down one after another in 2017. This approach has had a similar impact on potential insurers, with sixteen global insurance corporations refusing to do business with Adani thus far.

Jon Moylan got off with a $1000 two-year good behaviour bond. Whitehaven Coal Ltd is now disembowelling the Maules Creek sub-basin ten million tonnes at a time. In the Galilee Basin, and on frontlines everywhere, it has to be different. Cramer is pointing us to the most painfully exposed vulnerability across the whole attack surface: nervous, flighty, desperate capital. Burn the money and the whole edifice caves in.

Way back in 2015, no less a figure than Mark Carney, the governor of the Bank of England, warned an insurance industry audience at Lloyds of London: 'A wholesale reassessment of prospects, especially if it were to occur suddenly, could potentially destabilise markets, spark a pro-cyclical crystallisation of losses and a persistent tightening of financial conditions.'

A pro-cyclical crystallisation of losses. That's the sound of $4 trillion in unburnable fossil capital hitting the wall; one fund manager's sand-grain divestment kicking off a cascade that roars into an avalanche. Anyone's money that hasn't long since left the building is going to get crushed in that stampede, which in his own cautious way is what Carney was trying to say.

2015 feels like a long time ago. If we're still having this conversation, it means his audience wasn't listening. It means they still can't hear us. Refusing to leave through the door in an orderly fashion, so through the windows it is.

The rain is easing now, and it feels like the conversations outside are also different from what I'm used to. The fires, and then the rain, have re-ordered the acoustic field somehow; different languages occupying different frequencies. There is a lot more going on out there than there was before; squelchy songs of the Triassic joining a thousand voices from every age of the earth.

Rise, like lions after slumber
In unvanquishable number!
Shake your chains to earth like dew
Which in sleep had fallen on you:
Ye are many – they are few!

PERCY BYSSHE SHELLEY

in union

Our immune systems have no recollection of meeting it; our deepest genetic libraries contain no entries for the tiny replicator the World Health Organization will name SARS-CoV-2. Experts think this novel thing has an R number of maybe 2.63, but estimates go as high as 4.6. Recall that a number even a fraction above 1 indicates a runaway positive feedback cascade. The more people infected, the more people will continue to be infected – until everyone catches it, or something happens to push that number back below 1.

The virus moves with the speed of hyper-accelerated trade and aviation, coursing rapidly out of China's industrial heartland along the just-in-time sankey stripes of global supply chains. 'Dun & Bradstreet estimates that 51,000 companies around the world have one or more direct suppliers in Wuhan, while 938 of the Fortune 1000 companies have tier one or two suppliers in the Wuhan region,' writes Kim Moody for the journal *Spectre*. Six degrees of separation collapse into a frighteningly short distance as the people labouring within these enmeshed supply chains fall ill.

Something has shifted, and it won't be shifting back.

March 2020: helter-skelter shutdowns and lockdowns proliferate around the world as states crudely demarcate their workforces into essential and non-essential. Cardiac tremors in the coin stack: the global economy is sliding into recession. Central banks flood the system with freshly invented money, and the monopoly scramble shifts gear. 'What we've seen is a dramatic polarisation of fortunes. Billionaire innovators and disruptors in tech, healthcare, and industrials are fast and massively pulling ahead of the rest of the universe,' marvels Josef Stadler of UBS Global Wealth Management. Fucking Jeff has doubled his coins again.

The fossil sector's ashen corner of the universe is having a harder time. The industry is getting smashed as demand sags, driving it into deeper enmeshment with its captive states. Watch with horror as the parasite hive of think tanks and media platforms launch powerful disinformation campaigns demanding economies reopen so the oil can flow again. In post-truth strongman regimes such as the United States and Brazil, these efforts are so well targeted that within months, hundreds of thousands of people are dead.

Movements built on massed public gatherings are suddenly curtailed; flywheels of the extinction rebels and school strikers thrown briefly out of phase. But on other fault lines, other pressures are building. Footage of George Floyd's casual murder by Minneapolis police officers is the incendiary sand grain that reignites the Black Lives Matter movement, fury reverberating around the world as the mask slips on the violent superstructures of white supremacy. The uprising is met with tear gas and tentative concessions from New York to New Zealand; cold water feedbacks deployed against runaway rage. But it's too late; decades of advocacy for police and prison abolition are newly visible through the broken panes of the Overton window.

Now the pandemic opens a different kind of window into who's doing the real work in our stricken little village. Essential workers – healthcare professionals, teachers, delivery riders, supermarket night-fill staff, biomedical researchers: step up. Non-essential workers – Enterprise Solutions Architects, Fintech Quantitative Developers and Business Intelligence Engineers: go home.

For some, this means the loneliness of isolation, back-to-back video calls and home-baked sourdough. For others, an enforced return to workplaces infused with an unyielding and invisible menace; anxious eye contact above those awful masks; nightmare shifts in overwhelmed covid wards. Mass unemployment surges as the broken economy begins shedding workers into the ranks of unnecessariat, yet somehow, amid this astonishing species-wide trauma, the 1-per-cent villager is still demanding his rent, still demanding the interest on his coins.

And so the resistance flares spontaneously from the margins, far from the battered core of organised labour. In the United States, it erupts at the intersection of the pandemic and the Black Lives Matter uprising. Dispensing with formal votes and top-down union decision-making, non-unionised workforces are coordinating on social media networks to walk off the job. Black organisers are pioneering adaptive industrial action for the gig economy age: 'when workers get mad enough (or scared enough) about their working conditions they may simply stop working; if they are ordered to wade into a pandemic, they may simply refuse,' explains labour law professor Michael Duff. This is r-phase organising, fast and loose, without seeking permission from K-phase union hierarchies that are either too slow, too white or too wedded to the status quo to recognise the moment. 'I think the lessons for the traditional labor movement are that they are outdated and becoming more and more irrelevant,' argues union organiser Neidi Dominguez. 'If anyone is gonna strike or take more militant actions, it's going to be younger people.'

The strike is back. In defiance of an anticipated wave of evictions, IWW Kulin Nations organisers in Melbourne launch a rent strike petition. Nearly twenty thousand renters immediately sign this declaration of refusal, and so in March 2020 the prime minister announces a six-month moratorium on evictions. It's part of an astonishing wave of rent strikes rippling around the world, the concept of housing as a human right colliding with the concept of housing as just another asset class.

Some actions come from unexpected quarters. In August, the Australian Unemployed Workers Union pulls off a strike against the punitive system of 'mutual obligations' enforced by private employment agencies.

Hold on – the what union?

'Yes: unemployed people have rights. And governments are not very good at respecting or upholding those rights. So we need to band together so that we have strength in pushing back against that, and making sure that unemployed people aren't being abused by a welfare system that is supposed to support them.' That's Kristin O'Connell, a volunteer organiser with the AUWU.

This nuggety and fast-growing organisation was already filling a crucial niche before the pandemic dumped thousands of newly unemployed people out into the streets; now it is coming into its own. When the AUWU calls a strike, they are unprepared for the response: from other social justice organisations, more established union networks and – most importantly – thousands of people caught up in this degrading system. 'The stories have not stopped pouring in from people about what it meant for their mental health, what that act of solidarity meant, and how much more powerful people felt that they were taking a massive collective action, as opposed to trying to navigate the system on their own,' says O'Connell.

It's immediately clear why the oligarchs invest so heavily in automation and *divide et impera*. 'Ye are many – they are few,' Shelley wrote in 1819. So very few, in fact: an investor class of 2604 billionaires and twenty million millionaires counting coins and planning their passage to Alpha Centauri.

The 'defeat of organised labour throughout the core capitalist nations has perhaps been neoliberalism's most important achievement, significantly changing the balance of power between capital and labour', write Nick Srnicek and Alex Williams. Under this onslaught, union membership crashed in the latter part of the twentieth century across much of the industrialised world, falling from 30 per cent on average in 1985 to about half that rate today.

It's always been more than a numbers game, and defeat comes in many forms. K-phase unions captive to employer groups or political regimes can end up fused to the institutional furniture, or locked into decimal place contests over the minutiae of pay and conditions.

Now an offensive may be in the offing, carried on the same ember-laden winds that have mobilised the school strikers and the rest of this gathering storm. The International Trade Union Confederation (ITUC) is the largest federation of trade unions in the world, representing more than two hundred million working people through 331 affiliated organisations. Encompassing a vast diversity of sectors and contexts, the confederation's work on Just Transitions is rich and unambiguous. Amid the policy documents, resolutions, case studies and flashpoints, the opening line on its frontline campaign for climate justice and industrial transformation reads the same as our banner out front of the mining conference: 'There are no jobs on a dead planet'.

Even at the literal coalface, there is movement now. 'Communities grow around power stations and the mines that supply them. They are unique communities bonded in many cases by history, geography, difficult and dangerous working conditions and good unionised jobs. They are also uniquely vulnerable in their heavy dependence on the coal power industry,' writes Tony Maher, the national president of Australia's Construction, Forestry, Maritime, Mining and Energy Union (CFMMEU). In October 2018, it commissioned a study on the local costs of mine and power station closures in other parts of the world. 'Those costs would show up as unwelcome early retirements, unemployment, underemployment, insecure employment and work that is lower paid, less safe and less skilled,' the authors state. For an industry deliberately automating its workforce out of existence, the banner should maybe have read 'No jobs and a dead planet', since that seems to be what's happening. Fighting such deprivation is exactly why people join unions in the first place: it's from here that the ethic of just transitions emerges.

'The transition away from a heavy reliance on coal mining in Germany's Ruhr region, where forward planning, investment in industry diversification, staggering of mine closures and a comprehensive package of just transition measures delivered a major reshaping of the regional economy with no forced job losses,' writes Maher.

When students across the world borrowed the strike from the union repertoire, it invoked echoes of the 'green bans' that sparked across Australia in the 1970s. This is what should be keeping the investors awake at night: coal workers on the same side of a picket line as climate justice campaigners, striking in globally synchronised acts of refusal.

Something has shifted, and it won't be shifting back.

Stop imagining the apocalypse
Start imagining the revolution

PAVEMENT GRAFFITI

sovereign risk

Our search for the most productive forms of intolerable dissent is about to bring us full circle, back to our chambers of collective agency.

Investors hate it, and they complain about it endlessly: this thing they call sovereign risk. The phrase used to mean the risk of debt default by a sovereign government. If banks lent a stack of Anthropocene coinage to one of their comprador regimes who then blew it on mansions and military parades instead of paying it back: that was sovereign risk. Now it's just code for anything a government tries to do that investors don't like. When Australian prime minister Kevin Rudd tried to introduce a mining 'super profits' tax in 2010, they screamed sovereign risk and poured cyanide into the government's factional fault lines until he was gone. When prime minister Julia Gillard worked with the Greens and independents to introduce the *Clean Energy Act* in 2011, they screamed it again and installed Tony Abbott to make it disappear.

One of neoliberalism's most lethal kinks is to assume ideological control of public institutions and then run them into the ground. The rail network, the welfare agency, the health service, the primary school, the electricity grid. Pull the funding, cancel the maintenance, degrade the capability, and then use every breakdown and failure to argue that the private sector could do a more efficient job. Degrade it enough, people will give up and submit to privatisation; immediately the juice will be sucked out of the profitable parts, with the rest broken up and sold as scrap.

This isn't limited to your bus service. The core institutions of democracy are being run into this cold ground. They've now weathered five decades of neoliberal assault: funding pulled, maintenance cancelled, capabilities degraded until politics ends up loathed and despised. Run it down hard enough, we won't bother to vote, or we'll elect flyblown demagogues if they promise to drain the swamp. The corruption scandals, the graft, the desperate broad daylight incompetence, that's all part of the performance.

Enough. It's time we recaptured our decision structures at every level of the panarchy.

For those confronting assemblies full of men in military uniforms, or for campaigners trying to crack the slimy armour of communitarian, systemically corrupt oligarchies, this work can be risky and terrifying. But for those of us with greater degrees of freedom, even as the pandemic tilts the tables further against us, we have no excuse to abandon the field. The investment theory of party competition doesn't say that people with good heart will never get elected, it just warns us that the playing field is anything but level.

We don't campaign with cash transfers from the gas industry, or bot swarms and saturation promotion on the Murdoch platforms. We do it with patience and urgency, building grassroots networks, going door to door and talking to people, making thousands of calls. We do it by building movements: large-scale volunteer efforts instead of coal-industry coins. We do it with a million small donations, not with one large one. We do it with the power of collective organising at particular, targeted scales of governance.

Each election that rolls around, at all levels, is part of the attack surface, and no part of this story is a spectator sport. Back an independent candidate with the courage to throw themselves into this fight without a gas industry logo over their head. If all you see on the ballot paper are gas industry logos, then be that candidate. Otherwise, you could choose to work with a group of people who have spent more than twenty years building a feisty and resilient global grassroots network, a party that develops its platform deliberatively, a party that has never once banked a cheque from fossil capital.

Planet; peace; justice; democracy. That's the platform. If that party doesn't seem quite right, if you think its pitch is off-target or the logo is the wrong shade of green, join it and help us fix that shit up. There are vastly better ways to make decisions than brittle parliamentary machines, but while we're recapturing the old ways and experimenting with the new, these are the machines we count ourselves fortunate to have.

Some of the new ways are worth more than a passing glance. Professor Janette Hartz-Karp has spent years studying the conditions under which collective intelligence can be given political effect. She's now one of the country's foremost practitioners of a thing called 'deliberative democracy', which is helping communities from Australia to India to the United States use deliberative assemblies to resolve formidably difficult political problems. These assemblies are empowered to ask for whatever information they need; experts and subject matter specialists bearing data on tap, but the experts are there to inform, not to decide.

According to Hartz-Karp, the first condition to make such a thing work is diversity. You need a wide range of viewpoints represented in the room for it to succeed. The second condition is that these points of view have to meet; entrenched positions are challenged in the course of ordinary conversations. The third condition is that the assemblies must hold actual power; the decisions they make need to stick. It's agreeably consistent with the third demand of the extinction rebels: to convene citizens' assemblies on climate and ecological justice.

One example of an effective people's assembly comes from the UK, where a group of 108 randomly chosen citizens authored a strikingly coherent set of recommendations for steep decarbonisation pathways in September 2020.

There's now a solid basis of evidence that such assemblies, appropriately constituted, will always be wiser and fairer than the loudest expert in the room, for the same reason that the parliament was designed to be wiser and fairer than the King. Professor Hartz-Karp has facilitated dozens of these assemblies at local, state and national levels over more than twenty years. 'I think we incredibly underestimate people. I've never had a deliberative session – and I've run fifty, a hundred, I don't know how many, with randomly sampled people – I've never run one and felt let down.'

People's assemblies never resolve to throw children into the water. They are uniquely well-placed to guide the course of just transitions. They also have the benefit of not spawning career politicians. And while deliberative democracy sounds avant-garde, this may be the oldest form of collective decision-making there is. Recall a circle of elders and their allies, Uncle stirring at the fire with a stick, Aunties weighing up the fate of whole land-scapes. That's the risk that worries the investors most, perhaps; the ground shifting under the question of sovereignty itself.

This work isn't over until the old people around the campfire say it's over.

Every revolution – if it is an authentic revolution – is not only directed towards the future. It redeems, also, the past, failed revolutions. All the ghosts, as if the living dead of the past revolutions, which are roaming around unsatisfied, will finally find their home in the new freedom.

SLAVOJ ŽIŽEK

lacuna

My mind returns often to the dodge and weave of the systems game, still wondering what it's trying to teach us. One thing might be to abandon illusions of certainty and control. If two dozen people in a game with only one rule can give rise to chaotic dynamics, we have no hope of predicting the nonlinear jumps and twists of even near-future histories.

There is no historical inevitability to be found here; no shining path, no strategy guaranteed to prevail amid this cross-scale tangle of unintended consequences. Leaders who make claims on certainty should probably be automatically disqualified.

Another gift of the systems game is that every move of every participant matters to the outcome. Not as metaphor, but as gentle physical reality. The world would be different without you in it. There'd be an absence, a lacuna. Maybe you're a firebrand revolutionary, an overworked single parent or stuck at home with an undiagnosed chronic pain condition; your presence still matters in this deep old systems game.

We'll never know if we're the butterfly that stirs the hurricane, but it doesn't matter: now that we're in the hurricane business, the more butterflies the better. A movement sage in a teashop in Ranchi, a defiant teenager with a cardboard placard, an unbreakable Uncle sitting at a campfire. The network graphs we've been studying are inviting us to connect, especially with people outside our home villages; learn to synchronise wingbeats in time with all the others out there doing the same.

With a bit of craft, a bit of leverage, a bit of pressure and a bit of magic, maybe we are approaching that place where 'dragon-kings occur as system-wide events representing the tendency of the system to globally synchronize'.

What we're up against is certainly globally synchronised; from well-fields in the South Gobi to the utility selling power to the quiet house in the quiet street. It is densely interlocked and unified by a simple ideology: put every ecosystem, every human hour and every institution in service to coin-doubling growth.

By contrast, people working for the world that comes next are remarkably poorly connected at the planetary level, a consequence of centuries of *divide et impera*. Walled into competing nationalisms, divided by language barriers or just preoccupied with more locally immediate concerns: our networks of international solidarity are sparse and fragmented. So rather than reinventing these networks from nothing, let's begin with what we already have.

The United Nations provides a valuable superstructure for cross-border collaboration – the ICAN nuclear weapons ban treaty being one powerful example – and it also auspices life-or-death safety nets in places such as Kutupalong. With every nation represented and formal avenues for civil society participation, powerful agreement has already been sought on everything from disarmament to debt forgiveness to the far-reaching promise of the global goals.

But not everyone identifies with arbitrary nationalities inscribed by Westphalean aristocrats and monarchs, and many of those with a seat at these tables are only there through the repressive powers they wield at home. The planet's core multilateral architecture is also hamstrung by the existence of a 'Security' Council with a veto structure that ensures its five nuclear-armed permanent members will always place their own narrow interests above everyone else's. If our immediate future as a species depends on somehow igniting a globally synchronised challenge to the ubiquity of the coin-doubling game, these institutional chokeholds need to be bypassed somehow.

And so the question for those working to fan the intensity of global synchronies is a very old one: the question of scale.

There seems little appetite for the emergence of a global revolutionary vanguard party telling everyone what to do while gradually transforming into the ruling class it replaces. Without deep transparency and rigorous democratic pressure valves, it's evident that social movements, environment groups, trade unions and radical political parties are just as prone to K-phase conservatism and embrittlement as any other human institution, particularly when they reach scales sufficient to attract hostilities.

Does that mean we're doomed to stay small and largely disorganised? In *Inventing the Future*, Srnicek and Williams offer a confronting critique of what they term 'folk politics' – the thousandfold beautiful initiatives that somehow never manage to link arms with each other, rarely reaching scales approaching global synchrony. The forest blockade, the community garden, the anti-mining campaign; conflicts and initiatives that unfold at local scales of the panarchy but rarely trigger an upward cascade.

Commenting on the slow collapse of Occupy after its explosive proliferation in 2011, Srnicek and Williams note, 'The Occupy movements achieved real victories in creating solidarity, giving a voice to disenchanted and marginalised people, and raising public awareness. But they nonetheless remained an archipelago of prefigurative islands, surrounded by an implacably hostile capitalist environment.'

One by one, states moved to drown these islands with baton charges and pepper spray. So what then of global unity? How do we protect each other from the violence deployed against anyone who threatens the coin-doubling scam? And where are the networks and supportive infrastructures through which a truly post-national identity might arise?

A form of mutual aid at planetary scale: surely that's the missing piece of the architecture here; a lacuna so profound we barely notice its absence. For this emerging layer of our identity, the only border that matters is the one where the sky grades blue into deepest black; the boundary enclosing Luca's whole family tree.

Here's a specific demand that could help catalyse such an identity: the fossil industries setting everything on fire need to be shut down. Now. It's simple, short-term and terrifyingly necessary. It's a global demand, transcending the local by definition. It finds expression everywhere from the earth science community to investor briefings to hand-drawn placards in Guilin and Pushkin Square. It has drawn emerging social movements into alignment with much older ones: that's the advantage of a demand so defensible and direct.

Fossil is over. Focus on how.

The core of the network is there; has been there from the beginning. At the sites of extraction and destruction, First Nations communities have been holding the front line for generations. The rebellion has been underway on this ground since 1788; on other grounds since 1492. The campfires of ANFA; the campaign against Woodside's gas ambitions at Walmadan: these are the foundations for something enduring. Some communities are many generations into the fight against coin-doubling extinction, and some of us are perilously late to it.

'The foundation of social movement building is, first and foremost, friendship. The camaraderie is vital as it guards against self-interest and opportunism,' suggests Lena Anyuolo in her study of the Mathare organisers as they began to scale into a national network of social justice centres. The thing we discovered while puzzling over the repression paradox is that such an architecture also happens to be the most resilient to attack; combining tight-knit trust relationships with fast transmission to distant parts of the network. With leadership distributed and shared, so is the risk; none of us indispensable, but none of us ever unnecessary.

With unity of purpose and just the right amount of organisation, we begin to scale; not just horizontally, but also vertically. 'Levels in the panarchy are added over time,' Holling reminds us. 'If enough potential accumulates at one level, it can pass a threshold and establish another, slower and larger level.'

There it is: that larger, fleeting something emerging from the flow of the systems game; synchronised wingbeats of ten thousand social movements finding each other in every part of the world. More unified than r-phase folk politics; less institutionalised than deadening bureaucracy at the far end of the K-phase. Keep enough creative, democratic overturn within a movement's coordination faculties, and things can remain flexible and adaptive even as collaboration begins at this new, larger scale. What we're looking for lies at that fluid point of balance.

The network diagram may look sparse, but alongside the venerable structures of the United Nations are enduring long-distance ties across time zones, woven over decades by the World Social Forum, Friends of the Earth, Peace Boat, the Global Greens; human rights and trade union networks; successive Internationals.

Late in 2018, the Vermont-based Sanders Institute and Democracy in Europe Movement (DiEM25) issued a call for 'progressives of the world to unite'. What could have easily condensed into a trans-Atlantic alliance rapidly snowballed into something far more interesting, sweeping up old hands from the World Social Forum and new energy from active grassroots networks all over the world. In May 2020 the Progressive International was born; an online launch rolling across the time zones at the height of the pandemic's first wave. Namibian labour unions. The Colombia-based 'Peoples Congress'. Krytyka Polityczna, a central and eastern European network of writers and activists. The National Alliance of People's Movements, that venerable assembly of radical grassroots movements across India. Our dear friends from Mathare.

It's not a new social movement so much as the organisational scaffolding for those already out there doing the essential work. It's a subtle distinction but an important one: from a network perspective, what's needed here is to radically close the distance between dispersed parts of the village, to share the perspectives of people working in wildly different contexts, and to amplify and protect voices from the margins. An organising lattice through which a thousand other strands of this work can braid, without gentrifying into some brittle bureaucracy. Easy to say, hard to do, essential to try.

If we fail to arrest the momentum of the fossil coins, we plunge through a planet-wide brake failure. Societies, economies, ecologies in an omega discontinuity, deep tiers of the panarchy caving in all at the same time and not even the doomers know, really, what's down that abyss. Whether you're the activist holding the banner or the soon-to-be-unemployed truck driver screaming at her to get a job, we have perilously little time left to make common cause. 'Environmentalism without class struggle is just gardening,' declared Brazilian labour leader Chico Mendez. And class struggle without environmentalism is now just an argument over the spoils of collapse.

Shutting down fossil capital might go some way towards unity of purpose, but it's unlikely to be enough. The movement of 'one no, many yeses' that arose to challenge corporate globalisation in the late 1990s held its lack of a unified program as a strength; a hedge against sectarianism. Because what if we won? What does it look like on the other side of that? Who claims to know, with confidence, the world that comes next if we break this long incendiary fever?

We can't afford to wait for someone else to come up with the perfect manifesto, and our governments would have no interest in delivering it even if we did. 'Most obviously, the refusal to make demands was, quite self-consciously, a refusal to recognize the legitimacy of the existing political order of which such demands would have to be made,' writes David Graeber on the Occupy movement's intentional lack of a brittle ten-point plan. 'Direct action is, ultimately, the defiant insistence on acting as if one is already free.'

Unity of purpose might instead be found by turning, one last time, to the oldest book in the world – to the footprints our ancestors left on some of its uppermost pages, long before we lost our minds counting the coins of the Anthropocene.

family tree

Luca's daughter enfolded, suspended in an intimate darkness. A tumble of activity within; the stunningly complex descendants of those fluid Hadean dancers uncoiling, transcribing, multiplying; one becoming two in a ritual as old as life. For several hours, these new twins nestle side by side within the cocoon that bore them here; a pause, and then the inner whirl is redoubled. Before long, two have become four; now four will become eight, and now sixteen. They won't disperse into this interior ocean as their distant ancestors might have done: anchored here, sustained by a larger life, the generative script they follow is resolving into something more unified. The cells are differentiating, turning inwards as structure emerges; doubling, and doubling again; this we learned during the long Proterozoic. Within three weeks, it's as though a billion years have passed. The earliest formations of nervous, circulatory and digestive systems that arose during the Ediacaran are being replayed and remade in liquid fast-forward. An articulated spine; embryonic pharyngeal grooves briefly resembling gills that might have been; evolutionary memories of the Cambrian. For a few weeks, this curled possibility of a being will possess a tiny tail recalling amphibian ancestry; and then, unmistakably, mammalian features begin to predominate. Gifts of the Eocene; delicate and dextrous hands and feet, large brain and forward-looking eyes of a creature at home in forest canopy. Bipedal form recalling the cooling aftermath of the Miocene greenhouse pulse, when shrinking equatorial forests sent her ancestors ranging outwards onto the savannah.

Her body holds within it glimpses and after-images of the whole history of her lineage. Her mind is already forming around the dim impressions and sensory cues of sound and motion; music, her mother's voice. Already a social being; she will be born ready to learn.

She belongs here. Her ancestors belonged here, and her children will belong here. A species woven from the same fabric as every other creature that has ever lived, her cells reading biochemical scripts drafted in Hadean seas four billion years ago. Her first breaths of air are charged with oxygen exhaled by the trees she is born under. Her deepest memories will be of touch, and warmth, and movement, cradled by a campfire while the old ones sing. Her mother, her whole family, have paused in this birthing place as so many others have done before them; soon they will move with the rain across the contours of a changing landscape, following the footfalls of the creatures they have always shared this place with.

There's no detailed map of how she comes to be here, rocked to sleep by a campfire under East African skies. Multiple lines of evidence point to successive migration surges out of Africa beginning nearly two million years ago, with ancestral *Homo erectus* cousins making camp as far as northern China, Java and Spain by 1.4 million years ago. There are ghosts of other great dispersals from around a quarter of a million years ago, peoples who left only the faintest traces of their passage. But by around ninety thousand years ago, another migratory wave was on the move, with bands of *Homo sapiens* moving out across the Arabian Peninsula and into southern Europe and South Asia. Some of this story is told in footprints left behind in ash beds, by fragments of teeth and artifact scatters of spear points and fish hooks. Some of it is told in DNA sequencing: traces of cohabitation with other closely related subspecies; hook-ups that have left European and East Asian people with up to 3 per cent of their DNA inherited from our vanished Neanderthal cousins.

Orbital dynamics and the slow wobble in the earth's tilt may have played a role in driving these migrations. A cyclical touch more sunlight across the northern hemisphere shifts the rainbelts across North Africa and Arabia, creating twelve-thousand-year windows when these inhospitable regions bloom with life. New generations of travellers will move through these lush corridors, fanning outwards from their sub-Saharan homelands. When the earth gradually tilts back in the other direction and the rainfall shifts, these ecosystems revert through slow collapse to arid dunefields, cutting these sister populations off from each other until the next rainfall phase rolls around.

There are no written records of these extraordinary journeys: the fearsome retreats as ice ages advance and recede, the land-bridge crossings into new worlds, the astonishing skill of the first seafarers. The fossil record is patchy, contradictory and inconclusive, hinting only at a lost age of planetary discovery by people anatomically and genetically identical to us. Family. We know these stories are there, like submerged landscapes; it only takes an invitation to sit by a campfire to realise that some of them are still being told.

While the branches interlaced worldwide over tens of thousands of years, the trunk of this tree is firmly, deeply grounded. That's a truth we might try to hold on to now that the climate is on the turn once more: while there might be many branches, there is only one tree. When we begin to draw it, it fans out rapidly behind each of us – parents, grandparents, great-grandparents; the number of our ancestors doubling and doubling again with each generation we trace back. Before long, our families converge and intertwine. Unless we're even more closely related (hi, mum!), we're cousins, you and I. The maths says we're probably within the fifteenth-cousin range; certainly closer than fiftieth; I don't know, but there's a number. We're family.

Imagining every single human being alive at the moment I write these words; in the order of 7.8 billion of us. Brothers, sisters, cousins. Imagining now, all of our mothers; one generation back. Imagining all of their mothers; two generations back. Three generations; four – trace back the family tree now through matrilineage, watching it slowly converge from this vast number of individuals. Forty great-grandmothers ago we have traversed a thousand years back in time. In four hundred generations we are ten thousand years into the past; perhaps around the time of the founding of the fishing village that would become Byblos. An unbroken sequence of births, the family tree still converging backward in time; keep going; ten times longer; twenty.

Hold here. Eight thousand grandmothers, maybe around two hundred thousand years ago, the slender branches of this matrilineal tree – the tree that birthed everyone alive today – converge on one individual. Her place at this conjuncture is fleeting; a generation ago, it was someone else, and in a generation's time, it will be someone else again. But in this moment, there's someone there. Students of our deep ancestry refer to her as Mitochondrial Eve.

Imagining her now under East African skies, cradled by a campfire while the old ones sing.

> You never change things by fighting against the existing reality. To change something, build a new model that makes the existing model obsolete.
>
> BUCKMINSTER FULLER

morning in rabaul

Sunrise over Blanche Bay; long white liner gliding in on a mirrored sea. Bare volcanic cinder cones rise out of the jungle on the eastern shore, lush canopy down to the waterline. We slip by a pair of steep-walled rocky islands decked with trees, bearing through a rough-looking flotilla of tankers and trawlers at anchor. Tiny figures cast nets from outrigger canoes way out across the bay, waters churning with shoaling fish.

Leaning over the railing, I'm thinking of Fuller's well-worn quote about new models, wondering how I feel about it as we lean into the next stage of a fight against the existing reality that is reverberating all the way into the geological record.

Inbound, the smudge of a settlement resolving into a wide concrete landing, bulk cargo sheds, laneways running back towards town.

Far below, dockworkers throw ropes as thick as their arms over bollards. Shipboard winches pulling them taut, drawing us gently alongside. Rabaul, Papua New Guinea, morning air rich with the warmth of late summer. For ten hours, the liner will be the tallest structure in town, as though a Yokohama city block has broken away and washed in on the morning tide.

There's an improvised market one street back from the landing. Beaming vendors in bright clothes have arrayed local treasures on blankets and fold-out tables. An emerging platoon of foreigners are taking photos and blinking in the sun, carefully counting out bundles of unfamiliar currency. Leonard finds me there, warm smile and a shake of the hand. For a very reasonable sum, he's offered to be my guide for a couple of hours. He's maybe a little disappointed that I don't want to charter a taxi up to the volcano, that I'm content just to walk and breathe the air. We browse through a noisy open-air fresh-food market, hard work and volcanic soils having brought forth a wild abundance of produce. Where I'm from, the sellers would all be proudly certified organic; here, there's nothing to cert-ify, it's just how everything is grown. If you didn't bring your own, the bags all carry an oxo-biodegradeable logo – it's a plastic-free market. If Leonard is curious to know why I'm taking admiring photos of shopping bags, he's too polite to say so.

Next stop: this sunburned piece of white bread needs a hat. In a dusty car park, a shed as wide as an aircraft hangar, shelves stacked with every-thing from hats to honey to hardware under slow-turning fans. Something catches my eye: an entire aisle of solar panels, batteries, inverters, fittings and accessories. A 15-watt panel for 69 kina; 50 watts for 169.90. Nice. I'm scribbling that down, trying to work out the exchange rate in my head. Momentary comparison with the price of hardware, essentials; this gear is not outrageously expensive.

On a wide traffic island under shady palm trees, I'm trying betel nut and powdered lime for the first time to the evident hilarity of the small crowd of kids who've drifted in to sit with us. I must be making a weird face; evidently this is an acquired taste. The left side of my face is uncom-fortably numb and I'm attempting to pay attention as Leonard sketches how the place works. Cruise ships call through here every six weeks or so, dumping a fleeting shower of hard currency for the tourist operators, the drivers and souvenir vendors. The rest of the time, he and his family are farmers, working a smallholding not far from town. With the cash he makes showing noobs like me around, he is converting his farm pumps and electrics from diesel to solar. Next, he has his eye on a higher-capacity inverter and more batteries. He barely spends anything on diesel anymore, he tells me with a grin, firing a jet of betel juice out the corner of his mouth.

So he's still reliant on imports: the panels, a little diesel for back-up, and cashflow from fitful tides of tourists borne here on MDO-burning ocean liners. But he's made the jump: a farm-sized piece of Fuller's new model.

Late in 2019, Canberra – the capital city of the most carbon-intensive society on earth – went 100 per cent renewable. Three new solar farms within striking distance of town, five windfarms distributed from South Australia to Northern New South Wales, and five thousand embedded solar battery storage systems later: they've done it. 'This is a huge achievement in consolidating the ACT's reputation as Australia's renewable energy capital,' said climate change minister Shane Rattenbury when the last contracted piece fell into place. A well-organised grassroots network went door to door talking to people, got a Greens representative elected, and a decade later watched as he made the announcement on live television. Still reliant on imports, embedded in a national electricity grid heavily captive to coal and gas interests, but this strange sweet town has made the jump. A city-sized piece of Fuller's new model.

For decades, tracking the growth of clean energy has felt – to borrow a phrase – like mapping an archipelago of prefigurative islands, surrounded by an implacably hostile capitalist environment. A village here, a housing development there, but nothing approximating systems change. Raising our eyes then, to realise that a global-scale energy succession is underway. Spain's ten-year plan to phase out coal mining and burning was nearly accomplished in the first year, with emissions from the electricity sector crashing by a third in 2019. In Britain, where this whole story began, the coal industry is practically dead in the water, with only a handful of stations even remaining operable. This is part of a much larger shift: wind and solar generation overtook coal for the first time across the entire European Union in 2019, with coal generation dropping by a quarter in a single year. A continent-sized experiment in Fuller's new model.

Somehow, even in the midst of a political hellscape of gas fracking and state capture, the clean energy sector in the United States is still killing it. 'For the first time ever, in April 2019, renewable energy outpaced coal by providing 23 per cent of US power generation, compared to coal's 20 per cent share,' according to Deloitte's 2020 renewable energy industry outlook.

Japan still lags, a consequence of the energy policy paralysis exerted by the nuclear industry and the coal and gas sectors, but even here we saw how the Fukushima disaster opened a crack in the armour, through which surged the solar industry.

It is China that has emerged as the world's renewable energy superpower – by far the largest manufacturer of solar modules and wind turbines, and responsible for nearly half the world's renewable energy investment in 2017. 'China's installed wind power capacity doubled in the past four years . . . while installed PV capacity tripled,' says Shi Yubo, executive vice chairman of the China Energy Research Society.

India, some way behind, is still a place to watch, having set itself a gargantuan clean energy target in an effort to improve air quality and energy independence: 'India has set itself an ambitious target of 175 GW of renewables by 2022. This represents a massive increase, considering that India's total installed power generation capacity in October 2018 was only 346 GW, according to the International Renewable Energy Agency.

This surge isn't just about bright lights and big cities; it's also the quiet work of rural electrification in some of the poorest parts of the world: '60 per cent of the people becoming electrified between 2017 and 2030 will do so through decentralized systems, equally distributed between mini-grids and off-grid solutions based on solar photovoltaic (PV),' say IRENA.

These numbers will be outdated by the time you read them, but even this superficial traverse paints the picture: we are well past the prefigurative islands stage. Nobody in clean energy circles believes it is happening at anything like the pace we need it to, and the gas industry has emerged as the next serious adversary. But this is the real prize of exerting all the strength we have at the fossil and nuclear incumbents. Imagine, just for a moment, how fast things will turn when the oligarchs are evicted.

Standing on that busy street corner in Dhaka, waiting for the flow of traffic to clear and wondering why something felt different, I took a moment to figure it out. All of the two- and three-wheel traffic is silent, electric. A similar realisation in Shanghai, and in Kolkata: everything is changing. This isn't just about banks of PV panels on rooftops, or electric scooters and tuktuks; something much bigger and more interesting is afoot.

Imagine a sankey diagram the size of a planet, under an ashen sky. Pale stripes of the coin-doubling consumption torrent; colonial extraction of metal ores, cement, biomass, water. Immense waste streams piling up just out of shot. A great acceleration propelled by the motive power of fire, ghost forests of the Carboniferous unearthed and blown into the sky. Greasy stripes of coal, oil and gas doubling, and doubling again.

Now, watch as something profound begins to overtake the energy stripes, growing alongside them and abruptly throwing some of them into reverse. A field of giant turbines on the ridgeline, great arcs and grids of them standing offshore. Solar concentrators like glass mandalas under construction in Abu Dhabi, western China, the Atacama. Tesselated fields of photovoltaics from the steppes of Inner Mongolia to reservoirs in Chiba prefecture.

Instead of consuming fuel to stay alive, at the very brink of crisis, industrial society has learned how to photosynthesise.

The coal stripes powering London and Madrid, eliminated. The oil stripes powering Dhaka's two-wheelers and Leonard's farm, eliminated. Bankruptcies and plant closures tumbling in the wake of something too big to see, caught in the gaze of a child on the pillion seat of a scooter in Dhaka, bouncing past in perfect silence.

Narrow new stripes begin to swell on the diagram to service these new technologies, and as tempting as it is to ignore them, we can't. Rare earths for the turbine blades, lithium for the batteries, indium and gallium and selenium for the photovoltaic panels, alongside staples like iron and copper and aluminium for everything. This can't simply be an instance of another product stream being sucked into the coin-doubling game. This has to be something more evolved.

'The global PV market is still young, and PV systems typically last 30 years. Findings in this report show that a large increase in PV waste is projected to emerge globally around 2030,' writes Stephanie Weckend in a 2016 study of end-of-life management for solar panels. She's looking at predictions suggesting anywhere between sixty and seventy-eight million tonnes of PV panel waste going into landfill worldwide by 2050. Even this is likely to be an underestimate if we're successful in dramatically ramping up deployment.

So while our industrial metabolism learns to photosynthesise at scale, bankrupting fossil capital as it goes, it's going to have to perfect a new adaptation as it does it, since solar-powered extinction is still extinction. To bring this story full circle, watch as those one-way stripes on the sankey diagram begin closing into artful loops one by one. A linear consumption torrent folding into a circular economy before our eyes; Fuller's new model, at the scale of a planet.

unfurl

The evacuations, the mustard air, the polygon, they've receded like the edges of bad dreams fragmenting into a rough night's sleep. But I'm certain we didn't imagine it, even when the RFS began deleting the polygons they'd closed out on the map. We need a way of letting the grieving begin, to let go of residual internal polygons, so Flick suggests we walk one of the ridges to farewell the valley full of graceful tree ferns. In the rear-view mirror, Sirius nose-surfing the fresh air as we bump from our unburned refuge back onto the sodden fireground, feeling everything reverting to normal, everything changed forever.

I can't shake the image of that flow diagram, what it would mean if we got that right at scale. Stephanie Weckend's IRENA study on end-of-life for photovoltaics does more than just measure the pile of dead panels in 2050: it suggests ways of not doing that at all. When she rolls the principles of the circular economy over the life cycle of the panels, we end up somewhere very different. On the input side, swap out rare indium for more abundant tin oxide; use thinner cells that cut the use of silicon by half; screenprint the cells with copper, which cuts silver out of the process altogether. On the output side, use thermoplastics that can be melted down and reused, or drop polymers from the mix and start making panels that can be delaminated when they can't be repaired. With PV all the way at the bottom of the cost curve, focus design expertise now on panels resting within cradle-to-cradle product cycles: inputs sourced from materials already in circulation, outputs disassembled in dedicated PV recycling plants and pressed back into service.

Look what's happening out on the sankey diagram: the open loops are closing. Largely automated fabrication plants powered by sunlight, importing materials sourced mostly from recyclate streams, pressing them into PV panels to power thirty years of industrial photosynthesis, whereupon they are disassembled, the materials disaggregated and dropped back into the flow. Outputs of one process feeding the inputs of another.

These lines of thinking long predate the pile-up of dead solar panels, but we are scandalously late to this party. If we're to close the loops on the global flow diagram, we have to stop designing things with no known disposal path. There is no place for plutonium out on these maps, but no excuse for PV or turbine blades going into landfill either.

We'll never reach 100 per cent efficiency; the second law of thermodynamics will still tax every single transaction no matter how good we get at this. But that's probably where the real genius of this kind of work comes in: working out how not to need the panel or the turbine at all. Millions of years ago in 1990, Amory Lovins of the Rocky Mountain Institute calculated that industrial societies could save three-quarters of the electricity they generated by rolling intelligent energy efficiency measures and process redesign deep into plant and equipment and built form. Thermodynamics doesn't apply to the panel you don't need to use, he reasoned. This kind of thinking drove directly into coin-doubling headwinds, and he lost the argument.

Lovins' ideas were met with 'indifference or outright opposition' by private electricity utilities, whose entire existence was premised on driving demand up, not down. Flash forward to 2018: the International Energy Agency publishes a detailed study finding that 'the right efficiency policies could enable the world to achieve more than 40 per cent of the emissions cuts needed to reach its climate goals without new technology'. Nearly thirty years on from Lovins' pathbreaking work, the IEA is still confounded by the same headwinds, admitting that 'while energy efficiency is improving around the world, its positive impact on global energy use is overwhelmed by rising economic activity across all sectors'.

Don't let that astonishing admission just slip by like that. The IEA – a deeply conservative institution tightly welded to the status quo – assesses that 40 per cent of the pollution cuts we need to prevent the literal end of civilisation can be delivered by not burning anything at all. Free of the ruthless pressure for every part of the economy to be double the size in a generation's time, finally these ideas can bloom.

And so now we work our way across the flow diagram, end to end. Here's a general principle we could apply: 'A circular economy describes an economic system that is based on business models which replace the "end-of-life" concept with reducing, alternatively reusing, recycling and recovering materials in production/distribution and consumption processes, thus operating at the micro level (products, companies, consumers), meso level (eco-industrial parks) and macro level (city, region, nation and beyond).' It's a lumpy definition, but you get the picture. Closed loops, across scales. To use the more lyrical phrase adopted by William McDonough in his elegant 'cradle to cradle' design aesthetic, 'waste equals food'.

Instead of using coking coal, Swedish steelmaker SSAB is building a plant that uses renewable energy and hydrogen to make the world's first zero-emissions steel. Scale that up immediately. The Ellen Macarthur Foundation's 'New Plastics Economy' roadmap conducts a detailed global audit of all that detritus washing up on the beach, describing a three-fold strategy to 'Eliminate all problematic and unnecessary plastic items. Innovate to ensure that the plastics we do need are reusable, recyclable, or compostable. Circulate all the plastic items we use to keep them in the economy and out of the environment.' This beautiful work is sponsored in part by corporations such as Coca-Cola and Nestlé, whose strategy of predatory delay has done for the plastics industry what Exxon has done for oil. Maybe the experience of watching Exxon being hurled through the window will give this strategy the kickstart it needs to get delivered at scale.

Across the flow diagram we go, attention unavoidably caught by the scale of inputs and wastes and the deadening cruelty required to provide an expanding fraction of the world's population with a meat-based diet. Five seconds researching plant-based diets online delivers ten million hits on the avoidance of diabetes, heart disease, high blood pressure, high cholesterol and how good it is to not have colon cancer. If not having colon cancer still hasn't got you off the fence, it's hard to know whether fold-backs on an imaginary sankey diagram would do it, but here goes anyway. Animal agriculture is responsible for 18 per cent of global greenhouse gas emissions, an avoidably large wedge of the climate catastrophe pie chart, according to the UN Food and Agriculture Organization's report *Livestock's Long Shadow*. The land-clearing, pollution from fertiliser production to grow feed for livestock, the untreated sewage, pesticides, the antibiotics, the immense cumulative loading of all of it; time to wind it right back, and, for the love of god, get the chickens out of those cages.

It can happen fast: 'In May 2016, the Vegan Society commissioned Ipsos Mori to poll 10,000 people on their dietary habits and found that Britain's vegan population had increased from 150,000 to 542,000 in the space of a decade (alongside a vegetarian population of 1.14 million); *The Guardian* reported. 'Of those, 63 per cent were female and, significantly for veganism's future growth, almost half were in the 15–34 age category. What is astonishing is that the pace of change in the two years since the survey was carried out has been seemingly exponential – it seems plausible to speculate the number may have doubled again in that time.'

Coin-doubling, but for vegans.

From solar panels to seitan masquerading as crispy duck,[9] these are emerging fields; trends are hard to pick and subject to sudden reversals. System-wide adoption of closed-loop economic principles has been stunted and fragmented by the overwhelming logic of capital accumulation, but there's enough of an alternative ecosystem present to paint a picture of what might arise should that logic be shouldered aside and broken at long last.

One obvious problem is that the field of circular economics is arising in part as an attempt by some of the worst offenders to have their coins and grow them too. One study that analysed 114 different definitions of the circular economy found that 'The main aim of the circular economy is considered to be economic prosperity, followed by environmental quality; its impact on social equity and future generations is barely mentioned.' If we're to do this in a way that works for the whole village, we need to fix these principles firmly to the concept of supply chain justice. Circular economics without class struggle is just gardening.

Closed loops, cradle to cradle, circular production cycles, regenerative economics. If there's a reason this feels somehow familiar, it's because all this work attempts to harmonise our industrial flows according to the organic logics of the planet they are embedded in. 'Waste equals food' is the foundational organising principle of the biosphere – even the photosynthesisers for whom waste heat from a nearby star equals food. We're not doing anything cyanobacteria hadn't already figured out drifting in warm Archaean seas. It doesn't mean we couldn't take a little pride in seeing this ancient innovation scaled to the size of a city, industrial metabolism come full circle.

---

9   Fucking delicious, honestly.

As avant-garde as all of this sounds, First Nations societies in intimate dialogue with natural systems over tens of thousands of years hold a vastly more sophisticated understanding of landscape and its inhabitants across scales. A network of closed-loop trading societies undertaking large-scale cultivation and species stewardship, with ecological literacy coded in language and taught from the earliest age.

Colonisers and explorers took detailed records of the lands and nations they were overrunning, recorded widespread agriculture, breadmaking, networks of villages, extensive fish-trapping infrastructure, farm forestry and landscape-scale cultivation far in advance of anything they had ever seen before. Along with the violence, none of this has made its way into schools, or popular culture, or governance; institutional amnesia has rendered it blank.

It took Yuin author Bruce Pascoe's *Dark Emu* to resurface these colonial records. Some are ready to hear him, and some find his message so threatening they've launched a multi-platform character assassination. 'As I read these early journals I came across repeated references to people building dams and wells, planting, irrigating and harvesting seed, preserving the surplus and storing it in houses, sheds or secure vessels, creating elaborate cemeteries and manipulating the landscape – none of which fitted the definition of hunter-gatherer,' he writes.

On the eve of the ashfall that's soon to escalate into a megafire, he speaks at a public meeting in the coastal town of Bermagui. A question from the audience: what will it take for these bodies of knowledge to be placed back in service of land restoration? Pascoe doesn't hesitate. 'We need our land back.'

Some of what needs to happen now is new; unprecedented, genuinely revolutionary. But some of these things are old – as old as photosynthesis, as old as democracy, as old as a story from the Nyiting.

From the ridgeline, I'm braced. It burned hot here, out of control. While the bombers and the fire crews and the handful of locals who stayed behind were concentrating on human asset protection, this asset was reduced to a moonscape.

Flick sees it first, pointing in disbelief. The ashen columns of the tree ferns are unfurling bright new canopies against these dead black hillsides.

We wander, mesmerised, across the charred battleground, and the closer we look, the more we see. Emerging tiers of fast-moving brackens and small herbaceous plants. Shoots of brilliant green. Sirius eyeing flights of birds weaving across this reconfigured landscape, columns of ants and tentative pollinators hovering. Standing amid them now, under the emerging shade of these fire-adapted descendants of the Devonian. Survivors all, veterans of the Permian dying and the Chicxulub bullet; ancient, steadfast, delicate and absolutely metal as fuck.

Those who profess to favour freedom, and yet
deprecate agitation . . . want rain without thunder
and lightning. This struggle may be a moral one;
or it may be a physical one; or it may be both
moral and physical; but it must be a struggle.
Power concedes nothing without a demand.
It never did and it never will.

FREDERICK DOUGLASS

humble trash

There's beautiful trouble afoot in our village of a hundred people. The ash-fall, the floods, the heatwaves, the pandemic, and those new maps – the ones that showed us the money – have stirred up a mood. Not only is the village pissed, it has a focal point at which to direct the mood.

Remembering now, all those we're sharing this village with, look-ing them in the eye. Twelve of us undernourished. Ten of us in extreme poverty. A quarter of us with one or both feet in the informal economy, hustling to stay out of the ranks of the unnecessariat. Forty million slaves.

This map of the village is offensive enough. The map of the money is so obscene they'll probably try to have it banned. Where to even begin: $1.8 trillion dollars a year wasted on weapons spending and preparation for wars nobody can afford to fight. $72.9 billion of that blown on nuclear weapons that can never be used.

$650 billion a year on corporate tax avoidance: in 2016, that's the IMF's conservative estimate of how much is lost to government revenues every year. Now add the losses from personal income tax avoidance by the wealthy, estimate the cost of the rorts, manipulations and carve-outs from tax systems mutilated to suit the bottomless demands of the investors. Add the revenues that would accrue with a tax on global financial speculation, if global financial speculators stopped preventing it from being intro-duced. Now add the coins the investors suck out as profit every time they automate someone's job out of existence.

Add up the costs of predatory lending, crippling interest repayments, monopoly rents; the picture is already crystal clear but let's try not to miss anything big. Parasitic losses, engineers call them, energy sinks forcing all the other parts of the system to work much, much harder. 'If you look at the economic framework in terms of assets and debt, you find that the 1 per cent makes its money by holding the 99 per cent in debt. Or at least, you could say that the 5 per cent make its money by holding the 95 per cent in debt,' outlines the ever-reliable Michael Hudson.

Institutionalise this principle, back it with visible threats of destitution, and you have the working core of a coin-doubling flywheel. They spun it up through ascending tiers of the panarchy, found it worked on whole countries. Backed with credible threats of drone strikes and death squads, obedient comprador regimes were installed and armed to ensure the flywheel of extraction kept spinning. In the Global North the armatures of control are generally quieter; just investors renting political parties and slamming the Overton window down on the fingers of anyone who taps on the glass.

When we hurl the carbon oligarchs out into the street, all that glass gets broken. Seeing, clearly, that the one single guy who owns 45 per cent of the village has somehow accrued 18,446,744,073,709,551,615 imaginary coins, which he seems intent on riding all the way to Alpha Centauri, or downloading his brain into a jar, for reasons that make no sense at all.

Enough. Kate Raworth's *Doughnut Economics* lays out a rich menu of models more aligned with the reality of village life on a finite planet, including a range of strategies for dealing with the pathology of the coins. Demoting the Gross Domestic Product indicator so it's no longer the only light on the economic dashboard is a good start, she suggests. Redesigning the coins themselves so that they bear demurrage – a small holding cost – rather than accruing interest would return money to its place as a fluid medium of exchange, rather than a self-multiplying commodity to be stockpiled. 'Imagine, then, if a demurrage-bearing currency could be designed so that, instead of boosting consumption today, it boosted regenerative investments in tomorrow,' she says.

It's new language for an old idea; the $2 trillion Islamic banking industry rests on the ancient prohibition of *riba*, translating loosely as usury, or the charging of interest on loans.

In 1989, the Brazilian city of Porto Alegre pioneered the first city-scale experiment in participatory budgeting: applying deliberative democracy to municipal coin allocation in a city of 1.2 million people. Just as in other well-constituted aggregations of the wisdom of crowds, involving thousands of people in the development of city budgets was a runaway success, and has now been adopted in thousands of different contexts around the world.

The practice of debt jubilee – broad-scale cancellation – was a tool used by Babylonian rulers for more than two thousand years as each new ruler took the throne. 'A debt cancellation is needed when debts go beyond the ability to be paid, and all personal debts, all non-business debts, tend to mount up beyond what they can be paid,' says Michael Hudson, with one eye to the impossible burden of private debt carried by US businesses and individuals in the midst of the pandemic. 'They weren't egalitarians,' he says drily of the Babylonian kings. 'The reason you cancel the debts is you want to preserve stability.'

Debt cancellation as pressure valve. Now, do the whole planet. If they won't accept the idea quietly, there's always the debt strike. *Beautiful Trouble – A Toolbox for Revolution*, published in 2016, describes debt strikes as a kind of sleeper tactic, potential as-yet unrealised. As one, we just stop paying back the debt until the creditors come to the table. 'The outrage, organizers, techniques and tools already exist, and the tactic has perhaps never been more justified. The debt strike is out there, waiting to take the world by storm,' the authors write.

Seeds in the ground, everywhere. We know what we have to do, because Milton Friedman spelled it out for us: 'When that crisis occurs, the actions that are taken depend on the ideas that are lying around. That, I believe, is our basic function: to develop alternatives to existing policies, to keep them alive and available until the politically impossible becomes the politically inevitable.'

Humble trash of the Anthropocene, make your move.

Pull the remainder of that gigantic colonial windfall back into public circulation and stack it up in a completely different order. Much of it is bound for the Global South, where it came from. A universal basic income that's not conditional, not a mutual obligation, it's yours as a guarantee that human dignity and survival are no longer dependent on waged labour. We're good enough at this by now that many major essential services can be provided for free or at very low cost: water, food, even housing, when run on a not-for-profit basis.

Before it was colonised by surveillance capitalism, an internet buoyed on open protocols and the ethics of the free software movement had already begun fatally eroding intellectual property chokepoints; now it's time for another turn of that wheel. As Paul Mason points out in *Postcapitalism*, the ultimate potential of costless digital replication is to invert old scarcities and make content monopolies increasingly obsolete.

Working sector by sector, attacking debt-dependence from multiple angles: the profits of increasingly sophisticated automation socialised and ploughed back into dramatically reducing global inequality and the cost of living. Picking up the historic trajectory for shorter working hours that the union movement was progressing before the neoliberal assault, combining it with a menu of options for worker-owned enterprises. We're not abolishing waged labour necessarily; but as we begin to close the loops of the new model, participation in the market economy becomes increasingly optional.

Different strands and variations on these ideas are suddenly everywhere, folded into different understandings of what might constitute a global Green New Deal. Take the best of what Francis Perkins and Franklin D. Roosevelt managed to pull off the last time the politically impossible became the politically inevitable, only this time we stamp on the coin-doubling virus until the bastard thing stops moving.

requiem for the holocene

A lot has happened for the quiet house in the quiet street, while we've been away.

Someone got started planting trees; trees for food, trees for shade, trees for remembering. This doesn't look like the work of a lone activist; there are so many trees that this is nearly a closed-canopy street now. It has changed everything: the light, the air quality, the acoustic field, the whole sense of the place. But the biggest change is to the temperature; the shade and transpiration from this living corridor will be a lifesaver in the summers to come.

The home is a small power station now. A closed-loop solar battery system runs the lights, and a separate panel heats the water. They've torn down some of the fencing, so the shared front yard is a riot of flowers and bush foods, rain-fed from tanks tucked under the eaves. It's not perfect – energy retrofits can only take old building stock so far – but the place now costs essentially nothing to run.

In the cool of the evening, we'll take a ride down a wide new cycleway to discover that the tilt-up shopping centre and its acres of car parking, mercifully, is gone. That unforgiveable waste of space is a place again: a village square surrounded by four- or five-storey solar terraces stepped back into shady garden allotments and pocket parks. Some of the old building shells might still be in there, it's hard to tell, refashioned into workshops, micro factories and trigeneration infrastructure. The street frontage is alive with studio spaces, social service hubs and low-key retailers; aromas of the whole planet drifting in from nearby. Some kind of street festival is underway; I can't pick the cultural dress but there's a kids' dance troupe in the middle of the street and if I stop to ask, I'll discover they spent a year in Kutupalong before arriving here.

No street parking apart from a couple of bays reserved for an electric car-share co-op, but we're better off leaving the bike here and hopping on one of the trackless trams rolling towards us under a shady colonnade of Norfolk Island pines.

Imagining for a second a city that runs on sunlight, sipping just as much water as it returns to the landscape, growing a fair fraction of its own food, woven seamlessly into a mosaic of wetlands and native bush-land. It is a city of urban village centres with names thousands of years old, rising higher than I remember out of the tuart forest. Each of these centres nurtures its own subtle culture and flavour; some kicking on late into the evening, and each has regained the fine-grained mixed-use fabric of the genuinely accessible city.

The market square has overthrown the supermarket; industrial pharm-ing outcompeted by fresh produce grown locally on rooftop gardens and peri-urban farming co-ops. Each of these town centres has a comfortable degree of self-containment; you can work, eat, play within a kilometre of home if you wish, but you'd be missing out.

Bustling corridors link the compact urban villages like the one we've just left, up to four or five storeys high in most places, anchored by the electric transit network that was rebuilt after five decades of forgetful-ness. The major lines carry thousands of people down the corridors at five-minute intervals; the ease of access to major stops along the way has created fascinating urban microclimates, galleries and small bars patched into repurposed warehouses and showrooms. This transit system operates around the clock, reverting late in the evening to a precisely coordinated ballet of pulse timetabling from anywhere to anywhere. Realising, sud-denly, that there's no advertising in sight – the degrading bombardment of high-pitched commercial messaging infiltrating every sight-line is gone.

Quiet suburban greenbelts lie between these thriving transit corridors, served by frequent short-haul electric buses, distributed car-share services and a shady network of cycleways. Here the city breathes under the canopy of the urban forest we planted, away from the illuminated hustle of the town cores, alongside streams freed from brief memories of concrete culverts.

The old port still hums with activity; this is a trading city, as it ever was, but as we rediscovered the importance of knowing how to make some things for ourselves the whole tenor of trade reverted to high-value spe-cialised commodities.

This is a city that has deliberately and collectively awoken from the long, incendiary fever of fossil-fuel addiction. The grid crackles now with the swell of the ocean, the roaring sea breeze and fields of mirrors kilo-metres across, far over the escarpment towards the sunbelt.

It is a place that no longer calculates Gross Domestic Product; it tracks genuine progress indicators for social justice, health, energy and water productivity, and it grapples, year on year, with the dawning consequences of what the coins have unleashed.

The long, mild summer of the Holocene won't return; we live somewhere different now. Nothing can restore the places we've lost, the species permanently silenced, or the languages that will never be spoken again. All of us hold the memory of those we wish were with us to see this next page turn, but they are still here, in a way, because their presence in the world changed the balance of everything.

The trees they planted in the yard in Mathare, fully grown. The tower on Broadway overgrown with an alpine forest barely discernible amid the other buildings that have done the same. The wetland they remade on the edge of the cultural centre; it's just one reedy node in a network now that stretches from building forecourts to the steps of parliament, blended seamlessly back into the emerging urban forest. Boorlo, this place is called. Hyde Park, we call Boodjamooling again. Look what has regrown from the seed lodged in the pavement: if this future place feels familiar, it's because every part of it already exists, somewhere on Planet Earth, today.

Even the frogs perched on the edge of this reimagined wetland know that.

archipelago

Out in the archipelago, something new slipped into the trophic web and if we're not careful, we'll overlook its significance. Ecologists draw them like Mark Lombardi's lacework sociograms: interlock, but for marine food chains. Tiny sun beings at the foundations of it all, memories of the Archean adrift on great currents stirred by the same sunlight that powers their photosynthesis. Hunted by krill and swarms of tiny copepods, these formative beings are preyed on in turn by carnivorous zooplankton and cephalopods and shoals of fish. Map the ancient relationships between different species of fish, arriving at last at the largest creatures that ever lived: the great whales tracing their slow journeys across the whole extent of this imagined landscape.

Not long ago, a new arrival at the apex of this food web: a harpoon ship guided by a constellation of satellites, tracking its prey out in advance of a factory ship somewhere over the horizon. It took this newcomer and its kindred trawlers and longliners little more than a century to hurl these trophic webs sideways, but now there's an even more recent adaptation. Skull emblem on black flags streaming from the bow, a repurposed whaling ship crowdsourced and crewed by volunteers is racing to cut the harpoon ship off from her prey. For a moment, this Sea Shepherd Conservation Society vessel is the top-order hunter on these high seas; the harpoon ship tacking away and calling for backup.

We played the same desperate game in Wattle Forest, miniature figures bent in exertion under giant trees. Trophic webs of even greater complexity, a rich weave of collaboration and contention legible only to the Pibelmun and lifetime students of the subtle undercurrents of this place. In a blink, a new top-order predator is introduced: machines with tank-tracks and tungsten saws, reducing this place to a moonscape as effectively as an artillery bombardment. And so others, working to older imperatives, move to intercept these machines, cutting them off from their quarry with lock-on pipes and cars cemented into access roads.

Taking the long view, our interventions are vastly insufficient. The harpoon ships we turn back, the access roads we lock down, are just holding actions against the scale of the assault. It's done to prevent acts of destruction in the here and now, and so we press on. But the true purpose of this kind of work is to catalyse a wider field of action; to make common cause with others around the world, creating new instances of synchronisation in the global village square. Like the reimagined wetlands and the overgrown skyscraper, they are heraldic each in their own way, bearing hopeful significance way beyond their limited scale; prefiguring revolution.

Above the canopy, inconceivably far from this forest ringing with every kind of life, a great sweep of stars. A domain of physics and emptiness, a cloud of orbiting machines moving faster than bullets, showers of metallic Anthropocene debris. On a clear night, letting my eyes adjust, making out bright Sirius eight light years away, the Southern Cross, the dark emu. Night vision settling in properly, but still barely able to take in what it is I'm seeing. Dense shrouds of dust lanes lying across the galactic plane, whorls of the Magellanic Clouds balanced above the horizon. At impossible distances, other cradles, for worlds yet to be: the Lagoon Nebula, the Witchhead Nebula, outflung arc of Barnard's Loop.

In our own neighbourhood, a rusty spark traces a slow path across the starfield night after night. Mars, frosty desert world four light minutes from right where I'm standing – just one dusty island in this sun-warmed archipelago. Inward from here, Mercury's scorched plains and the sulphuric sauna of Venus; outward, ringed gas giants and ice giants, and then, just this sparse, midnight penumbra of worldlets drifting in the paths our long-distant Hadean sun set them on.

Here, though, life's deep continuities have somehow brought forth a marbled world, a place unlike anywhere else. While it seems likely – formally, mathematically almost certain – that the galaxy's spiral arms are teeming with life, we'll never know anywhere like this. From Luca's daughters to the lyrebirds, the whole place sensate and alive on every level. Pausing to feel it, the watchfulness; that sense of multitudes of eyes-on. Every one of us pushing uphill in defiance of entropy's cold gradient; none of us indispensable, but none of us ever unnecessary.

Enough prefiguring. Whatever your idea is, big or small, do it now. See you out in the village square.

Scott Ludlam

22:11, 16 January 2021

find the others

Who knows what you might learn from taking
   a chance on conversation with a stranger?
Everyone carries a piece of the puzzle.
Nobody comes into your life by mere coincidence.
Trust your instincts.
Do the unexpected.
Find the others.

TIMOTHY LEARY

acknowledgements

Much of this book was written on the occupied lands of the Yuin people. I acknowledge the elders past and present of all the places on which I've lived and worked, Country over which sovereignty was never ceded.

Properly acknowledging everyone who made this book possible would require a whole separate volume; even though this will only scratch the surface, here goes.

Dear Mum and Dad, you have been so supportive from beginning to end, it's hard to think of a way to thank you. How supportive? Remember when you bought me bags of cement for my birthday so that we could use it to block access roads into the forest? That supportive. Also, for not freaking out when I sent you my travel itinerary; it wasn't half as nuts as yours but thank you for being good about it even so. Glen, for being as steady af no matter what, and for raising such a thoroughly joyful human being. Riley, for being exactly who you are but also for reminding us why we do this work in the first place.

Flick played a singular role here that's impossible to overstate: no Flick, no book. From a mini-inception at the Cooge that turned post-Senate malaise into something with purpose, to the offer of a writers retreat that turned into a home; from fundraising and itinerary wrangling to deep moral support and the ruthless pursuit of wayward apostrophe's. If you see her, please thank her, because I mean it: no Flick, no book. Hoping we never have to go through a birthday party like that again, but may there be many more pavlovas to come.

Thank you to Sirius for being a Good Boy even when you were scared during the fires.

Paris, for that first, remarkable election campaign, for real talk on digital campaigning and the politics of the internet, and small things like pulling me out of the bottom of a bucket when things could only have got worse.

Ray, for your pointed suggestion a decade ago that it's not fair to dump the coin-doubling game on people without at least gesturing at some possible solutions – but also for the way you've been turning possible solutions into practical reality for as long as I've known you. Chantal, for proving you can combine policy nuance with gleeful network building, for doing it with lols and for reminding us that we're all out of time to play small. Trish, for love and continuity in equal measure, especially when things got hard.

To Rici and Trevs the bush sage, for long conversations, fresh perspectives, book loans and safe harbour when we needed it; I hope this was worth the wait.

Joana, for your gentle but consistent encouragement, and for helping illuminate the process of turning imaginary meat trays and trifle metaphors into the full parma. Somehow, here it is, cubes and all, so much better for having you in it.

Sticky, for the jun and the firefighting and for being there for the trees; Thompson, for the puppy and the firefighting and for being there for us.

Kat, for helping make the shit-show of 2020 so much lighter than it might have been, for weightless forays out of Carpini, debriefs on the red moon and for placing Sovereignty at the centre of everything; I'm so looking forward to seeing what happens with what we're making now.

Larissa, for bringing the rebellion and giving it heart, for the timely nudge to give Occupy its due respect, for the gems of Graeber, and for everything you do: love and rage.

Amy, for such positive feedback on the early pieces and for not letting my annoying grammar get in the way of our friendship – and obviously also for pepper chips and histology. Matilda, for the end-to-end view, and for shining light into some of the book's blind spots. Fran, for the year in owls, for believing in this work and for unfailing encouragement always. Felicity, for introducing me to seitan masquerading as crispy duck, for being my word-count-accountability buddy when I was stuck, and for not hating the first bits of the book in Berlin.

And dear Kara, for the opportune spark that started this project. Thank you for suggesting – no, insisting – that those scrappy essays should be made into a book all that time ago, and for caring enough to make sure I actually stuck with it.

Loz, for your eye on Wattle and for your unfailing excellence; Jess, for never giving up on these places. All those who rallied under sky-blue flags, the school strikers and rebels and ratbags; the FANG crew and WANFA warriors and everyone working to close down the nuclear industry: change never comes from the comfortable centre. It comes from you.

Kristin and everyone at the AUWU – thank you, from a proud member. Janette, for sharing your appreciation for more evolved forms of democracy; a conversation to be continued, I hope. Marieke, for just being you, and for believing in this when I wasn't sure if I did or not.

Dear Dave, for two decades on the campaign trail from Pine Gap to the top end to quiet moments in Preston; thank you for your insights and your friendship. Yuk, for living the work and always keeping an eye out for me. Nicola, for thoughts on direct action from direct experience and for many years of steam-engine appreciation. Court, for your care and support. Nat and Arun, for Melbourne refuge; it's been too long. Gill, for relaying your grandfather's words; what a remarkable honour.

Thank you, Jo, for being such a patient mentor to me and so many others, for showing what it means to be an activist legislator, and for introducing us to Joanna and the work that reconnects all that time ago. From Joanna, comes the systems game, the evolutionary remembering in 'family tree', and the practical application of these ideas in confronting power.

Claire, for taking the time to school a noob on the workings of money; Sam and George, for giving me the time and space to dig into the mechanics of state capture. Marjolein and Geoff, for everything in the old days, and for the fast-forward intro to process design just before I set sail.

Bob and Christine and Rach and Larissa and all my former colleagues, for teaching me everything about that place and for never giving up despite days of 39–33, or worse. To Robin, for giving me my start, and to every volunteer doing the largely invisible work on which movements are founded: the tipping points are out there, and every single action matters.

Michelle and Giz, for suggesting the Lebanon trip; your timing could not have been better, because pulling that thread ended up grounding the whole book. Michelle, for opening doors from Beirut to Ulaanbaatar; Keli, for making connections with the wider Global Greens network.

To Nada and everyone in the Greens Party Lebanon, who welcomed me like family; thank you. Najah and Vanda in Beqaa; Mazen and Dima in Shoef, Pierre and family in Zgharta: you are changing the balance of everything. Riwa, for translation and orientation and making sense of that dear city, and everything since then. Imad, for a spellbinding day walking back through the layers of Byblos, and for knowing where to find the oldest book in the world.

Jessica, for getting things moving on the trip to Palestine; Miranda, for making it actually happen. Thank you to dear Baha, Yasser and Mohammad, for the precious glimpse of the West Bank, and for your courage every single day. I can't recommend To Be There highly enough as an introduction to life under Occupation. In Jerusalem, Hagai, for your clarity and determination; and Sahar, for being such a powerful voice for peace.

Meri and Kawasaki-san, for finding a place for me on the ship; Michi and Matt, the CC team and everyone onshore and on board for making it so absolutely unforgettable. Part of me is still in that deranged piano bar waiting for you to show up with wine. Yoshioka-san for bringing Peace Boat into being, and making time for me amid all the work you do. Caitlin from CNIC, for such a valuable grounding in the politics of nuclear power. Dear Karina and Miyake-san, for your extraordinary testimonies; for holding these memories and being willing to share them in service to these weapons never being used again. To Rico, for the owls of Ikebukuro.

I'm forever grateful to Shriprakash for steering me right all that time ago in Bangalore, then making this most recent trip possible, and for demonstrating the power of activist film. Dayamani Di and the heroes of Satel village: thank you for passing on your extraordinary story to a stranger from far away, and for the example you set for everyone to follow. To Ghanshyam, for welcoming me into your home, and for your powerful resistance over decades; Ashish, for taking up the fight and the early morning start; Anupam, for rice beer, superb photos and friendship. Johar. Reecha and Ayesha, for quiet times and campaign inspiration in Delhi.

Sarah, for making the connection to Cox's Bazar; Naveed, for trusting the idea; and Nadirah and the whole MedGlobal team, for granting me a small window into the extraordinary work that you do. Thank you for introducing me to the city of children. Mansur, for unforgettable Dhaka orientation and for getting me out on the water.

Boldbayar made my time in Mongolia too memorable to really capture in words: a whirlwind I'll never forget. Jagar and Saruul, for the view from the grassroots; and Boem, for the national context (and the shoes). Deeply grateful for the opportunity to meet with Mr Enkhbayar for your unique perspective and resolve over such a long period.

Peter turned cafe hangs in Berlin into a meditation on what a safe climate future looks like in the places they're actually building it; thank you for sharing your expertise and for your perfectly pitched scepticism. Jayne, Giles and James, for the Karlskrona book club, and the introduction to Goran and the urgent work of BTH. I hope you like how the cities stuff turned out and that this is a useful addition to the bookshelf. Vanesse, for quiet Auray time to catch a breath and for La ZAD; Valerie, for your unique expertise, and for the space and time to write. Birgitta the poetician, for showing different ways of doing this work; Mar and the European Greens crew, for building the world we want in real time. Adam – for writing *Radical Technologies* – but also for being okay with my unforgivable lateness and sage advice on keeping things lyrical. Taniel, for somehow being across everything from nuclear abolition to feminist economics to rebellious street occupations, and for finding Alan Turing with me. Stella and Joseph and Jen and Kristinn, for such steadfastness in this long unbearable campaign; Julian, for making the map and for hanging on until we can get you out.

Ray and Tim and Dim and the ICAN crew, you aren't just an inspiration: you've changed international law. Anna, for plain talk on movement building, and everyone at Purpose, for such beautiful work behind the scenes and for taking the time and helping open doors. Tiago and the crew from Thoughtworks in Belo, for arranging the trip to Paracatu, with gratitude to Letícia and everyone who made time to meet with us. Maria, for explorations of peace and memory in Medellin.

To the Mathare Social Justice Movement crew: Gacheke, J.J., Micko and Juliet, thank you for demonstrating the power of grassroots organising and for your generosity with your time. Dr Njoya, for naming the monsters with such clarity; Inge, for straight talk about state capture.

Thank you, Leonard, for finding me on the docks and introducing me to the new model. To David and Renata, and all those working with the Progressive International and allied networks, thank you for being there at exactly the right time.

I've been humbled to be supported by extraordinary people, not just in friendship and mentorship but also financially. Flick and Ruth, Chilla and

Jo, John and Dan, and my dear folks. Trish and Rob, Giz, Hilary, George, Julian, David, Harold and Alex. That's what made this whole thing possible.

Nick, for giving me a chance in *The Monthly*, but also for cheerful persistence in suggesting that Black Inc. could be a good home for a book. And to Chris, for turning that possibility into something real. Presented with an unruly shambles of five different books trying to coexist in the same place, thank you for giving me the latitude to explore these ideas while perfectly timing the interventions that brought it back on the rails. Neil Gaiman reckons the second draft is where you make it look like you knew what you were doing all along; this one took until the third, and thank goodness you could see that when I couldn't. Kirstie, I'm in awe of your patience, for putting up with occasional precocious behaviour, and for how much you threw at making this the best piece of writing it could be. Julia, for the sharpest eyes in the business and for saving me from some pretty embarrassing mistakes at the last minute, and Kate and Irene for organising the book's actual introduction to the world.

To dear Rob and Annmarie, for everything since.

There are so many others whose wit, wisdom and practical support made this book what it is, but whose names and words aren't referenced directly. For reasons of space alone, huge amounts of material were cut from the manuscript in the process of drafting; you're deeply appreciated nonetheless.

This book was written on occupied territories; largely on the traditional lands of the Yuin people on the south coast of New South Wales, and it was shaped by forty years on the lands of the Whadjuk Nyoongah. Thank you, Uncle Noel, for your gentle guidance while we tried to articulate a different kind of vision for the city, and for the stories from the Nyiting. Uncle Kev, Auntie Sue and the whole ANFA family; the Muckaty mob and the Mirarr, for everything you taught me going right back to the beginning.

This work isn't over until the old people around the campfire say it's over.

notes

fireground

3   'Recent projections': Ross Garnaut, *The Garnaut Climate Change Review: Final report*, Commonwealth of Australia, 30 September 2008.

3   'It's one of sadness': Garnaut, quoted in Nick Baker, 'How a climate change study from 12 years ago warned of this horror bushfire season', SBS (online), 6 January 2020.

part 1: the motive power of fire

13   increased methane levels from rice cultivation in China: William F. Ruddiman and Jonathan S. Thomson, 'The case for human causes of increased atmospheric CH4 over the last 5000 years', *Quaternary Science Reviews* 20, no. 18 (December 2001): 1769–77.

14   'We no longer live': Rolf Lidskog and Claire Waterton, 'Anthropocene – a cautious welcome from environmental sociology?' *Environmental Sociology* 2, no. 4 (October 2016): 395–406.

14   'Only beyond the mid-20th century': Will Steffen, Wendy Broadgate, Lisa Deutsch, Owen Gaffney and Cornelia Ludwig, 'The trajectory of the Anthropocene: The great acceleration', *The Anthropocene Review* 2, no. 1 (April 2015): 81–98.

16   metallic ores: The following data on extraction of metal ores follow material flow analysis conventions which record 'gross ore extracted' – that is, it includes mine tailings wastes in addition to usable metal content: Fridolin Krausmann, Christian Lauk, Willi Haas and Dominik Wiedenhofer, 'From resource extraction to outflows of wastes and emissions: The socioeconomic metabolism of the global economy, 1900–2015', *Global Environmental Change* 52 (September 2018): 131–40.

21   this game: Joanna Macy, 'The systems game', Work That Reconnects website, 1 December 2017, https://workthatreconnects.org/the-systems-game/.

22   'We may therefore state': Sadi Carnot, *Reflections on the Motive Power of Fire: And other papers on the second law of thermodynamics*, edited by E. Mendoza, New York: Dover Publications, 2005.

23   'Reality is irreversible': Mikhail Volkenstein, *Entropy and Information*, transcribed by Abe Shenitzer and Robert G. Burns, *Progress in Mathematical Physics*, Birkhäuser, 2009.

24   'a regularly interacting': Merriam-Webster online dictionary, accessed 22 April 2019.

37   wild melange of chemicals: B.S. Palmer, 'A review on the spontaneous formation of the building blocks of life and the generation of a set of hypotheses governing universal abiogenesis', *International Journal of Astrobiology* 12, no. 1 (January 2013): 39–44.

39 three qualities *and* some form of enclosure or boundary: John F. Padgett, 'Autocatalysis in chemistry and the origin of life' in John F. Padgett and Walter W. Powell, *The Emergence of Organizations and Markets*, Princeton and Oxford: Princeton University Press, 2012: 38.

36 'If history shows anything': David Graeber, *Debt: The first 5,000 years*, Brooklyn, NY: Melville House, 2011.

43 'People everywhere': Bernard London, *Ending the Depression through Planned Obsolescence*, 1932.

44 'Advertising helps': Quoted in William Leiss, Stephen Kline and Sut Jhally, *Social Communication in Advertising: Persons, products & images of well-being*, Psychology Press, 1990.

45 'The future of business' and 'industry's conscious attempt': Stuart Ewen, *Captains of Consciousness: Advertising and the social roots of the consumer culture*, 25th anniversary edn, New York: Basic Books, 2001.

45 'I think the child': Adriana Barbaro & Jeremy Earp (dirs), *Consuming Kids: The commercialization of childhood*, Media Education Foundation, 2008.

46 US$532-billion-dollar industry: IMARC, *Global Advertising Market Report, Trends & Forecast 2019–2024*, IMARC, www.imarcgroup.com/global-advertising-market, accessed 12 December 2019.

45 FACT: Larry Kramer, 'FTC officer delays children's advertising hearing', *The Washington Post*, 29 December 1978.

46 'We never know': Louise Story, 'Anywhere the eye can see, it's likely to see an ad', *The New York Times*, 15 January 2007.

46 Facebook retargeting: Dan Hecht, 'A beginner's guide to retargeting ads', https://blog.hubspot.com/marketing/retargeting-campaigns-beginner-guide, accessed 20 August 2019.

47 'a distinct self–non-self recognition mechanism': Eugene V. Koonin and Kira S. Makarova, 'CRISPR-Cas: Evolution of an RNA-based adaptive immunity system in prokaryotes', *RNA Biology* 10, no. 5 (May 2013): 679–86.

49 Bacterial chemotaxis: Daniel Koshland, *Bacterial Chemotaxis as a Model Behavioral System*, Raven Press, 1980.

51 'Henry Ford said': Michael Hudson, 'How bankers became the top exploiters of the economy', CounterPunch.org, 15 March 2017.

52 total global workforce: The numbers in the following section are mostly derived from the ILO's remarkable World Employment and Social Outlook database – 'Data Finder – World Employment and Social Outlook', www.ilo.org/wesodata/. Taking 2020 workforce projections and dividing them by the estimated global population in 2020 according to the *World Population Prospects 2019, Volume I: Comprehensive Tables*, United Nations, Department of Economic and Social Affairs, Population Division 1 , 2019.

53 seventy-seven cents: UN Women, 'Equal pay for work of equal value', www.unwomen.org/en/news/in-focus/csw61/equal-pay, accessed 2 November 2019.

53 two and a half times more hours per week: UN Women, 'Women in the changing world of work – facts you should know', https://interactive.unwomen.org/multimedia/infographic/changingworldofwork/en/index.html, accessed 2 November 2019.

53 'It is peasants': Ariel Salleh, 'Green economy or green utopia?' *American Sociological Association* 18, no. 2 (2012): 141–5.

53 without access to basic services: UN Water, *UN-Water GLAAS 2019: National systems to support drinking-water, sanitation and hygiene – global status report 2019*, 23 August 2019.

53 one of the villagers is a slave: 'What is modern slavery?' Anti-Slavery International, www.antislavery.org/slavery-today/modern-slavery/.

54 This one white guy: 'Global inequality', Inequality.org, https://inequality.org/facts/global-inequality/, accessed 3 November 2019.

54 twenty million millionaires: Knight Frank, *The Wealth Report – Insight Series 2019*, www.knightfrank.com/research/the-wealth-report-6505.aspx, accessed 3 November 2019.

54 2604 billionaires: *Global billionaire population: The Billionaire Census 2019*, Wealth-X, www.wealthx.com/report/the-wealth-x-billionaire-census-2019/, accessed 3 November 2019.

56 passing segments of DNA back and forth: Alex Mira et al., 'The bacterial pan-genome: A new paradigm in microbiology', *International Microbiology*, no. 13 (2010): 45–57.

57 the first photosynthesisers *and* perfects a version of this trick: Tanai Cardona, 'Early Archean origin of heterodimeric photosystem I', *Heliyon* 4, no. 3 (March 2018): e00548.

58 wild array of new minerals: D.A. Sverjensky and N. Lee. 'The great oxidation event and mineral diversification', *Elements* 6, no. 1 (1 February 2010): 31–6.

59 a bacterium starts living inside an Archean: Andrew J. Roger, Sergio A. Muñoz-Gómez and Ryoma Kamikawa, 'The origin and diversification of mitochondria', *Current Biology* 27, no. 21 (November 2017): R1177–92.

59 eukaryotes invent sex: Joseph Heitman, 'Evolution of sexual reproduction: A view from the fungal kingdom supports an evolutionary epoch with sex before sexes', Fu*ngal Biology Reviews* 29, nos 3–4 (December 2015): 108–17.

59 evolution's tempo quickens: Richard Boyle, 'Eukaryotic origins and the proterozoic earth system: A link between global scale glaciations and eukaryogenesis?' *Earth-Science Reviews* 174 (November 2017): 22–38.

62 'can be regarded': Roger D. Congleton, 'The median voter model' in *The Encyclopedia of Public Choice*, edited by Charles K. Rowley and Friedrich Schneider, Boston, MA: Springer US, 2004: 707–12.

63 'Competition between blocs of major investors': Thomas Ferguson, *Golden Rule: The investment theory of party competition and the logic of money-driven political systems*, Chicago: University of Chicago Press, 1995.

64   'There is a strong, direct link': Lynn Parramore, 'Stark new evidence on how money shapes America's elections', Institute for New Economic Thinking website, 8 August 2016.

64   'both major party presidential hopefuls': Thomas Ferguson, Paul Jorgensen and Jie Chen, 'Party competition and industrial structure in the 2012 elections', *International Journal of Political Economy* 42, no. 2 (1 July 2013): 3–41.

64   'This leads to a significant conclusion': Michael West, 'The Minerals Council, coal and the half a billion spent by the resources lobby', Michael West website, 2 October 2017.

65   'According to our estimations': Yasmine Bekkouche and Julia Cagé, The *Price of a Vote: Evidence from France, 1993–2014*, Working Paper, Institute for New Economic Thinking, January 2018.

66   'Oligarchy is when': Aristotle, *Politics*, Book III, translated by William Ellis, full text by Project Gutenberg.

66   the parties that spent the most money: Kate Griffiths, Danielle Wood and Tony Chan, 'How big money influenced the 2019 federal election – Grattan Institute', *The Conversation*, 4 February 2020.

69   'A long view of human history': C.S. Holling, 'Understanding the complexity of economic, ecological, and social systems', *Ecosystems* 4, no. 5 (1 August 2001): 390–405.

72   visible to the fossil record: D.H. Erwin, 'Early Metazoan life: Divergence, environment and ecology', *Philosophical Transactions of the Royal Society B: Biological Sciences* 370, no. 1684 (9 November 2015): 20150036.

76   11,000 watts per person: Geoffrey West, *Scale: The universal laws of life, growth, and death in organisms, cities, and companies*, New York: Penguin Books, 2018: 13.

78   A map of this slow haulage: Shipmap.Org, www.shipmap.org.

79   we mined 6.5 billion tonnes: Fridolin Krausmann, Simone Gingrich, Nina Eisenmenger, Karl-Heinz Erb, Helmut Haberl and Marina Fischer-Kowalski, 'Growth in global materials use, GDP and population during the 20th century', *Ecological Economics* 68, no. 10 (August 2009): 2696–705.

79   We quarried: Fridolin Krausmann, Christian Lauk, Willi Haas and Dominik Wiedenhofer, 'From resource extraction to outflows of wastes and emissions: The socioeconomic metabolism of the global economy, 1900–2015', *Global Environmental Change* 52 (September 2018): 131–40.

79   we slaughtered: 'Animal slaughter and meat production – global', Terrastendo (blog), 12 January 2018.

79   we caught and killed: FAO, *The State of World Fisheries and Aquaculture 2020: Sustainability in action*, Rome, Italy: FAO, 2020.

79   we were diverting and desalinating: Hannah Ritchie and Max Roser, 'Water use and stress', Our World in Data, https://ourworldindata.org/water-use-stress, accessed 20 November 2017.

part 2: new silk roads

90 It only employs 4 per cent: European Bank for Reconstruction and Development Evaluation Department, *Cluster Evaluation – Mining Operations in Mongolia*, Approach Paper, EBRD, February 2019.

90 A recently-agreed IMF stability package: European Bank for Reconstruction and Development, *EBRD Extractive Mining Industries Strategy 2018–2022*, 13 December 2017.

91 closer to one in two: 'Mongolia's 2018 poverty rate estimated at 28.4 percent', World Bank, 21 June 2019.

94 'This is an incredibly important milestone': 'WSJ Update: Mongolia Scraps windfall profits tax on copper, gold', Dow Jones Institutional News, New York, 26 August 2009.

95 70 per cent of Mongolians: David Stanway, 'Democratic but deadlocked, Mongolia braces for "inevitable" political change', *Reuters*, 26 June 2019.

98 Four out of ten people live below the poverty line: 'Jharkhand: Here is why India's richest mineral state is not even close to development', dailybhaskar, 30 March 2014; *Jharkand: Economic and Human Development Indicators*, UNDP factsheet, accessed 12 March 2021.

98 'transforming tomorrow': 'At a glance', ArcelorMittal website, https://corporate. arcelormittal.com/who-we-are/at-a-glance, accessed 10 December 2019.

103 one of Shriprakash's superb, timely films: 'Buddha Weeps at Jadugoda (Ragi: Kana: Ko Bonga Buru)', Kritika Productions, 1998, published to YouTube 1 July 2017, www.youtube.com/watch?v=FxO_LlHaYvs.

110 'prohibit . . . the burning of seacoal': J.U. Nef, *The Rise of the British Coal Industry*, Routledge, 1966.

110 London Brewers Company: William M. Cavert, *The Smoke of London: Energy and environment in the early modern city*, Cambridge University Press, 2016.

112 'whatever measures are needed': Naomi Roht-Arriaza, 'Measures of non-repetition in transitional justice: The missing link?' SSRN Scholarly Paper, Rochester, NY: Social Science Research Network, 10 March 2016.

113 'The annual material': The data for this section were all sourced from Fridolin Krausmann, Christian Lauk, Willi Haas and Dominik Wiedenhofer, 'From resource extraction to outflows of wastes and emissions: The socioeconomic metabolism of the global economy, 1900–2015', *Global Environmental Change* 52 (September 2018): 131–40.

114 informal workforce up to ten thousand strong: Peter Yeung, 'The rich world's electronic waste, dumped in Ghana', Bloomberg CityLab website, 30 May 2019.

114 fifty million tonnes of e-waste: *The Global E-waste Monitor 2020*, http://ewastemonitor.info/, accessed 28 August 2019.

114 'The smoke is a very big problem': Emmanuel Asampong, Kwaku Dwuma-Badu, Judith Stephens, Roland Srigboh, Richard Neitzel, Niladri Basu and Julius N. Fobil,

'Health seeking behaviours among electronic waste workers in Ghana', *BMC Public Health*, 16 October 2015.

117 termination paperwork: Julie Bort, 'Amazon's warehouse-worker tracking system can automatically fire people without a human supervisor's involvement', *Business Insider*, 26 April 2019.

118 seventh straight year: Yuan Fang, 'China is largest market for industrial robot application', China.org.cn, 22 August 2019.

119 'thrown into the street': Karl Marx, *Capital: Volume 1*, trans. Ben Fowkes, London: Penguin, 1976: 764

119 'From where I live': Anne Amnesia, 'Unnecessariat', More Crows than Eagles blog, 10 May 2016.

119 27 per cent of the imprisoned: Paul Gregoire, 'A world without bars: The prison abolition movement', Sydney Criminal Lawyers, 29 April 2017.

119 'convict leasing': Joy James, 'From the prison of slavery to the slavery of prison: Frederick Douglass and the convict lease system' in *The Angela Y. Davis Reader*, Maiden, Mass.: Blackwell Publishers, 1998.

119 'Robots are not killing jobs': Brian Merchant, '"Robots" are not "coming for your job", management is', *Gizmodo*, 3 June 2019.

122 'The professionalization of political science': Steven Peterson and Albert Somit, *Handbook of Biology and Politics*, Edward Elgar Publishing, 2017.

123 'We accept and welcome': Andrew Carnegie, '1889: Survival of the Fittest', *Lapham's Quarterly* website, accessed 5 November 2019.

123 'The growth of a large business': John D. Rockefeller, quoted in Peter Corning, '"Survival of the Fittest:": Herbert Spencer (and friends) got it wrong', Institute for the Study of Complex Systems, ComplexSystems.org, 3 September 2018.

123 'struggle for existence' 'overrating its narrow meaning': Pyotr Alexeyevich Kropotkin, *Mutual Aid: A Factor of Evolution*, edited by Jhon Duran, CreateSpace Independent Publishing Platform, 2017.

part 3: continuities

132 'Of the 248,000 kilometres of land borders': Michel Foucher, *L'obsession des frontières*, Paris: Perrin, 2012.

132 '(1) the government of each country': Seyom Brown, *International Relations in a Changing Global System: Toward a theory of the world polity*, 2nd edn, Boulder, Col.: Westview Press, 1995.

133 'The British and the French divided up the Middle East': Manlio Graziano, Stanford, CA.: Stanford Briefs, 2018.

134 'Nationalism is founded': 'What is the left case for open borders?' *Political Critique* blog, 13 February 2019.

140 1 per cent of its GDP: 'Bangladesh is a unique example of climate vulnerability, resilience: PM Hasina', bdnews24.com, 8 September 2020.

140 'Europe of Nations': Agence France-Presse, 'Le Pen's national rally goes green in bid for European election votes', *Raw Story*, 21 April 2019.

141 'The climate crisis is the foundation': Kate Aronoff, 'The European far right's environmental turn', *Dissent* online, 31 May 2019.

141 'The power of population': Thomas Malthus, *An Essay on the Principle of Population*, 1798.

141 'With savages': Charles Darwin, *The Descent of Man, and Selection in Relation to Sex*, revised edn, Princeton University Press, 1981.

143 'we are all the descendants of thieves': Garrett Hardin, 'Lifeboat Ethics: The case against helping the poor', *Psychology Today*, September 1974.

144 'When the lifeboat is full': 'Pentti Linkola: Ideas', Pentti Linkola website, www.penttilinkola.com/pentti_linkola/ecofascism/, accessed 16 March 2021.

144 'wealthy, busy': 'Pentti Linkola interview from Quadrivium #6 (2014): Abridged Version', Quadrivium blog, 12 June 2015, https://qvadrivivm.blogspot.com/2015/12/pentti-linkola-interview-from.html.

144 'We are a plague': Louise Gray, 'David Attenborough – Humans are plague on Earth', *The Telegraph*, 22 January 2013.

145 'The Misanthropocene': www.themisanthropocene.com, accessed 23 July 2019.

147 'From ancient times': Vandana VaShiva, Maria Mies, Pnina Werbner, Richard Werbner and Ariel Salleh. *Ecofeminism*, 2nd edn, London: Zed Books, 2014.

147 'Although also shown': Beth Kinsella, 'Secondary education for females: A primary way to prevent overpopulation', *Harvard College Global Health Review*, 17 November 2011.

147 'Unlike women': Aparna Mitra and Pooja Singh, 'Human capital attainment and gender empowerment: The Kerala paradox', *Social Science Quarterly* 88, no. 5 (December 2007): 1227–42.

148 'Go, then': Homer, *The Odyssey*, Scroll 1, Line 7, edited by Samuel Butler, based on public domain edition, revised by Timothy Power and Gregory Nagy.

148 'the way Western culture': Douglas A. Vakoch and Sam Mickey, *Ecofeminism in Dialogue*, Lexington Books, 2017.

148 'seized control': Michelle Murphy, *Seizing the Means of Reproduction: Entanglements of feminism, health, and technoscience*, Duke University Press Books, 2012.

148 'Our schools': Robert J. Marzano, Tony Frontier and David Livingston, *A Brief History of Supervision and Evaluation*, ASCD, 2011.

149 more than 80 per cent: Monique Villa, 'Women own less than 20% of the world's land. It's time to give them equal property rights', World Economic Forum website, 11 January 2017.

149 89 per cent of the world's billionaires: 'Gender economic inequality', Inequality.org, https://inequality.org/gender-inequality/, accessed 4 December 2019.

149 'women shall be considered': Cyndy Baskin, 'Women in Iroquois Society', *Canadian Woman Studies / Les Cahiers De La Femme* 4, no. 2 (1982): 43.

149 Minangkabau people: Peggy Reeves Sanday, *Women at the Center: Life in a modern matriarchy,* Ithaka, NY: Cornell University Press, 2003.

149 'for thousands of years': Ambelin Kwaymullina, 'You are on indigenous land: Ecofeminism, indigenous peoples and land justice' in Lara Stevens, Peta Tait and Denise Varney (eds), *Feminist Ecologies: Changing environments in the Anthropocene*, Springer International Publishing, 2018: 193–208.

151 60 per cent of marine species: Yukio Isozaki and Thomas Servais, 'The Hirnantian (Late Ordovician) and End-Guadalupian (Middle Permian) mass-extinction events compared', *Lethaia* 51, no. 2 (April 2018): 173–86.

152 Tentative lines of evidence: Charles H. Wellman and Paul K. Strother, 'The terrestrial biota prior to the origin of land plants (embryophytes): A review of the evidence', edited by Andrew Smith, *Palaeontology* 58, no. 4 (July 2015): 601–27.

153 tiny Rhyniognatha insects take flight: B. Misof, S. Liu, K. Meusemann, R.S. Peters, A. Donath, C. Mayer, P.B. Frandsen et al., 'Phylogenomics resolves the timing and pattern of insect evolution', *Science* 346, no. 6210 (7 November 2014): 763–7.

156 'We had to know what the Japanese had done': Jennifer Chan, *Another Japan Is Possible: New social movements and global citizenship education*, Stanford University Press, 2008.

157 Japanese textbooks: Kathleen Woods Masalski, 'Examining the Japanese history textbook controversies', *Japan Digest*, National Clearinghouse for United States–Japan Studies, 2001.

158 'We heard the big bomb': Dijana Damjanovic, 'Aboriginal activist, nuclear campaigner Yami Lester dead at 75', ABC News (online), 22 July 2017.

158 'The first step': Milan Kundera, *The Book of Laughter and Forgetting*, New York: Harper Perennial Modern Classics, 1999.

159 detailed maps: Nick Evershed, Andy Ball, Lorena Allam, Ciaran O'Mahony, Jeremy Nadel and Carly Earl, 'The Killing Times: A massacre map of Australia's frontier wars', *Guardian Australia*, 4 March 2019.

162 'people who move around': James C. Scott, *Seeing Like a State: How certain schemes to improve the human condition have failed*, New Haven, Conn.: Yale University Press, 1999.

162 'the globally interconnected': 'Global Information Grid – Glossary', Computer Security Resource Center website, https://csrc.nist.gov/glossary/term/global_information_grid accessed 12 January 2021.

162 'full spectrum dominance': Jason Cantone, Natasha Fields, Brandon Iske, Kristin Phaneuf, Karen Poyer, Daniel Reynoso and Ann Sawatzki, *Measuring the Health of the Global Information Grid*, May 2009, 106.

164 'Until we know': 'The War on Journalism: The case of Julian Assange', PeerTube, https://video.emergeheart.info/videos/watch/f2467447-f5a8-45c9-8d08-804d6a2d4747, accessed 3 October 2020.

164 Australian spies wiretapped: Ian Cunliffe, 'East Timor Bugging Scandal: Attorney general's push for secret trial diminishes us as a nation', Michael West blog, 19 August 2020.

167 'It's the basic intellectual dynamic': Michael Hudson, 'The Democracy Collaborative', Michael Hudson website, 28 March 2017.

170 'Failed investment': 'An existential question of terrestrial habitability and human survivability: An interview with Peter Droege', EuropeNow website, 6 June 2017.

171 'comparing the priesthood' and 'the Senate-belly': Joëlle Rollo-Koster, 'Body politic' in *Encyclopedia of Political Theory* by Mark Bevir, Thousand Oaks, CA: SAGE Publications, 2010.

171 'for three centuries': Stefanie R. Fishel, *The Microbial State: Global thriving and the body politic*, Minneapolis: University of Minnesota Press, 2017.

173 'Factory occupations': Steve Fraser, 'The new deal in the American political imagination', *Jacobin* website, https://jacobinmag.com/2019/06/new-deal-great-depression, accessed 24 December 2019.

174 'federal old-age insurance': 'Chronology', Social Security Administration website, www.ssa.gov/history/1930.html, accessed 24 December 2019.

175 'Only a crisis' and 'When that crisis occurs': Milton Friedman, *Capitalism and Freedom*, 40th anniversary edn, University of Chicago Press, 2009.

176 total bailout commitment: James Felkerson, *$29,000,000,000,000: A detailed look at the fed's bailout by funding facility and recipient*, Levy Economics Institute of Bard College Working Paper No. 698, 9 December 2011.

177 'A positive' and 'Positive feedback': Donella Meadows, 'Places to intervene in a system (in increasing order of effectiveness)', *Whole Earth* 91, (1997): 78–84.

178 US platform monopolist Amazon: Matt Day and Jackie Gu, 'The numbers behind Amazon's market reach', Bloomberg website, 27 March 2019.

178 'Lower prices led': Brad Stone, *The Everything Store: Jeff Bezos and the age of Amazon*, New York, NY: Back Bay Books, 2014.

178 'The only way': Mike Murphy, 'Jeff Bezos thinks his fortune is best spent in space', MarketWatch website, 1 May 2015.

179 'At the point': Hudson, 2017.

182 white rot Agaricomycetes fungi: D. Floudas, M. Binder, R. Riley, K. Barry, R.A. Blanchette, B. Henrissat, A.T. Martinez et al., 'The Paleozoic origin of enzymatic lignin decomposition reconstructed from 31 fungal genomes', *Science* 336, no. 6089 (29 June 2012): 1715–19.

183 Skagerrak-Centered Large Igneous Province: M. Doblas, R. Oyarzun, J. López-Ruiz, J.M. Cebriá, N. Youbi, V. Mahecha, M. Lago, A. Pocoví and B. Cabanis, 'Permo-carboniferous volcanism in Europe and northwest Africa: A superplume exhaust valve in the centre of Pangaea?' *Journal of African Earth Sciences* 26, no. 1 (January 1998): 89–99.

184 cynodont: J. Botha, F. Abdala and R. Smith, 'The oldest cynodont: New clues on the origin and early diversification of the cynodontia', *Zoological Journal of the Linnean Society* 149, no. 3 (March 2007): 477–92.

184 likely wearing fur: Piotr Bajdek, Martin Qvarnström, Krzysztof Owocki, Tomasz Sulej, Andrey G. Sennikov, Valeriy K. Golubev and Grzegorz Niedźwiedzki, 'Microbiota and food residues including possible evidence of pre-mammalian hair in upper permian coprolites from Russia', *Lethaia* 49, no. 4 (October 2016): 455–77.

185 'Started up six major projects': BP, 'Our strategy', BP website, www.bp.com/en/global/corporate/what-we-do/our-strategy.html, accessed 29 December 2019.

185 'There is evidence': Kert Davies, 'Mining Congress Journal, August 1966 – Air pollution and the coal industry', *Climate Files* (blog), 22 November 2019.

186 The oil men knew: Neela Banerjee, Lisa Song and David Hasemyer, 'Exxon's own research confirmed fossil fuels' role in global warming decades ago', InsideClimate News, 16 September 2015.

187 'At the point': Hudson, 2017.

part 4: power laws and dragon kings

192 more than two million people: Fridays For Future, 'List of Countries', Fridays for Future website, https://fridaysforfuture.org/what-we-do/strike-statistics/list-of-countries/, accessed 11 March 2021.

192 largest climate demonstration in history: '7.6 million people demand action after week of climate strikes', 350.org press release, 27 September 2019.

193 'One person holds a poster': Matthew Taylor, Jonathan Watts and John Bartlett, 'Climate Crisis: 6 million people join latest wave of global protests', *Guardian Australia*, 27 September 2019.

193 'I feel planting trees': 'China's First Fridays for Future sees teen planting trees', *Deutsche Welle* website, 30 October 2019.

194 'mentally ill Swedish child': Zachary Pleat: 'Right-wing media launch unhinged attacks on Greta Thunberg', Media Matters for America website, 24 September 2019.

194 'I have never': Amanda Meade, 'Greta Thunberg Hits Back at Andrew Bolt for "deeply Disturbing" column', *Guardian Australia*, 1 August 2019.

195 'Tase and arrest her': Pleat, 'Right-wing media launch'.

195 'Their denial': Isolde Raj-Seppings, 'I'm the 13-Year-old police threatened to arrest at the Kirribilli house protest. This is why I did it', *Guardian Australia*, 20 December 2019.

196 'a nonviolent rebellion': 'Over 1000 people block Parliament Sq to launch mass civil disobedience campaign demanding action on climate emergency', Extinction Rebellion (blog), 31 October 2018.

197 'the moment of the whirlwind': Sanford D. Horwitt, *Let Them Call Me Rebel: Saul Alinsky, his life and legacy*, New York: Vintage, 1992.

197 'the defining attribute': Mark Engler and Paul Engler, *This Is an Uprising: How nonviolent revolt is shaping the twenty-first century*, New York: Bold Type Books, 2016.

197 invited to meet with the mayor of London: Fiona Harvey, 'Extinction Rebellion: Michael Gove admits need for urgent action', *Guardian Australia*, 30 April 2019.

198 In 2008: David Spratt and Philip Sutton, *Climate Code Red: The case for emergency action*, US edn, Carlton North, Vic.: Scribe US, 2008.

198 first local government authority: 'Darebin Climate Emergency Plan', City of Darebin website, accessed 30 June 2019, www.yoursaydarebin.com.au/climateaction.

199 'allowed governments': Jeff Sparrow, '"Climate Emergency" endangers democracy', *Eureka Street*, accessed 30 June 2019.

199 'We have no choice': 'Why environmentalists must be antifascists', *Earth First! Newswire* (blog), 21 April 2017.

201 John Gorton's warning in 1969: Alex Mitchell, 'Untold story of Canberra's first coup: The political assassination of PM John Gorton – Part 6', Come the Revolution website, 14 February 2019.

201 'contentious politics': Sidney G. Tarrow, *Power in Movement: Social movements and contentious politics*, 3rd edn, Cambridge, New York: Cambridge University Press, 2011.

201 'openness of the regime': Charles Tilly, *Contentious Performances*, Cambridge University Press, 2008.

202 'Particular groups': Tarrow, *Power in Movement*.

204 Some interpretations: David P.G. Bond and Stephen E. Grasby, 'On the causes of mass extinctions', *Palaeogeography, Palaeoclimatology, Palaeoecology* 478 (July 2017): 3–29.

204 Three extinction waves: Sarda Sahney and Michael J Benton, 'Recovery from the most profound mass extinction of all time', *Proceedings of the Royal Society B: Biological Sciences* 275, no. 1636 (7 April 2008): 759–65.

204 Seven million square kilometres: Alexei V. Ivanov, Huayiu He, Liekun Yan, Viktor V. Ryabov, Artem Y. Shevko, Stanislav V. Palesskii and Irina V. Nikolaeva, 'Siberian traps large igneous province: Evidence for two flood basalt pulses around the Permo-Triassic boundary and in the middle Triassic, and contemporaneous granitic magmatism', *Earth-Science Reviews* 122 (July 2013): 58–76.

204 oceans overheated and starved of oxygen: Kimberly V. Lau, Kate Maher, Demir Altiner, Brian M. Kelley, Lee R. Kump, Daniel J. Lehrmann, Juan Carlos Silva-Tamayo, Karrie L. Weaver, Meiyi Yu and Jonathan L. Payne, 'Marine anoxia and delayed earth system recovery after the End-Permian extinction', *Proceedings of the National Academy of Sciences* 113, no. 9 (1 March 2016): 2360–65.

205 it will take thirty million years: Sarda Sahney and Michael J Benton, 'Recovery from the most profound mass extinction of all time', *Proceedings of the Royal Society B: Biological Sciences* 275, no. 1636 (7 April 2008): 759–65.

205 the continental interior is mostly arid: Nereo Preto, Evelyn Kustatscher and Paul B. Wignall. 'Triassic climates – state of the art and perspectives', *Palaeogeography, Palaeoclimatology, Palaeoecology* 290, nos 1–4 (April 2010): 1–10.

206 Venturing out: Gideon H. Groenewald, Johann Welman and James A. MacEachern, 'Vertebrate burrow complexes from the Early Triassic Cynognathus Zone (Driekoppen Formation, Beaufort Group) of the Karoo Basin, South Africa', *Palaios* 16, no. 2 (April 2001): 148–160

209 Prime minister Yoshihiko Noda will declare: 'In wake of Fukushima disaster, Japan to end nuclear power by 2030s', *LA Times* blog, 14 September 2012.

214 'As the pile is built up': Per Bak, Chao Tang and Kurt Wiesenfeld, 'Self-organized criticality', *Physical Review A*, 38, no. 1 (1 July 1988): 364–74.

215 'three natural hazards': D.L. Turcotte, B.D. Malamud, F. Guzzetti and P. Reichenbach, 'Self-organization, the cascade model, and natural hazards', *Proceedings of the National Academy of Sciences* 99, Supplement 1 (19 February 2002): 2530–37.

216 'An earthquake': Mark Buchanan, *Ubiquity: Why catastrophes happen*, New York: Broadway Books, 2002.

216 population distribution of the world's cities: Luci Ellis and Dan Andrews, *The Distribution of City Sizes: RDP 2001-08: City sizes, housing costs, and wealth*, Reserve Bank of Australia, 31 July 2015.

216 Per Bak's 1996 summary: Per Bak, *How Nature Works: The science of self-organized criticality*, New York: Copernicus, 1999.

217 'Unfortunately': 'So you think you have a power law – well isn't that special?' Three-Toed Sloth blog, http://bactra.org/weblog/491.html, accessed 8 February 2019.

217 'finding common statistical distributions': Juan Camilo Bohorquez, Sean Gourley, Alexander R. Dixon, Michael Spagat and Neil F. Johnson, 'Common ecology quantifies human insurgency', *Nature* 462, no. 7275 (December 2009): 911–14.

217 'extreme behaviors emerge': D. Sornette and G. Ouillon, 'Dragon-Kings: Mechanisms, statistical methods and empirical evidence', *The European Physical Journal Special Topics* 205, no. 1 (May 2012): 1–26.

219 Prime minister Naoto Kan: Naoto Kan, *My Nuclear Nightmare: Leading Japan through the Fukushima disaster to a nuclear-free future*, translated by Jeffrey S. Irish, Ithaca, London: Cornell University Press, 2017.

220 'It was a crucial moment': 'Tokyo faced evacuation scenario: Kan', *The Japan Times* online, 19 September 2011.

220 'to determine': International Atomic Energy Agency, *Development and Application of Level 1 Probabilistic Safety Assessment for Nuclear Power Plants*, IAEA Safety Standards Series No. SSG-3, 2010.

220 Reactor pressure vessels are fail-proof: David Lochbaum, *Nuclear Plant Risk Studies: Failing the grade*, Union of Concerned Scientists, August 2000, 33.

220 measured either by cost or by radiation release: Ichizo Aoki and Ogibayashi Shigeaki. 'Probability of nuclear power plant accidents with respect to radioactive fallout', *Journal of the Society of Multi-Disciplinary Knowledge*, no. 1, 2015: 14.

220 'We . . . document' and 'there is a 50 per cent chance': Spencer Wheatley, Benjamin Sovacool and Didier Sornette, 'Of disasters and dragon kings: A statistical analysis of nuclear power incidents and accidents', *Risk Analysis* 37, no. 1 (January 2017): 99–115.

222 'system-wide events': Didier Sornette and G. Ouillon, 'Dragon-kings: Mechanisms, statistical methods and empirical evidence', *The European Physical Journal Special Topics* 205, no. 1 (May 2012): 1–26.

223 'Transgressive contention': Michael Biggs, 'Strikes as forest fires: Chicago and Paris in the late nineteenth century', *American Journal of Sociology* 110, no. 6 (May 2005): 1684–1714.

224 'Civil unrest contagion': Dan Braha, 'Global civil unrest: Contagion, self-organization, and prediction', edited by Yamir Moreno, *PLoS ONE* 7, no. 10 (31 October 2012): e48596.

224 'What happens next': Dmitry S. Zhukov, Valery V. Kanishchev and Sergey K. Lyamin. 'Application of the Theory of self-organized criticality to the investigation of historical processes', *SAGE Open* 6, no. 4 (October 2016).

224 'The probability': Biggs, 'Strikes as forest fires'.

225 'primary group' and 'Researchers used to say': Charles Dobson, 'Grassroots rot', *The Citizen's Handbook* (online), www.citizenshandbook.org/wilt.html, accessed 27 December 2019.

229 'Numbers may matter': Erica Chenoweth and Maria Stephan, *Why Civil Resistance Works: The strategic logic of nonviolent conflict*, New York, NY: Columbia University Press, 2012.

235 'We look forward' and 'As the town changes': 'Politicians step up for Jabiru and Kakadu', The Gundjeihmi Aboriginal Corporation website, http://mirarr.net/stories/jabiru-business-case, accessed 28 December 2019.

236 Everything in sight is dead: Robert A. DePalma, Jan Smit, David A. Burnham, Klaudia Kuiper, Phillip L. Manning, Anton Oleinik, Peter Larson et al., 'A seismically induced onshore surge deposit at the KPg Boundary, North Dakota', *Proceedings of the National Academy of Sciences* 116, no. 17, 23 April 2019: 8190–9.

236 Photosynthesis collapses: Johan Vellekoop, Appy Sluijs, Jan Smit, Stefan Schouten, Johan W.H. Weijers, Jaap S. Sinninghe Damsté and Henk Brinkhuis, 'Rapid short-term cooling following the chicxulub impact at the cretaceous-paleogene boundary', *Proceedings of the National Academy of Sciences* 111, no. 21 (27 May 2014): 7537–41.

236 Worldwide the complex food webs and ecosystems: Peter Schulte et al., 'The Chicxulub asteroid impact and mass extinction at the Cretaceous-Paleogene boundary', *Science* 327, no. 5970 (5 March 2010): 1214–18.

236 Terrestrial dinosaurs are wiped out: Daniel J. Field, Antoine Bercovici, Jacob S. Berv, Regan Dunn, David E. Fastovsky, Tyler R. Lyson, Vivi Vajda and Jacques A. Gauthier, 'Early evolution of modern birds structured by global forest collapse at the end-cretaceous mass extinction', *Current Biology* 28, no. 11 (June 2018): 1825–31

237 the world briefly belongs to the ferns again: Douglas J. Nichols and Kirk R. Johnson, *Plants and the K–T Boundary*, Cambridge: Cambridge University Press, 2008.

237 Vast stands of conifers *and* a weird temperature spike: B.A. Schubert, A.H. Jahren, J.J. Eberle, L.S.L. Sternberg and D.A. Eberth, 'A summertime rainy season in the Arctic forests of the Eocene', *Geology* 40, no. 6 (1 June 2012): 523–6.

238 Global temperatures jump: Marcus Gutjahr, Andy Ridgwell, Philip F. Sexton, Eleni Anagnostou, Paul N. Pearson, Heiko Pälike, Richard D. Norris, Ellen Thomas, and Gavin L. Foster, 'Very large release of mostly volcanic carbon during the Palaeocene–Eocene Thermal Maximum,' *Nature* 548, no. 7669 (August 2017): 573–7.

240 a hundred and fifty social relationships: R.A. Hill and R.I.M. Dunbar, 'Social network size in humans', *Human Nature* 14, no. 1 (March 2003): 53–72.

241 numbers have held approximately true: Pádraig MacCarron, Kimmo Kaski and Robin Dunbar, 'Calling Dunbar's numbers', *Social Networks* 47 (October 2016): 151–5.

242 Euler had eliminated: Rob Shields, 'Cultural topology: The seven bridges of Königsburg, 1736,' *Theory, Culture & Society* 29, no. 4–5 (July 2012): 43–57.

242 'why some communities organise': Mark S. Granovetter, 'The strength of weak ties', *The American Journal of Sociology* 78, no. 6. (May 1973), pp. 1360–80.

243 'collective dynamics': Duncan J. Watts and Steven H. Strogatz. 'collective dynamics of "small-world" networks', *Nature* 393 (1998): 440–2.

244 succinct traverse: Mark Buchanan, *Nexus: Small worlds and the groundbreaking science of networks*, New York: W.W. Norton & Company, 2003.

244 'We should think': S. Milgram, 'The small world problem' in G. Carter, *Empirical Approaches to Sociology*, Boston: Pearson (2004[1967]): 111–18.

247 Germany: Mishael Milaković, Simone Alfarano and Thomas Lux, 'The small core of the German corporate board network', *Computational and Mathematical Organization Theory* 16, no. 2 (June 2010): 201–15.

247 Brazil: Wesley Mendes-Da-Silva, 'Small worlds and board interlocking in Brazil: A longitudinal study of corporate networks, 1997–2007', *SSRN Electronic Journal*, 2011.

247 Singapore: Phillip H. Phan, Soo Hoon Lee and Siang Chi Lau, 'The performance impact of interlocking directorates: The case of Singapore', *Journal of Managerial Issues* 15, no. 3 (2003): 338–52.

247 'thousands of directors': Johan S.G. Chu and Gerald F. Davis, 'Who killed the inner circle? The decline of the American corporate interlock network', *American Journal of Sociology* 122, no. 3 (November 2016): 714–54.

248 'an invitation only club': Ben Butler and Nick Evershed, 'Australia's biggest companies are being run by a "directors' club", study finds', *Guardian Australia*, 25 October 2020.

248 principally from privileged classes: Philip Stanworth and Anthony Giddens, 'The modern corporate economy: Interlocking directorships in Britain, 1906–1970', *Sociological Review* 23, no. 1 (1975): 5–28.

248 'Does a unified': Joshua Murray, 'Interlock globally, act domestically: Corporate political unity in the 21st Century', *American Journal of Sociology* 122, no. 6 (May 2017): 1617–63.

248 'Interlocks are considered': J.P. Sapinski and William K. Carroll, 'Interlocking Directorates and Corporate Networks' in Andreas Nölke & Christian May (eds), *Handbook of the International Political Economy of the Corporation*, Edward Elgar Publishing, 2018.

249 'We must remember': C. Wright Mills and Alan Wolfe, *The Power Elite*, New York: Oxford University Press, 2000.

252 'on the verge': Jeff Schechtman. 'The mysterious death of an artist whose drawings were too revealing', WhoWhatWhy (blog and podcast), 4 December 2015.

253 'Any student': John Bierman, 'Crackdown in China: The leadership pursues a purge of dissidents and Canada recalls its ambassador', *Maclean's*, 26 June 1989.

253 upwards of four million members: Ziyang Zhao, *Prisoner of the State: The secret journal of Zhao Ziyang*, New York: Simon & Schuster, 2009.

253 'Repression is the process': David A. Siegel, 'Collective action in social networks', *The Journal of Politics* 73, no. 4 (October 2011): 993–1010.

257 'In this process': Gene Sharp and CRDB, *From Dictatorship to Democracy: A conceptual framework for liberation*, Committee for the Restoration of Democracy in Burma, 1994.

257 Her only public appearance: 'Lest we forget: The missing Chinese activists of 2019', *Made in China Journal* blog, 23 December 2019.

260 Their report: 'Who is next?', Mathare Social Justice Centre website, www.matharesocialjustice.org/who-is-next/, accessed 13 January 2020,

263 comprador: *Oxford English Dictionary* online, accessed 14 January 2020.

part 5: full circle

270 'The real issue': 'Climate activists like Greta Thunberg just want to "upend society"', Sky News Australia, 14 January 2020.

271 'a long view': Holling, 'Understanding the complexity of economic, ecological, and social systems'.

273 This time the hot zone: Ann Holbourn, Wolfgang Kuhnt, Karlos G.D. Kochhann, Nils Andersen and K.J. Sebastian Meier, 'Global perturbation of the carbon cycle at the onset of the Miocene climatic optimum' *Geology* 43, no. 2 (February 2015): 123–6.

274 Every conceivable frequency: Bryan C. Pijanowski, Luis J. Villanueva-Rivera, Sarah L. Dumyahn, Almo Farina, Bernie L. Krause, Brian M. Napoletano, Stuart

H. Gage, and Nadia Pieretti. 'Soundscape ecology: The science of sound in the landscape', *BioScience* 61, no. 3 (March 2011): 203–16.

275 the world has somehow become alive: Gunther Witzany, *Biocommunication of Animals*, New York: Springer, 2013.

279 'Tell the prime minister': Amanda Schaffer, 'The firefighter whose denunciation of Australia's prime minister made him a folk hero', *New Yorker*, 18 January 2020.

282 'When states': Niccolò Machiavelli, *Discourses*, London: Penguin Classics, 1984.

282 'We may see': Qian Sima, *Records of the Grand Historian: Han Dynasty I*, translated by Burton Watson, 3rd edn, Hong Kong: Columbia University Press, 1993.

282 'The eternal struggles' and 'The principle of division': Robert Michels, *Political Parties: A sociological study of the oligarchical tendencies of modern democracy*, translated into English by Eden Paul and Cedar Paul, New York: The Free Press, 1915.

283 'The first is an overall increase': Holling, 'Understanding the complexity of economic, ecological, and social systems'.

288 'The rallying and chaffing': '1920s Monopoly', The Monopolist website, https://themonopolist.net/tag/lizzie-j-magie/, accessed 26 December 2019.

289 'A positive feedback loop': Donella Meadows, 'Places to intervene in a system (in increasing order of effectiveness)', Whole Earth; San Rafael, no. 91 (1997): 78–84.

289 'In a short time': Mary Pilon, 'Monopoly was designed to teach the 99% about income inequality', *Smithsonian Magazine*, January 2015.

289 'what has destroyed': Henry George and John Burns, *Progress & Poverty: An inquiry into the cause of industrial depressions, and of increase of want with increase of wealth; the remedy*, London: William Reeves, 1884.

289 other, more egalitarian, set of rules: Mary Pilon, *The Monopolists: Obsession, fury, and the scandal behind the world's favorite board game*, New York: Bloomsbury, 2016.

290 now the world's bestselling proprietary board game: Christopher Ketcham, 'Monopoly is theft', The Stream – *Harper's* (blog), 19 October 2012.

292 'Let the children': '1920s Monopoly', The Monopolist website.

297 'We ask you': Stephanie Convery, 'Perth Festival: Artists step up protests against sponsorship by fossil fuel companies', *Guardian Australia*, 6 February 2020.

298 'The campaign was not won': 'Case Study: James Price Point/Walmadan – A huge win', CounterAct website, https://counteract.org.au/resources/creating-change-in-australia/case-study-james-price-pointwalmadan-a-huge-win/, accessed 9 February 2020.

299 'This was not a top-down community organising model': Annie Kia and Aidan Ricketts, 'Enabling Emergence: The Bentley Blockade and the struggle for a gasfield free Northern Rivers', Volume 00, (2018): 26.

300 'I announced': Sarah McVeigh, '"I wanted to stop the mine": Jonathan Moylan and the $300 million hoax', triple j *Hack* website, 3 October 2017.

301 'integrity of financial markets': 'ASIC must call to account those who undermine market's integrity', *The Sydney Morning Herald*, 8 January 2013.

301 'the full force': Clive Hamilton, 'ASIC and he great coal hoax', RenewEconomy website, 21 December 2013.

301 'The fossil fuel industry': Bill McKibben, 'The case for fossil-fuel divestment', *Rolling Stone* blog, 22 February 2013.

302 'Climate is the top issue': Werner Hoyer in Frank Jordans, 'EU Bank to stop funding fossil fuel projects in 2 years', The Associated Press, 15 November 2019.

302 European Investment Bank will have completely phased out: 'EU Bank launches ambitious new climate strategy and energy lending policy', European Investment Bank press release, 14 November 2019.

302 'Australia and Canada': Quoted in Kelsey Johnson, 'Climate change fears drive sell-off of Australian bonds', *Reuters*, 14 November 2019.

303 'A wholesale reassessment': Mark Carney, 'Breaking the Tragedy of the Horizon – Climate Change and Financial Stability', speech at Lloyd's of London, London, 29 September 2015.

304 R number of maybe 2.63: Elisabeth Mahase, 'Covid-19: What is the R number?', *BMJ* 369 (12 May 2020).

304 'Dun & Bradstreet estimates': Kim Moody, 'How "Just-in-time" capitalism spread COVID-19', *Spectre* (online), 8 April 2020.

304 'What we've seen': James Phillipps, 'Billionaires' wealth surges to a record $10.2 trillion during the pandemic', *Forbes*, 6 October 2020.

306 'when workers': Michael C. Duff, 'New labor viscerality? Work stoppages in the "new work", non-union economy', *SSRN Scholarly Paper*, Rochester, NY: Social Science Research Network, 28 June 2020.

306 'I think the lessons': Mike Elk, 'How black & brown workers are redefining strikes in the digital COVID age', *Payday Report* (online), 8 July 2020.

306 Nearly twenty thousand renters: Charlotte Lam, 'Australia's coronavirus lockdown has renters and landlords in a bind', SBS News (online), accessed 10 April 2020.

307 'defeat of organised labour': Nick Srnicek and Alex Williams, *Inventing the Future: Postcapitalism and a world without work*, revised edn, London: Verso, 2016.

307 Under this onslaught: Niall McCarthy, 'The state of global trade union membership', *Forbes* (online), 6 May 2019.

307 'There are no jobs': 'Climate Justice and Industrial Transformation', International Trade Union Confederation, accessed 8 February 2020.

308 'Communities grow', 'Those costs' and 'The transition away': Peter Sheldon, Raja Junankar and Anthony De Rosa Pontello, 'The Ruhr or Appalachia? Deciding the future of Australia's coal power workers and communities', October 2018.

313 'dragon-kings occur': D. Sornette and G. Ouillon, 'Dragon-kings: Mechanisms, statistical methods and empirical evidence', *The European Physical Journal Special Topics* 205, no. 1 (May 2012): 1–26.

320 1.4 million years ago: Nicole Boivin, Rémy Crassard and M.D. Petraglia, *Human Dispersal and Species Movement: From prehistory to the present*, Cambridge: University Press, 2017.

320 up to 3 per cent: Benjamin Vernot and Joshua M. Akey, 'Resurrecting surviving neandertal lineages from modern human genomes', *Science* 343, no. 6174 (28 February 2014): 1017–21.

320 New generations: Axel Timmermann and Tobias Friedrich, 'Late Pleistocene climate drivers of early human migration', *Nature* 538, no. 7623 (October 2016): 92–5.

320 *Homo erectus* cousins: Tim Urban, 'Everyone on earth is actually your cousin', *Quartz* (online), 18 December 2015.

321 Mitochondrial Eve: Rebecca L. Cann, Mark Stoneking and Allan C. Wilson, 'Mitochondrial DNA and human evolution', *Nature* 325, no. 6099 (January 1987): 31–6.

324 'This is a huge': Australian Greens. 'Final infrastructure in place as ACT set to deliver on 100% renewable electricity target', The Greens wesbite, 1 October 2019.

324 crashing by a third in 2019: Manuel Planelles, 'Greenhouse gas emissions drop in Spain as power plants ditch coal', *El País*, 6 January 2020.

324 crashing by a quarter: 'The European Power Sector in 2019: Coal collapses, overtaken by wind and solar', http://ember-climate.org/project/power-2019, accessed 15 March 2021.

324 'for the first time ever': Deloitte, *2020 Renewable Energy Industry Outlook*, Deloitte Development LLC, 2020.

324 'China's installed wind power capacity': Renewable Energy World, 'End of the year wrap-up: Five figures show China's renewable energy growth in 2019', Renewable Energy World website, 12 January 2019.

325 'India has set itself': Global Commission on the Geopolitics of Energy Transmission, 'A new world: The geopolitics of the energy transformation', http://geopoliticsofrenewables.org/report, accessed 12 February 2020.

325 '60 per cent of the people': International Renewable Energy Agency, *Tracking SDG7: The Energy Progress Report 2018*, IRENA, May 2018.

328 more than 40 per cent: Michael Mazengarb, 'Canberra's green machines: ACT reaches 100% renewable electricity target'. RenewEconomy (blog), 30 September 2019.

328 plant and equipment and built form: Amory Lovins: 'Negawatt revolution', Rocky Mountain Institute website, https://rmi.org/insight/negawatt-revolution/, accessed 14 February 2020.

328 'the right efficiency policies': IEA, *Energy Efficiency 2018: Analysis and outlooks to 2040*, IEA, Paris, 2018.

329 Swedish steelmaker SSAB: SSAB, 'First in fossil-free steel', SSAB website, www.ssab.com/company/sustainability/sustainable-operations/hybrit, accessed 14 February 2020.

329 'Eliminate all problematic and unnecessary plastic items': New Plastics Economy, www.newplasticseconomy.org.

329 Animal agriculture: Henning Steinfeld, Pierre Gerber, T. Wassenaar, V. Castel, Mauricio Rosales and C. de Haan, *Livestock's Long Shadow: Environmental issues and options*, The Livestock, Environment and Development Initiative, Food and Agriculture Organization of the United Nations, 2006.

329 'In May 2016': Dan Hancox, 'The unstoppable rise of veganism: How a fringe movement went mainstream', *Guardian Australia*, 1 April 2018.

330 'The main aim': Julian Kirchherr, Denise Reike and Marko Hekkert, 'Conceptualizing the circular economy: An analysis of 114 definitions', *Resources, Conservation and Recycling* 127 (December 2017): 221–32.

331 It took Yuin author: Bruce Pascoe, *Dark Emu: Aboriginal Australia and the birth of agriculture*, US edn, Scribe, 2018.

331 'As I read these early journals': Bruce Pascoe, 'Decolonising agriculture: Bruce Pascoe's "Dark Emu"', *Foreground* (online), 1 November 2017.

333 $72.9 billion: *Enough Is Enough: 2019 global nuclear weapons spending*, The International Campaign to Abolish Nuclear Weapons, May 2020.

334 'If you look at': Michael Hudson, 'The democracy collective', Michael Hudson website, 28 March 2017.

334 'Imagine, then': Kate Raworth, *Doughnut Economics: Seven ways to think like a 21st-century economist*, White River Junction, Vermont: Chelsea Green Publishing, 2017.

335 Just as in other well-constituted aggregations: Ernesto Ganuza and Gianpaolo Baiocchi. 'The power of ambiguity: How participatory budgeting travels the globe', *Journal of Deliberative Democracy* 8, no. 2 (30 December 2012): 8.

339 'They weren't egalitarians': David Brancaccio and Daniel Shin, 'To avoid a depression, forgive debts, one economist says', Marketplace website, 2 April 2020.

index

#MeToo 227
#StopAdani 302

Abbott, Tony (Australian prime minister) 309
ABC 301
Abe, Shinzo (Japanese prime minister) 209
Aboriginal and Torres Strait Islanders 119, 149
Aboriginal Tent Embassy 230
Accra (Ghana capital) waste disposal 113–14
activists 7–8, 19, 40, 156, 211, 260, 297–8
Adani, Gautam (Indian billionaire) 302
adaptive cycles 24–5, 70, 271, 276–8, 280,
    282–3, 285, 293
ADD Armed Response (South Africa) 126
Adivasi (Jharkhand people) 98, 100, 106, 235
Adnyamathanha land 233, 235, 299
advertising industry 40, 42, 44–6
Aesop ('The Belly and the Members') 171
Albanese, Tom (Rio Tinto chief executive) 94
Aleixo, Letícia (lawyer) 112, 263
Alliance Against Uranium 231, 234
Alpha Centauri 16, 34, 307, 334
Amazon (US platform monopolist) 117, 178
Amazon Basin 186
Amnesia, Anne (blogger) 116, 119
Amnesty International 94, 260
Antarctica 198, 205, 207, 237, 273–4
Anthropocene epoch 3, 14, 19, 41, 50, 63, 80,
    113, 145, 177, 191, 309, 319, 335
Anyuolo, Lena (study of Mathare) 316
ANZ bank 300
'apophenia' 161, 165, 279
ArcelorMittal 98–101, 104
Archean eon 57–59, 71, 109, 153
Aristotle 66
Aronoff, Kate (freelance journalist) 141
Arrernte nation 133
Assange, Julian (WikiLeaks) 164
Atlas Foundation 250
Attenborough, Sir David 144
Australia 29, 140, 207, 237, 311
Australia Frontier Wars 159
Australian Conservation Foundation 232
Australian Greens 66, 271, 279
Australian House of Representatives 194
Australian Nuclear Free Alliance (ANFA) 234,
    316
Australian parliament 3, 16, 61
Australian Petroleum Production &
    Exploration Society 251

Australian Unemployed Workers Union
    (AUWU) 306–7
autocatalytic set 38–9, 47, 49, 56, 177
Avenida Atlântica 108–9

Baha (To Be There collective) 135–6, 139
Bak, Per (*How Nature Works*) 214–16
Ban Ki-moon (UN secretary) 198
Bandt, Adam (Green Party MP) 194
Bangladesh 117, 134, 143, 145–6, 176
Bardella, Jordan 140–1
Barla, Dayamani (Jharkhand) 97–101, 113, 263
Basel Congress 1897 135
Beard, Mary (*Women & Power*) 148
Beautiful Trouble – A Toolbox for Revolution
    335
Beeliar Wetlands (Aboriginal meeting ground)
    75
Beijing Students Autonomous Federation 253
Beit Sahour (Palestine) 135
Bekkouch, Yasmine (French economist) 65
Belmarsh Prison 164–5
Bentley gasfield blockade 298–9
Bento Rodrigues village (Brazil) 111
Beqaa Valley (Lebanon) 83–5, 150
Berkman, Michael (Qld Green Party MP)
    144–5
Berlin 132, 175
Berlin *Stolpersteine* 169
Bertalanffy, Ludwig von 23–4
Beverley uranium mine (Adnyamathanha land)
    233, 235, 299
Bezos, Jeff (Amazon CEO) 178–9, 289–92, 305
BHP Billiton 111, 296
Biggs, Michael (sociologist) 223–4
Bilderberg Group 250
biomass 79, 277, 325
biosphere 280, 294, 330
Birulee, Ashish 106–7
Birulee, Ghanshyam (Santhal elder) 102–7
Bituminous Coal Research Inc. 186
Black Lives Matter 227, 305–6
Boldbayar (Mongolian Green Party) 87–2, 95,
    113, 263
Bolsonaro, Jair 112, 115
Bolt, Andrew (Murdoch columnist) 194–5
BP 185, 268, 296
Brandeis University 132
Bretton Woods agreement 175
Brexit 134

Bronze Age 12
Brown, Seyom (professor) 132
Brumadinho mine disaster (2019) 115
Buchanan, Mark 216, 244
bush fireground 1–3, 9–10, 185, 228, 267, 270, 279, 286–7, 293–5, 331–2
Byblos (Arabic: *Jbeil*) fossil gallery 12–14, 25, 121

Cagé, Julia (French economist) 65
Cambrian period 72–3, 76, 121–2, 124, 151, 154, 204–5, 319
Canavan, Matt (minister for coal) 270–1
capitalism 53, 62, 115–16, 270–1, 286, 289, 293–4, 336
carbon 37, 62, 170, 186–7, 198, 204, 238, 295, 301
carbon dioxide 14, 28, 32, 152–3, 182–3, 185, 204, 238
Carboniferous age 181–3, 204–6
Carnegie, Andrew ('Survival of the Fittest') 123, 289
Carney, Mark (Bank of England governor) 303
Carnot, Sadi (*Reflections on the Motive Power of Fire*) 22–3
Carroll, Dr Valerie (feminist scholar) 148
Carroll, William (*Handbook of the International Political Economy of the Corporation*) 248, 250
Carter, Jimmy (US president) 45
centrists 19
chaos school theory 24
Chapple, Robin 231
Charren, Peggy (Action for Children's Television) 45
Chenoweth, Erica (professor) 225–6, 229
Chernobyl 220–1
Chevron 296
Chicxulub crater 238, 332
Chile 68
China 88, 90, 93, 96, 253, 286, 304
China Energy Research Society 325
China People's Liberation Army 253
Chindi, Kennedy 'J.J.' (Mathare Social Justice Centre) 259
Chinese Communist Party (CCP) 159, 193, 253
Chocolate Manufacturers Association 45
Chu, Johan (US researcher) 247, 250
civil uprisings 225–9
Civilian Conservation Corps 174
Clarke, Arthur C. 30
Clausius, Rudolf (German mathematician) 23
Clean Energy Act 2011 62, 66, 309

clean energy reforms 4, 198, 323–5
climate campaigners 83, 202, 209–11, 297, 307–8, 311
climate change 3, 183, 191, 199
climate crisis 10, 141, 198–9, 283–4
climate denial 140
CNBC 'Mad Money' 300
coal 4, 14, 17, 19, 23, 62, 78, 90–1, 93, 98, 159, 164, 182, 201, 251, 268–9, 271, 296, 302
Coca-Cola 329
colonialism 16, 79, 123, 126, 133, 144, 159, 234, 294, 325, 331, 335
community and collectives 124, 127, 133, 135–6, 156–60, 159, 169, 171, 180, 201–3, 240–4, 255–6, 271, 274, 311
'complex adaptive systems' 24
Congleton, Roger (economics professor) 62–3
conservatism 285, 315
Construction, Forestry, Maritime, Mining and Energy Union (CFMMEU) 308
consumerism 18, 30, 40–5, 50–1, 113–14, 165
Copacabana 108–9, 113
copper 77, 90, 93
corporations and corporate elites 168, 247–50
Cretaceous period 13, 207–8, 236–7
Cryogenian ice ages 71
CSS Tactical (South Africa) 126
Cubberley, Ellwood P. (Stanford University) 148–50
cybernetics 24

Darebin Council (Melbourne) 198
Darrow, Charles (Monopoly game) 290
Darwin, Charles (English naturalist) 122–3, 142
Darwinian survival of the fittest 171
Davis, Gerald (US researcher) 247, 250
Davis, Professor Angela (US prison abolitionist) 119
Defence Legislation Amendment (Enhancement of Defence Response to Emergencies) Bill 2020 199
deforestation 8–10, 13, 127, 284
deliberative democracy 311
Demnig, Gunter (German artist) 169
democracy 10, 62, 66, 69–70, 92–3, 125, 199, 248, 271, 282, 309, 311, 331 *see also* deliberative democracy
Democracy Now! 163
deoxyribonucleic acid (DNA) 47, 56, 59, 72
Devonian period 153–4, 181–3, 208, 267, 332
Dhaka (Bangladesh) 140, 143, 325–6 6
Dickinson, Roy (US journal *Printers' Ink* 1930) 44

dissipative structures study 23, 28
Doce River disaster Brazil 2015 112, 235
Dominguez, Neidi (union organiser) 306
Dow Jones Industrial Average 173
Droege, Professor Peter 170–2
Duff, Michael (labour law professor) 306

Earth First! 145, 199
Earth System and earth system scientists 14
ecofascism 145
ecologists 25, 69–70, 278, 280, 340 *see also*
adaptive cycles; hierarchies; *Kapazitätsgrenze*
economic systems 51, 117, 172–9, 206
circular economics 326, 329–30
'jobless recoveries' 118
proletariat 118
precariat 118–19
'surplus populations' 116
'unnecessariat' 119, 176, 305
ecosystems 70–1, 75, 151, 153–4, 186–7, 202,
205–7, 235, 269, 276–8, 280
Ecosystems journal 69–70
Ediacara Hills (SA) 71–2
Ediacaran era 319
Eggington, Robert 230–1
Ehrlich, Paul (*The Population Bomb*) 147
Eisenhower, Dwight D. (US president) 249
El-Ad, Hagai (director-general B'Tselem) 137,
139
Ellen Macarthur Foundation ('New Plastics
Economy') 329
Emergency Banking Act 174
Engler, Mark and Paul (*This is an Uprising*) 197
Enkhbayar, Nambaryn (Mongolian prime min-
ister) 92–5, 164
entropy 23, 44, 116
environmentalism 85, 144–5, 298, 317
Eocene era 237–8, 319
Eora nation 133, 159
Erdenet copper mine (Mongolia) 90
ESP (London artist) 'extinction symbol' 196
'Estranged Labour' 1844 (Karl Marx) 117
eugenics 122, 142
Euler, Leonhard (Swiss mathematician) 242
see also graph theory
Europe 192, 207, 237, 250
European Bank for Reconstruction and
Development 90
European Investment Bank (EIB) 302
European parliamentary elections (2019) 140
evolution 48–9, 57, 59, 77, 142, 152
extinction 9–10, 14–15, 19, 46, 58, 69, 149,
181, 204, 206 *see also* mass extinction
Extinction Rebellion XR 11, 194–7, 199–201,

211, 223, 227, 257, 311
ExxonMobil 186, 296, 329

Facebook 46, 241
FACT: Families Against Censored Television
45
Fair Labor Standards Act 174
fascism 168–9, 175, 282
Federal Reserve Bank 173
Federal Trade Commission Improvements Act
(1980) 45
feedback loops 38–9, 56, 127, 170–1, 177–9,
195, 212, 217, 223, 226–7, 248, 280, 289, 291,
296, 304, 329
Ferguson, Thomas (political scientist) 63–5
Ferriera, Rosetânia 112, 235
financial systems 33–5
function of money 18, 177–8
loans and interest 33–6, 50, 334–5
'structural adjustment' 35
universal basic income 335–6
First Nations societies 211, 271, 298, 316, 331
Fishel, Stefanie (international relations scholar)
171
Fisher, Irving (economist) 173
Floden, Martin (European Investment Bank)
302
Floyd, George 305
Ford, Henry 51
Foreman, David (Earth First! founder) 145
forest fire *see* bush fireground
Forestry Corporation 1
fossil capital 140, 170, 198, 201, 294, 297,
300–1, 303, 305, 310, 315, 317, 326
fossil fuels 78, 182, 185–6, 300, 338
fossil records 13, 71–2, 121–2, 151, 154, 208,
238
Foucher, Michel (*Border Obsession*) 132
Fox News 194
Fraser, Steve (Australian writer) 173
French Office du Travail 223
Friedman, Milton (economist) 175, 335
Friends of the Earth 317
Fukushima Daiichi Tokai nuclear reactor
209–10, 219–21

Gachihi, Gacheke (Mathare Social Justice
Centre) 260–2
Gallagher, Shaun (University of Memphis) 166
game theory 24
Garnaut, Professor Ross 3–4
Garvey, James R. (Bituminous Coal Research
Inc. president) 185–6
gas 4, 17, 19, 30, 164, 201, 302

Gazprom 296
general systems theory 23
geneticists 39
genocide 122
Gentile, Giovanni (fascist philosopher) 168
geochemists 39
geological memory 13–14, 121, 154
George, Henry (economic philosopher) 289
German Nazi Party 123, 142–3
Germany 29, 44, 132
Germany Ruhr region coal mining 308
Ghandi, Mahatma 257
Gillard, Julia (Australian prime minister) 66, 309
Githabul land (NSW) 298–9
global civil uprisings 191–4, 228
global economy 17, 90, 113, 119, 146, 170, 176, 333–4
Global Greens 317
Global Information Grid (GIG) 162–3
global mass surveillance network 163–5
Global North 79, 113, 145, 176, 192, 248, 334
Global South 79, 147, 335
global supply chain 76, 178
global unity 314–15
Gobi Desert 83, 87–8, 90
gold 77, 90, 108, 126–7, 159
Gondwana supercontinent 71, 205, 207, 237–8
Gorton, John (prime minister) 201–3
Graeber, David (Debt: The First 5,000 Years) 35–6, 318
Granovetter, Mark ('The Strength of Weak Ties') 242
graph theory 24, 242, 246
Graziano, Manlio (scholar of geopolitics) 133
Great Depression 1932 11, 43, 173–5
Great Tohoku earthquake (Japan) 209, 216, 218–19
Green New Deal 336
Greenpeace 251
Grocery Manufacturers Association 45
Gross Domestic Product (GDP) 18, 334, 339
Guardian, The 193, 330
Gujarat oil refinery complex 79
Gutenberg-Richter law for earthquakes 215–16

Hadean eon 11, 27, 39, 47–9, 122, 204, 283, 319
Hardin, Garrett ('Lifeboat Ethics') 143–5, 150, 294
Hariri, Rafic (Lebanese prime minister) 86
Hartz-Karp, Professor Janette 311
Hasina, Sheikh (Bangladeshi prime minister) 140

Haudenosaunee Confederation 149
Hayek, Friedrich (Mont Pelerin Society founder) 249
Herald Sun 194
Hidankyo Japanese confederation 156
hierarchies 70, 271, 280, 306
Hiroshima atomic bombing 155–6
Hitler, Adolf (Mein Kampf) 17, 142
Hobbes, Thomas (Enlightenment philosopher) 171
Hobhouse, Emily 16–17
Hoffman, Nicholas von 197
Holling, Crawford Stanley (ecologist) 69–70, 86, 271–2, 277–8, 280, 283, 285, 3316
Holocaust 143
Holocaust Memorial (Berlin) 169
Holocene era 13, 14, 175, 339
Holy Roman Empire 132
Homo erectus 320
Homo sapiens 320
Honeymoon uranium mine (Adnyamathanha land) 233, 235
Hoover, Herbert (US president) 173
Howey Ou (youth climate striker) 193
Hoye, Werner (European Investment Bank) 302
Hudson, Michael (historian) 51, 167, 179, 187, 334–5
human population 17–18, 140–4, 147
Huronian glaciation 59
Husliin Khairkhan mountain 87
Huxley, Aldous 95
hydrogen 17, 26–7, 37–8, 219

Ibn Khaldun (Kitab al-'Ibar: Book of Lessons) 282, 285
ICAN nuclear weapons ban treaty 314
ice ages 12–13, 58–9, 74, 151, 154 see also Huronian glaciation; Nyiting (the cold time); Pleistocene Ice Ages
Ienaga Saburō (historian) 157
Incidence Project on the Mining Agenda 112
India 79, 134, 237, 311
industrial metabolism 109, 115, 126–8, 167, 170, 180, 250, 296, 326, 330,
industrial world 31–2, 41–2, 76–80, 90, 117–18, 126–8, 176
IndyMac 176
International Atomic Energy Action 220
International Bank for Reconstruction and Development 175
International Chamber of Commerce 249
International Energy Agency 328
International Geosphere-Biosphere Programme (IGBP) 14

International Labor Organisation (ILO) 52–5
international law 112, 132, 133
International Monetary Fund (IMF) 35, 90,
   175–6, 333
International Renewable Energy Agency 325
International Trade Union Confederation
   (ITUC) 307
Ipsos Mori poll 329
Iraq war 211, 225, 229
'iron law of oligarchy' 282
iron ore 16, 28, 37, 90, 98, 159
Israel 85
IWW Kulin Nations 306

Jabiluka Action Groups 231
Jabiluka uranium mine (Mirarr country)
   231–3, 235, 299
Jabiru township 235
Jadugoda (Jharkhand) 102, 120
Jagalingou people (Qld) 268
Japan 44, 155–7, 192, 209–10, 218
Japanese *hibakusha* (explosion-affected people)
   156–7, 161
Japanese *uyoku dantai* (ultra-nationalists) 211
Jharkhand (India) 97–8, 104–7, 111, 299
Jharkhandi Organisation Against Radiation
   104–5
Johannesburg (South Africa) 125–6
Jurassic period 207–8
Just Transitions 307

Kakadu National Park (Mirarr country) 231–3,
   235
Kan, Naoto (Japanese prime minister) 219–20
Kapazitätsgrenze 277
Kar, Anupam (Jadugoda photographer) 107
Karra block (Jharkhand) 98
Katona, Jacqui 231
Kenya 259–64
Kenya Tuitakayo Movement 263
Kenyatta, Uhuru (Kenyan president) 262
Kerala (India) 147–8
Khövsgöl (Mongolian province) 92
Kia, Annie 299
Kinsella, Beth (*Harvard College Global Health
   Review*) 147
Klein, Naomi (the 'shock doctrine') 286
Knowles, Michael 194
Kolkata (West Bengal) 97
Korzybski, Alfred (mathematician) 133
Kropotkin, Pyotr Alexeyevich (*Mutual Aid
   1902*) 123–4, 274, 289–91
Krytyka Polityczna 317
Kuarna lands 159

Kundera, Milan 158–9
Kupa Piti Kungka Tjuta 235
Kutupalong refugee camp 146, 150, 261, 294,
   337
Kwaymullina, Ambelin (Palyku scholar)
   149–50

La ZAD de Notre-Dames-des-Landes 299
labour market 51, 53–4, 117
Laurasia supercontinent 205
law of conservation of energy 22
laws of thermodynamics 22–23, 25, 328
Le Figaro 140
Le Pen, Marine (National Rally president) 140
Lebanon 68, 83–6, 150
Lebanon Green Party 83–84
Lehmann Brothers 176
Lester, Karina 155, 158–60
Liechtenstein Institute for Strategic
   Development 170
Linkola, Pentti (Finnish deep ecologist) 144,
   150
Linnit, Carol (Canadian blogger) 145 *see also*
   'Misanthropocene'
Livy (Roman historian) 171
Lloyds of London 303
Lombardi, Mark 246, 251–2, 295, 340
London, Bernard (real estate broker) 43–4
London Brewers Company 110
Lorenz, Konrad (Nazi military psychologist)
   143
Lovins, Amory (Rocky Mountain Institute)
   328
Luca (last universal common ancestor) 47,
   56, 59, 72, 109, 124, 127, 151, 153, 205, 208,
   280, 319

Machiavelli, Niccolo 282, 285
Macy, Joanna (US author; anti-nuclear cam-
   paigner) 21, 201, 212, 240, 268 *see also*
   systems game
Madison, James (US constitutional drafter;
   slave owner) 166, 248
Magie, Lizzie J. (Monopoly game) 288–91, 293
Maher, Tony (CFMMEU national president)
   308–9
Makichyan, Arshak (#FridaysForFuture) 192–3
Malthus, Thomas 141–2
Mandela, Nelson 202–3
Margarula, Yvonne (Mirarr senior Traditional
   Owner) 232–3, 235
Mars 20, 27
Marx, Karl 117–18, 178, 249, 290–1
Mason, Paul (*Postcapitalism*) 336

mass extinction 13, 151, 153–4, 181, 204, 206, 228, 267, 332
Mathare Art for Social Change 261
Mathare Green Movement 261
Mathare Social Justice Centre 11, 259–62, 316–17
mathematical chessboard analogy (coin doubling) 16–18, 19–21, 24, 34, 36, 41, 44, 50, 55, 69, 77, 113, 118, 120, 127–8, 141, 172–3, 175–7, 180, 186–7, 195, 267, 293–4, 309, 314–15
Maules Creek coal (Whitehaven Coal Ltd) 300–2
McCormack, Michael (deputy prime minister) 194
McDonough, William 329
McKibben, Bill (US environmentalist) 301
Meadows, Donella (*The Limits to Growth*) 177–8, 289, 291
Mediterranean 12, 83, 86
Mendez, Chico (Brazilian labour leader) 317
Merchant, Brian (*Gizmodo*) 119
metabolism 39, 48–9, 59, 72, 76–7, 127, 148, 170
metallic ores 16–17, 27, 325
Metgasco gas fracking 298–9
methane 13–14, 58, 204, 238
Mexico 134
Michels, Robert (German sociologist) 282–3
microbiologists 39, 47
Mid-Miocene Climate Optimum 273
Mies, Maria 147
Milgram, Stanley (US psychologist) 242–4
militarism 10
Miller, Stephen (US blogger) 195
Mills, Charles Wright (Columbia University sociologist) 248–9
Minangkabau people (Western Sumatra) 149
Minas Gerais (Brazil) 11, 111–12
Mineral Council of Australia (MCA) 65–6, 251, 269
mining 4, 93–4, 102–4, 231–2
Mining Congress Journal 186
mining leach sites 88–9, 233
mining slag heaps 126
mining tailing dams 102, 105, 115, 120, 127
Miocene epoch 272–5
Mirarr country (NT) 133, 231 –3, 235
'Misanthropocene' 145
Mitochondrial Eve 321
Mitra, Aparna (University of Oklahoma) 147–8
Miyake, Nobuo 155–6 *see also* Peace Boat project

Mohenjo-daro (Indus Valley) 109
Mongolia 11, 87, 90, 94–6
Mongolian Democratic Party 93
Mongolian Green Party 87, 91–2
Mongolian People's Party 93
Mont Pelerin Society 175–6, 180, 249
Moody, Kim (*Spectre* journal) 304
moon 27, 37
Moukheiber, H.E. Ghassan 85
Moylan, Jon 300–1
Muckaty traditional owners 234
Murray, Joshua (Vanderbilt University) 248, 250
Mussolini, Benito (wartime dictator) 168
Myanmar 146

Nabanardi, Simon (Mirrarr Traditonal Owner) 235
Nagasaki atomic bombing 155–6
Nagatacho climate activists 209–211, 221
Najah (Lebanon Green Party) 83–4, 150
Nakba (Palestinian exodus) 135
National Alliance of People's Movements 317
National Police Service (Nairobi) 259
National Socialist Teachers League 142
National Soft Drink Association 45
National War Memorial 159
nationalism 133–4, 140, 142, 165, 211, 314
nation-state borders 132–5, 138–9, 143, 148, 167
neocolonialism 176
neoliberalism 45, 175, 179, 249, 279, 293–4, 309
Neolithic era 12
Neoproterozoic era 59–60
Nestlé 329
network analysis 243, 246
New Century financial institution 176
News Corp 251, 269–70, 279, 301
Nexus (Mark Buchanan) 244
Njoya, Dr Wandia (Daystar University senior lecturer) 262–4, 289–91, 293
Noda, Yoshihiko (Japanese prime minister) 209
nonlinear dynamics 24, 313
North America 29, 41, 143, 207, 273
nuclear reactors 102, 170, 209–10, 219–21 *see also* probabilistic safety assessment (PSA)
nuclear weapons and testing 14, 103, 158, 231
Nyiting (the cold time) 74–5, 331
Nyoongah warriors (Dumbartung) 230–1

Obama, Barack (US president) 64
obsolescence 42–4

Occupy movement 118, 197, 202, 315, 318
O'Connell, Kristin (AUWU volunteer) 306–7
oil 17, 19, 35, 41, 79, 88, 90, 186, 302, 305
oligarchy 66, 85–6, 125, 283, 293, 296, 307, 310
  see also 'iron law of oligarchy'
Olympic Dam copper/uranium mine 233
Orano (French nuclear giant) 88
Ordovician period 151–2, 204
Origin of the Species by Means of Natural
  Selection (Charles Darwin) 122
Orwell, George (Nineteen Eighty-Four) 159
Oslo (Accordance) 135
Overton, Joseph P. (US public-policy thinker)
  19
Overton window 19–20, 176, 297
oxygen 37–8, 58, 60, 76, 153, 181, 204
Oyu Tolgoi copper mine (Mongolia) 90, 94–5

palaeontologists 14, 109
Palaszczuk, Annastacia (Qld premier) 201, 203
Paleocene epoch 236–8
Paleocene-Eocene Thermal Maximum 238, 273
Palestine 85, 133–4, 136–7
panarchy 25, 70, 271, 276–8, 280, 283, 286,
  310, 315–17
Pangaea supercontinent 181, 183, 205–7, 235
Paracatu village (Brazil) 111, 113, 296
Paris, Nicola (CounterAct founder) 298
Parker, Paul (volunteer firefighter) 279
Parramore, Lynn (researcher) 64
Pascoe, Bruce (Dark Emu) 331
Patel, Priti (UK Home Secretary) 134
Peace Boat project 156–7, 159, 317
'Peace of Westphalia' 1648 132–3
'Peoples Congress' (Colombia) 317
Perkins, Frances (US Secretary of Labor) 174,
  290–291, 336
Permian period 13, 183–4, 204–6, 238, 332
Perth and Perth Fringe Festival 74–5, 297
Peterson, Steven A. (Handbook of Biology and
  Politics) 122–3
Philippines 117, 176
photosynthesis 57, 59, 152, 236, 326, 330–1
Pibelmun Noongar 7–9, 340 see also Wattle
  Forest
Pilbara (WA) 25, 109
Pitjantjatjara land 157, 160
Planet Earth 3, 14–15, 27, 28, 37, 51–2, 58, 172
Pleistocene Ice Ages 13
politics and electoral systems 11, 67–9, 84, 86,
  286, 301
    investment theory of party competition
      63–6, 85, 90, 93–5, 310
    median voter theorem 62–3, 65–6

political 'centre' 62
public choice scholars 63
'sensible centre' 62–3
poverty 10, 54, 91, 98
power laws 216–18, 223, 227–8, 243–4, 247
President Suharto (1967) 17
probabilistic safety assessment (PSA) 220
Progressive International 317
Proterozoic eon 58, 71, 319
Public Works Administration 174

Queensland Galilee Basin coal mine 268–9,
  271, 302–3
'quorum sensing' 56, 127

Rabaul (Papua New Guinea) 322–3
racism 122, 143, 165, 199
radiation 104, 220
Radio Times 144
radioactive isotopes 14, 19, 103, 107
radioactive waste 105, 231
radionuclides 89, 107
rainforest 181–183, 186
Raj-Stepping, Izzy 195
Raman, Parvathi (SOAS Centre for Migration
  and Diaspora Studies) 131
Ranchi (Jharkhand capital) 97, 100, 113
Rand, Ayn 123
Randburg (South Africa) 126
Ranger uranium mine 232–3, 235
Rattenbury, Shane (Minister for Climate
  Change and Sustainability) 325
Raworth, Kate (Doughnut Economics) 334
Reagan, Ronald (US president) 45
recycling systems 19, 113–14, 328–9
resource sector investors 3, 263, 279, 286, 295,
  299–300
Ricketts, Aidan 299
Rio Tinto 94–5, 164, 233, 235
Robinson, Joan (British economist) 115
Rockefeller, John D. 123, 171, 289, 293
Rodinia landmass 71
Roht-Arriaza, Naomi 112
Romney, Mitt (US Republican nominee) 64
Roosevelt, Franklin Delano (US president)
  174, 336
Rottnest Island (Wadjemup) 74
Roy, Arundhati (Indian author) 36
Rudd, Kevin (Australian prime minister) 65–6,
  309
Rural Fire Service (RFS) 1, 327

Salleh, Ariel (Australian sociologist) 53
Samarco (iron ore mine) 111

Sanders Institute and Democracy in Europe Movement (DiEM25) 317
sankey diagrams 79, 113, 115, 127, 170, 296, 304, 325, 327
Sant Maral poll (Mongolia) 95–6
Santayana, George (philosopher and essayist) 211
Santhal (Jharkhand people) 102–4, 235
São Paulo (Brazil) 116, 120
Sapinski, J.P. (*Handbook of the International Political Economy of the Corporation*) 248, 250
SARS-CoV-2 pandemic 179, 226, 304–6
sarvanim (Israeli conscientious objectors) 138
Saudi Aramco 296
Schemm, Hans (National Socialist Teachers League) 142
School Strike 4 Climate movement 4, 191–5, 202, 211, 223, 227, 292, 307
Scott, James (*Seeing Like a State*) 162
Sea Shepherd Conservation Society vessel 340
Securities and Exchange Commission 174
Shadow State 125
Shahab, Nyah (School Strike 4 Climate) 192
Shalizi, Cosma (physicist and statistician) 217
Sharma, Nandita (associate professor of racism, migration, transnationalism) 134
Sharp, Gene (*From Dictatorship to Democracy*) 257
Shenhua 296
Shi Yubo (China Energy Research Society) 325
Shiva, Vandana 147
Shripakash (documentary filmmaker) 97–106
Siberia 204–5
Siegel, David (political science professor) 253–8
Silurian period 152, 205
Sima Qian (Han dynasty historian) 282, 285
Simmons, Skyler (Earth First!) 199
Singh, Pooja (independent Indian researcher) 147–8
Slaby, Jan (Freie Universität Berlin) 166
small-world networks 243–4, 246–8, 256
Smith, Adam (economic thinker) 178
Snowden, Edward (former CIA subcontractor) 163
SOAS Centre for Migration and Diaspora Studies 131
social graphs 241–2, 254, 285, 293
social media 1, 3, 46, 193, 195, 197, 241, 252, 306
social networks 4, 11, 195, 197, 223–4, 226, 229, 235, 244, 263, 296, 301, 307–8, 310, 315, 317

and 'contentious politics' 201–3
the 'Dunbar number' 240–1
and 'repertoires of contention' 202, 228
repression of 104, 201–2, 227, 242, 253–9, 316
Social Security Act 174
social-Darwinist thinking 142
social-ecological systems 70, 271
sociograms 241, 245–7, 251, 295
solar photovoltaic (PV) panels 325–7
Somit, Albert (*Handbook of Biology and Politics*) 122–3
South Africa 109, 125–6, 202, 205
South America 207
South Korea oil refinery complex 79
Sovereignty of the Gadigal people of Eora nation 159
Soviet Union (USSR) 87, 90, 93, 159, 286
Soweto (South Africa) 126
Sparrow, Jeff (Australian writer) 199
Spencer, Herbert (philosopher) 122–3
Spratt, David (*Climate Code Red*) 198
Srnicek, Nick (*Inventing the Future*) 307, 315
SSAB Swedish steelmaker 329
Stadler, Josef (UBS Global Wealth Management) 305
Standing, Guy (economist) 118
Standing Rock reservation 299
Steffen, Professor Will 14
Stephan, Maria 229
Strogatz, Steven (mathematician) 243
Sükhbaatar Square (Mongolia) 95
Summers, Lawrence (World Bank) 114
Sutton, Philip (*Climate Code Red*) 198
Sweeney, Dave (Australian Conservation Foundation nuclear campaigns coordinator) 232–3
Sydney Morning Herald, The 301
symbiogenesis 59, 124
Syria 83, 85
systems game 21–2, 25, 201, 212, 240, 268, 293–4, 313, 316
systems theory 21–2, 179, 215, 217, 283, 293
see also cybernetics; dissipative structures; general systems theory; sankey diagrams

Tarrow, Sidney (US political sociologist) 201–3
Tavan Tolgoi coal deposits (Mongolia) 90, 96
tectonic seams 56, 83, 216, 221–3
Telemachus (in *The Odyssey*) 148–9, 150, 166, 167
TEPCO 219
Tethys Sea 13, 205, 207–8, 237
The Citizen's Handbook 225

The Descent of Man, and Selection in Relation to Sex (Charles Darwin) 142
thermodynamics 53, 109, 328
Three Mile Island 220–1
Thunberg, Greta (climate campaigner) 191–2, 194–5
Tiananmen Square (China) 68–9, 159, 253, 257
Tilley, Charles (political sociologist) 201–2
Tōkai nuclear reactor (Japan) 209
Tovuusuren, Saruul 92
Transgondwanan Supermountain 72
Triassic period 204–7, 236, 303
Trilateral Commission 250
Trump, Donald (US president) 135–6, 168

Ubiquity (Mark Buchanan) 216
UBS Global Wealth Management 305
UK House of Commons 198
Ulaanbaatar (Mongolian city) 90–1, 93, 96
UN Climate Change Conference (COP24) 192
UN Food and Agriculture Organization (*Livestock's Long Shadow* report) 329
Union of Concerned Scientists 220
United Nations 94, 149, 164, 269, 301, 314, 316
United Nations Charter 132–3
United Nations COP 15 (2009) 17
United States of America (USA) 64–5, 85, 119, 134, 140, 166–8, 192, 236, 250, 286, 306, 311
Uranium Corporation of India Limited 102
uranium 40, 77, 89–90, 98, 102–7, 126, 231–5
urban metabolism 77, 110, 127, 172
urban streetscape 29–35, 40–1, 43, 46, 50, 74–8, 80, 113, 126, 337–8
US Bureau of Labor Statistics 223
US civil rights movement 257
US Democratic National Convention 174
US Department of Defence 162
US Federal Reserve Bank 54, 173, 176
US Federal Trade Commission (1979) 45
US Homeland Security 167
US House of Representatives 166
US Immigration and Customs Enforcement 167
US National Security Agency (NSA) 163
US Senate 166, 168
US State Department 94–5, 164, 226

Vale S.A. 111, 115
Vallentine, Jo 231
Vardi, Sahar 137, 139
Vegan Society 329–30
Venezuelan oil refinery complex 79
Volkenstein, Mikhail (Russian biophysicist) 23

Wadjemup (Rottnest Island) 74
Wage, Labour and Capital 1847 (Karl Marx) 117
Walatina community 158
Walmadan gas complex (WA) 297–9
Wangan people (Qld) 268
Wanjira, Juliet (Mathare Social Justice Centre) 259–61
Waseda University (Tokyo) 156–7
waste 19, 31, 44, 62, 76–7, 80, 88, 105, 108–10, 113–15, 170, 204, 295–6, 325, 327–9
water 27–8, 31, 38, 76, 199, 325, 336, 339
water treatment plants 78, 79
Wattle Forest 11, 21, 68, 127, 186, 299, 340
Watts, Duncan (sociologist) 243
Wealth-X Billionaire Census 54
Weckend, Stephanie (IRENA study) 325–7
West, Michael (journalist) 65, 251
white supremacy 122, 140, 142, 199, 294
WikiLeaks 94, 164
Williams, Alex (*Inventing the Future*) 307, 315
Willowmore, Inge 125
wind turbines 325–6
women 148–50
Wong, Tobias (New York artist) 108
Wood, Jonathon (Control Risks consultant) 298
World Bank 114, 175
World Business Council for Sustainable Development 250
World Council for Renewable Energy 170
World Economic Forum 250
World Health Organization 304
World Heritage Committee 232–3
World Social Forum 97, 317
World Trade Organisation 17
World War II 41, 44, 132
Wright, Jai Allan (climate campaigner) 192

Yankunytjatjara land 157, 160
Yeelirrie uranium deposit (WA) 235
Yoshioka, Tatsuya 156–7 *see also* Peace Boat project
Yue Xin (labour organiser) 257
Yuin country (NSW) 1, 133, 185, 191, 267

Zaarour, Nada (Lebanon Green Party leader) 85–6
Zhao Ziyang (CCP general secretary) 253
Zuckerberg, Mark (Facebook) 241
Zuma, Jacob 125
Züünbayan (Soviet-era military base) 87, 89

Photograph by Jean-Paul Horré

SCOTT LUDLAM was a senator from
2008 to 2017 and served as deputy leader
of the Australian Greens. He has also worked
as a filmmaker, artist and graphic designer.
This is his first book, the fruit of a life
of activism, study and travel.